Charles Fraser-Mackintosh

Letters of Two Centuries

Chiefly Connected With Inverness and the Highlands From 1616 to 1815

Charles Fraser-Mackintosh

Letters of Two Centuries
Chiefly Connected With Inverness and the Highlands From 1616 to 1815

ISBN/EAN: 9783744771672

Printed in Europe, USA, Canada, Australia, Japan

Cover: Foto ©ninafisch / pixelio.de

More available books at **www.hansebooks.com**

LETTERS OF TWO CENTURIES.

PRINTED AT THE "SCOTTISH HIGHLANDER" OFFICE, INVERNESS.

LETTERS

OF

TWO CENTURIES

*CHIEFLY CONNECTED WITH INVERNESS
AND THE HIGHLANDS,*

FROM 1616 TO 1815.

EDITED, AND EACH INTRODUCED WITH EXPLANATORY
AND ILLUSTRATIVE REMARKS,

BY

CHARLES FRASER-MACKINTOSH
OF DRUMMOND, M.P., F.S.A. Scot.,
AUTHOR OF "ANTIQUARIAN NOTES";
"INVERNESSIANA"; ETC.

INVERNESS: A. & W. MACKENZIE.
MDCCCXC.

PREFACE.

———:0:———

WHEN the *Scottish Highlander* was first projected I agreed to contribute a series of articles under the title of " LETTERS OF TWO CENTURIES." These appeared, with one interval, regularly for four years, beginning in July, 1885, and they are now reprinted in this form.

Giving a letter for each year has many advantages, and that plan has been adhered to; but not having my collections of letters inventoried when the series commenced, I found as I went on that my letters for some years were uninteresting, though obliged to give them; and for some twenty years of the entire series I had to go outside my own collection.

The issue in its progress has brought me into communication with many new friends, notably in New England, in consequence of the letter of 1739.

The index, which is full and well executed by Mr. William Simpson, of the *Scottish Highlander*, will, it is hoped, be found generally useful.

The printing, etc., is in every respect satisfactory; but this was to be expected from the enterprising publishers.

C. F.-M.

LOCHARDILL, INVERNESS,
February, 1890.

CONTENTS.

———:o:———

LETTERS— PAGE.
I. SIR DONALD MACKAY of Strathnaver - - 1
II. GEORGE, First Marquis of Huntly - - - 4
III. GEORGE, Earl of Caithness - - - - 5
IV. SIR LACHLAN MACKINTOSH of Torcastle - - 6
V. LORD MACKENZIE of Kintail, and the Bishop of Ross 8
VI. SIR ROBERT GORDON - - - - - 11
VII. THE VIRGINIAN SETTLERS - - - - 12
VIII. ANNA CAMPBELL, Second Marchioness of Huntly - 13
IX. GILBERT VAUS, writer, Burgess of Inverness - - 15
X. THE EARL of Arundel and Surrey, and King James' funeral - - - - - - - 17
XI. GEORGE VILLIERS, Duke of Buckingham - - 18
XII. SLAVERY IN NEW ENGLAND - - - - 20
XIII. KINGSMILN'S DISPUTES - - - - 22
XIV. THE FIRST LORD REAY - - - - 24
XV. WALTER ROSS and the Laird of Kincraig - - 25
XVI. JOHN DUNBAR of Bennetsfield - - - 27
XVII. SIR ALEXANDER GORDON and the Second Marquis of Huntly - - - - - - 29
XVIII. GEORGE, Earl of Seaforth - - - - 30
XIX. WILLIAM ROBERTSON of the Inshes family - - 32
XX. LORD REAY - - - - - - 34
XXI. DUNCAN FORBES of Culloden and his wife Janet - 36
XXII. JOHN NICOLL, writer, Edinburgh - - - 38
XXIII. MR. KAY, Doer for Lord Reay - - - 39
XXIV. CHARLES I. - - - - - - 42
XXV. THE EARL, afterwards first Marquis, of Argyll - 43
XXVI. ROBERT INNES of Rosskeen - - - - 45
XXVII. JAMES, third Earl of Moray - - - - 46
XXVIII. JOHN, thirteenth Earl of Sutherland - - - 48
XXIX. SIR ROBERT GORDON - - - - - 48
XXX. THE EARL and COUNTESS of Sutherland - - 50
XXXI. JOHN ROBERTSON, first of Inshes - - - 51
XXXII. THE EARL of Sutherland and Sir Robert Gordon - 53

LETTERS—	PAGE.
XXXIII. ALEXANDER LESLIE, Writer, Edinburgh	55
XXXIV. The Slanders of JAMES CUTHBERT of Little Drakies	56
XXXV. A. MUNRO, Writer, Edinburgh	57
XXXVI. CHARLES II.	59
XXXVII. A. LESLIE and the Good Wife of Inshes	60
XXXVIII. COLLECTOR WATSON, of Inverness	61
XXXIX. A. MUNRO, Writer, Edinburgh, Doer for the Lady Inshes	62
XL. Messrs. ROSE, FORBES, and PATERSON, of Inverness	63
XLI. ALEXANDER BAILLIE of Dunain	65
XLII. JOHN CUTHBERT of Castlehill	66
XLIII. ALEXANDER MACKINTOSH of Connage and his tenants in Sutherland	68
XLIV. A. LESLIE, writer, Edinburgh, and the Laird of Inshes	69
XLV. LORD LORN and his friends	71
XLVI. ALEXANDER ROSE, Town Clerk of Inverness	75
XLVII. H. ROBERTSON, merchant, Inverness	76
XLVIII. DAVID BAILLIE, first of Dochfour	77
XLIX. HEW ROBERTSON of the Inshes family	82
L. BAILIE FOWLER of Inverness Inshes, and Glenmoriston	83
LI. THE EARL OF ARGYLL	84
LII. THE EARL OF MAR	86
LIII. OLD LOVE LETTERS, W. R. and M. R.	87
LIV. LORD STRATHNAVER	88
LV. H. ROBERTSON of Nairn and Lord Strathnaver	90
LVI. THOMAS LINDSAY, an inmate of Cromarty Prison	91
LVII. HENRY SINCLAIR, writer, Edinburgh	92
LVIII. BAILIE WILLIAM MACBEAN, of Inverness	94
LIX. J. MACKINTOSH, from the Castle of Moy	95
LX. SIR GEORGE MACKENZIE of Rosehaugh	97
LXI. ALEXANDER MACKINTOSH of Connage	98
LXII. CULLODEN and his co-proprietors of the Kingsmilns	99
LXIII. KENNETH MOR, third Earl of Seaforth	101
LXIV. THE MARQUIS OF HUNTLY, and the goodwife of Dochgarroch	102
LXV. A. ARNELL	103
LXVI. ALEXANDER CHISHOLM, Sheriff-Depute of Inverness-shire	105
LXVII. CAPTAIN ROSS and his Thieving Recruits	107
LXVIII. SIR DAVID FORBES, Advocate	109
LXIX. SIR DAVID FORBES, Advocate	111
LXX. WILLIAM BAILLIE, Commissary of Inverness	112

CONTENTS.

LETTERS— PAGE.
LXXI. THE MAGISTRATES of INVERNESS and the Arms on the Stone Bridge - - - - 114
LXXII. WILLIAM ROBERTSON of Inshes and his Stolen Cattle - - - - - - 116
LXXIII. The Rev. ANGUS MACBEAN of Inverness - - 117
LXXIV. JOHN GRAHAM of Claverhouse, Viscount Dundee 119
LXXV. LIEUTENANT R. INNES and the Pluscardines - 120
LXXVI. WILLIAM HAY, last Bishop of Moray - - 122
LXXVII. HEW FRASER of Balnain - - - - 124
LXXVIII. The LAIRD of GORDONSTOUN'S Stolen Cattle - 125
LXXIX. The GOODMAN of CUTTLEBRAY and Borlum Castle 128
LXXX. PROFESSOR HUTCHESON of Edinburgh - - 130
LXXXI. A COLLEGIAN to his Father for Supplies - - 131
LXXXII. LORD SALTOUN, and Brodie, anent the Dowager Lady Lovat - - - - - 132
LXXXIII. JOHN ROBERTSON of Lude - - - 134
LXXXIV. SIR DAVID FORBES, Advocate - - - 135
LXXXV. LADY MACDONELL and Aros - - - 137
LXXXVI. The EARL of PORTMORE - - - 138
LXXXVII. The LAIRD of LETHEN - - - - 139
LXXXVIII. AN INDIGNANT FATHER to his Son - - 140
LXXXIX. KENNETH MOR MACKENZIE, first of Dundonell - 141
XC. Principal WILLLIAM CARSTARES - - - 143
XCI. AN INVERNESS WATCHMAKER - - - 144
XCII. SIR DONALD GORME of Sleat - - - 146
XCIII. COLL MACDONELL of Keppoch - - - 147
XCIV. SIR HARRIE INNES, Baronet - - - 148
XCV. GEORGE, first Earl of Cromartie - - - 149
XCVI. Brigadier WILLIAM MACKINTOSH of Borlum - 152
XCVII. DR. ARCHIBALD PITCAIRN, the Scot - - 153
XCVIII. ALEXANDER, Marquis of Huntly, afterwards second Duke of Gordon - - - - 156
XCIX. The PARLIAMENTARY DEBATES on the Succession 158
C. MR. JONATHAN FORBES, son of Dr. Forbes, of Elgin - - - - - - 162
CI. SIR HUGH CAMPBELL of Calder - - - 163
CII. WILLIAM MACKINTOSH, an insurgent of 1715, Lieutenant in Borlum's Battalion - - 165
CIII. The Rev. LACHLAN SHAW, Historian of Moray - 166
CIV. LADY ANNA STUART or ROSS of Balnagown - 168
CV. ALEXANDER, second Duke of Gordon - - 170
CVI. SIR ARCHIBALD CAMPBELL of Clunes and John Cuthbert of Castlehill - - - 171
CVII. The Rev. LACHLAN SHAW, Historian of Moray - 175

LETTERS— PAGE.
CVIII. The MAGISTRATES of INVERNESS and their criminal
jurisdiction - - - - - 177
CIX. MACKINTOSH and "Nisbet's Heraldry" - - 179
CX. ARCHIBALD CAMPBELL, writer, Edinburgh, and the
Laird of Calder - - - - 180
CXI. DANIEL BARBOUR of Aldourie - - - 182
CXII. DAVID ROSE of Holm - - - - 184
CXIII. JAMES BRODIE of Inshock - - - - 185
CXIV. LACHLAN MACKINTOSH of Kyllachy - - 187
CXV. LACHLAN MACKINTOSH of that Ilk - - 189
CXVI. ALEXANDER MACKINTOSH of Kyllachy - - 191
CXVII. ALEXANDER BAILLIE, writer, Edinburgh - - 193
CXVIII. JOHN FORBES, Fourth of Culloden - - 196
CXIX. JOHN CAMPBELL of Cawdor - - - 197
CXX. JOHN POLSON, advocate, late of Kinmylies - 199
CXXI. SIMON LORD LOVAT - - - - 200
CXXII. JOHN MACKINTOSH of the Holme family - - 203
CXXIII. Mrs. SIBELLA ROBERTSON, Carie - - - 204
CXXIV. SHAW MACKINTOSH, Sixth of Borlum - - 205
CXXV. EWEN MACPHERSON of Cluny, the younger - 211
CXXVI. JOHN BAILLIE of Leys, Clerk to the Signet - 214
CXXVII. PROVOST HOSSACK of Inverness - - - 216
CXXVIII. LADY ANN MACKINTOSH of Mackintosh - - 219
CXXIX. JOHN BAILLIE of Leys and Lord Lovat - - 220
CXXX. JOHN, second Earl of Breadalbane - - - 222
CXXXI. LORD H—— to his sister in France about Prince
Charles and his lady supporters at Inverness 223
CXXXII. Lieutenant NORMAN MACLEOD of Raasay - 228
CXXXIII. WILLIAM MACKENZIE of Gruinard and the High-
land dress - - - - - 229
CXXXIV. Bailie JOHN STEWART, Inverness, of the Kincardine
family - - - - - 231
CXXXV. The Rev. ÆNEAS SAGE, of Lochcarron - - 233
CXXXVI. JOHN MACKENZIE of Delvin, C.S., and Ross of
Kinmylies - - - - - 235
CXXXVII. Mrs. NAOMI ROSS of Pitcalnie - - - 236
CXXXVIII. ALEXANDER BAILLIE of Dochfour - - 237
CXXXIX. J. M. on his Matrimonial Disappointment - - 240
CXL. The MAGISTRATES of INVERNESS and impressing
for the Navy - - - - - 245
CXLI. The PROVOST of INVERNESS and Coal Discoveries 247
CXLII. The MAGISTRATES of INVERNESS and their Im-
provements - - - - - 248
CXLIII. The Rev. JOHN CLARK of Stornoway - - 249

CONTENTS. xi

LETTERS— PAGE.
CXLIV. JAMES MACKINTOSH of Farr - - - 251
CXLV. JAMES BAILLIE, son of Dochfour - - - 253
CXLVI. The Honourable MRS. GASCOIGNE - - - 255
CXLVII. GENERAL FRASER of Lovat - - - 258
CXLVIII. D. F. and E. F.—To Marry or not to Marry - 259
CXLIX. WILLIAM FRASER of Balnain - - - 260
CL. MR. WM. ROBERTSON of the Inshes family - 262
CLI. THOMAS FRASER of Gortuleg - - - 263
CLII. The Rev. ÆNEAS SHAW of Forres - - - 266
CLIII. SIR ALEXANDER GRANT of Dalvey, Baronet - 267
CLIV. The CAMERONS in Auchindaul - - - 269
CLV. LORD FORBES - - - - - 271
CLVI. The Rev. ROBERT MACQUEEN, Laggan - - 272
CLVII. LORD GEORGE GORDON - - - - 277
CLVIII. WILLIAM MACKINTOSH, son of Dalmigavie - 278
CLIX. JOHN MACPHERSON of Ballachroan (the Black Officer) 280
CLX. Captain ALEXANDER GOODSMAN of the 89th Highlanders - - - - 282
CLXI. JAMES BOSWELL of Auchinleck - - - 288
CLXII. JOHN MACKINTOSH of Corrybrough, Captain 42nd, on the American War - - - 290
CLXIII. General SIMON FRASER of Lovat - - - 294
CLXIV. Colonel WILLIAM BAILLIE of Dunain - - 295
CLXV. CHARLES FRASER, of the Balnain family - - 297
CLXVI. LORD CORNWALLIS and the Rev. Dr. Alexander Webster, Edinburgh - - - - 299
CLXVII. DUNCAN MACKINTOSH of Castle Leathers - 300
CLXVIII. SHERIFF FRASER of Farraline and the Year of Scarcity - - - - - 303
CLXIX. Governor ALEXANDER SHAW of Tordarroch - 305
CLXX. FRANCIS HUMBERSTON MACKENZIE of Seaforth - 307
CLXXI. ARTHUR FORBES of Culloden - - - 309
CLXXII. ANNE MACRA, the "Wise Woman" of Beauly - 310
CLXXIII. MRS. MACDONELL of Glenmeddle and the Knoydart Evictions - - - - 311
CLXXIV. SIR JOHN MACPHERSON, Bart., and the Inverness Academy - - - - - 313
CLXXV. Captain SIMON FRASER of Fanellan, on the barony of Drumchardiny - - - - 315
CLXXVI. SIR JAMES MACKINTOSH and the "Vindiciae Gallicae" - - - - - 317
CLXXVII. Colonel JOHN BAILLIE of Leys - - - 320
CLXXVIII. LADY MACKENZIE of Grandvale - - - 325
CLXXIX. GLENGARRY and the Men of Knoydart - - 327

LETTERS—

CLXXX. JAMES FRASER of Gorthlick, C.S., and the Lowland Sheep-Grabbers - - - 329
CLXXXI. MUSIC TEACHING in INVERNESS. The Kirk-Session and the Magistrates - - 331
CLXXXII. LANDING of the FRENCH in WALES, and their Capture by Lord Cawdor - - - 333
CLXXXIII. RARE DOINGS in INVERNESS in early May - 334
CLXXXIV. SHERIFF FRASER of Farraline, and the state of crime in Inverness-shire - - - 337
CLXXXV. The Rev. EDMUND MACQUEEN, of Barra - 339
CLXXXVI. JAMES CLARK of Naples, painter - - 340
CLXXXVII. SIR GEORGE STUART MACKENZIE of Coul - 340
CLXXXVIII. The Hon. COLONEL ARCHIBALD C. FRASER of Lovat - - - - - 342
CLXXXIX. The LORD and VICE-LIEUTENANT of Inverness-shire on the threatened invasion in 1804 - 346
CXC. A DAUGHTER of the MANSE on her Liverpool Experiences - - - - - 348
CXCI. EWEN MACLACHLAN, Poet and Scholar - 351
CXCII. LACHLAN MACKINTOSH of Raigmore - - 353
CXCIII. Colonel HALKETT and GLENGARRY and Rothiemurchus - - - - - 357
CXCIV. Captain CHARLES MUNRO, late 42nd Regiment 357
CXCV. The Hon. ARCHIBALD FRASER of Lovat - 359
CXCVI. An Alleged BREACH OF PROMISE of Marriage - 362
CXCVII. Captain ENEAS MACDONELL, 6th Royal Veterans, Fort-Augustus - - - - 364
CXCVIII. JOHN MELVILL, Island of Isay - - - 367
CXCIX. JOHN LAMONT, Priest at Aberchalder - - 369
CC. COLL MACDONELL of Barisdale - - 371

APPENDIX.

NO. 1. MACDONALD of Sleat - - - - - 375
2. DR. COLIN CAMPBELL, of Inverness - - - 377
3. LETTER No. CXXXI., Kennochan in Athole - - 378
4. LETTER No. CLVI., Translation of Gaelic Songs by Margaret Cameron - - - - - 380
5. Lieutenant THOMAS FRASER of Errogie - - - 383
6. JAMES MACKINTOSH and GENERAL MACKINTOSH of Savannah - - - - - 386
7. SHERIFF TYTLER - - - - - 388

LIST OF SUBSCRIBERS.

———:0:———

Aitken, Dr., District Asylum, Inverness
Asher & Co., Messrs, booksellers, London
Blair, Sheriff, Inverness
Brand, Sheriff, Chairman, Crofters Commission
Brown, Mr. William, bookseller, Edinburgh (2 Copies and 1 Large Paper)
Burgess, Peter, Esq., banker, Glenurquhart
Burns, Wm., Esq., solicitor, Inverness
Cameron, Charles, Dr., M.P.
Cameron, D. M., Esq., merchant, Inverness
Cameron, D., Esq., Moniack Castle
Cameron, James A., Esq., M.D., Edinburgh
Chisholm, Colin, Esq., Namur Cottage, Inverness
Chisholm, The, Tavistock Square, London (Large Paper)
Cran, John, Esq., F.S.A., Scot., Bunchrew.
Donaldson, H. T., Esq., solicitor, Nairn
Douglas & Foulis, Messrs., booksellers, Edinburgh (6 Copies)
Duncan, Colonel P., Brighton
Elliot, Mr. Andrew, bookseller, Edinburgh
Forbes, Duncan, Esq. of Culloden
Fraser, Donald, Esq. of Millburn, Inverness
Fraser, Donald, Esq., registrar, Inverness
Fraser, ex-Provost, Inverness
Fraser, Leslie J., Esq., surgeon dentist, Inverness
Fraser, Major-General Hastings, C.B., of Ardachie (2 Copies)
Fraser, Sir Wm., K.C.B., LL.D., Edinburgh
Fraser, William, Esq., M.A., Broad Street Avenue, London, E.C.
Gall, J. H., Esq., architect, Inverness
Grant, Colonel J. A., C.B., London
Grant, Dr. Ogilvie, Inverness
Hart, George, Esq., F.S.A., Scot., Procurator-Fiscal of Renfrewshire

Head, Mrs. James, of Inverailort
Holland, Richard D., Esq., London (Large Paper)
Holland, Stephen G., Esq., London
Hossack, Wm., Esq., Crofters Commissioner
Innes, Charles, Esq., solicitor, Inverness (Large Paper)
Jenkins, R. P., Esq., solicitor, Inverness
Kyllachy, Right Hon. Lord, Edinburgh
Macandrew, Sir H. C., ex-Provost of Inverness
Macbain, Alex., Esq., M.A., Inverness
Macdonald, Allan, Esq., LL.B., Antrim, Ireland
Macdonald, Allan, Esq., M.A., solicitor, Inverness
Macdonald, Alexander, Colonel, Portree
Macdonald, Duncan, Esq., J.P., Inverness
Macdonald, Ewen, Esq., Inverness
Macdonald, Kenneth, Esq., Town Clerk, Inverness (Large Paper)
Macdonald, Lachlan, Esq. of Skaebost
Macdonald, W. C. R., General, C.B., London
Macdonell, Eneas R., Esq. of Camusdarroch
Macgillivray, Alex., Esq., London
Macgregor, Alex., Esq., solicitor, Inverness
Macgregor, Wm., Esq., Caledonian Bank, Inverness
Macintyre, P. B., Esq., Crofters Commissioner
Mackay, John, Esq., C.E., J.P., Hereford
Mackay, William, Esq., solicitor, Inverness
Mackenzie, Bailie, Inverness
Mackenzie, Burton, Colonel, of Kilcoy
Mackenzie, Dr. F. M., Inverness
Mackenzie, Hector Rose, Esq., Crofter Commission
Mackenzie, J. A., Esq., burgh surveyor, Inverness
Mackenzie, Mrs. Jas. H., bookseller, Inverness (2 Copies)
Mackenzie, W. Dalziel, Esq. of Farr
Mackenzie, Wm., Esq., Cabarfeidh House, Inverness
Mackenzie, Wm., Esq., Secretary, Crofters Commission
Mackenzie, Roderick, Esq., London
Mackintosh, Æneas, Esq., The Doune, Daviot
Mackintosh, Angus, Esq. of Holme
Mackintosh, D., Esq., Bank of Scotland, Inverness
Mackintosh, Eneas, Esq. of Balnespick
Mackintosh, C. Keir, Esq. of Dalmigavie
Mackintosh, Hugh, Esq., merchant, Inverness
Mackintosh, Miss, London
Mackintosh, Mrs., of Mackintosh, Dunachton
Mackintosh of Mackintosh, Moy Hall (Large Paper)
Maclachlan & Stewart, Messrs., booksellers, Edinburgh (2 Copies)
Maclean, Major Roderick, Inverness

LIST OF SUBSCRIBERS.

Macnee, Dr., Inverness
Macritchie, Andrew J., Esq., solicitor, Inverness
Mactavish, Alex., Esq., merchant, Inverness
Matheson, Sir Kenneth J., Bart. of Lochalsh (Large Paper)
Melven Bros., Messrs., booksellers, Inverness
Milne, A. & R., booksellers, Aberdeen
Mitchell Library, The, Glasgow
Moray, Right Hon. the Earl of, (3 Copies)
Munro, Bailie David, Inverness
Munro, Sir Hector, Baronet, of Foulis
Murray, Frank, Esq., The Lodge, Portree
Napier and Ettrick, Right Hon. Lord, K.T.
Noble, Mr. John, bookseller, Inverness (1 Copy & 1 Large Paper)
Ramsden, Sir John, of Byram, Bart.
Reid, Hugh G., Esq. of Warley Hall
Ross, Alex. M., Esq., Inverness
Ross, James, Esq., solicitor, Inverness
Ross, Provost, Inverness
Sinton, Rev. Thos., Dores
Shaw-Mackintosh, Alex., Esq., Hadley, Barnet
Skues, Wm. Mackenzie, Esq., M.D., Brigade-Surgeon, London
Smart, P. H., Esq., Muirfield, Inverness
Smith, ex-Bailie, Inverness
Sutherland, Provost, Wick
Thin, Jas., Mr., bookseller, Edinburgh (3 Copies)
Thomson, James, Esq., Inverness
Vass, Dr., Provost of Tain
Warrand, Lieut.-Colonel Alexander, of Ryefield
Whyte, David, Esq., Inverness
Wyllie, D., & Son, Messrs., booksellers, Aberdeen

LETTERS OF TWO CENTURIES.

No. I. ANNO. 1616.

SIR DONALD MACKAY OF STRATHNAVER.

No more interesting or, in many respects, amusing books connected with the North are to be met with than the Histories of the Houses and Clans of Sutherland, and Mackay. They ought to be read together if the reader wishes for amusement. The deep, subtle, and experienced Sir Robert Gordon not only managed the Sutherland and his own affairs to admiration, but actually for the benefit, though not enlightenment, of posterity, wrote a history, just as much to be depended on as Macaulay's Romances, published under the names of Histories. To understand Sir Robert, read the Mackay History, a valuable, painstaking work.

Sir Donald Mackay, afterwards created Lord Reay, had been knighted in April, 1616; a few months prior to the date of the letter after quoted, communicated by Mr. Dunbar Dunbar. Sir Donald stands out so prominently in history that it is only necessary to make one or two observations on matters contained in the letter. The dubious and uncomplimentary references to his wife, daughter of Lord Kintail, are not easy of interpretation. He does not seem to have been successful in his matrimonial ventures, having attempted to divorce his second wife, an English gentlewoman, as she is described, named Rachel Winterfield, but who successfully vindicated her position. The third wife bore the unaristocratic name of Elizabeth Tamson, and is described as of mean birth, which, indeed, the name in itself would denote. The burning of Sandside, which occurred in the month of November, 1615, directed by the Earl of Caithness against Lord Forbes and his tenants, was not in itself a great affair, but entailed lasting effects on the Caithness family, who, ere they got rid of the civil and criminal processes arising out of the burning, had to pay large sums, and yield up all their valuable and extensive jurisdictions. The head of the Clan Gunn, who had been asked by the Earl to commit the burning of Sandside, indignantly declined to do so, but readily offered to murder the tenant.

Two years after the date of this letter, Sir Donald fell out with his uncle, and endeavoured to form a combination with the Earl of Caithness, against the Sutherland interests.

Follows the letter referred to, the old spelling being observed :—

Rytt. Wy. Sr. and Loveinge Unkill,—I resaifit ane Letter off yors on the sext day off this instant qlk Letter was wrettin fre Bouilie ye 4 of Agust Qrbe I understoud ytt. yr. is sindry Letteris miscarryit till ous boithe. I never resaifit ne Letteris of yors sen Gorge Gray, came bot this last Letter and ane uther. I gat nane that was sent to Allexr. Watsones. All the heids yt. we craifit of ye Lord off Chathnes is grantit bot only conseninge my good moyr, and yt. we gat ne catinors for ye some bot Berrydell his awine band. My Lord Erll of Chathnes sayes or he laiff ye Kingi's dominyeons yt. you or I sall pay for ye sinis of ye peipill. He will not byd be nothinge yt. we haiff done willingly. He employett wtin. this aucht dayis (one of) ye name off Cadell to stay at lexr. Devisone & some uthers of ye clan joine. Ye Cadels reveilitt ye same, so yt. his Lo/ is very neir ye

secound staip to French Sie. My cousinge Angus McKy, is wt.
my selff now. Ye clan Kenze & I is lykly not to sort weill.
Anent my wyff, schow is becoum to bed of ane boy qlk be all
resoune & liklyhoud I haiff nothinge ado wt. Ye Bischop of
Chathnes is gone to Court as I heir for he was not resafit to
Aberdine as I heir at this Assemly. I wrett tua sindry tymes to
your wif off befoir, to hold you in memory off Mr. Ion Gray to gett
hem ye Bischoprik of Chathnes, for I am persoudit yt. his Magistie
wald grant ye same at ye first, giff he war weill informit off yt.
man his delygence for ye weill off ye Keirke in this Deyossie ; as
lykwayis yt. he is ye only man to plant thir countryes giff he hed
yt. scharge. As lykwayis he wad be ever resident at ye Cathedirall
Chourche qlk nane as yit hes evir done in thir parts. I dout not
Unkill bot you knaw yt. ye Hous of Sutherland will nevir gett in
our tyme ane in yt. Scharge, so loveinge as he, and for my part I
rader treist hime yr. then ony I knaw (so help me God) for I ame
assurit yt. he wt. my awine help wald reforme this country, Unkill.
I nor nane neids not to requyst you to do for this mater bot yor.
wor. will be ye better to be thus far haldine in memory. I haiff
not beine in Sutherland sen I cam home, so yt. I wett not Mr. Ion
his awine mynd heirine, bot I dout not bot his father and brothers
will wrette at lenthe to yor wor. anent this. As for country nowis
I heir none, bot that yor mother, brother, and good-sister agryes
not as I wald wis. Ye perticoulers I refer to them selffis. I pray
you to wrett to yor. brother ernastly to get me at Mertimes ye
silver yt. yor wor. rests me for Ion Morray. I lmervell that I heir
ne word frome my brother : giff he coumis to England hest hem
home wt. all dilygence. Ye service of Lochaber gois slawly ford-
wartt. All ye tyme yt. ye Douk his Grace was in Edr. I could not
wine doune to ye Abey to sie hem, be resoune of ane soir back yt.
I hed, the qlk moufit me pertly to coum home be sie. I pray you
forgett not my hors qlk he promist. Remember my hartly kyndnes
to Sr. Wm. Balfour, and assur hem giff evir I may be abill to
plesour him yt. ye same is abyding his plesour. I rest,
    Youris wor. loveing Nephue till daithe,
        (Signed)   DONALD McKIE.
Doirnes ye 3 off Septer., 1616.

The goodman of Broumis, yor cousinge, informit me, yt. yor
umquhell brother, my Lord, was his Souperyour of ye lands of
Broumis at ye tyme yt. my Lord sald ye Foue lands to ye Erll of
Chathnes, so yt. now ye Erll of Chathnes is his superyor. He is
feirit yt. Chathnes be forfititt for this fyr of Sansyds.* Therfor he
prayis yor. wor. giff this falls yt. you sout his lands of Broumis
frome ye King. He sayes becaus ye mother yt. bouir hem was ye

---

 * The lands of Sandside formed part of Barony of Reay.

Erll of Sutherland's dochter, yt. he rader haiff you to be his master than ony uther sourty. Richartt was evir to his pouer ours. Yrfor. forgett hem not, giff it falls.—D.

   Addressed—To Ye Rytt. Wor. and my lovinge Unkill,
    Sir Robert Gordoune, Touter off Sutherland.

P.S.—Remember my bouits.

No. II. Anno. 1617.

GEORGE, 1st MARQUIS OF HUNTLY.

The writer of the letter after given, George 6th Earl of Huntly, created Marquis in 1599, was one of the leaders in the battle of Glenlivet. Born in 1562, he died peacefully in 1636, and though he had a chequered career, was more fortunate in his end than his son George, 2nd Marquis, who was executed 22nd March, 1649.

This letter refers to two matters. The first, a case of witchcraft, Lord Huntly, though a Catholic, makes short work of. The strange and intolerant charges of witchcraft were practically unknown in Great Britain before the Reformation; and for encouragement in its belief, James the Sixth is much to blame.

The second point refers to sport, and shows that in the Braes of Mar, at least, wolves were to be found at the period in question. These gatherings must have been very enjoyable. Freedom from care, life in the open air for days and nights together, violent exercise in the chase, song and dance at night, all tended to health and strength.

The Gordons had their hunts in various parts. For their Castle lands it was on Dochnacraig, or Lochend; and in the final sale of superiority to Colonel Baillie of Dunean, at the close of last century, there is reserved, but long obsolete, that in remembrance and perpetuation of the ancient ties betwixt the Gordons and Baillies, the Duke and his successors shall be entitled to hunt in the heights of Craig Dearg, according to use and wont. Follows the letter referred to :—

Right Special Cousin,—After my very hearty commendation, according to the desire of your letter, I have sent to the Gudeman of Buckie, my cousin, and has willed him to do justice on the witch which you wrote to me has bewitched Golspitaire's son. Therefore you may advertise Buckie whensoever he comes to Inverness for that effect.

As for the white hound you wrote for, he cannot be sent to you at this time, because the morn eight days, I have appointed ane wolffe huntis in Mar, and am to hunt myself there, ten or twelve days thereafter, and we are scarcer of hounds here nor ye are there. So my loving commendations remembered to my lady, my aunt, your mother, I will commit you most heartily to God—Your most loving cousin, (Signed) HUNTLYE.

Huntly, the 17th of August, 1617.

Addressed—"To my Right Special Cousin, Sir Robert Gordon of Kinmonavie, Knight."

No. III. Anno. 1618.

GEORGE, EARL OF CAITHNESS.

OF old, the counties of Sutherland and Caithness were practically owned by the families of Caithness, Reay, and Sutherland, and their respective cadets.

One only has thriven by English inter-marriage; of the other two, one has been expropriated, and the other has dwindled to comparative insignificance.

No race of the nobles of Scotland has such a record as that of Caithness. The Earls were able, but so unscrupulous and tyrannical, that in course of time they lost jurisdictions, lands, caste, and influence.

The writer of the annexed letter was engaged in many a misdeed, although he writes to his creditor in a very soft tone. The sword was more familiar than the pen, there being a singular lack of smoothness or elegance in the language. The letter is but short, yet in it the words "your Lordship" occur about ten times.

One of the most curious episodes in the Caithness history, was that where one of the Earls tried to sell, not only his estates, but also the title, to Lord Breadalbane. The last Earl has unhappily alienated the estates from the title.

It would appear from the letter that at the period the present of a hare, fine of its kind, was considered not an unsuitable gift from one noble to another.

Follows the letter referred to :—

My Very Special Good Lord and Cousin,—I received your Lordship's letter, and, according to my promise to your Lordship in Edinburgh, I shall fulfil unto your Lordship in all parts according to my more nor bound duty. I know your Lordship has sold your land and paid for me—I were more nor ingrat if I were unthankful to your Lordship. I protest to God since my home-coming, I never had an idle hour to do the uttermost of my power to give all contentment to my creditors, and if I were letten to do my best, I hope in God to pay all my debts in shorter space than is expected. I have written to Ronald Murray to inform your Lordship what I have heard. Your Lordship shall be assured, and I be not stayed by what I wrote to Ronald, your Lordship shall have experience of my true meaning. I have sent my man to your Lordship with ane fyne hare of kynd. So to your Lordship's next advertisement I end, and ever shall remain, yours so auive to be commandit,

(Signed)   G. CAITHNES.

Berriedale, 23 June, 1618.

Addressed—" To My Most Special Good Lord and Cousin, My Lord of Skoone. These."

No. IV. Anno. 1619.

SIR LACHLAN MACKINTOSH OF TORCASTLE.

THE system of holding of lands in Scotland and other countries, where the feudal laws prevailed, was perhaps in no sense so oppressive, as in the casualty of marriage. The unfortunate owner of land must either take the wife offered by the favourite who procured the gift, or pay a heavy fine. Such marriages were also frequently forced on, when the bridegroom or bride, as the case might be, was much under the age of twenty-one. The Mackintosh family for three successive generations were victims of this pernicious system. Lachlan Mor Mackintosh was quite a youth when Mackenzie of Kintail made him marry his daughter Agnes. In like manner Lachlan's eldest son, Angus, had to take the Earl of Argyll's daughter, and lastly Sir Lachlan, the writer of the letter after given, had to marry the Laird of Grant's daughter. I have no means of knowing whether these marriages, contracted so early and under such conditions, were or were not happy; but this is certain, that every one of these connections, brought trouble and permanent loss to the family of Mackintosh.

The Frasers of Lovat have been so long dominant in the Aird, that the possession of much of it by other families is unknown or forgotten. Lachlan Mor Mackintosh before referred to, who did so much to enlarge and consolidate the family estates, though he made a pathetic appeal to the Laird of Grant in 1568 to let him have, at a fair price, Rothiemurchus, which he describes as "his own most native country," alluding to its possession as early as 1236 by his family, first as lease-holders and afterwards as owners, and which had fallen into Grant's clutches, was also most anxious to have a good hold in the low country of Inverness-shire. He had immense estates in the higher parts, but little corn lands. Therefore he bought Culloden, and should have had Ardersier were it not for the perfidy of Calder. As early as 1520 Lachlan, then laird, had acquired a considerable estate in the Aird, chiefly by purchase from the Baron of Moniack, whose place of residence still goes under the name of "Larach-Tigh-a-Varran." In the year 1568 Lachlan Mor settled upon his son Angus those parts of the baronies of Drumchardiny and Beauford, called Holm, Craggach, Drumchardiny, Kinneries, and Eskadale. In Anderson's *History of the Frasers*, page 101, he says—"The family of Mackintosh held large possessions in the Aird."

It is no doubt in reference to those estates that some

debt appears to have remained due by Lachlan Mor, at his death in 1606, to Fraser of Phopachie, and for which Fraser was pursuing Sir Lachlan as heir of his grandfather.

Follows the letter referred to, conceived in courteous and dignified terms:—

Right trusty friend,—My commendations remembered. These presents are to show that your officer Patrick Strachan, gave me a charge in your name concerning some gear that was betwixt my gud sir (grandfather) and you, and Malcolm Ego, my servant, showed me that you spoke to him at Inverness that you were not willing to trouble me over muckle, till you spake with my self thereanent, that you might know what I would do to you in that errand. Which continuation I have gotten of your courtesy, till now that the officer has made intimation to me of new. Wherefore, seeing you have continued the same so long, I will request you cause your officer oversee me to Martinmas that I speak with yourself in respect of my adoes in Murray presently, which I have no doubt you will. So rests your assured good friend.

(Signed)   Sir La: M Kintosche
off Torcastell.

Addressed—"To his right trust friend, James Fraser of Puhoppochie."

On the back—"Sir,—Please you to send some silver with this bearer, for my pains because I have adoes, so rests.

(Signed)   P. Strathauchin.
Mess."

Thus endorsed—"Mackintosh's letter sent to James Fraser, for continuation of his letters, to Martinmas next, 1619 years."

No. V. Anno. 1620 (Circa).

LORD KINTAIL AND THE BISHOP OF ROSS.

The letter after quoted, communicated by Mr. Dunbar Dunbar, has no date, but we assign to it, about 1620, as Lord Kintail was created Earl of Seaforth in 1623. The ability in composition shown by some of the noted men of the North, one, two, and three hundred years ago, is well illustrated by this letter of Lord Kintail's.

It is known, as matter of history, that the Clan Kenneth

pressed out many of the old proprietors of Ross, and notably the Bishops of Ross, even to the very doors of their residence. All the Channon lands fell into their hands, step by step; and wisely, to consolidate and retain their power, the family of Seaforth made Chanonry their own chief residence. The struggles, harryings, and spuilzies which occurred are historical, yet here we find Lord Kintail heartlessly speaking of the poverty of the Bishop, thus—"he and his few company and sober convoy (which is very small) comes to his cathedral to visit his diocesans." The Bishop in question was Patrick Lindsay, of the honourable family of Edzell, who was afterwards translated to Glasgow, and of whom Keith says—"In both these Sees, he exercised his office with great lenity."

Like that of a lady, Lord Kintail's postscript to his letter is not the least interesting. The information to his correspondent, Sir Robert Gordon, Tutor of Sutherland, of whom he was asking a favour, "that all friends are well, and your foes as you would wish them—most miserable," is admirable in its delicate flattery.

Follows the letter referred to, the old spelling being observed :—

Honll. Sr.,—Upon the assuirance I have of your favour, by resoune of your manifold courtieseis schawin to me, I thocht it requiset to remember my affectioun to you, as likwayis to schaw you as my new freind, how I am crossit by the Bischope of Ross, as I declared to you at our last meiting; now he is directit with the Archbischope of Gleskow to His Majestie as Commissionaris fra the Generall Assemblie to schaw of thair proceidingis. In the meantyme I am assuired that the Bischope of Ross will prease to mak som erronius informatione of me to His Majestie concerning his house of the Chanonrie of Ross, quhereof I am heritable constable as my predicesors hes bein of befoir, altho no just occasioune is given him, for he ever was reseairt, interteinict, and acknawledgit as the just awner thairof quhen as he and his few cumpanie and sober convoy (quhilk is verie small) cummis to his Cathederall to viseit his diocesians.

My umquhill grandfather, to his great losse, coft the heritable constabilrie with certane landis adjacent therto fra the Laird Buquheane to quhom Bischope Ihone Leslie fewit the samen.

Thairefter my umquhill father behovit to give ane secund compositione, and that my reat to Mr Wm. Leslie as I think His Majestie himself is in recent memorie thairof. Nocht theless, quhen, as the Bischops in the Parlament of Perthe, 1606, war restorit to thair auld privelegis at His Majestie's desyir, my father behovit to give his geir in great to Mr David Lindsay, last Bischope of Rosse. No theless this bischope intendis to truble me now, hoiping thairby to get sum neidles geir of me, nochtwithstanding of the sufficiencie of my richt, to helpe to by his new conqueis in Angus & not to helpe his cathedrall kirk altogither ruinus nor to viseit his house of Channonrie quhilk had been ruinus lyk the cathedrall kirk thairof, war not the great charges my father and grandfather mead thairon. Quherfoir my earnest requeast to you is that gif the Bischope go to Court, as I doubt not to misrepresent to His Majestie of me, that ye stand my freind in this occasioune as ye have doin evir hitherto and deleat to His Majestie sick as I have wretin to you quhilk, I will avowe the least word I have wreatin to you to be your warrand. As lykwayis I beseeche that ye wald mein to His Majestie his wicked intention in this purpose & my thraild esteat at the present, always in all respects I sall be law byding to him. For I knaw it is not His Majestie's will that new richts be taine from everie intrant Bischope quhen as his leigis hes sufficient richt fra thair predicessouris confermit be His Majestie. I have wreatin to my Lord of Fentown in the same particular, and I have directit his letter with this to my Lord Chancellar to sie giv it be expedient that it be directit to my Lord Fentoune. Give it gois to Lord Fentoune or not I knaw not. Yit I doubt not bot at my requeast ye will schaw heirof and hald him in memorie of the same. As likwayis I luik that ye will schaw the same to suche utheris your freinds as ye think hes the King's ear, that ye and they may deleat my honest pairt to His Majestie. Quherfoir ye may be assuired ye sall have me and all I may do, to do you all kynd of dewtie as your employments and my abilitie sall requear. Sua assuiring myself of your courtious acceptatioune of this my heamlines I end, not doubting of your freindlie dealing with me in this and in all other thingis quhilk sall and dois obleis me ever to remain in to yowe as

Yr. assuired ever to his power,

(Signed)　Kintaill.

I have no newis to wreat to you bot that all freinds are weill, and your foes as ye wald wisse them—maist miserable.

I wald have wreatin to Sir George Hay in this particular war not I know at the deat heirof that he is not cum'd home. Alwayis I doubt not bot ye will schaw him al the meireit of this caus quhairbe he may assist you in deleating the same to His Majestie.

I request you earnestlie to excuis me for putting you to this pains. Alwayis gif ye have ado in Scotland I myself and all I may do sall back your guid actioune.

I entreat you heast you home, and bring your bedfellow heame with you. I think ye remainit long aneuche at the Court.

Addressed on the back—"To the Ryt. Honll. His maist special Freind Sir Robert Gordoun of Kinmonthy, Knit."

No. VI. Anno. 1621.

SIR ROBERT GORDON.

THE letters of the able and busy Sir Robert Gordon are always interesting, He had much to do with the Mackay family, and while always affecting to befriend them, yet it so happened that ultimately the family of Sutherland had all the benefit.

The letter after given finds him engrossed in the affairs of others, notably that of the Earl of Sutherland. Lords Elphinstone and Forbes had at this time an interest in the county of Caithness, from which they ultimately retired, these families never having taken any real root in the country.

The letter is a good specimen of Sir Robert Gordon's easy and courteous style, and contrasts most favourably with that of the Earl of Caithness, No. III.

Other letters from or to Sir Robert, will be given afterwards. Sir Robert laid the foundation of that wonderful library, the prices at its sale, nearly a century ago, being quoted in all the book manuals, as indices of values of many rare and curious works.

Follows the letter referred to :—

My Lord,—I have all this while delayed to write to your Lordship, and also stayed hitherto my journey to England, expecting a meeting of Mackay. All that I can draw him to, is to have a free communing in this town, the 5th of October next, which is better than to leave all loose when I am in England, for of a free communing there may come better. As to a submission, he refuses altogether, but I think friends will persuade him to it when they meet. Therefore I will entreat your Lordship to take pains to be in this town on the 5th of October next, by twelve hours, for without your Lordship I will be loath to end any matter. I confess the time of the year is not very proper for a man of your Lordship's years, yet the fault is not in me.

My Lord Forbes likewise and the Earl of Caithness will have a diet the same time here, which also will be a part of your Lordship's coming hither. I was of late three nights in Castle Sinclair; I drew on the meeting betwixt the Earl of Caithness and my Lord Forbes; your Lordship shall know all particulars at meeting. The 22nd of this month was first appointed, but because it was ower short time to advertise your Lordship, it was continued to the 5th of October. If this diet holds not, I shall advertise your Lordship before the 26th of this instant, lest your Lordship should take such a journey in vain. I am now in haste going to the bog* with the Lord Chancellor, so that I cannot write at such length as I would; only that I would intreat your Lordship to keep this tryst because it concerns the Earl of Sutherland so far; and remembering my service to my good lady, I rest, your loving cousin to serve you,

(Signed)   ROBERT GORDON.

Elgin, the 6th of September, 1621.

Addressed—"To my very good lord, my Lord Elphinstone."

No VII. Anno. 1622.

THE VIRGINIAN SETTLERS.

SETTLERS began to flock in great numbers to Virginia, towards the close of the reign of Elizabeth, and the flow continued during King James reign.

The official records and documents of the period are full of complaints on the part of the Settlers. The Crown gave grants and monopolies to favourites, resulting in discontent and misery. In 1622 Sir Nathamie Rich was a leading personage in Virginian matters, as also in those of the Bermudas, then called the Summer Islands. The Settlers in the Summer Islands, many Nonconformists, complained that they "were defrauded of the food of

* The Bog, now Gordon Castle.

their souls," as they had only one minister, and had never more than two for 1500 souls dispersed into a length of twenty miles, and those two "always shortened in their promised entertainment." Again, when their parents died, "the children were held as mere drudges to their landlords, in order to discharge their fathers' debts."

King James, as is well known, was a strong opponent of tobacco smoking and wrote against the habit. Yet it is found that he was not above having a royalty on all sales, as may be seen from the following extract of a document in 1622. Selling tobacco in paper packets was a fair thing to the ordinary consumer, who would have tobacco pure, and not as at present, previously steeped and impregnated in water and oil, so as to increase its weight :—

The King was to have the pre-emption of all tobacco and allow adventurers and planters 2s 6d per lb. clear of all customs, payments, or impositions. Some persons who would become the King's merchants would allow him 5s a lb., and would in return have the sole power to license retailers. All tobacco sold at alehouses was to be in paper, sealed with the seal of a licensed retailer, who was to sell it to the alehouses in penny papers, thirteen to a dozen, so that the ale-house keeper might get a penny in the shilling.

In a subsequent letter I will deal with the transportation of British subjects to America and the West Indies, an atrocious system which preceded the Negro slave trade, and give an indenture as late as 1716, into which Mackintosh of Balnespick's brother had to enter as the result of engaging in the Rising in 1715.

No. VIII. Anno. 1623.

ANNA CAMPBELL, 2ND MARCHIONESS OF HUNTLY.

THE writer of the letter or ticket after given, was daughter of Archibald, seventh Earl of Argyll, and married, when

Lord Gordon and Earl of Enzie, George, second Marquis of Huntly, who was executed in 1649.

The document is holograph of the lady, and shows she was well up in legal matters. The writing on its back must have been added after she became Marchioness. The ticket, not of value in itself, was found enclosed in an interesting document, being the agreement for sale of Dochnacraig, or Lochend, to Alexander Baillie of Dunain in the year 1619. The consideration money was only three hundred merks, and the deed is very special in conveying the alehouse and alehouse croft of Dochnacraig, with its fishings in the Loch and water of Ness, and its grazings in the Mount of Caiploch.

It is not uncommon in old deeds to find special conveyances of alehouses, but this of Lochend is the oldest I am familiar with in the United parish of Inverness and Bona.

The disgraceful abundance of public houses and drink houses along the public roads can hardly be credited by the present generation. Unfortunates who perhaps had quite enough in Inverness, returning to their homes by the Urquhart Road, were met within a mile by the Three Merry Boys, at Tomnahurich Bridge; beyond the fourth mile stone there was a public house at Dochgarroch, and beyond the sixth, the house at Lochend. Taking the Dores Road, the house, Back of the Islands, within a mile, was first met, next one at Scaniport, next at Dores, next at Inverfarigaig, and so on. Going to Stratherrick, Back of the Islands was convenient; drink could be had at Slack na Mearlaich of Holme; there was a house at Essich, and a noted one at Achnabat. Achnabat was a centre of interchange for produce in cattle, horses, sheep, etc., for a large district, and no house within miles of Inverness had a worse reputation for clan, township, and personal feuds and bloodshed amongst the frequenters, than Achnabat. By the old Edinburgh Road change houses were found at Hilton, Faillie, Ballintruan, etc.; and perhaps the worst road of all was that to the east, beginning with the famous Scridain. On the other hand, good accommodation was wanting. There being no proper house between Aviemore and Inverness, the Inn at Freeburn was built in 1799, chiefly by public subscription, Ulbster, Seaforth, and other northern gentlemen using the Perth road, contributing liberally.

The Baillies of Dunain had been settled there long anterior to the period in question, but they had held up to Alexander's time, on wadsets and other redeemable rights.

This Alexander, who lent the forty pounds to Lady Huntly, was in great favour with the Huntly family, and acted as their Chamberlain for some time over their Castle lands, and the Lordship of Lochaber, some of his accounts being preserved. He also got charters to all his lands, and established his family on a permanent footing. From his second son, David, the present family of Dochfour springs.

Follows the letter referred to :—

We by these presents grants me to have received from Alexander Baillie, the sum of forty pounds, which we oblige us to pay twixt this and Martinmas, in the year of God, sixteen hundred and twenty-three years. By this our ticket, subscribed with my hand at Inverness, the twentieth of July, 1623 years.

(Signed) ANNA CAMPBELL.

Endorsed—" My Ladie Huntlie's Tickat for 40 lb."

No. IX. ANNO. 1624.

GILBERT VAUS, SON OF ROBERT VAUS, WRITER, BURGESS OF INVERNESS.

THE annexed interesting letter from Hungary seems to be the earliest preserved by the Inshes family, and was indeed addressed to the head of that family ere it had acquired any part of Inshes.

The name of Vaus or Waus, originally " De Vallibus," is of long standing in Inverness, and the writer was son of that Robert Vaus who so deeply offended the author rities of Inverness by his purchase, in 1591, from Lesslie of Balquhain of the lands of Drumdivan, lying within the Barony of Lochardill.

There was a close connection, by marriage and otherwise, 'twixt the Vauses and Robertsons; indeed, one part of the Inshes property is described in the old titles as "Martin Vaus's Inshes," to distinguish it from the other, or "Paterson's Inshes."

The writer did not return, and the once powerful family of Vaus, degenerating into "Vass," has become almost extinct. Part of this letter appeared in a northern paper between forty and fifty years ago, being contributed by the late accomplished Mr. George Anderson. Mr. Anderson made the curious mistake in the signature of writing "Miller," instead of "Wretter." Another transcriber made the Town Council of Inverness a couple of centuries ago order "the bee-hives" in the Islands to be repaired, instead of "The Cruives."

Follows the letter referred to:—

Laus Deo Semper,
December 10th, 1624.

Dearlie and well-beloved Eme,—After my hearty commendations, please you to wit that I am in good health, God be praised, wishing to hear and see the like of you and all your good friends.

I marvel ye are unkind grown since your passing away from here, that you never wrote to me of your own proceedings there, and of the state of your own friends and mine together. I have formerly, in the month of May, written to you concerning the reversion of the quarter of the Water of Ness, which reversion my good brother and sister has in keeping. According as I have promised it to you I have written home to my good brother and sister to deliver you the reversion, and with it what ye please to my meeting and coming home; and if it please God that I never come home, I think the same well bestowed on you, by reason you are mor etender of blood and kin to me, nor the honest man is that had it in wadsett of four hundred merks.

Loving Eme, I pray you write to me if ye have gotten the same or not, for I have written to them both most earnestly to deliver you the same, for they have no means of their own to relieve it. If ye have gotten the reversion write to me, and I shall send you an assignation, wherebe that James Cuthbert will

pursue his own moneys according to the reversion, and laws of the country, and you to intromit with the same even as if I were then present myself personally without any trouble or skaith. Loving Eme, seeing ye have written to me and spoke to me that it will be to your profit, I rather ye have the same in your custody and possession on the condition he has it, nor he nor any other. And I doubt not that, if it please God that I come home, but that ye will restore me the reversion back again, and put me in my own place, so that I give you as meikle money as ye disburse on it, or else some more content? nor he would give me that has it. For, under God, I lippen in you more nor in him by reason ye are of kin and blood to me, and in case it please God to wisie (sic) me here, ye shall bruik the same for ever. But I request you, Eme, to be good to my poor sister, who is your aunt of blood, and help her, seeing God has blessed you. She has written to me that ye coft her as meikle as was her ain coat of grey cloth, and has given her ane plaid, which I hope in God, God will bless you the better, seeing I lie off far from her myself, and I am not well to the fore. God, if I might pleasure you more, God forgive your Eme and mine, William Paterson, who was my wrack as I was last in Scotland. No more, but my hearty kindness to yourself and to all my friends and yours from Bucko, besyde Posuay, the 10th day of December, 1624. Your loving Eme. (Signed) GILBERT VAUS,
 Son to Umquhile Robert Vaus, Burgess and Writer of Inverness.

Addressed—"To his loving Eme John Robertson, William's son, Burgess of Inverness."

No. X. Anno. 1625.
THE EARL OF ARUNDEL AND SURREY, AND KING JAMES' FUNERAL.

THE wise King, James the Sixth, was not much regretted at his death. Royal funerals even at this day are celebrated with great pomp. In King James' time the funeral of private persons, was a great and expensive event.

The custom of giving gloves and bands has hardly died out in these days.

The annexed most curious letter has been preserved among the collections of a Welsh lady.

It seems hardly credible that any one in the rank of a noble could think of applying for black cloth and not attend the Royal funeral, although it is known there were many hungry and impoverished persons hanging about King James' Court.

The letter speaks for itself, and indicates either that abuses had crept in, or that there was to be close economy in the future.

His Majesty's will (Charles I.) is, that he is pleased that the nobility of this kingdom shall attend the funeral of our late Sovereign, King James, as mourners, so that it be intimated to every man that shall send for blacks, that none, upon pain of his high displeasure, keep the blacks, which will not or can not really mourn, and do honour to the funeral, as well in the proceeding, as at the ceremony in the church. And as every one is to have notice given of this command at the Wardrobe, so no doubt all will obey it, and not take these blacks, when they know their occasions will not permit them to attend the service.

Dated 24th April, 1625.

Every now and then mutterings of discontent are heard at the retention of ancient and by no means time-honoured customs of perquisites even of clothing, jewellery, etc., in favour of bishops, deans, sinecurists, and pluralists, though they do not take the distinctness of the order above quoted.

No. XI. Anno. 1626.

GEORGE VILLIERS, DUKE OF BUCKINGHAM.

THE extraordinary rise of the first Duke of Buckingham has never been equalled in British History. The title has been a favourite one, and in the year 1889 has again disappeared from the rolls.

George Villiers was second son, by his second marriage, of Sir George Villiers of Brokesby. In 1615 the honour of Knighthood was conferred upon him; in 1616 he was made Viscount, in 1617 Earl, in 1618 Marquis, and in 1623 Duke of Buckingham.

In 1626 he was elected Chancellor of the University of Cambridge, and on 6th June, in acknowledging the distinction conferred upon him by the Professors of learning, whose good opinion he prizes highly, notwithstanding his want of scholarship, adds, "Yet I cannot appreciate the honour to any desert of mine, but to the sacred memory you bear to my dead master, the king of scholars, who loved you and honoured you oft with his presence, and to my gracious master, now living, who inheriteth with his blessed father's virtues, the affection which he bore to your University."

So the Duke was not unmindful of the King, who did so much for him, and whom he terms "the king of scholars." After the Duke's assassination in 1628, there was presented to the University a rare collection of Arabic manuscripts, procured in remote countries by the industry and diligence of Erpinius, a famous linguist. These manuscripts the Duke had acquired in Holland with the object of presenting them himself to the University.

The Duke of Buckingham had great and valuable properties in London, leading from the Strand to the Thames. While the lands were laid out in streets, each street or lane was called thus, "George" Street, "Villiers" Street, "Duke" Street, "Of" Court, and "Buckingham" Street, running "George Villiers, Duke of Buckingham" in succession. Some of these remain to this day.

The dissolute life and unhappy end of the second Duke of Buckingham are well known. The Earls of Surrey and Clarendon are descended from an elder brother of the first Duke.

By curious destinations the nephew of the last Duke of Buckingham who died in 1889, became Earl Temple, while the eldest of the Duke's three daughters became Lady Kinloss in the Peerage of Scotland

No. XII. Anno. 1627.
SLAVERY IN NEW ENGLAND.

PRIOR to the great exodus on the part of Nonconformists and others to the States, the previous settlers were much dissatisfied with their position, as may be seen by the authentic Government and private records extant.

Favourites received grants and monopolies, as I mentioned in a former letter, and the object was to extract as much wealth, and within as short a space, as possible.

Later on, in the seventeenth century, the systematic deportation of criminals and political prisoners had come to a great pitch, as the planters and colonists were always in straits for labour.

I take this opportunity of giving papers connected with Mr James Mackintosh of Kinrara, brother to the Laird of Balnespick, a young man who, unhinged by the death of his wife, took a commission in Borlum's battalion in 1715, was taken prisoner at Preston, and afterwards transported to Virginia.

The first paper is a note holograph of Kinrara, prepared after his return, a most interesting record of the events of that period. It is titled on the back, "A note of all my losses in the year 1715," and is as follows :—

A NOTE OF ALL MY LOSSES IN THE YEAR 1715, BEING TWO YEARS ABROAD, ONE YEAR IN PRISON, AND ANOTHER IN VIRGINIA.

	lbs. Scots.		
Imps.—Lost two good working horses at Burntisland	50	0	0
Item—A new saddle, with furniture, crossing the Forth	50	0	0
It.—Lost of clothes and linen at Leith and at Preston	40	0	0
It.—Cost going to England, and in prison there ...	100	0	0
It.—Paid for my freedom and transportation to Virginia	182	0	0
It.—Paid for expenses in Virginia and my passage home	100	0	0
It.—Paid coming home, in Ireland and Scotland ...	40	0	0
It.—My good pistol, sword, target, and dirk	60	0	0
It.—Having left in disorder, being a widower at the time of horses, cows, and sheep to the value of	600	0	0
And never got any of them, and of crop also	100	0	0
	£1,322	0	0

Here follows the Indenture, which is printed, and on stamped paper :—

The Indenture of a person transported for rebellion against our Most Gracious Sovereign Lord, King George (which, upon the humble petition of the rebel herein mentioned, was most mercifully granted by His Imperial Majesty, upon condition of serving seven years, and other conditions) is as follows, viz. :—

This Indenture made the twenty-eighth day of June, *Anno Regni Regis Georgii Magn. Brittan*, &c., *Secundo Annoque Domini*, one thousand seven hundred and sixteen, between James Mackinkintosh of Kinrara, in the parish of Alvie, in the county of Inverness, gentleman, on the one part, and Henry Trafford of Liverpool, in the county of Lancaster, merchant, on the other part, witnesseth that the said James Mackintosh doth hereby covenant and agree to, and with the said Henry Trafford his executors, and assigns to serve him, the said Henry Trafford, and his assigns from the day of the date of these presents, until his first and next arrival at Virginia, or any other of His Majesty's plantations, and after, for, and during and unto the full end and term of seven years from thence next ensuing, fully to be complete and ended, there to serve in such service and employmennt as he, the said Henry Trafford, or his assigns shall employ him in, according to the custom of the country in the like kind. In consideration whereof the said Henry Trafford doth covenant and agree to and with the said James Mackintosh to pay for his passage, and to find for and allow him meat, drink, apparel, and lodging, with other necessaries, according to the custom of the country. In witness whereof the parties aforesaid to these presents interchangeably, their hands and seals have put, the day and year first above written.

      (Signed) JA. MACKINTOSH, [L.S.]

Sealed and delivered in presence of
      (Signed) CHA. PETERS.

Before the Worshipful William Squire, Esquire, Mayor of Liverpool, and attested by him.

      (Signed) WM. SQUIRE.

I assign unto Mr. Joseph Chamberlain, or his assignees in Virginia, the within Indenture, and all my right and title to the service of the within named James Mackintosh upon the terms and conditions within mentioned. Witness my hand.

      (Signed) HENY. TRAFFORD.

Readers will be glad to know that after his return Mr Mackintosh fell on his feet, to use a common expression, and marrying the well-dowered relict of Macpherson of Uvie, lived, though always in valetudinary health, to a great age, and long after the 'Forty-Five.

No. XIII. Anno. 1628.

KINGSMILN'S DISPUTES.

I HAVE more than once had to note the keen disputes which took place in the neighbourhood of Inverness, regarding milns and miln dues.

After the removal of the original milns from the Haugh to the valley of the Millburn, the property of the milns was feued out by the Burgh, and came to be held in five parts, as is, I believe, the case to this day. The feu duty for each portion was 42s. Scots. John Robertson, first of Inshes, whose predecessors had been considerable burghers of Inverness, had, as early as 1628, become possessor of one half of the milns.

His rights to miln dues were not only questioned by the mode of abstraction, but as detailed in the annexed Royal letters, Lord Lovat for the Leys, Glenmoriston for Culcabock, Cuthbert of Easter Drakies, and the feuars and tenants of the Castle lands went further, and threatened and molested Inshes and his head miller.

Nor did the doings of Cuthbert stop at that point, for he is accused of breaking Inshes' miln lades, interfering with his dams at the Leys, and carrying away the water that should serve the King's milns, to a miln newly erected by him. This miln was probably Midmills, or the smaller one further down the stream. That the Provost of the Burgh should act in so high-handed a manner as to call for the King's letters against him can not be much wondered at, when we find, just about this period, Baillie of Dunain's assassination attempted by his own brethren, on the road between Inverness and Dunain.

Follows the letter referred to :—

Charles, by the grace of God, King of the United Kingdom of Great Britain, France, and Ireland, Defender of the Faith, to our Lovites William Ross, messenger, our Sheriffs in that part conjunctly and severally. Specially constituted greeting—Whereas it is humbly meant and complained to me by our Lovite John Robertson, merchant burgess of our Burgh of Inverness, heritable proprietor of all and whole the just and equal half of our miln in our said Burgh, astricted thirled multures, and knaveships of the same, and Thomas Mac Comis, master miller of the said John Robertson's, half thereof, upon our right trusty cousin, Simon Lord Lovat, James Cuthbert of Easter Drakies, Provost of our said Burgh of Inverness, Mr. John Rose, Burgess there, Robert Baillie, Burgess there, Finlay Taylor and James Macallister, servitors to the said James Cuthbert, Malcolm Fraser of Culduthel, and John Grant of Glenmoriston. That where the said John Robertson as heritor of the equal half of the said miln has good and undoubted right in and to all and sundry, the thirled multures of the corns growing within the town's territory, and parochin of Inverness, which suffers fire and water within the same, and to the thirled multures of the corns growing upon the Castle lands of Inverness, as his rights and securities of the same purport. Notwithstanding whereof our said trusty cousin, Simon Lord Lovat, and remanent persons above mentioned, daily by themselves and their servants, complices and others in their names of their causing sending hounding out and ratihabition, intercepted the corns thirled to our said mill of Inverness, casts the lades of the streams, and violently and perforce compels the growers of the said corns to come to such mills as they have in their possession, and albeit they are all thirled to our said miln of Inverness ; likeas also the foresaid persons above complained upon, though their corns are thirled to our said miln of Inverness, yet abstract the same therefrom, and not content therewith, but troubles and molests said complainers in taking away the water, that should cause the miln grind out at the said John Robertson his miln dam, daily and nightly, and by abstracting and breaking down the dams of the said lands at the Leys, and carrying the same down to the miln of Drakies, newly built by the said James Cuthbert, which is prejudicial to our miln of Inverness, and also threatens and menaces the said complainers for their bodily harm and slaughter, in proud contempt of us, our

authority and laws, and instil example to others to commit the like, unless timeous remeid be hereto provided.
Edinburgh, 4 June, 1628.

No. XIV. Anno 1629.

THE FIRST LORD REAY.

Sir Donald Mackay of Farr, afterwards first Lord Reay, was the most celebrated of his family. He had been engaged in many important diplomatic undertakings, and was much in repute at home as an arbiter. The letter of acquittance after given, relates to a transaction with the Danish monarch, and sufficiently explains itself.

The subsequent heads of the Mackays by no means distinguished themselves in the history of the country, and, finally, the sale of their vast estates destroyed the unity of the clan as a distinctive body.

It is a moot question who is, or ought to be held and accounted, "the real Mackay;" indeed the term has become proverbial. A meeting of those of the name was lately held in Glasgow for the purpose of refounding the clan. Mr John Mackay, Hereford, is a true Mackay; the Bonanza King is another, and so may be the holder of the title, and his next heir, the Dutch Baron. But I should fancy the "real Mackay" will not appear with general acceptance, until he become owner of the Reay Forest and of the parish of Farr. The name is numerous, not uninfluential, and it may be hoped the rehabilitation of the clan will not be a thing of the far future.

Follows the letter of discharge referred to :—

Whereas His Most Excellent Majesty of Great Britain (my dread Sovereign) hath been graciously pleased to give me assurance by several Privy Seals of the payment of the sum of eighteen thousand three hundred and four Rix dollars, amounting to the sum of four thousand five hundred and seventy-six pounds sterling, assigned unto me by the King of Denmark by letters of His Majesty dated the 4th day of October, 1628, whereby the said

King of Denmark doth recognise that payment of the said sum should be made unto me, and deducted out of any such monies as should rest upon accompt as due from the King of Great Britain to the King of Denmark. I do hereby acknowledge myself fully satisfied in the King of Denmark's behalf for the said sum of money, and shall have patience to attend the time set down by His Majesty's Privy Seal for the payment of the said money, but in accounting the thousand pounds allotted me in consideration of the Sheriffship of Strathnaver, in the country of Scotland, as part of my money. Given at Greenwitch, the first day of May, in the year of our Lord sixteen hundred and twenty-nine.

(Signed)   REAY.

Endorsed—"The Discharge given by the Lord Reay unto the hands of my Lord Viscount Dorchester for the King's use."

No. XV. Anno. 1630.

MR. WALTER ROSS AND THE LAIRD OF KINCRAIG.

As the writer of the letter after given signs "Mr.," I presume he was a clergyman. His name does not appear, however, in the Ross-shire Presbytery Records. Colin Mackenzie, of Kincraig, to whom the letter is addressed, was a man of importance in his day. A younger son of the first Baron of Redcastle, he, in the year 1644, appears owner of lands in five parishes. The earliest paper I notice extant, connected with Kincraig, is dated in 1589, being a charter by Sir William Keith of Delnie, to Andrew Monro of Dochcartie in life-rent, and Andrew Monro, his second son, in fee. The lands only remained with the Monros until about 1630.

A very formal contract of marriage is drawn out in 1643 between Colin Mackenzie of Kincraig and his daughter, Florence, with David Cuthbert, Town Clerk of Inverness. Florence gets the very considerable dot of 4500 merks, but is unable to write her name. The witnesses to this deed, signed at Inverness on 24th October, are Roric Mackenzie of Redcastle ; Duncan Forbes of Culloden, Provost of Inverness, Duncan Forbes, son to Culloden ; John Cuthbert of Castlehill, John Cuthbert of Wester Drakies, Alexander Dunbar of Bennetsfield, and John MacRobbie, writer in Inverness, and of the deed. The name of Duncan, son of the first Culloden, is very seldom met with.

The circumstances of the Kincraig family would appear to have become straitened, for, in 1672, when Agnes, daughter of Colin, the second Kincraig, married Alexander Bayne of Knockbayne, her tocher is only 2000 merks. The direct line of Kincraig failed in the person of John the sixth. The succession then devolved, by Deed of Provision, in the year 1760, upon John, Captain in Lord Macleod's Regiment, second son of Ruari Ban, seventh Baron of Redcastle, whose grandson is the present possessor. The ancient spirit of the Redcastles was well kept up in Kincraig, the descendants of the above John being essentially a fighting race. Miss Mary Mackenzie of Redcastle, whom Mr Mackenzie in his history records as having died at Lettoch in 1828, aged 96, and who modestly styles herself in the year 1826 as "86 years and upwards," in an interesting paper gives some particulars of her family. For some time before her father's death in 1785, he lived at Inverness, and, being latterly blind, Mr. Mackenzie of Woodside used to come and read the newspapers to him. Redcastle had been Collector of Customs at Inverness, but his affairs were much embarrassed, partly through the extravagance and high-handedness of his son, Captain Kenneth, who was killed in a duel in 1789. This Kenneth was the terror of Inverness mothers, and the aversion of Inverness tradesmen. He had great power in inveigling and cozening young men and apprentice boys to enlist. Several papers on this point are in my possession. His name was as opprobrious in Inverness as that of the " Black Officer" in Badenoch, and it was the general belief that he would come (as he did) to a bad end. Captain Kenneth's son, Roderick, the last

Redcastle, was never practically owner, for, in 1790, the year following his father's death, the estate was sold. Bailie Inglis of Kingsmills, writing from Edinburgh, where he happened to be, under date 26th June, 1720, says—" There is nothing going on here but the bustle of politicks. This day the Lord Advocate was unanimously elected member for the county. Last night Mr Grant of Sheuglie bought the Red Castle estate for £25,450, which is thought cheap."

It was indeed cheap, being sold within fifty years thereafter for upwards of five times the price given in 1790. Sir William Fettes, the purchaser, had made a considerable fortune as an army contractor. Both he and his predecessor, Cheape, had large dealings in the North connected with the various forts in Inverness-shire.

Follows the letter referred to :—

Right honourable and affectionate Gossip, my hearty duty remembered. Please the present is declaring you that I have forgot yesterday to speak with you anent my fuel. Therefore, sir, the present is requesting you that it will please you to licentiat my tenants and servants to lead my fuel as ye and my wife condescended, as I will gladly willing to obey you hereafter. Assuring myself of your furtherance herein, I commit you heartily to God. I rest your ever obedient Gossip in all dewtie.

(Signed)   MR. WALTER ROSS.
Rosskeen, 11 July, 1630.
Addressed—" To the Right Honourable Collein Mackenzie of Kincraig. These."

No. XVI. ANNO. 1631.

JOHN DUNBAR OF BENNETSFIELD.

OF the numerous, wealthy, and influential heads and cadets of Dunbar, in the north and east of Scotland, they as landowners have, with two or three exceptions, dwindled into insignificance.

The Dunbars of Bennetsfield held for some time a respectable position in the county of Ross.

The writer of the letter after given, refers to an old practice, common but reprehensible, of signing in blank, bonds, deeds of trust, and other important documents.

If such deeds fell into improper hands, names were filled in contrary to the views of the granters, and great mischief and wrong occurred.

Titles were made up in this way, on which adjudications followed, the object being to avoid representation of deceased persons, whose debts, real or fictitious, might be unknown.

The practice leading to fraud and wrong, was put a stop to. For a long period, nothing can be legally inserted in a deed after its execution, except the testing clause.

The letter, holograph of Bennetsfield, is a beautiful specimen of caligraphy.

It is not often that one writes his own contract of marriage, and the case of Alexander Bayne of Knockbayne, who married Agnes, daughter of Kincraig, in 1672, is the only case within my observation where the like occurs. This contract is lengthy and formal, as if the work of a professional.

Follows the letter referred to :—

Loving and assured friend, my best affection remembered. I long very much to hear of your master's good company, and his own healthful return. Please you wit that having the commodity of this bearer, my brother-in-law, Kincraig, I thought meet to write over these lines to you, requesting you to take the pains to seek out the last blank infeftment of the Inche of Killene and Blairfoyd, which I sent over to your master, to have filled up my name therein, by Mr. John Pope, younger, who wrote the infeftment, and seeing he was scrupulous to do the same at your master's desire, ye shall give the infeftment to this gentleman to see if he can get my name inserted therein; seeing I have coft the land, for I hope he will get more done than any other; and so to your diligence there anent, and your advertisement how Alexander Brodie has ended the bargain of our teinds, recommends you heartily to God and rests.—Your loving friend at all power,

(Signed)   JOHN DUNBAR of Benethfield.

Kiltearn, 16th of April, 1631.

I pray you inform this gentleman what ye know has been betwixt your master and Mr. John Pope here anent.

Addressed.—"To his loving and assured friend George Stewart, servitor, to Walter Hay of Droulay, Advocate. These."

No. XVII. ANNO. 1632.
SIR ALEXANDER GORDON, AND THE 2ND MARQUIS OF HUNTLY.

AT the period of the letter after quoted, the Huntly family had become much embarrassed. The writer appears to have been one of the family agents, and his advices as to feuing and letting of lands, selling of woods, etc., were wise and ahead of the times. Lord Gordon, who was shortly to succeed to the Marquisate, was not above being open to taking a sinecure seat on the judicial bench. He was executed in 1649, and after his death his relation and great opponent, the Marquis of Argyle, and his son Lord Lorne, under covert of being creditors, possessed for many years the Gordon estates, and lived at The Bog.

Students of Scottish history know but too well how freedom was crushed and progress frustrated by the excessive powers given or extracted from the weakness of the sovereigns by many of the nobility. In 1660, at the time of the Restoration, the Huntly family owed a million, which would have finished their career, had not Charles II. weakly discharged this enormous debt. He also restored to favour the Earl of Argyll, and thus an opportunity of freeing the West and North of Scotland from the oppression of two unduly powerful nobles was lost, and material progress impeded and delayed.

A singular specimen of bigotry and malice on the part of the Gordons recently came under my notice when assorting a collection of papers regarding the family.

It is well known the Gordons were Catholics up to the time of the second Duke. In a set of the Barony of Kincardine, made in 1747, a clause is inserted that the tenants are not to harbour "rebels or papists," under pain of irritancy. The old possessors of Kincardine, Baron and people, were Catholics, and this was the case with John Roy Stuart, and his men in the '45. This villainous clause began the expropriation of the people, and was the more marked, seeing that sets of the same period in Badenoch contained no such clause.

Follows the letter referred to :—

My Lord,—That you did not receive a letter from me by Mr. Adamson when he went out of this, was merely Mr. Adamson's fault, for I showed my letter written to your Lordship in my own chamber, and did then offer it to him, but he would not take it at that time, because he said he would come for it before he went away, and he forgot to call for it and so was gone, a day before I knew of his departure. There were only two things I entreated your Lordship to have a care of, one to get a protection for yourself and your cautioners signed by the King for two years before you came to this Kingdom, that you may have leisure in that time to take order with your creditors for their satisfaction. The other, that you would put in for power to sit in the Session as the Duke had, when one of the four extraordinary places are vacant, which are now filled by my Lords of Lorne and Alexander, by the Bishop of Ross, and Clerk Register, with a warrant to prefer you to the first extraordinary place that shall be vacant. Were your Lordship at home, I am confident that in a short time you should be able, by selling some lands, feuing others, and selling your woods, and setting long leases of your Lowland lands, to pay many of all your Scottis debts. If your Lordship resolve to make any long stay at the English Court I should wish to know, that I may do my best to make a start up to kiss your Lordship's hands.

Mr. Innes, bearer hereof, can inform your Lordship of all passages here. So, wishing your Lordship all health and happiness, I continue your Lordship's most humbly devoted servant,

(Signed)   SR. ALEXR. GORDON

Edinburgh, 16th March, 1632.

Address—" To the Right Honourable, My Lord Gordon."

No. XVIII. Anno. 1633.

GEORGE, EARL OF SEAFORTH.

THE following letter summoning the Earl of Seaforth to the Scottish Parliament, is interesting, inasmuch as it explains the formalities then in use.

The Parliament of Scotland sat in one hall as one

body, but corruptions arose by the appointment of committees which went under various names—" Lords of the Articles," etc., etc.—and exercised all real power. These Committees were packed according to the views of the Ministers for the time, and whatever they reported or recommended was subserviently agreed to.

I was much struck with the enormous extent of the possessions of the Seaforth family, as contained in the service of Kenneth Mackenzie as heir to his father, Colin Mackenzie of Kintail, expede at Inverness in the month of September, 1594. The family, it will be recollected, had not the Lewis at this period, but at same time the extensive grants to younger children had not greatly spread. Kenneth Mackenzie, created Lord Kintail in 1610, inherited the Barony of Eileandonan, which originally consisted of ten davochs and thirty-six merks land, in itself a magnificent estate; as also such disjoined lands as the davoch of Cro of Kintail, and the three merk lands of Kinlochluichart and Corrievoullie, the three davochs of land lying betwixt the water of Keppoch and the water of Luing, and the three merk land of Inverchouran, etc., etc.; twelve merks of lands in possession of Glengarry in Lochaber; Monar and Neid, described as waste or forest lands; Castle Leod estates; Lochalsh estate; Meikle Brahan estate; Lochbroom Parish; Foddertie's and Ussie's lands; half of Lochcarron; the greater part of the lordship and barony of Dingwall; the two Scatwells; Urray; Kinchulladrum; and Ord; the estate of Coul; parts of Tarradale; Strathvaich; the estate of Applecross; the Bishop of Ross's Bishopric lands of Applecross; Allangrange, and others; the barony of Assynt; the lands of Rhindoun; various lands near Fortrose; and the right of patronage to the churches of Kintail, Lochalsh, Lochcarron, Applecross, Gairloch, Lochbroom, Assynt, etc.

Notwithstanding this magnificent estate, fifty-two years had not elapsed since the service of 1594, ere the family was sunk in debt. This continued, notwithstanding numerous sales and the rise in values, to be the normal state of affairs.

Follows the letter referred to :—

After our very hearty commendations to your good lordship,—Whereas the King's Majesty is resolved, God willing, in this approaching summer, to honour this his ancient kingdom with his Royal presence, as well for receiving of his Crown as for holding of ane Parliament, which is proclaimed to be at Edinburgh, and to begin upon the 28th June next (1633) with continuation of days. At the which solemnity His Majesty looks that the nobility of this kingdom, out of their dutiful respect to His Majesty's obedience and the honour and credit of this country, will give their presence and assistance, and therefore according to His Majesty's direction sent unto us in this matter. These are therefore to desire and require your good lordship to prepare yourself and to be in readiness to keep the appointed time of these solemnities in that settled and decent form as becometh the dignity of such actions, vizt., with your robe of crimson velvet, emerald, and your crown at the Coronation, and with your scarlet robe, at the Parliament. And noways doubting that ye will be wanting in anything which to your duty in so important a business, and which so nearly concerne His Majesty in honour and estate, is the first that has occurred in this kingdom of that kind belongeth. We commit your lordship to God.

From Holyrood House, the 6th day of March, 1633. Your lordship's very assured good friends,

(Signed) HADDINGTON.
(,,) WINTOUN.
(,,) LORNE.
(,,) ERSKINE.
(,,) DUNKELD.
(,,) ARCH. ACHISON.

Addressed—"To our very Honourable good Lord, the Earl of Seafort."

No. XIX. Anno. 1634.

MR. WILLIAM ROBERTSON, OF THE INSHES FAMILY.

As stated in these letters, many scions of the Inshes family spread themselves on the Continent in the seventeenth century.

The letter after given is written in a reverent style, as if from one who had suffered much in body, and had turned for relief to the true quarter.

Notwithstanding his critical state of health at the period referred to, Mr. Robertson lived for many years, and settled in Poland, where he left descendants.

At this period, the Robertsons, who had for some time been considerable Burghers of Inverness, had only acquired the lands of Easter Inshes. By this Laird of Inshes and his son, William, were acquired the other lands of the family, viz.—Wester Inshes, Culcabock, Easter Leys, the two Hiltons, and others, last as a whole vested in the person of Arthur, grandfather of Arthur John, late laird of Inshes.

Follows the letter from Edinburgh referred to :—

Laus Deo,
Anno. 1634, the 17th March.

Right loving and well-beloved cousin,—My love and entire affection remembered unto yourself, your loving bedfellow, and whole family.

You shall witt that I received your letter from John Mill, and has paid him his hyre.

Loving cousin, I am purposed to do all things as I wrote unto you of before, concerning my will. I am purposing, God willing— March being ended—to go by the sea to Dantzic, although I be as yet heavily diseased. Let God work His holy will incalling me, or in prolonging me to further life, for here there is no remeid for me, for I have sought all means to my great charges, and done me no good. I am not well to write for the present ; therefore I end committing yourself, your loving bedfellow, and family, to God's holy protection, your loving and well affectionate cousin to death,
(Signed)   WM. ROBERTSON.
From the Channongait, the 17th March.

If, that Gilbert Fraser come and ask for the key, he shall have it, but, if not, I am of purpose to leave it beside William Gray till your coming, for I did speak with him concerning that. I render you many thanks for entertaining my brother's son so long beside you. I pray God that both he and I may be thankful unto you for it. You shall receive from the bearer three pound of powder (pudir). I cannot bestow it upon a surer friend. More, you shall receive a wax candle. I know not what way to requite your kindness,

34   LETTERS OF TWO CENTURIES.

I am so much beholden to you. Yet I hope to remain thankful, altho' altogether I cannot requite for the present. God of His mercy grant us one blyth meeting.
Addressed—" To his loving and well affectionate cousin, John Robertson of Easter Inshes. This to be delivered to his hand."
(Memorandum on back)—"William Robertson K   from Poillonia."

No. XX. ANNO 1635.

LORD REAY.

THE letter after given, communicated by Mr. Dunbar Dunbar, is very interesting, referring as it does to so many important matters. Lord Reay, though much distressed and harrassed in his own affairs, takes a kindly interest in his relatives, and those dependent upon him. The postcript, referring to the infant heir to Foulis, shows Lord Reay in a pleasant character. Even at this comparatively settled period, rights of succession were subject to many dangers and risks. Needy and heartless relatives, the exaction of the superior, debts unclaimed during life, all pressed upon the heir to an estate, and, if an infant or minor, with dangerous consequences. The proverb about the friend in need is stated thus by Lord Reay—"There is no friend (equal) to a friend in need." His description of his uncle "as arch in his own particulars" or affairs, is a vivid rendering of the Gaelic word " Eolach,' generally used to denote the person who is knowing in his own business and adoes.

Follows the letter referred to, the old spelling being preserved :—

Very Honobill. and loveing Unkill,—I resaived tow of yor letters. Yor last wretin cam first to my hands. I hav wrettin to Sir Parce Corsby and to Sir James Heay to caus atend ye last commission for Iyrland. I hav send fyftye pounds to Mr. Doctor Reiffis yat he may send one of his owine to Iyrland to attend it, and on ye 20 off October I sall hav ane at you wt. moir moneyes. In the meintyme iff ye bissines requyr it giff you tounty pounds to Doctor Reiffis or to Mr. Dethik, my proctor, and on yor advertisement it sal be payed thankfouly. Sir James gav 23 pounds to them at severall tymes ondesyrit be me to defray ye chargis of yt. Court. Yit I wrett to you severall tymes and they have not wretin any grant from you, qroff. I mervell, seing you nor non alyff was never interest in me a peny, nor never sall so long as I hav a farding. Seeing it stands me to my lyff and honour, it's no tyme to me to stand on meines. Therfor kyithe in this as you wis my fall or standing. Yr. is no frind to a frind in neid. You neid not feir ye caus, for its just befoir God and man. Sir, I most be frie wt. you. I did sie a letter of yors wrettin to Gorg Teilor's agent in Edr., in favours of Mrs. Mary Linsay, qrat I touk exceptione. I hav nothing ado wt. it, bot thoyes yt. wald street my frinds yat stands be me I think wishes not me weill (having no entres off yor owin). Its no tyme to you to laiff me now, standing all this tym for me. Nether feir nor gretnes sall never mak me laiff you so long as I braithe. I know you ar arche in yor owin perticouler, yit in this I hop yors sall coum off wit creditt. I end, and sall ever reman to daithe, your loveing Nephew to serff you.

(Signed)   D. REAY.

August ye 28th, 1635.
Carbis-dell.

James Innes hes plaid ye knaiff wt. me. I will send ye band to you to sik order of hem wt. ye nixt ocation.

My sister, ye Lady Ffoulls, is brocht a bed off a goodly boy quhom we hav callit Hector, efter his father. We hav hed a miting heir wt. the Lord Lovad & son (some?) off the name of Monro. Some stands firm for ye chyld—uthers not. Lovat is bot a waik man, and we feir he may be brocht ower stayds to ye chyld—uthers not. Lovat is bot a waik man, and we feir he may be brocht ower stayds to ye chyld his prejedus. Yr. is no way to previn this bot to enter ye chyld as eair to his unkill Robert & consolet ye es esteit in ye chyld's persone, and tak it out off Lovat's hands absolut. This I dair not heasart on except we hed his ward and maryage, wche. I pray you to sik for as you lov ye chyldis standing or his hous. I hav wrettin to ye Erll off Morton not to dispon on it to ye chyld's prejedus ; therefor deill wt. Mortone iff he be yr.; giff not, deill wt. ye King hemseliff. Iff it may be hed for a littill thing we will tak yt. cours. Iff not, we most let it ly in Lovatt's hands as it is. Iff you could gett this wrocht we sould all heir stand volens nolences. Iff he be my sister son he is yor sister's grandchild, so do as you may and try it.

(Signed)   D. REAY.

Qtever. coums off this, keip it from ye Grayes, for they and hem

evir gois on way, and Lovat and them evir rines on fours.
D. R.
Addressed on the back—"To my very Honobill and Deir Unkill Sir Robert Gordoun, Knytt and Baronett, one of His Maty. Privie Consellors off Scotland, at Court, or at Robert Carall's Hous in King Street, at Brudrs. Yard, ye 6.
Answered Oct., 1635.

No. XXI. Anno 1636.
DUNCAN FORBES, ESQ. OF CULLODEN, AND HIS WIFE (JANET FORBES).

There are numerous documents extant connected with this worthy couple, and also some floating reminiscences. Among the latter, Duncan Forbes is yet known by some Gaelic-speaking ancients as *Donnachadh nam Boicnean* (Duncan of the Skins), as he chiefly dealt as a home purchaser, in that formerly important article of commerce in the Highlands. That Mr. and Mrs. Forbes were clever, thrifty, and intelligent to a high degree is shown by the letters after given, addressed to Sir Robert Gordon, the first created Baronet of Scotland and Nova Scotia, communicated to us many years ago by Mr Dunbar Dunbar. The letter of the good lady is not inconsistent with the tradition of her being so hard, even to penuriousness, that the easier Duncan's home was not so comfortable as it might. Having on one occasion, in course of business, gone to Holland, Mr Forbes found himself so comfortable, that he wrote, according to tradition, to his wife at Inverness, stating he did not intend to return, unless temper and table were improved.

The lady stood out for three years, as the story goes, finding, in the excitement of money-making, a substitute for the want of her husband. She at last relented, promised amendment, Duncan returned, and the couple lived thereafter a happy, united, and prosperous life, leaving to the eldest son, John second of Culloden, a name and estate which has flourished for upwards of 250 years.

Follows the letter, the old spelling being preserved :—

Rycht Worll.,—My hartly dewtie remembrit. Heiring of yor gaing out of the countrey, I haiff written this letter desyiring you to send me with this berar that contrak quhilk is betwix your Worship and me ondistroyit, seing that I haiff thankfully performit my pairt thairoff. Sir Siklyk, I desyir you to send me with this berar sick money as I debursit in Edinburgh at the desyir off your letter, the compt thairoff you will knaw be Allexr. Lintoun's letter, and his compt thairin derect to you quhairunto I giff crydeit togidder with your awin discretioun. I remember I gaiff your Worschip ane Band upon sick money, as I restit you of that contrack quhairoff I send you fyiff hundreth merks with my awin servand, and the rest off that Band, lat it be peyet with that moneyis I debursit in Edinburgh, and cifter just compt and rackning, send me the superplus togidder with that Band ye haiff of myn. Your Worschip alledgit that off that mony I send you thair was rebait on the gold, quhilk my servand refuisses awayis. I refer that differ to your awin descretioun. Bot remember I send you the fyiff hundreth mark lang afoir the term. Sua Sir adverteis me in wreit quhat you send, and referris all forder till it pleis God to send you weill hame again.—To the quhilk meiting, I rest your awin assurt.

(Signed) DUNCAN FORBES.

Resaiff your awin Letter derect to me to Edinburgh, for anscring that money. [No date.]

Addressed—" To The Ryt. Woll., Sr. Robt. Gordoun off Kinmonouy, Knyt.

———

Richt Woll.,—Pleis, efter receipt of yor Wo/ and my husband's Lres., I did my best devoir for getting als much money to the most as you required, bot in respect of the apoyntment my husband had maid with your brother, Sr. Alexr., for paycing thois moneyis at Edr., and our compt being so layed that such moneyis as we had besyd us heir we imployed utherwayes, as I dout not my husband hes alreddie showen you. Yit, notwithstanding, to doe Yor. Wo/ pleasur, and for pirformance of my husband's promeis hes purchaseit six hundreth merkes, quhich pleis Yor. Wo/ recave from the beirar and give your recept thairupon.—Sory that I could not giv Yor. Wo/ full satisfactioune, I rest, Yor. Wo/ loveing frind,

(Signed) JONET FORBES.

Inverness, this Wedenisday, seventeint of Sepr., 1636.

Yor. Wo/ sall pleis pay the boy for his paines.

Addressed—" To the Richt Woll. Sr. Robert Gordoune, of Kinmonavie, Knyt. and Barronet. These."

JANET FORBES.

No. XXII. ANNO 1637.

MR. JOHN NICOLL, WRITER, EDINBURGH.

THE family of Inshes owed much of its stability to the wealth and ability brought to it by the Caithness lady, Miss Sinclair. She appears, by many letters preserved, to have been competent to carry on a legal correspondence with men of business in her husband's absence. In this she shared the same remarkable ability as that possessed by the first Mrs. Forbes of Culloden, her contemporary. The annexed letter refers to the frequent litigations carried on by the proprietors of the King's Milns against the heritors and suckeners. The privilege of Milns became latterly such an instrument of oppression that thirlage was abolished. It is quite surprising to see in old rentals what a large sum of money was paid for mill rents in proportion to the other rents of an estate.

Letters of this period from lawyers are generally couched in restraining language, and advising that clients should not be too rigorous.

Follows the letter referred to :—

Sir,—This bearer, William Tulloch, has been at me showing me the letters of horning executed against him and his neighbours for the Miln multures, and has shown me that he has agreed with you, and therefore desyred me to pass through a gift of his escheat. As for answer thereto, ye shall understand that I have compounded already the escheat of all these five persons that ye hav given me up in roll for three hundred merks, as I advertized you of before, whereof this bearer, William Tulloch, is one. And if he shall pass this gift by himself, it will be above two hundred merks unto him at the least. Wherefore, seeing there is one gift already passed for the escheat of five for three hundred merks, it were fittest that all these five should go on together, and contribute among themselves to pay the three hundred merks, and so much more as will pass the seals, and raise a declarator thereupon. This being done, you shall see I shall despatch all to you in order and very good cheap, and far better and better cheap nor if you should separate them in diverse gifts, for many good causes which I could show you if ye were here. But you have forgot all which I showed you at our last meeting, and I have had very great pains and trouble to get that turn done, both in writing and attending the Lords of Exchequer, which were langsome to write. Wherefore, I think it best that with all possible diligence, ye expede the gift for the haill five, and if the rest will not transact with you, ye may use the rigor against them. And as for this man ye may dispose to him his own part of that gift, so far as concerns his own escheat, and reserve the rest to yourself.

I have shown some of these particulars to Duncan Forbes, Provost, who allows very well of this course, and thinks I have got this matter very cannily through, to whose relation I refer the rest, because it would be langsome and tedious to write all the particulars. So committing you to God, I rest yours to serve you.

(Signed) JON. NICOLL
Edinburgh, 17 June, 1637.

Remember your cousin James of that which I disbursed for his letters against McRanald. And if this bearer be agreed with you for these Myln multures, for which he was denounced to the horne, then ye may subscribe this discharge that I have penned to him.

Addressed—"To his much respected friend, John Robertson of Inshes. These."

No. XXIII. ANNO 1638.

MR. KAY, DOER FOR LORD REAY.

THE following patient and sensible letter, to the first Lord Reay, one of the most fickle of men, from his man of business in Edinburgh, has been preserved. The uncle referred to was the famous Sir Robert Gordon, first baronet of Scotland. In a former number I referred to Lord Reay and his unfortunate matrimonial experiences. Amongst certain papers which belonged to his lordship, I find the following bond.

The Seaforth family were anxious for the match, but the lady being very young, the marriage was postponed. To bind the Fiar or Master of Reay, whom report alleges to have been very unkind to his wife, some of the tocher was advanced :—

Be it kend to all men by these present letters, we, Huchoun

Mackay, life-renter of Farr, and Donald Mackay, Fiar of Farr, my son and heir apparent, with consent of me his father, tutor, guider, and lawful administrator, for my interest, and we both, with one consent and assent, and also I, the said Huchoun, taking the burden on me for my said son,—That, forasmickle as we, being justly indebted and owing to our good friend, Mr Wm. Forbes, of many, divers, and sundry great sums of money extending in the whole be just compt. and reckoning to the sum of four thousand pounds money. For the which sum of four thousand pounds money, and in satisfaction to the said Mr. Wm. Forbes thereof, I, the said Donald, with consent of the said Huchoun, my father, have made and constituted the said Mr. Wm. and his heirs, our undoubted cessioners and assignees, in and to the sum of four thousand pounds money, as rest and remnant of the sum of six thousand pounds money, obliged to be paid to me, the said Donald, my heirs, executors, and assignees, by Kenneth McKenzie of Kintail, in name of tocher good with Barbara McKenzie, his daughter, with whom I am contracted in marriage, conform to the contract of marriage made thereanent, betwixt us, on the same one part, and the said Kenneth and his said daughter on the other part, of the date the eleventh day of Octr., the year of God sixteen hundred and seven years; and, conform to a posterior contract made betwixt us and them for continuing of the said marriage to be completed betwixt me and the said Barbara, until the sixteenth day of October next to come. By the which assignation, we have given power to the said Mr. Wm. Forbes to uplift the said sum of four thousand pounds money as rest of the said sum promised to me in name of tocher, as said is, as the said assignation of the date of these presents bears; and seeing that in case either I or the said Barbara decease, or otherwise either of us refuse and complete not the said marriage, as the same is contracted, the said Kenneth Mckenzie will be free of the said sum of four thousand pounds money, as rest of the said tocher promised to me, so that therefore the said assignation hereof made by us to the said Mr. Wm. in satisfaction of the like sum indebted by us to him will be of no avail and ineffectual. Therefore, in case in any sort it shall happen the said marriage to dissolve, and not to be completed as said is, or that the said Barbara die, as God forbid, within year and day after the marriage, so that the said four thousand pounds be not received, we oblige us conjointly and severally, and our heirs, executors, and successors to consent and pay to the said Mr. Wm. and his foresaids the said sum of four thousand pounds money foresaid betwixt and Whitsunday the year of God sixteen hundred and eleven years, together with   of expences in case of failure. And we consent these presents be registered in the Books of Council, and decerned to have the strength of any decreet of the Lords thereof that letters of horning upon a simple charge of six days allenarly, poinding and others, the one without prejudice of the other, may pass hereon, and for that registering constitutes   conjunctly and severally our procurators *promitten de rato*. In witness whereof we have subscribed these presents, written by Robert Pringle, writer in Edinburgh, at Edinburgh, the   day of March. 1610 years.

Doubtless Mr. Forbes got his money as he acted so formally, taking both assignation and bond.

Follows the letter referred to :—

My Lord,—It may please your lordship that since your uncle his coming to Edinburgh, he and I have had several conferences anent those mistakings betwixt your lordship and him. He complains heavily that without any just deserving your lordship should have so wronged him in his honour and credit as to have alleged against him that so unjustifully and unhonestly he would have wronged your lordship.

He does also regret that besides he was your lordship's uncle, that, as a gentleman of your friendship and acquaintance, you should have so little esteemed him as not to have reserved an ear to himself, and if he should not have purged himself of any fault that your lordship could have laid to his charge, it had been then time to have written and spoken against him according to any warrant that your lordship had found.

This and the like conferences has passed betwixt him and me. He did show me also the copy of a letter he had written to your lordship, answering to the reports and informations that he had heard concerning your lordship's proceedings against him, and clearing himself of all those imputations by very many kind and loving expressions.

I did likewise answer, that in his proceedings here, I had neither seen nor known of anything that he or Sandside had done to your lordship's prejudice, but had carried themselves kindly and friendly for the discharge of that trust your lordship had committed to them. I did further show him how your lordship having wrettin to me of that purpose, I had returned answer to your lordship declaring theirs and my part and proceedings in all that business ; and that the letter delivered to the counsel was drawn and made up by the advise of all your lordship's friends here ; and farther, I could not write but remitted me to my letter containing this and all other particular proceedings in the business concerning your lordship.

I thought good to advertise your lordship of these particulars humbly, yet as if before, entreating your lordship to consider thereof and so keep friendship with your lordship's friends where ye find not occasion of offence.

Not else but wishing your lordship all happiness I shall ever remain your lordship's servitor.

        (Signed) W. KAY.

19 June, 1638.

Addressed—"To the Right Honourable and my very good Lord —My Lord Rea."

No. XXIV. Anno 1639.

KING CHARLES I.

CHARLES had not been long on the throne before differences arose with the ruling authorities in Scotland. His pressing of Episcopacy in itself was a grave error, but it was only one of several causes of disagreement.

The King could not rely on many of the nobility, notwithstanding the gifts of ecclesiastical properties lavishly bestowed. These nobles were in most cases selfish, grasping, and envious of each other. The leading clergy were, or had been forced to become, fanatical and intolerant. With all this, and Scotland torn by dissensions, the common people suffered, and progress was impeded.

In 1639 the then Earl of Holland was a prominent statesman. Certain difficulties betwixt the Crown and the Scottish leaders had apparently been adjusted, and the latter sent a deputation to the King of a complimentary character. Some behind the throne appear to have poisoned the King's ear, so that he declined to receive the commissioners. The Earl of Holland, writing to Lord Mandeville on 16th July, 1639, expresses his deep regret "that the King had been advised to spoil or destroy the honourable and happy accommodation with the Scots." The writer was full of anxiety, and unwilling to trust to paper all that he thought and knew. On the 13th November Lord Loudoun wrote to the Earl complaining of the manner in which his fellow-commissioner, Lord Dunfermline, and himself had been treated. "They had been debarred His Majesty's presence, and their Parliament condemned before they were heard."

This conduct, to say the least, was highly discourteous, and could only lead, as it did, to further discussion and bitterness.

No. XXV. ANNO 1640.

THE EARL, AFTERWARDS MARQUIS OF ARGYLL.

WHAT reader of Scottish history, or what lover of Scottish song is not familiar with "The Bonnie House of Airlie?"

The words, simple and pathetic, have been admirably set to music, and will be popular so long as Scottish nationality exists, not only among the noble Ogilvies themselves, but every lover of right.

The words, as known to me in childhood, in part ran:—

> Lady Margaret looked o'er the Castle wall,
> And, oh, but she lookit sairly;
> For there was Argyll wi' three hundred o' his men,
> Come to plunder the bonnie House o' Airlie.

* * * * * * * *

> "Come down, come down, Lady Ogilvie," he cried,
> "Come down and kiss me fairly."
> "I wadna kiss ye, fause Argyll
> Tho' ye left na a stannin' stane in Airlie."

The circumstances of the burning of Airlie House and of Forther, are perfectly authentic.

James, 8th Lord Ogilvie, was in 1639 created, by Charles the First, Earl of Airlie, and, in consequence of his strong Royalist proclivities, had in 1640 to quit Scotland.

The Covenanting rulers in June, 1640, despatched a

force to demolish the Castle, but this force having no great heart for the work, after exchanging some shots with Lord Ogilvie, afterwards the second Earl, retired. This gave much offence, and the great man of the party, Archibald, first Marquis of Argyll, who had an hereditary grudge against the Ogilvies, willingly resumed hostile proceedings. Lord Ogilvie, finding resistance unavailing, vacated Airlie and made his escape, whereupon the destruction shortly followed. Lord Ogilvie had one daughter, Margaret, who may have been the Margaret referred to in the song, his first wife's name being Helen, and the second, Isobel.

It would have been just after Lord Ogilvie quitted Airlie, and possibly immediately after the place was burnt, that the letter after given was written, dated 7th July, and addressed to the Laird of Inverquharity. The letter is in possession of the Laird's representative at Baldovan, and is mentioned by Sir Wm. Fraser in his report to the Historical Manuscripts Commission upon the Argyll muniments.

It is now given with the spelling modernised, not only on account of its own value, but also because its bearer, Colin Campbell, commonly called of Ardersier, who died in 1642, was connected with our own neighbourhood. On failure of heirs male of his eldest brother, Colin's son Hugh, carried on the Calder line.

Whether Lord Ogilvie was in the house of Inverquharity or not, he was not caught. Argyll's character, fawning and threatening, is well shown in the letter. He received his *interim* reward, the title of Marquis, shortly after.

Follows the letter referred to :—

<small>Loving friend,—Since your parting from this, I have gotten certain information that my Lord Ogilvie is this night in your house, from the which cause I could do no less than direct a company to be about your house till it be searched, whereat I entreat you to take no exception, for I do no ways doubt you, only I will give you this warning, that if ye press to conceal my Lord Ogilvie in your house at this time, it will be more to your prejudice than you are aware of, and so I hope ye will be wise. The gentleman that is commander of this</small>

company is Colin Campbell, Calder's son. So referring this to your consideration, I rest your affectionate friend.

(Signed) ARGYLL.

From my camp at Airlie, 7th July, 1640.

No. XXVI. ANNO 1641.
ROBERT INNES OF ROSSKEEN.

As lands came under cultivation, and grass was hained, lack of peats became a serious question in localities like Easter Ross.

Over and over old letters are found to contain requests or "Tolerances" as they were termed, by one proprietor to another, for liberty of fuel. Many have speculated upon the future of St. Kilda—but that is certain. There is not much soil on the Island, a deal is necessarily washed away yearly, and yearly is a considerable quantity used up for fuel, so that the time when it will become an uninhabited rock, is almost matter of accurate counting.

In the letter after given, the then Laird of Rosskeen asks for liberty of fuel, and the composition is that of a well educated man. He speaks of his portion of the parish as a "Room." This is an old Scottish legal designative for lands of a limited extent, and is found included in a general description of lands such as "mosses and muirs," "tofts and crofts," "rooms and possessions," etc., but I have not often met with it in a mere letter from one gentleman to another. There is another curious expression, which seems to be proverbial in Easter Ross, connected with one Katharine Gordon. She, it seems, would not want her "thicking for the seeking"—that is, I infer; when she wanted thatch for her biggings, she, far and near, by hook or crook, by fair means or foul, hesitated not to seek for the attainment of her object.

Follows the letter referred to, dated from Chanonry of Ross :—

Honourable and loving Gossip,—My love rememberit to you and

all yours. I am informed by my tenants in Roskeine that ye have stayed them from fuel casting, which I know is only done by you, that I might write to you for an attolerance which by these presents, intreats you to let my men have the old custom from you as they had before.

And although I be not so powerful to please you as my predecessors who had the Rowme, yet I shall not be deficient to be as kind as I may for all the eases I will be necessiated to seek from you, and shall think myself obliged for all your favours, and hope that betwixt you and Inner Brekie, ye will not see me want wherein I stand in need for me and my tenants; for it is not only in this element I will be a solicitor, but for all other things necessary that you may please me. Because necessity will make me resemble Katherine Gordon who would not want her thicking for seeking. I will send over my wife to use the rest of the solicitation within two or three days. To which time I rest and do remain your loving Gossip,

(Signed) ROBERT INNES.

Chann., the 6 July, 1641.

Addressed—"To my honourable and loving Gossip, Collene Mackenzie of Kincraig."

No. XXVII. Anno. 1642.

JAMES, THIRD EARL OF MORAY.

THE following letter holograph of the Earl of Moray is a wonderful production from a person not a lawyer, at the early period of 1642. It may be taken for granted that few Scottish Earls, even at the present day, could put together such a well-couched and correctly-framed legal communication to his chamberlain. The Earl, who succeeded in 1638 and died in 1653, was evidently displeased at his good name being called in question. It is a pity that the letter of the clever lady, which evoked this remonstrance, has not been preserved. In her time, and through the fortune she brought from Caithness, and her own thrift, the family of Inshes was at its highest. The son, William Robertson of Inshes, received an excellent education at Leyden, having many distinguished men as his cotemporaries. He lived to a great age, carefully preserving his varied correspondence. He was an excellent Latin scholar, and composed a number of fugitive pieces in that language still extant, but not of much value, as they referred to passing events and objects, which have lost interest. The race of Dunbars, prominent merchants, and high burgal authorities in Inverness, for the hundred years from 1640 to 1740, has long been extinct as such. It is to be feared that the house of one of them, James Roy Dunbar of Dalcross, built in 1700, at the south-west corner of the new street now being built, to connect Academy and Church Streets, will soon disappear.

Follows the letter referred to, the old spelling not being observed :—

James Dunbar,—In regard Janet Sinclair. spouse to John Robertson of Inshes, has complained to me upon you, who has detained their annual rents due to them by me for these moneys borrowed by my umquhile father from them, and that for certain terms and years bye past, which is far contrary to my will and command given you. Therefore fail not, upon sight hereof, instantly to make payment and give to them, on her husband's sufficient discharge to me, as heir to my father, the full and haill annual rents due and resting to them of all years and terms bye past, for the said moneys borrowed, as said is, and that yearly and termly hereafter, so long as ye have charge under me, and in my affairs, and that they shall not be paid of the principal sum by me. That they be thankfully and completely paid as said is, of all their due annual rents, in all time coming, allowing for the monies of that time past for their annuals as is ordinary and due to others and no more. Let me hear no more hereanent hereafter, and be more tender of my credit and honour, and not suffer those in the north come to the south and crave me, where I have given timely order to satisfy them. So this without delay do, and fail not, as ye will be answerable, except ye will fail to yourself.—I rest, your maister,

(Signed) JAMES, EARL MURRAY.

Canongate, 25 June, 1642.

Addressed—"To James Dunbar, my servitor and chamberlain of my lands of Murray."

No. XXVIII. Anno 1643.

JOHN, 13TH EARL OF SUTHERLAND.

MUCH of the northern correspondence during and immediately prior to the usurpation, concentrated in and about Sir Robert Farquhar, and a good deal has been preserved.

This Earl of Sutherland, the writer of the letter after given, was twice married. A conjunct letter by him and his second wife will be hereafter given.

The Earl, guided by his sagacious uncle, steered his way cautiously through the troubles, coming out unscaithed.

He was born in 1609, and is described as "a man of considerable note." He died in 1663, having married Lady Jean Drummond, a great beauty, who died in 1637. The Earl married secondly, in 1639, Anne, second daughter of Hugh, ninth Lord Lovat, by whom he had no issue. Anne, Countess of Sutherland, was aunt to the famous Simon Lord Lovat.

Follows the letter referred to :—

Right Worthy and Loving Uncle,—These are entreating you to deliver Mr. Robert Farquhar his ticket wherein he obliges himself to deliver me in Mr. Ross his behalf six thousand merks, as I did write formerly unto you with James Farquhar ; seeing from the said James I have received satisfaction in the said sum, this hoping you will obey, I shall ever continue your very Loving Nephew to serve you.

(Signed)   SUTHERLAND.
Dornoch, the 19 day of March, 1643.

"Addressed—" For the Right Honble. and my most affectionate uncle, Sir Robert Gordonne of Gordonstoune, Knight and Baronet. For delivery of Mr. Robert Farquhar's ticket. These."

No. XXIX. Anno. 1644.

SIR ROBERT GORDON.

IT might be very agreeable for the Sutherland family, its adviser Sir Robert Gordon, and other Covenanters, to fall in with all the plotting and scheming of the clergy to obtain universal sway, so long as this could be done quietly, and by the exercise of the pen.

A painful and disagreeable business had to be gone through with in Orkney and Zetland, and the Assembly thought they could, as a fitting instrument, rely on Sir Robert Gordon. But indisposition, that oft resorted to fiction when the will is adverse, is brought up by Sir Robert, in the laboured communication to one of his agents in the Black Friars' Wynd, Edinburgh, of which a copy is given.

In other parts of the letter, reference is made to his various transactions with neighbours and others who, by hook or crook, he desired to expropriate in order to enlarge and square off, in a proper manner, the bounds and limits of the Barony of Gordonstoun, and fittingly establish and perpetuate his line.

Follows the letter referred to :—

Right Assured Friend,—I have sent you the packet, if you be at Edinburgh, if not, I have directed it to George Gordoun in your absence. I have sent this bearer with a letter to Mr. Robert Douglas (Moderator of the committee of the General Assembly), to excuse my going into Orkney and Shetland this spring, by reason of my indisposition. I have directed him to go to you, and in your absence to George Gordoun, that either of you might deliver my letters by Mr. Robert Daglishe, his advise, and to get me an answer from Mr. Robert Douglas. I have directed my London letters to Henry Seton, who will also send me what letters he hath from thence for me. You shall likewise know that I have agreed with Archibald Innes; therefore ye shall not go on further in that action against him. I hope you will write to me what you have done this Candlemas at Edinburgh with Alexander Heburne and Mr. James Wallace; or if you have received the money for the two letters of exchange from George Forbes.—And so I rest ever your assured friend, to my power,

(Signed)   ROBERT GORDON.

Gordounstoun, the 23 of January, 1644.

Addressed on back—"To my assured good friend Alexander Linton, writer, at his house in the lower end of the Blackfreir Wynd, at Edinburgh.'

No. XXX. Anno 1645.

THE EARL AND COUNTESS OF SUTHERLAND.

THE granting of a boll of victual, in name of yearly annuity, no extravagant allowance, forms the subject of the letter after given.

Money values in 1645 as compared with 1889, may be estimated twenty-fold, but to a poor man the boll then and the boll now is practically the same, allowance only being made in so far as the imperial boll is less than the old or Scots boll.

It would be interesting to know what services Ogilvie performed for which he got this grant, whether a lifelong service or some special transaction.

The bestowing of an alias in the Highlands was very common, sometimes personal, sometimes hereditary. Many curious aliasses have been met with, some of which may be named. Towards the end of last century, one Margaret Macdonald in Inverness was termed, alias "Dialach,"—a family of Mackenzies, in Biallid of Kingussie, alias "Sallach."* These were personal and offensive. Amongst those personal, but honourable, may be mentioned the Mackintoshes at Kinreay of Dalcross, "Torre," their predecessor being he who four hundred years ago bored the holes through the cofferdam at the west of Loch Moy, erected by the Comyns, to drown the Mackintoshes in the Isle—and the Mackintoshes "na Brataich," from Donald Mackintosh, the hero who saved the Mackintosh colours at Culloden. Donald's great-grandson, Charles Mackintosh at Craggie of Daviot, kindly presented me several years ago with the sword used by Donald on the fatal day—I need not say a highly valued chattel. Other aliasses are family ones. I observe that Colonel Archi-

* It has been suggested to me by Mr. Mackenzie, of Ardgowan, that the word here is "Tàllach," as it was not unusual for Kintail men when settled in other places to have the alias of "Tàllach," or "Kintail" men.

bald Fraser of Lovat, having fallen out with one of the Lovat trustees, General Simon Fraser, commonly styled of Bruiach, who had served with distinction in the army of Portugal, took legal proceedings to dispossess the General. In a paper sent to Colonel Archibald Fraser to revise I see he introduces, after the General's name, wherever it appears, "alias Mac Isaac"—a piece of grim humour not unlike that of his father, Simon Lord Lovat, who refers to Major James Fraser, Castle-leathers, as "Major Cracks," an habitual drawer of the long bow.

Follows the letter referred to :—

Right Worthy and Loving Uncle,—These are intreating you to give the bearer hereof, Alexander Ogilvie, alias Casayfourd, ane boll victuall either in bear or meal as he requireth it yearly, during his lifetime, beginning the first year's payment for crop 1645, which shall be allowed in any accounts shall fortoune to be betwixt us, or thankfully paid, by their presents written and subscribed with our hand at Dounrobin, the 9 of September, 1645 years.

(Signed) SOUTHERLAND.
ANNA SOUTHERLAND.

On back—"Warrant for Sir Robert Gordon in Alexander Ogilvie alias Casayfourd his favors of ane boll victuall yearly during his lifetime. 1645."

No. XXXI. ANNO 1646.

JOHN ROBERTSON, FIRST PROPRIETOR OF INSHES.

THE letter which follows, shows the class of men who rose to wealth and position in the seventeenth century in the North.

It is addressed to Inshes' lawyers in Edinburgh, and deals in a very clear manner with various concerns. He wishes his titles to be examined by an Advocate, and all put in order. He is distressed and damnified in his shop properties by one Kenneth Macpherson, who stopped up water and kept middens; and is concerned as to abstracted multures from the King's Milns, of which he possessed a share.

There was a long-standing feud betwixt Glenmoriston and Inshes regarding the barony of Culcabock, upon which, and his other lands, Glenmoriston had borrowed largely from Inshes. In these circumstances it seems curious that Glenmoriston was able to lend the Laird of Grant. Glenmoriston possessed at this period considerable lands in Urquhart, and was wadsetter of Balmacaan. The energy and capacity of the earlier Grants of Glenmoriston enabled them to hold their own with ease. On the other hand, to those conversant with the history of the Lordship of Urquhart, it seems marvellous that notwithstanding its curious sub-divisions, and its jealousy, if not hatred, of the weak and distant nominal heads, the Lordship should have continued with the Grant family.

Follows the letter referred to :—

Loving Cousin,—My love remembered to you, and to Mr. William Lauder. These are requesting that you be so good as to see all my rights, and take one of the best Advocates you can have, to advise thereupon, to see all put in order. And in the minute that is between me and Gilbert Robertson, that Robert Munro write eik to it this clause, that if there be an inhibition belonging to the good man of Carron Grant, to evict from me the lands that I comprised for James Robertson his oye, that I be made free of the sums of monies that I must pay to the said Gilbert Robertson, who is take burden for the said umquhile James Robertson his oye of and their father, Walter Robertson, his eldest lawful son, and especial Gilbert Robertson who takes burden bearer for them their tutor conjunct with me, as testament can show you at more length, that is in Mr. William Lauder's custody. And sicklike to cause letters raised at my instance against James Marchand, burgess of Inverness, and against Kenneth Macpherson, who did buy the biggings holding of me in fee as my charters will testify, to raise summons against them to produce their evidents holden of my father, and, good sir, William Robertson, my father, and John Robertson, my good sir, burgesses of Inverness. And sicklike to make mention in the summons to present all their discharges that they have since my father departed, and my own discharges in like manner. The feu duty is resting by them to me, I trow, above thirty years, and to raise lawburrows against Kennoch Macpherson for wronging my booths in letting in water through my house, which does to the merchants great harm. They want to have salt in behind their presses in their booths, and now, in respect that he casts his water and makes a dam of water at the back of my house, and much middings, he does me and my tenants much harm. Sicklike consult about my decreet that you know that I purchased against Drakies about mill multures, for I served a horning and inhibition against him registered in the Sheriff Books of Inverness by George Lesslie.

And now the guidman of Multovie Mackenzie coft these lands, I must pursue him for abstracted multures in like manner since his entry.

You shall consult with your advocates concerning the lands of Urquhart, belonging to Glenmoriston, for I comprised Bellamaka, the Clune, Culin-Kirk, and the mill. This Bellamaka pays yearly 400 merks holden of the Laird of Grant. He is to redeem at Whitsunday for 3000 merks. See what course you will have me to do thereanent.

I was desired by George your brother, and Muirtown, to arrest these monies, in the Laird of Grant his hands. Consult thereon with the rest. My bedfellow will give you both content for your pains, and pay advocates and other necessaries. You must excuse me, I can not win in to you at this time. At meeting I will show you of all our proceedings. I rest your friend and cousin both,

(Signed) JOHN ROBERTSON OF INSHES.

Addressed—"To my loving cousin, Alex. Lesly and Mr. William Lauder. These."

No. XXXII. ANNO 1647.

THE EARL OF SUTHERLAND AND SIR ROBERT GORDON.

SIR ROBERT GORDON kept his papers methodically, and, however attached to the family of Sutherland, failed not to look after his own interests, as may be seen by the paper after given.

Implicit faith was placed in his judgment and integrity, and as he had the handling of a good deal of monies, public and private, he was able to accommodate a friend, always on security, and at good interest. Upon the ruins of the Mar family in Aberdeenshire, together with personal penuriousness, Duff of Braco, chiefly made his great fortune. His end was as inglorious as his life. Sir Robert Gordon wiped out a good number of lairds, calling their lands by his name; yet, for all this, it is long since these lands passed to another family and name.

The grand old house of Gordonstoun and Sir Robert, the third baronet, styled "The Wizard," are referred to in the impudent production of that unctuous placeman, Sir Thomas Dick Lauder, called "Lochandhu."

Lord Braco and Sir Robert Gordon, fourth Baronet, had a severe contest as to roads and marches between their Baronies of Pluscardine and Dallas about the year 1750. In course of this contest it was complained by Sir Robert that William Taylor, writer in Edinburgh, his agent and doer, was forcibly stopped by Lord Braco's men when upon the ordinary road, he having gone there on purpose to view the roads and to make himself acquainted with the situations thereof. What Sir Robert Gordon did in consequence may be narrated in Lord Braco's own words :—" Two days thereafter, Mr Duff, the Lord Braco's agent, and Stewart of Lessmurdie, his Lordship's factor, and his servants were stopped (by Sir Robert's men) on a road that leads to a fishing upon the Spey, in going to execute a commission from the Court, *and were poinded like so many cattle, and detained till they paid half a merk each.*"

Follows the paper referred to :—

Addebted to me by the Earle of Southerland.

Imprimis, a band of seven thousand marks, payable at Martinmas, one thousand six hundred forty-eight years, with five quarters' annual rent thereof.

Item, a bond of seven thousand merks payable at Whitsunday, one thousand six hundred forty-eight years, with three quarters' annual rent thereof.

Item, a bond of six thousand merks payable at Martinmas, one thousand six hundred forty-seven years, with a quarter's annual rent.

ROBERT GORDON.

On back :—" A note of the Earle of Southerland's bands to Sr. Rob. Gord., 1647."

No. XXXIII. Anno 1648.

MR. ALEX. LESLIE, WRITER IN EDINBURGH.

THE Lairds of Inshes were sorely distressed by the Laird of Glenmoriston. Twice within an interval of twenty years were their houses destroyed and crops devastated.

For the first, the Laird was in some degree compensated by an Act of the Scottish Parliament.

The particular grievances complained of in the year 1648 are contained in the clear and precise letter after given, from one of Inshes' lawyers.

The writer was no Highlander evidently, or one having much sympathy with Highlanders—indeed he uses such language as a Lowlander who both feared and held in contempt at the same time his neighbour Highlander.

The expression of " honest men having their own " occurs in the letter, giving to it, and, as mentioned in another letter to a different saying, a respectable degree of antiquity. At this period, John Forbes, the second Culloden, was Provost of Inverness, but in his after life, the burgh had no more energetic opponent in many an encounter.

Follows the letter referred to :—

Cousin,—Yours I received, which I have considered, and takes the same to run upon these three :

1. That Carron, Invercauld, and the rest of Glenmoriston's friends, intend to elide your apprysing, by an Inhibition, upon a former engagement.
2. If you may legally suit your cautioners, notwithstanding of your comprising.
3. What course may be expected by you, anent your vastation, and if you ought not to be free of local quartering, &c.

For answer—

To the first, it is conceived that the first diligence should carry the business, since the estate of Glenmoriston is able to compense all, and though there were former inhibitions, yet they cannot be prejudicial to you in respect the cause whereupon the same is grounded, is not discussed and cleared whether Glenmoriston be liable thereto or not, so that you must arm yourself with patience, and let them discharge themselves of their great courses, which may in time evanish.

To the second, you may charge your cautioners, and compryse their estates also, and use all other manner of execution against them.

To the third, I have sent to the Provost, young Culloden, an extract for you containing an Act of Committee, which I think will do your turn anent your losses, for there is no farther granted to others. He will show you the price, for upon his desire I have sent him for himself, you, and other three, five extracts, to ilk man ane.

There can be no perfect resolution given anent Glenmoriston, except we were acquainted with their wiles. Since they are going in direct courses against you, fall ye upon the cautioners, for I suspect some of them has a hand therein. They nor Glenmoriston will not win by your decreet, in regard their estates will be able to pay all, at the least well near all. This same week there has ane practik passed here, which will work for you, so that it is your best to be doing against the cautioners for their pains. And to hear well from you rest, resting confident that honest men ought to have their own, which all their Highland tricks will not avert, for so is the opinion of your affectionate Cousin,

(Signed)　　AL. LESLY.

Edinburgh, 7 January, 1648.

Cousin, I pray you remember me to your bed-fellow.

Addressed—"For my very real and affectionate Cousin, John Robertson of Inshes. These."

No. XXXIV.   Anno 1649.

THE SLANDERS OF JAMES CUTHBERT OF LITTLE DRAKIES.

THE following letter relative to an old scandal, has neither address nor place indicating where written, but it is endorsed, "A letter Mr. R. and David Rattra," 1649, in an unfamiliar hand.

I have no clue to the writers, or to the person to whom addressed. The letter is couched in a friendly spirit, showing very good feeling towards a lady and her relatives, it is to be hoped unjustly traduced. The lady probably did not belong to the north, as I cannot see any vestige of truth in the charges as connected with an Inverness family at the period, unless, herself a stranger, she may have married a north country man.

It will be seen that Cuthbert of Little Drakies was well up in bad language and innuendo, and the letter is of some value as indicating the thoughts and expressions of an angry and unprincipled man, two hundred and fifty years ago.

There were two Drakies, possessed by families named Cuthbert. One of these at an early period, became absorbed in Castlehill, and the other passed through numerous hands during the eighteenth century.

Follows the letter referred to :—

Right Honourable Sir,—Please you to know that I was in company with your good daughter when she was upraided, and very scandalously, by one called John Cuthbert of Little Dreakie, ane neighbour of hers, which offended me very much, for there was no just occasion offered to him upon her part, which I am very much ashamed to utter till herself inform you, and I and my servant being present at the time, shall testify whensoever it shall please her to pursue him for the slander.

He objected to her that her guidshir (grandfather) was taken over ane craig, and was never seen again ; that her father hanged himself for getting of her in adultry ; that her father's brothers were all hanged ; and that she was once casting herself over the Brig of Inverness, and that she was for hangand herself.

So wishing you all happiness, I remain yours assured at command,
(Signed)   J. ROSE,
(„)   DAVID RATTRA.

No. XXXV. ANNO 1650.

MR. R. MUNRO, WRITER, EDINBURGH.

THE circumstances connected with the letter after given refer to family disputes, arising out of a second marriage.

The case here was one of common occurrence. A person marries when young well and happily ; children arriving in due time, and all on both sides of the house contented. The wife after a long and happy married life dies, and although the husband has a grown up family, unhappily marries a second time, and almost as a matter of course, one who is objectionable to the children and their friends. Annoyed at this, the second wife circumvents her husband, and gets him to make a settlement greatly benefiting her and her children. After death comes the fight, and the friends of the first wife's family, in the words after given, "take hold of the business," and will not let the unhappy trustee off "so lightly as he supposes." The letter is addressed to Mrs. Robertson of Inshes, and is as follows :—

Mistress,—I have written to you lately with Castlehill, which I hope is come to your hands ere now, so that I cannot write much more now than what is written already; only receive here enclosed a summons at Walter Robertson's bairn's instance, and at his as administrator of law to his bairns, against Gilbert Robertson and your husband; which summons, immediately after receipt thereof, you shall cause Andrew Sutherland or William Cumming execute upon 21 days' notice, for the first diet, and upon six days thereafter for the second diet according to the will of the letters. Andro Sutherland or William Cumming will do the same handsomely and deliver sufficient copies to your husband and Gilbert Robertson for to hear and see that money declared to appertain to Walter Robertson's bairns, and to none else; and immediately after execution thereof, send the same with the execution back here again with the first occasion, and delay no time. Direct your letter in my absence to Mr. William Lauder whom I have appointed as agent for you. Mistress, if you please you may tell Gilbert Robertson that his brother's bairns' friends here of their mother's side, has taken hold of their business and his carriage; and will not let it pass so lightly as he thinks.

Thus leaving to fash you with idle writing, wishing you to use diligence in returning this summons with the execution back here again.—I rest and am, Mistress, yours affectionate to serve,

(Signed)   R. MONRO

Edin., 29th Dec.

No. XXXVI. Anno 1651.

KING CHARLES II.

THE faint support given by Scotland to Charles the Second in his first attempt to regain the Crown was rewarded by its absolute and complete subjugation by the Usurper. This period (1650-1660) in Scottish history is not a pleasant one to contemplate, the chief extenuating matter being in the satisfaction that the arrogant clerics of the day had met their match, and had to walk carefully and circumspectly.

The following letter from Charles the Second, addressed to the Laird of Mackintosh, explains his views on the state of affairs :—

CHARLES R.

Trusty and well-beloved,—We greet you well. Having resolved, God willing, to come in our Royal person to our city of Aberdeen against the 12th of February, we have thought fit to give you this timely notice of it, hoping that it will stir you up to hasten your levies against that time that they may be ready to march southward the nearest and most convenient way. Your former testimonies of affection to us makes us believe that you will give at this time and in this business most careful and ample proof of it, when we are resolved to cast ourself and kingdoms upon the good Providence of God, not doubting but He will at length arise and have mercy upon us, and will for His own namesake deliver this and our other kingdoms from the barbarous oppression and usurpation they have so long groaned under. And as we are confident of your own interests, of religion, lives and liberties, will be powerful arguments of your activity and forwardness, so we do assure you that your loyalty and love shall be fresh in our memory in the day that God Almighty shall enable us to express our kindness in those real effects that may be most agreeable to you. Thus expecting you will answer the good opinion and hopes we have of your zeal to God's cause, your duty to us aud your regard to your own and your country's welfare, we bid you heartily farewell. Given at our Court at Perth, the 31st day of January, 1651, and the third year of our reign.

No. XXXVII. Anno 1652.

MR. A. LESLIE AND THE GOOD WIFE OF INSHES.

NOTWITHSTANDING the political troubles of the Usurpation, and that Inverness was in subjugation, garrisoned by aliens, business continued to be conducted, as may be seen by the letter after given from Mr Leslie. The afterwards notorious Colonel Lilburn and Colonel Man were frequently called upon to decide disputes betwixt neighbours, even of controverted marches. Amongst the Maclean papers is a submission betwixt the Lairds of Dunain and Dochgarroch, and decree pronounced by Colonel Man thereon. The line of March as fixed by him began at a "gob" of land, as it is termed, running into the river Ness, and terminating at a spring, the source of the burn now called Bunchrew Burn. Much land to the north west of the old Urquhart road, appears to have been lost by the estates of Dunain and Dochgarroch within the last two hundred years, and acquired by the estates of Bunchrew, Lovat, Newton, and Reelig.

The concerns of the Lady Inshes and the Laird continued to require their constant attention, and husband and wife are regularly writing or receiving letters connected with business.

Follows the letter referred to :—

Mistress,—I delivered the writs to William Fleming, and received from him our Bond, wherefrom I have riven my name, and which it will please you receive, together with William Fleming's Bond to you of one thousand merks, a letter to Mr. Dundas for anwering thereof, and the inventory of the writs, subscribed by William Fleming, so that you have all which is due to you. Albeit William Fleming wants the power which you promised to have sent to him, I am to write the same, and to send it to you, and am confident you and your husband will subscribe and return it here, since assurance is given for that effect by your affectionate friend,

(Signed) A. LESLIE.

Edin. 16th Sep., 1652.

I pray you permit these to remember my best respects to your husband.

Address—"For my very affectionate good friend, the good wife of Inshes. These."

No. XXXVIII. ANNO 1653.
COLLECTOR WATSON OF INVERNESS.

THE disputes betwixt Inshes and Glenmoriston were not finally settled until long after 1653, but at this time, in virtue of wadsets and adjudications, Inshes was in possession of the barony of Culcabock, under a defeasible title. He was consequently liable for the taxations, and the letter of acknowledgment after given, was for the proportion due by James Macpherson, one of the tenants of the barony.

For about two centuries a family of Macphersons were respected tenants in Culcabock, and the present representative is well known, not only in his adopted country of Canada, but also in Britain. In former times, in and about Inverness, pecularities in families and individuals were conspicuous, and more closely noted than now. The Culcabock Macpherson family peculiarity was to be always late in arriving at church. In my younger days I sat in a table seat in the High Church. On the opposite side sat the Nicol family, and in one corner was a pillar. The moment the sermon began, Dr. Nicol, to my great admiration and considerable envy, drew up, side and head, to this pillar, and slept soundly till it was over.

Follows the letter of acknowledgment referred to :—

Received by me, from James Macpherson, burgess of Inverness, the sum of six pounds eighteen shillings, Scots money, for the cess of his proportion of land occupied by him within the parish of Inverness, some time belonging to John Grant of Glenmoriston, and now belonging to John Robertson of Ishes, and that for nine months' cess, collector's fees, and clerk's dues, with the Commissioners' charges. Whereof I grant the receipt and discharges him thereof. As witness my hand at Inverness, the first day of January, sixteen hundred and fifty-three. (Signed) THOMAS WATSON.

I say received 6 lib. 18 sh.

Endorsed—"Letter of Discharge of nine months' cess, from the 1st of June, 1652, to the 1st of March, 1653."

No. XXXIX. ANNO 1654.

MR. A. MONRO, WRITER, EDINBURGH, DOER FOR THE LADY INSHES.

IN another letter reference is made to the business capacities of the Lady Inshes. That family was much involved in litigation, and during the seventeenth century generally successful.

The cautious and self-satisfied characteristics of an Edinburgh writer are well displayed in the annexed letter. It has been selected for that purpose, not otherwise being of much moment.

Keppoch is referred to as a debtor, and it is rather humiliating that almost all the references to Highland lairds and families during the seventeenth century, which have been preserved in writing and have come under my notice, concern their debts and obligations. Family and private letters are unfortunately very scarce.

A number of very interesting letters from Colonel Hill, commanding at Inverlochy, at the time of the Massacre of Glencoe, have recently come under my notice, and may be referred to hereafter, but even these are chiefly taken up with deficiencies in payment of cess, and consequent quarterings upon unhappy heritors and districts.

Follows the letter referred to:—

Mistress,—These are desiring you to haste over here that summons, which I sent you with Donald Buy, against Gilbert Robertson and your husband, duly execute. Cause the messenger write his executions formally, and send both the summons and executions here with the first occasion, and direct your letter in my absence to Mr. William Lauder, who will be very careful thereof.

Gilbert Robertson's lawyers are labouring to catch all the advantage they can by stealing in quietly the process to avizandum. But they need not make much rings of their game as yet. Gilbert Robertson has written (as I am certainly informed) to his lawyers that he will prove his action against your husband by the writer of the assignation which he gave to him, to wit, George Leslie, and by the witnesses thereanent, viz., James Rose of Merkinch, John Robertson, messenger, and I, and therefore desires his lawyers to refer nothing of that action to your husband's oath, whereby ye may perceive that he is very diffident of your husband's honesty in the particular. But he is too busy, for the business is not come that length as yet, neither knows he whether it will be referred to his probation or no, nor how the business will go, for he is as far from his intention now as at the beginning, for all his boast, and will not be much wiser in this session.

I cannot understand why you nor your husband did never write to me since my coming here. If the fault be my own, I will be sorry for it, but howsoever it be, I expect ye will tell me of it hereafter. So, leaving to fasche you with unnecessary writing, I rest and am, mistress, your affectionate to serve you.

(Signed) A. MONRO.
Edr., 3 January, 1654.

No. XL. Anno 1655.

MESSRS. ROSE, FORBES, AND PATERSON, OF INVERNESS, INVOLVED IN LEGAL TROUBLES.

WHEN a merchant in Inverness waxed rich, he bought land, and if he and his descendants retained their balance, they prospered. From wealth accumulated in Inverness sprung the landed Cuthberts, Forbesses, Robertsons, and others. Many retained, and wisely, their interest in trade. This gave rise to heart-burnings and jealousies among other traders, who could not endure that the produce and purchases of the extra burghal owners came and went free of taxation, in respect they were also free burghers. About the middle of the seventeenth century, the burgesses of Inverness pure and simple, as they may be termed, having a majority at the Council, imposed certain heavy taxations upon all externals, whether these were or were not free burgesses, being non-resident. It is in reference to the serious question which consequently arose that the letter after given was written. The dispute lasted many years, and ultimately in a process of declarator at the instance of Culloden, Inshes and others, the imposts by the Burgh of Inverness were declared illegal. The number of litigations of interest connected with public matters in and about Inverness, during the last three hundred years, is extraordinary. One regarding those supposed to be astricted to grind their corns at Kingsmills gave rise to a protracted struggle. Another, most amusing in some of the details, was the interdict of the coble proprietors against the Skinner Incorporation, to prevent the latter from polluting the river in drying and dressing of skins. In a word, the materials for a history of litigations are universal.

Follows the letter referred to :—

Much honoured friends,—We cannot but admire that we should have no return to our last letter from you ; and now, since new occasion has presented, we do again present our best respects to both of you, and do earnestly entreat, seeing we have willingly engaged ourselves in so needful a plea of law, that ye will prove very effectual to the promoting of your own and our interest. We are very confident the business once tabled, will not bide great tosting. Yet, however, we entreat you that you will not be wanting in anything that is your own proposition, for we have already contributed indifferently, and purposes to persevere. Mistress, you know that whatever we do in this was by your advice ; and to testify our obligement that whatever ye debursit in that particular we would proportionally satisfy you. Wherefore we entreat you again that you will not only be as our neighbour in this, but also a labouring and painful agent for them, who will be both kind and thankful to you. Thus taking leave we rest your very loving neighbours.

                    (Signed)   R. ROSE.
                    („)   JOHN FORBES.
                    („)   ALEXR. PATERSONE.

Inverness, Decr. 7th, 1655.

Mistress, we do entreat that you will send us a new summons for great reasons.

Addressed—" For our much honoured friends, John Robertson of Inshes, and Janet Sinclair, his spouse."

No. XLI. Anno 1656.

ALEXANDER BAILLIE OF DUNAIN.

THE letter after given, from Alexander Bailie of Dunain, in the year 1656, is not without interest in itself; but is to me more valuable from the place where it was written. It will be observed that it is dated Dochnacraig, the old name for the lands of Lochend and Bona, and I infer that the letter was actually written within the walls of the ancient Castle Spioradail. I am rather disposed to believe in this, because David Baillie, second son of Alexander, the writer, and first of the family of Dochfour, to whom his father gave the lands of Dochcairn in patrimony, lived at the Castle.

I am in possession of a legal summons against David Baillie whereon the messenger, being unable to find him personally, leaves it with a servant, at "his residence of Castle Spioradail."

Hardly a vestige of the Castle now remains, it having been demolished by the operations of the Caledonian Canal Commissioners; but in 1808, as appears by an elevation on the corner of the plan signed with reference to the conveyance by Dunain to the Canal Commissioners, a very considerable part of the Castle remained, windows up to the third story being shown. There was no reason for the Castle being shown at all, but evidently the draughtsman was a person of taste, and, struck with the picturesque ruin, happily preserved it. The old house of Dunain, to which the family removed in the time of Alexander's successor, was but a thatched house, situated on a terrace some distance higher up than the present mansion near the fine garden, and stood until lately.

The circumstances referred to in the letter were connected with the long-standing dispute betwixt the families of Glenmoriston and Inshes as to the possession of the Barony of Culcabock.

Follows the letter referred to :—

My Flure of ye Forrest,—Thinking long to hear from you, and more long to see you here before any greater alteration comes to me, some were showing me you were to be here shortly yourself, which is my wish, but if this letter come to you as you are, be extreme well resolved before you agree with Strechyn in ye business of Glenmoriston, for there are sundry things in it which cannot be shown by paper till your Northcoming. Donald Fowler and I knows of it. He has a mind to write to your husband concerning it, but his business in Ross obstructs him, so, if you resolve to do your own will, and to be rightly informed by friends, continue all till your Northcoming, and if you do shall avail you much, which is the great desire of

Your loving friend,
(Signed) ALEX. BAILLZIE of Dunzeane.
Dochnacraigie, ye 20 Apryle, 1656.

Addressed thus :—" To my worthy and loving friend, ye goodwife of Inshes."

No. XLII. Anno 1657.

JOHN CUTHBERT OF CASTLEHILL.

THE annexed well-written letter from the Castlehill of the day to his neighbour Inshes then in Edinburgh, refers to law proceedings connected with the claims of the Kingsmills proprietors, or, as they are here termed, farmers. These milns had been originally granted to the town of Inverness, and by the authorities feued out in divisions, latterly confined to five. No subject connected with Inverness gave rise to greater or more protracted litigation than these milns. The properties supposed to be thirled to these milns were widespread, covering all except ecclesiastical property. The family of Huntly had their mill for the Castle lands at Altnaskiah, and all their feuars claimed exemption from the Kingsmills. This gave rise to great litigation, and it may be said that from 1600 down to the beginning of this century, and the period when the Thirlage Act was passed, there was constant litigation.

It will be observed that Castlehill speaks of his family as being "small and great," and that he could not afford to spend much in law. What he meant by the above quaint expression was that his children were young and numerous.

The Cuthbert lands were held chiefly of the town, those holding of the Crown being, according to the Roll of 1691, under the value of £200 Scots per annum. Nevertheless they were freeholders or barons, in respect these lands being near the town, were ascertained of the value of forty shillings of old extent, according to ancient retours. Some of the Highland chiefs, who made a good figure in their day, were not freeholders. Thus Sir E. Cameron of Lochiel latterly held his lands of Argyle and Huntly; Lord Macdonell of Aros, of Argyle, Huntly, Lovat, and the town of Inverness; and others might be named.

Follows the letter referred to :—

Much respected Cousin,—My love being remembered to yourself and bedfellow, I received your letter showing me that you will pass from prosecuting anything against me, anent the Kings milns, for which I cannot but render you many thanks, and I hope ere I die to show you and yours a greater courtesy before I die. And since ye pass from me yourself, I would entreat you, cousin, to be instrumental and to befriend me in making the rest of the farmers to desist from pursuing me, since my right is good, and in possession past prescription. Hoping you will write to the rest of the farmers in my favours to desist, for ye know, cousin, I have no need of spending, my family being small and great. But yet, before I suffer the least prejudice in the business, I shall not be wanting to defend myself, altho' I am little obliged to those who put me to it. I know not if I be called or no as yet, till my men of law acquaint me, or whether I shall be forced to go south or not this session. So, cousin, I would entreat you to acquaint me what is done in the business, and to signify your mind anent me to Mr. John Barrie, or to my advocate. I expect all that lies in your power you will do it for me in that matter, for if I go south and spend, I shall quarter upon you to my commer. So to your answer I remain, your assured cousin to my power,

(Signed)   Jo: CUTHBERT of Castelhil.

Inverness, 11 of January, 1657.

No. XLIII. Anno 1658.

ALEXANDER MACKINTOSH OF CONNAGE AND THE TENANTS OF SUTHERLANDSHIRE, Etc.

THE position of Scotland between the years 1650 and 1660 is not a pleasant subject of contemplation. The tyranny of the Stuarts is a constant theme to this day; but how little is said of the cruelties of the Usurpation?

Inverness benefitted perhaps as much as any other locality, in consequence of the great amount of money spent in connection with the building of the Citadel, and the maintenance of a large garrison. Colonels Man, Lilburn, and others were very influential, and acquired property, although the only alien family connected with this period, which took root in Inverness, was that of Scott of Seabank.

Much of the history of Scotland is taken up with the preying of one section of the community upon the other. The Roundheads were not a whit behind in persecuting the so-called Malignants when they had the opportunity, as may be seen by the letter, or ticket, as it is styled, after given. Friends of the Usurper had to be quieted, and what more convenient mode than by the escheating and despoiling of those who did not agree with them? However, it must be done with an air of legality, and the gathering in, in the first instance, must be by the recognised administrative officers of counties.

Though a mere band, yet these officers had a good deal to say, and could ease friends, as is shown in the case of the Sutherland and Gordonstown tenants after referred to :—

I, Alexander Mackintosh, younger of Connage, Donator to the gifts of escheat of all the delinquents and criminal persons denounced rebels within the shires northwards of the River Spey, do by these presents promise and engage that I shall not put the said gift in execution to the full against the maillers and tenants of the Earl of Sutherland and Sir Lodovick Gordon, Knight, and that I shall not escheat and inbring all their goods and gear, and apply the same to my own use. But for the respect I bear to the said noble Earl and the said Sir Lodovick, shall go on fairly with their tenants, dwelling presently on their own lands (not being feuars, or wadsetters, or heritors), and with the advice of the said Earl and the Lord Strathnaver, his son, and the said Sir Lodovick, shall compone and agree with their said tenants, and shall take such reasonable composition for the escheats of their tenants, as may be suitable to their fines, in a discreet manner, and not destructive to their livelihood, and that by the advice of their said masters. Provided that the said Earl, his son, and the said Sir Lodovick concur with, assist, and further me in the same, and direct their tenants readily to satisfy me as aforesaid, and not obstruct or retard the said business, or the prosecution of the said gift against others, or against their own people, as is above written, and not otherwise. In testimony whereof I have written and subscribed these presents at Edinburgh, the second day of March, 1658.

(Signed)   ALEXR. M'CINTOISHE.

Endorsed—"Ticket, McKintosh anent E. Sutherland and Sir Lod. Gordon."

No. XLIV. ANNO 1659.

MR. A. LESLIE, WRITER, EDINBURGH, AND THE LAIRD OF INSHES.

THE annexed letter was, I think, really written in 1660, after the Restoration, as there is reference to the King's Advocate. During the Usurpation, letters ran in name of the Lord Protector, and one important advance characterised this period, namely, that all legal documents were ordered to be couched in the English language. At the Restoration, Latin was again introduced, and in Crown writs continued until during the present reign.

Lawyers are always ready to receive their fees, and it

did not matter whether these were paid in gold or silver, as Mr. Leslie truthfully says.

The reference to the meeting of Parliament, and to the closing of the Exchequer and Signet offices all point to the year 1660.

The letter is more gossippy and diversified in its contents than that of the ordinary letters of lawyers. Styling a "junior" counsel a "common" counsel is curious.

Follows the letter referred to :—

> Honoured and affectionate cousin,—I received yours and your token, for which I give you thanks. And for a return of yours be pleased to know that our Parliament is to sit down the 12th of December next, before which time it is thought that the Signet will not be opened—and though it should be opened then, yet ye will do well to come over when the Parliament sits, since knowledge and sight may be had by your being here at that time.
>
> As for employing the King's Advocate, or any else, unless ye shall have a consultation with them, it is inexpedient, in respect they will forget anything given them. But if ye would have them fixed for you, it will be fit to bring with you all your writs, viz., your Decreet of Apprysing, the Charter and Sasine following thereupon, with what else you are to make use of, and take a consultation thereanent with the Advocates ye mind to make use of, to whom you must give, as use is. For which they will set down an information what is to be done, and thereby they will be secured for you; besides that ye may prosecute before the session sit down, that which they shall prescribe for your further security, and bettering of your right.
>
> You and your mother is bound in Kennedy's bond, principals, conjunctly and severally, and she not to relieve you. Patrick Nicoll expects for the money at the term, otherwise ye may be assured of a Charge of Horning, how soon the Signet opens.
>
> Dollars will be as acceptable to advocates as gold, if gold cannot be had. Calder is not yet come, and I conceive ye must have two chief advocates, whereof the King's Advocate must be one, and a common advocate to have a care of the proofs. Yourself may be agent with my advice.
>
> The committee has adjourned until the last of this instant. There will be a great committee here the 15th November. It is reported that Commissioners from Shires and Burghs will be here at that day, so that if ye think fit ye may come along with them, and have the consultation before the Parliament sit.
>
> We are all idle at present, there being neither Exchequer nor

Signet patent, but it is hoped we shall have our idleness turned into employment for writs and process, which is much longed for by all and amongst the rest by your affectionate cousin,

(Signed)   A. LESLIE.

Edinburgh, 22 Oct., 1659.

I pray you permit these to remember my very best respects to your mother.

No. XLV. Anno 1660

LORD LORN AND HIS FRIENDS.

AMONGST a bundle of pedigrees, narratives, and glorification-of-Campbell papers which at one time seemed to have belonged to Sir Hugh Campbell of Calder, who died in 1716, I found the annexed copy letter, written on a very faded sheet of large paper. With it is also copy of a curious letter from Queen Elizabeth to the Earl of Argyll in 1594. I am not aware whether either has been published, but the letter of 1660 is of sufficient interest to warrant its publication now. The Marquis of Argyll had been tried and sentenced, and this letter was in form of an intercession by Lord Lorn and his friends with Charles the II. It is fulsome and insincere. Lord Lorn himself was tried and sentenced a few years after the date of this letter, but Charles II. who, by reports, never said a foolish thing and never did a wise one, spared him, created him Earl of Argyll, and nurtured a deadly foe, who expiated his treason in due time. The references in the letter to Queen Mary are meagre, and close the account of pretended loyalty, so warm in the time of Somerled.

Follows the letter referred to, which is incomplete in some sentences, through decay of the paper:—

Most gracious Sovereign,—The son of Cressus having been dumb from his nativity, yet notwithstanding when in a battle he perceived a soldier ready to sheath his sword in his father's bowels, his vehement zeal for his father's preservation, burst asunder those ties which so far had bound up his tongue from speaking, and made him cry out for safety to his dear father.

The like affection hath laid a force upon us the cadents, kinsmen, and branches of the house of Argyll, hearing of that sudden desolation and calamity which is come upon that house. To break off silence in all humility, to represent to your Majesty the constant, uninterrupted, inbred loyalty and fidelity borne by our chiefs and forefathers to your royal predecessors, which they have testified to in many noble services in past ages. (Here the paper for a couple of lines has decayed.) . . . Gilchrist, the Earl of Angus, being sent by the King against him (Somerled) with an army, was eminently assisted by our chief, friends, and followers. Somerled, the rebel, was overthrown, and forced to flee to Ireland, where, gathering a new power, he returned with the like hostility as before, was subdued upon the river Clyde, suffered due punishment at Glasgow, for his proved treasonable attempts.

In the year 1306 that renowned prince, King Robert Bruce, shortly after his coronation, being routed at Methven, near Perth, by Sir Henry Vallence, Lieut.-Governor to King Edward of England, and forsaken of the most part of his friends, his Queen being made prisoner in the Tower of London, his brethren put to death, and the small remainder of his army which conducted him being again routed at Strath phillan, by John McDougall of Lorn, descended from Sommerled; our chief at that time, Sir Neil Campbell, with a most constant loyalty adhered to King Robert in his greatest extremity with his kinsmen and followers, conducting him first to Argyle, then to Kintyre, and from thence to the Isle of Rathin, near Ireland (being still followed by the said John), where he wintered, and was preserved for a time, until he raised some forces, returned next year to the Isle of Arran, and from thence landed in Carrick, surprised the Castle of Turnberry, from thence went to Inverness by the mountainous way, and ever after did prosecute his victories with many wrestlings, till in end he routed Edward II. of England at Bannockburn, near Stirling, delivered Scotland from a long and cruel bondage, got in Stirling Castle, and all the strongholds of the lands, being always strongly assisted by Sir Neil Campbell, our chief, and his kinsmen, upon whom that royal prince bestowed his royal sister, Lady Marjory Bruce, in marriage, put many marks and favor of his princely love upon him, and his house and children.

It was at this time, in Sepr., 1308, that these three valiant knights—Sir Neil Campbell, Sir Alexr. Setoun, and Sir Gilbert Hay made indentures yet extant, subscribed with their hands, and sealed with their seals, at the Abbey of Cambus Kenneth, and did bind themselves to stand to the uttermost in defence of their sovereign, King Robert, against all deadly, as the indentures bear, as well French, English, or Scots.

King David Bruce succeeding to his father's Crown a child of seven years old, in the beginning of his reign anno 1332, then Edward Baliol, assisted by many English and French and many Scots also, did usurp the Crown of Scotland, and thereafter, supported by Edward III. of England, force King David to fly to France for safety, his party in Scotland being brought so low as to have lost all the strength of this nation except four, when none durst avow King David to be King.

The first check to their usurping authority was given by the Lord Robert Stuart, your Majesty's Royal predecessor, who then was very young, but in the great extremity faithfully assisted by our Chief, Sir Colin Campbell and his friends, who by force invaded the Castle of Dunoon, in Cowall, in his assault.

This good success was fortunate and so well improven by the Regents of King David, still assisted by our Chief and his friends, that in end they established King David on his throne; for the which service, this generous and kind Prince bestowed many evidences of his royal bounty upon our Chief, as his evidences yet extant do bear, as the heritable keeping of this place with a yearly pension for the same. As also he did create John Campbell, son to Sir Neil, Earl of Athole.

King James I., of eternal and blessed memory, being 18 years retained prisoner by the English, his uncle Robert, Duke of Albany, and his son, Duke Murdoch, had in the opinion of all men settled themselves. (Here the paper is again decayed and illegible). . . . and inbred loyalty of our Chief, then Sir Robert Campbell, that, notwithstanding of his alliance of his eldest son, Sir Duncan, in marriage with Lady Marjorie Stuart, Duke Robert's daughter; yet he rather improved this opportunity of friendship to the advantage of his imprisoned Sovereign, than to that of his alliance or private respect, and never ceased, till he brought them to condescend to the ransoming and re-establishing of King James on his father's throne.

King James II. in his young years being reduced to great straits by the binding of many. men against his authority, our Chief, then Earl of Argyll, did adhere most constantly to his sovereign lord, laying out himself to the utmost for bringing down so dangerous a rebellion, and settling the crown in security to his Sovereign. His son also, Earl Archibald, died fighting valiantly near his Sovereign Lord and Prince James IV. in the fatal battle of Floddoun.

Neither is it to be overpast that King James V., in his younger years, as he was to take the government in his own hands, was plunged in many difficulties and crossed in his designs by many nobles of the greatest power of this Kingdom, notwithstanding our Chief, Colin, Earl of Argyll, stood constant and firm to the maintenance of the royal authority, and in the end was made Lieut.-General of all the south shires, in which service (assisted always with his kinsmen and friends), he so behaved himself, that within few days, he brought all the King's enemies either to absolute submission, or then to betake themselves to banishment out of the realm, for which service the King put a high mark of favor on him, that the charter of his reward beareth these words "for holding the crown upon our head."

Queen Mary, mother to King James VI., of happy memory, escaping prison out of the Castle of Lochleven, A.D., 1566, being forsaken (for the most part) by the nobility in a most dangerous backsliding time. Yet our Chief, Archibald, Earl of Argyll, retaining his antient inbred loyalty of their house, was not wanting to her in her great extremity, and was General of her army, adhering still constantly to her party thereafter, till such times as her son, King James, came to be offered the throne, from whose authority thereafter he did not shrink.

We shall not vex your Majesty by making mention of many horrid insurrections and rebellions of islanders and remote mountainous men, that have been broken, destroyed, and overthrown by our chiefs and their friends, and how many notorious malefactors and cruel oppressors have been brought from their strongholds and inaccessible places, otherwise hardly to be overtaken, without great bloodshed and expence, and yet have been overcome and brought by our chiefs to condign punishment, yea, we may, with all confidence and credit, avouch that never any of our chiefs of the house of Argyll or their cousins or cadents have been tainted to this day with the least mark of disloyalty or disobedience to their sovereign lords, the Kings of Scotland, but by the contrar, they have been most willing to set themselves for bearing down the insolencies of the remote, rebellious, lawless men, much occasioned by the remoteness and distance of these places of the land far from the law and justice (the horrors of rocks, woods, and mountains contributing much unto these). Let the most ancient of men be consulted, and all the progress of the history of this nation be consulted, and all that we have said shall be found to be certain and manifest. This moved the wisest of princes in his time, King James, of happy memory, to give this testimony of our family, that it was the soundest and most loyal family to the Crown of Scotland that he ever saw.

And now, sir, when your sacred Majesty, after so many bad sufferings, has so fully tasted of the sweet mercies of Jesus Christ who hath lifted up your head above all your enemies round about you, by a miracle of unexampled mercy, and when you are next God, over these kingdoms; even so, sir, it shall be your glory to be like unto God, whose mercies are over all His works. Remember our Chief, now, in his low condition. (Here the paper is destroyed for a couple of lines) . . . hath done to your Majesty's Royal progenitors so many acceptable services, in so many ages constantly continued, without any crack, backsliding, or remission—then it shall be no grief to your Majesty, nor offence of heart, that you have not rooted out so loyal and ancient a family, who, in most backsliding times, have still retained our loyalty and integrity. And it shall be our daily prayer to our God to make unto your Majesty and your royal posterity a sure house. And this we do all subscribe upon the knees of our heart, and tears in our eyes, as your Majesty's most humble and obedient subjects and servitors.

Endorsed—" Double letter Lord Lorn and his friends to King Charles II. 1660."

No. XLVI. ANNO 1661.

ALEXANDER ROSE, TOWN CLERK OF INVERNESS.

A GOOD deal of money was spent in Inverness during the period of the Usurpation. The only good result of this disastrous period as regards in especial several ancient buildings in the North, was the founding, as is commonly said, of that purity in speaking the English language which has long been a characteristic of Inverness. The inhabitants, and in especial the authorities, were probably too happy at the Restoration to get rid of the Aliens. The demolition of the Citadel was ostensibly at the instance of the Highland Chiefs, and seems to have been gone about in an indifferent manner. There is a curious protest among the Grant papers, taken on the part of the Laird of Grant, to the effect that whilst he had by command his quota of men in readiness to proceed with the demolition, for days running, there was not one in authority present to give the necessary orders.

The letter of discharge after given refers to cess which in some of its phases, was a source of difficulty and litigation. As mentioned in a former letter, the Town vassals holding lands outside the Burgh or Royalty, were unwilling to pay stents or cesses for intra mural objects, and ultimately were successful in their contention. Illustrations of the cesses, objected to by Castlehill, Culloden, Inshes, and others were, these—Cess of a thousand pounds for wood from Glenmoriston, and labour in re-erecting the Wooden Bridge which had fallen. Cess for a sum raised to repel the Earl of Moray's oppressions in consequence of the Burgh siding with the Mackintoshes. Considerable cess for "a new Prick for the High Kirk steeple." Cess to resist the Earl of Moray and Mackintosh of Holme, who stopped the Burghers from taking stone, feal, and divot on the Muir adjacent to the River Ness, beyond the Burgh's haugh.

It must be admitted, that with the exception, perhaps, of the Bridge, the other cesses were purely of a burghal character, and for the benefit of the burgesses.

Follows the letter of discharge referred to :—

Inverness, Nov. 21st, 1661.

"Received then from Thomas Dunbar, merchant in Inverness, the sum of ten pounds ten shillings Scots money, and that in name and behalf of Mr. Wm. Robertson of Inshes for three months cess imposed on the said Mr. William by the Town of Inverness. As witness my hand, day, year, and place aforesaid.

(Signed) ALEX. ROSE, Clerk.

No. XLVII. Anno 1662.

MR. H. ROBERTSON, MERCHANT, INVERNESS.

THE annexed lengthy letter from an Inverness merchant, to the Laird of Inshes, then in Edinburgh, is almost verbose in its directions.

There are two matters dealt with, one on account of the writer's pupil, and the other personal. The chief matter is that to be intented against John Forbes, second of Culloden, as representing his father, and against Sir Robert Farquhar.

Sir Robert Farquhar had been appointed by the Committee of Estates of Parliament, which had usurped power during the latter part of the reign of Charles the First, and until they, having fulfilled Cromwell's aims, were summarily discharged. Farquhar's business was to levy cesses in the north, from Aberdeen to Caithness. They were levied most arbitrarily, the Cavaliers having hard times of it, of which we now hear very little, during the usurpations. After the Restoration the Royalists had their turn, and Sir R. Farquhar was called to refund many a sum, so that he had reason to rue the day he took office. The first Culloden's views were strictly in accordance with those of Farquhar, and he had a good deal to do with cesses of Inverness, Ross, and Nairn. It is with reference to receiving excessive imposts that the letter after given deals.

Follows the letter referred to :—

Inverness, 6th June, 1662.

Much Honoured Cousin,—Yours I received of date, the 7th of May last, whereby ye showed me that ye received in my behalf five pound sterling, but that both my letters and money were too late of coming, for such reasons as ye wrote of. I received in like manner the whole papers which I sent you in relation to my pupils particulars, together with the two Advocates informations, queries, and resolutions, whereupon I have given receipt as ye desired by your letter to Andrew Sutherland. I perceive by your letter and the Advocates resolution, that the business relating to my pupil cannot be pursued at his instance as we intended, but the Executors of umquhile William and Gilbert Robertson's, grandfather and father to the minor must pursue jointly as heir, and that there is a difficulty in pursuing of Culloden, and Sir Robert Farquhar alike in one proof. So that it is necessary that every one of them be pursued severally for their own parts. I have sent your letter, together with the Haill instructions and informations for my further satisfaction to be advised by our cousin David Fearne, who sent me the form of a factory drawn up by himself, and written by his own hand, wherein he inserts, as well the heir as the executors of the deceased Gilbert Robertson, and desiring me with all speed to send the same south with some money whereby ye may employ Maister John Bayne and Maister William Lauder, as agents for the heir and executors, since ye cannot gudlie attend it yourself, as ye inform me by your letter. Wherefore I have sent you herewith all the papers ye sent me—to wit the principal bond, the Committee of Estates receipt and discharge, the petition and procuratory, together with this new procuratory subscribed by the heir and myself, Matthew and Francis Robertson as executors, but I have kept the town of Inverness receipt by me, since it was your desire that it should be destroyed for the reason contained in your letter. And as for the petition ye are to cause, draw it up yourself, according as ye shall be informed by the agents which ye are to employ. For David Fearne has written to me that it would not be so formally drawn up here as elsewhere, so that it is necessary that it be drawn up by the agents advice. Because as he informs me that there is no necessity that the petition should be subscribed here, since the factory warrants them who are entrusted in our behalf to do in that as they shall think most convenient. The factory is not subscribed so as I would wish it, by reason, I and the heir subscribed it, and the witnesses have subscribed the same under our subscriptions, and Matthew and Francis Robertson has subscribed under the witnesses, which may be thought somewhat unfortunate. Yet I hope since all hands do it, it will not be a reason to retard the business. Ye shall know that umquhile William Robertson made not a testament, neither can we yet find out his confirmed testament if any be, so that it cannot be sent south to instruct the action at this time, but if ye think it necessary, ye may have my brother, Gilbert Robertson, his confirmed testament whenever ye will. But in the meantime, I think neither of these testaments can instruct anything of these monies for which Culloden is to be pursued, since the same was not confirmed in testament. All the testament can do, is to instruct that such men were executors to umquhile Gilbert and William Robertson. Well, as for these things, I remit all to yourself, and to such agents as ye please to employ in this particular of the heir my pupil, and the executors of umquhile Gilbert and William Robertson, my father and brother, against Culloden for their money received by him, and his umquhile father from them, and desire you earnestly that ye cause prosecute the same against Culloden in so far as can be done in law. And to that effect according to David Fearne's desire by his letter to me, ye employ the foresaid Maister John Bayne and Maister William Lauder as agents in the said particular. And for furthering of the pursuers, be pleased to receive from this bearer, the number of twenty-three rix dollars being one hundred merks money, and what more shall be necessary, acquaint me and

ye shall have it. I entreat you, be as diligent in this particular as you can. You inform me that ye have passed the bills in my own particulars, and my cousin, Walter Robertson, against Sir Robert Farquhar for these monies wrongfully received by him from us. I hope ere now there is something done in it, if it lay in your power. I entreat ye, have a special care to see that action of ours against Sir Robert Farquhar prosecute to the full, and if ye think that the laws may be obtained in his contrar, spare not your charge to get your intent, as well in my particular, as in my cousin Walter Robertson's particular also, for the Lord knows in what necessity he stands at this time, albeit he was forced to pay these monies now craved by him, to Sir Robert Farquhar. I have no farther to add at the present, remitting the care of all these particulars to yourself, but that I am and still continue.—Your affectionate loving cousin to serve you.
(Signed)   H. ROBERTSON.

Addressed—" For his honoured and loving cousin Maister William Robertson of Inshes, for the present at Edinburgh. These."

No. XLVIII. ANNO 1663.

DAVID BAILLIE, FIRST OF DOCHFOUR.

SOME notice of a family which has acquired great possessions in the north, may not be without interest. The first Baillie I find connected with Dochfour was one Alexander Baillie, doubtless of the Dunain family, whose name appears in 1606. In 1637, William Baillie, portioner of Dochfour, with consent of Marion Maclean (sister of Dochgarroch) grants a charter to Alexander Fraser, son to Malcolm Fraser of Culduthel. In 1657, David Baillie, described as of Dochfour, younger son of Alexander Baillie of Dunain, is infeft in Easter and Wester Dochcairns, upon charter by his father. Dochcairns are bounded on the south by the burn of Lochend or Dochnacraig, and on the north by a run of water finding its way to Little Loch-Ness, now called Loch-Dochfour, near the boat-house—the lands 'twixt this run and the burn of Dochfour, being Dochfour proper. The

present house of Dochfour stands upon Dochcairn, the
old house having stood near the burn, at the place called
Bal-na-cruick. The Baillies have thus had a heritable
and irredeemable right to Dochcairns since 1657, but
their indefeasible right to Dochfour goes back only
towards the end of last century.

I find David first named in 1629, when a marriage
contract is entered into between Alex. Baillie of Dunain
taking burden upon him for David Baillie, his lawful son,
with his consent, and with consent of Katherine Munro,
spouse to the said Alexander, on the one part, and
William Paterson, Burgess of Inverness, for himself, and
taking burden upon him for Janet Paterson, his lawful
daughter, on the other part, dated Inverness, 1st December of said year. The tocher was the handsome one of
3000 merks. There was probably no surviving male issue
of this marriage, for in 1659, David grants a disposition
of Dochcairns to himself and to Janet Fraser, his spouse,
in conjunct liferent, and to Alexander Baillie, their son,
in fee.

I have several letters written by David Baillie, one of
which is given. He, as I formerly mentioned, lived at one
time in Castle Spioradail, according to a messenger's execution, and at another at Kinmylies. In 1672, he granted
a lease to John Fraser in Bunchrew, of all and haill the
upper half of the farm and lands of Dochfour. On 28th
May, 1673, Mr. Alexander Clark and Mr. James Sutherland, ministers of Inverness, testify "that David Baillie of
Davochfour, is an excommunicated Papist, and lies under
the stroke unrelaxed the space of these 8 years byepast,
without any hopes of being reclaimed or returning to the
bosom of the true Christian Reformed Church." In consequence of this certificate, Mr. Baillie's evidence as a
witness, was refused by the Court of Session in a legal
process, in an objection raised by the Burgh, pursuers in
the cause. Alexander, the second of Dochfour, was in
1689, or previous thereto, married to Mary Grant, whose
mother was Catherine Ogilvie, described as relict of Alex-

ander Grant, in Milltown of Ballachastell, and they had a son called William. In the year 1727, a herd named Alexander Urquhart entered Alexander Baillie's service, where he remained four years. Urquhart, speaking in 1793, describes his master as old and blind, when the witness was herd at Dochfour, 1727-1731. This Alexander appears to have married, for the second time, Hannah Fraser, one of the Reelig family, by whom they had a son named Alexander living in 1711. In 1733, old Alexander is dead, and his eldest son, Hugh, and his wife, Emilia Fraser, are infeft in Dochcairns. Hugh was succeeded by his son Alexander, who was succeeded, as purchaser, by his younger brother Evan. Evan was succeeded by his grandson Evan, and this last Evan by his grandson James. The present Dochfour is not heir male or head of the Dochfour *stirps*, there being male heirs of an elder brother of Evan Baillie, first above referred to, which Evan was a purchaser.

It has been often asked who is the heir male of the last Dunain, and consequently head of all the northern Baillies. This I cannot answer, as at the present moment, but in 1797, the late Jas. Fraser of Gortuleg, W.S., mentions that the nearest agnate of the last Dunain, who died in 1869, was "Mr Baillie, brewer in London." His heir male, if he exist, is the head.

Follows the letter referred to :—

Honourable Cousin,—Concerning our discourse yester night, if ye get me payment at this time of the principal, I shall quit the annual, with a little more, if you please, so as to be certain of payment at this term of the stock, or thirty pounds less, it would much pleasure me and oblige your affectionate cousin and servant,

(Signed)   D. BAILLIE.

3rd of June, 1663.

No. XLIX. ANNO 1664.

HEW ROBERTSON OF THE INSHES FAMILY.

THE annexed letter is of interest as showing that an Inverness-shire laird was sufficiently enterprising upwards of two hundred years ago to engage in a salmon exporting transaction with the Continent. The laird had an important fishing on the Ness, which towards the close of the sixteenth century had belonged to a family named Macphail. The writer became a leading merchant and one of the bailies of Inverness. He was one of the Robertsons of Shipland, an important burghal family, as were their successors, the Alves family. The property is now divided. The mansion-house of Shipland is an interesting part of Old Inverness, and, as Dr. Alves, who died about 1788, lived in Church Street, it may be safely assumed the house was built by his father, Mr. Thomas Alves, if not by his grandfather, the well-known Bailie who early last century was deputed by the Council of Inverness to visit and report upon the state of the burgh of Dingwall, and whose portrait still exists.

Follows the letter referred to :—

Paris, 16 May, 1664.

Very loving brother,—My love being heartily remembered to you, I received yours whereby you show me of your acceptance of the bill of the two hundred livres, which I desired might be given to Thomas Crawford. Be pleased to know that the salmon monies I have had thankfully paid me here with that of James Graham. Also by reason the most part thereof was engaged before your return came. I wrote to you long ago of my receipt of James Graham's bill, but it seems you had not received my letter at your writing. Sir, the disposing of the money upon my necessar occasions, with sundry things also that I am necessitated to be provided of, has brought to great extraordinars. But I hope the worst is past. Sir, I hope this will meet you at Edinburgh, as I learn by your letter. I have given Mr. Kinloch a bill of one hundred and eight pounds for money to carry me to London. I entreat you to excuse this trouble. Rest satisfied ere long it will draw to an end.

The shortness of my time makes me brief in my intelligence, but from London I shall give you a larger account to whatever place you shall write to me immediately at your receipt of this; for, God willing, I intend to take journey to-morrow for Dieppe. You may address your letter to Mr. Alexander Blair's, in Rood Lane, at the sign of the Salters and Chandlers, and let me hear from you, I pray, in all haste, how my mother is in her health. So rests this in haste, your loving brother to death.
(Signed)   HEW ROBERTSON.

No. L. ANNO 1665.
BAILIE FOWLER OF INVERNESS, INSHES, AND GLENMORISTON.

THE old feud 'twixt the families of Inshes and Glenmoriston, regarding the barony of Culcabock, culminated in the famous burning of the Inshes barns, by a party of Grants. It brought matters to a climax, and Inshes got peaceable possession of the lands under favourable circumstances. The story will be told elsewhere, so I do not refer to it more particularly at present. The Laird of Inshes had gone to headquarters to obtain justice, and the receipt of the letter after given from a friendly correspondent and connection at Inverness, that Glenmoriston had been apprehended, must have been very gratifying.

The family of Fowler were for a long time influential burghers of Inverness, with property chiefly in Bridge Street and Gordon Place. The south gable of "Bailie Fowler's house" is frequently referred to as the northern boundary of the Castle Shot Fishings. Mr. Fowler shows his interest in the Robertson family and connections by his anxiety as to the state of the title to the estate of Robertson of Kindeace, cadet of Inshes.

Follows the letter referred to, addressed "To my honoured cousin, Mr. William Robertson of Inshes, present in Edinburgh:"—

Inverness, 16th Oct., 1665.

Honoured Cousin, Sir,—Saluting you with my kind respects, I

doubt not but ye have heard of Glenmoriston how he was apprehended by the Robertsons of Athole, and carried to the Justice General, who taking pity on him, as also the gentleman that apprehended him taking pity on, did dismiss him on his bond to appear at Clunye in Badenoch, against the second day of November, with two of his friends, where they are to meet him with two of the friends for taking cognisance in your affairs and debates and for removing of the same. The failure is six thousand merks. This is all the information we have here in the premises. I doubt not but by this time, you have letters, and you would do well to advise with your friends in Athol hereanent and what your carriage shall be in that business. They should not be neglected that owned your quarrel and interest. You would do well to send an express to them to know their minds hereanent, for once that people has espoused your quarrel, they will not see you wronged, but own you to the full. Therefore they should not be met by ingratitude nor forgetfulness.

There is another business fallen out I believe by Achnacloich's instigation, as you may perceive by David Robertson's letter in relation to Kindeace's ward. Therefore you will be pleased to search out the mystery of the matter, whether or not Kindeace be ward land, and if ward, you may try the Exchequer books whether or not Kindeace's widow or Life-rentrix be entered by the superior; and what else is needful to be done therein, let it be done and defended to the full. Since there is but few of you heirs, you ought to stick the closer together, at least as far as law can carry you, for preventing the insolencies of malicious persons. I need not enlarge, but refer you to David Robertson's letter and David Fearne's, which will show you more large. All your relatives here are in good health. Your brother Hew is at Elgin at the writing hereof. This is all addressed from, sir, your humble servant,

(Signed)   JA: FOULLER.

No. LI. Anno 1666.

THE EARL OF ARGYLL.

THE fate of Archibald, Marquis of Argyll, did not, so soon as his son was taken into favour, deter or prevent the latter from continuing the old family trade of coveting their neighbours' lands, and interfering for their own advancement whenever and wherever they could.

The feeble support given to the Laird of Mackintosh in 1665, when he went for the last time to Lochaber to recover Glenlui and Loch Arkaig, would not have lost him these lands, were it not for Argyll's interference. The Earl sent Campbell of Glenurchy with a party and an intimation that his full strength would be thrown for Lochiel if Mackintosh opposed a sale of the lands; and this, unhappily for Mackintosh, turned the scale, and compelled him to submit.

The Earl became purchaser, and he and his successors' family proved hard masters to Lochiel. The Earl was most anxious to have the estates, but had not the whole money. Mackintosh had to lie out of a considerable part of his money for nearly twenty years. He had to put the rigour of the law into execution, and, to enable him to do so, had to borrow on the Earl and his cautioner's bond.

The letter after given, written in answer to Mackintosh's demand for money, or to cancel the agreement of sale, is civil enough and sufficiently apologetic. But observe how he treats the idea of cancellation; he will not do so, though it might not be against his pecuniary interests, but pretends he could not bear to be laughed at.

Follows the letter referred to :—

Loving Friend,—You see everybody is not so frank with you as I, yet do not use me the worse. I have written very earnestly the Earl of Moray to do all your desires. I have sent back the bond signed by Glenurchy and me to Aberuchill, and have desired the Earl of Moray to sign a bond relating to it, and corroborating it, because I will not send it North again, but, if he refuse to put in Petty, stand not against it. You have Glenurchy and me. Before I got your last, your 8000 merks was in Lochaber, on the way to Innernesse. The want of this, and the money at Edinburgh, would be so greatly a disappointment to you, that I should be very sorry for it. Yet it will not make the minute void, which I will not discharge, not because of any advantage I have by it, but that I be not laughed at by those who wish not you and I to settle about it.—I rest your loving friend and servant.

(Signed) ARGYLL.

Inneraray, April 17, '66.

So Mackintosh lost the great heritage which came to his family through his ancestress, Eva, heiress of Clan Chattan, nothing of it remaining to him but the title "of Torcastle" during his life, which was specially reserved.

No. LII. Anno 1667.

THE EARL OF MAR.

THE Laird of Mackintosh having a commission to vindicate his rights in the Brae of Lochaber, applied to friendly supporters for their assistance. In response he received the very prompt and satisfactory answer after given from the Earl of Mar. It must have been particularly gratifying to Mackintosh that the men of Mar were put under Invercauld, himself the head of one of the tribes composing Clan Chattan. The letter is interesting as showing the power great landlords had or assumed over their tenants and vassals. The Mackintoshes were able to repay the obligation of 1667 very handsomely in 1715, when they arose in strength to support the then Earl of Mar in the gallant effort made for the restoration of the Stuarts.

Follows the letter referred to :—

Much honoured cousin,—In obedience to your entreaty, sir, I have written to Innercald to take along with himself my whole vassals and feuars in Braemar, Strathdee, and Glengairne, to attend you and accompany him in what you may have to do in Lochaber.

And as this is the best and most effectual order I can send them to make testimony hereof, as my will, by Innercald, who is my bailzie in these countrys, so shall I be ready, sir, to witness my respects to you in a greater manner when occasion offers, as sir, your very affectionate cousin to serve you.

         (Signed) MAR.
Tillifour, Nov. 26th, 1667.
Addressed—"For my much honoured cousin the Laird of Mackintosh."

Readers may contrast this letter with the famous notice issued by Lord Mar in 1715 to "Jock" his bailie at Kildrummie to raise his men.

No. LIII. Anno 1668.
OLD LOVE LETTERS, W. R. AND M. R.

THE letters after given are part of a series which the loving hands of the descendants of the gentleman have preserved with care, and had pasted in a book. He was a scholar and ready penman, and, though kept at a distance for a while, yet, by the final letter, carried his point. The lady, unfortunately, died within a year of the marriage. Both parties belonged to the North, and though there is nothing in the letters demanding concealment, yet, as there are numerous representatives of both families now living, it is thought better not to give names. Love letters of this early date are uncommon, particularly as regards northern families, hence those given will, no doubt, be perused with interest.

Follow the letters referred to :—

Accomplished lady,—As I need not offer to vie compliment in the tender and illustration of my suit with such a well qualified lady as yourself, whom I ever eyed as ane mirror of all accomplishments, yet if you will accept of ingenuity, in lieu of encomiastick strains, quaintness of expression, and rare embellishment of discourse, I am obliged to tell you, dearest lady, that my thoughts are still confined under a strong obligation to your virtues. And ever since our last interview, my passions have been so violent that I am constrained to remitt them by a line, as through a conduit, or channel, till once they adventure to dilate and exoner themselves in the profoundest abyss of your heart and best affection, where I wish they be concentrated and sealed up for ever, with such success and prevalency, to the utter extirpation of whatsoever aversions and thoughts of repugnancy, to the hopes of your favour and conquest of my love. Wherefore, generous lady, if my fixed thoughts be entertained, let it be signified and me refreshed by a line from your own hand. If not, yet notwithstanding, write with the bearer whom I appointed to attend your pleasure. Both await your discretion to refresh or confound my mind, to embrace or renounce my suit. But the best resolution, I mean acceptance, is only hoped, and most passionately longed for, by dearest lady, your most passionate lover, and most humble servant,

(Signed) W. R.

———, 11 Feby., 1668.

Sir,—I have received many testimonies of your respect, for which I confess myself much obliged to you; and shall take it as the greatest proof of your affection that you would banish those unprofitable thoughts out of your mind and will. I assure you that henceforth I will neither hear nor listen to any matter of that nature. So, for this is my final resolution, I wish you much joy in your choice, and rests your assured friend and servant,

(Signed) M. R.

Sir,—I have put your affection to trial often, but if it has not been stricken by this last blow, I shall never question the sincerity thereof, but persuade myself of your constancy, and rest more your friend than you imagine.

(Signed) M. R.

P.S.—Above all, I conjure you, by the love you bear me, do not let any alive know of this.

Marked—"Received upon the 2nd of March, 1668."

No. LIV. Anno 1669.

LORD STRATHNAVER.

THE annexed letter from Lord Strathnaver, shows that people travelling southwards from Sutherland and Caithness did not travel by Inverness, but crossed the Moray Firth. The letter is sent to Mr Clerk, one of the ministers of Inverness, who had been at one time minister of Latheron, and thus well known to the writer. Mr Clerk was laureated at Aberdeen in 1646, appointed minister at Latheron in 1652, and translated to Inverness in 1665. From his being Master of Arts, he carefully prefixed " Mr."—*Magister*—before his signature. The worthy clergyman must have been a good deal put about by having to attend to secular matters, late on a Saturday afternoon. The old idea was that the minister was not to be disturbed on Saturday, he being understood as engaged in the preparation of his sermons. I was rather amused lately by reading a long letter from a clergyman—one of the most correct of men—who rarely, if ever, was caught tripping, written on a Sunday morning about 80 years ago, and apparently in the Session House of Inverness, which he hastily concludes by saying the bells have been ringing for some minutes, and he must prepare himself for his duties.

Lord Strathnaver's letter is carefully written, and shows all those signs of caution and circumspection in his affairs characteristic of the family since the admixture of Gordon blood.

Follows the letter referred to:—

Dunrobin, 26th October, 1669.

Right Reverend,—I am still troublesome to you, and at this time, seeing I am on my journey south, I have sent this bearer to receive your commands, south, who is to meet me in Moray. I entreat that you may see him deliver the three hundred and forty-four pounds to Inshes, that I have sent with him as complete payment of the interest of four thousand three hundred merks Scots for two years, which is all that is owing at Whitsunday last since the former discharge, which is till Whitsunday, 1667, as the former discharge, which I have also sent with the bearer, will show. Let the discharge narrate the whole progress of the bond, and to Inshes' own right to it, and let it be delivered with all diligence to the bearer, who is to meet me with it in Moray on Saturday. Pardon this freedom, and wherein I can serve you, you may command your affectionate friend to serve you. (Signed) STRATHNAVER.

Addressed—" For Mr. Alexander Clerk, minister at Inverness. These."

On the blank leaf of the letter the minister writes—

Honoured Sir,—Here there is a letter come from my Lord Strathnaver to me, to see some money delivered to you, and receive your discharge. Seeing this is Saturday, I cannot see you, and my lord being bye, I shall entreat you to receive your money, and discharge my lord as he hath deserved. This is all in haste, but that I continue your well-wishing friend and servant.

(Signed)   MR. A. CLERK.

Inverness, 30th Oct., 'twixt 3 and 4 afternoon, 1669.

No. LV.   Anno 1670.

H. ROBERTSON OF NAIRN AND LORD STRATHNAVER.

THE title of Lord Strathnaver, as a leading one, has been dormant for a good deal more than a century, but a son having been happily born to Lord Stafford, it might be well to revive in his person the ancient and historic title of Lord Strathnaver.

It is doubtful whether there are bailies or merchants in Nairn at the present day able to lend a Highland nobleman or gentleman the sum of five thousand pounds sterling. Yet, we find that upwards of two hundred years ago, there was at least one bailie able to lend a sum in these days equivalent to the figure just mentioned.

The name of Suttie took root in Edinburgh and the Lothians, and flourishes even in these days of change. Lord Strathnaver was a prompt payer, for though the letter or precept is only dated 16th June, it is paid in Edinburgh on 23rd August.

Follows the letter referred to:—

My Lord,—May it please your lordship after sight hereof, to pay or cause to be payed to George Suttie, Bailie of Edinburgh, the sum of two hundred and fifty-eight merks, Scots, and his receipt with these presents, shall oblige me, my heirs, and successors, to deliver to your lordship, or any other in your name, having the said Bailie George Suttie's receipt of the sum above mentioned, with these

presents, a sufficient discharge of one year's interest of the principal sum of four thousand three hundred merks, Scots money, and that from Whitsunday sixteen hundred and sixty-nine to Whitsunday sixteen hundred and seventy years, and all years preceding, and that with warrandice, and all other clauses needful. Make good and thankful payment upon the account of, my lord, your lordship's most obliged and most humble servant,
                        (Signed)   H. ROBERTSON.
Nairne, 16th June, 1670.
For the Right Noble Lord the Lord Strathnaver.

Edinburgh, the 23rd of August, 1670 years. Then received the contents of the within written bill by me.
                      (Signed)   GEORGE SUITTIE.

No. LVI. ANNO. 1671.
MR. THOMAS LINDSAY, AN INMATE OF CROMARTY PRISON.

THE annexed pitiful letter, from a prisoner confined in the prison of Cromarty, is not without interest.

He appears to have only been cautioner for a debt, whilst the principal was a considerable landed proprietor in Caithness-shire.

The circumstances are not detailed, and it seems inconsistent with the Laird of Inshes' general character to have been pressing the cautioner so hard, while allowing the principal debtor to get out of prison.

I have nothing to show who the writer was. The letter is holograph, and the writer must have been a man of good education. Cromarty was at one time a thriving port, but has long fallen from its former state, without much chance of prosperity again reverting to it. No more humane laws have passed in modern times than those gradually doing away with the horrors of imprisonment for civil debt. No doubt it is frequently hard to lose money for goods supplied, and otherwise. But the true remedy is to take all the debtor's property; and in my own time, and to some extent with my help, the last vestige of imprisonment for civil debt, which the debtor, from misfortune and not fraud, is unable to pay, has been swept away. In trade, over-credit is an evil to which no encouragement ought to be given.

The saying "put the saddle on the right horse," it will be seen, is of respectable antiquity.

Follows the letter referred to:—

Much honoured sir,—I am informed that you have given Dunskaith ane respite of time of his captivity, and yet I am kept in close prison, which truly I think strange of, seeing he is the principal, and I am but cautioner of mere goodwill, without any kind of benefit, though I hear you are misinformed of the contrary, which I declare, is truly untrue. Wherefore I most earnestly entreat you may grant me a timeous releasement, for I can do nothing to farther your payment while I am in this condition. But if I were at liberty I should be very willing and active to further your payment, and I beg it of you to put the saddle on the right horse, for truly I am evil used, as severals can inform you, more nor I mind to write for the present. You need not think I will flee, for I am neither of intention nor in ability so to do. Wherefore, again I entreat you for a timeous releasement, that I may go where that man is, and put him to it. For since we were taken, I have not seen him nor heard from him. I humbly entreat you will not put me to ruin, seeing the man himself is in ability to pay his own debt; and if I were at liberty I shall be very active—he will either sell or wadset a part of his land. I shall very much further your speedy payment, but while I am in captivity I can do nothing. Your kindly answer is expected by him who is your assured friend and servant,
(Signed) T. LYNDESAY.

From the Prissone in Cromertie, 15 Feby., 1671.

Addressed—"For my much honoured and worthy friend, Mr. William Robertson of Inshes. These."

No. LVII. ANNO 1672.

MR. HENRY SINCLAIR, WRITER, EDINBURGH.

THE annexed letter is interesting in respect it gives an account of a debate before the Court of Session upwards of two hundred years ago. The pros and cons are stated very clearly, as well as the decision. The debate was *in presentia*, that is, in presence of the whole Court, and it would be curious to know whether the counsel for the Laird of Inshes argued subsequently with the Lord President in Court, or privately. It would almost seem as if the latter had been the case, and, in any view, it is clear the President was inclined to be curt.

The letter is most indistinctly written, and some of the words are doubtful. In pressing for money to carry on the process, the writer dwells on the fact that counsel and their clerks must be paid.

Follows the letter referred to:—

Edinburgh, 18th January, 1672.

Worthy Sir,—Having the occasion of the bearer altho' I have not had no line from you this long time, I thought it my duty to let you know that the Reductions, at your instance against Mr. James Robertson, was called and discussed in the Inner House the 9th of this instant, and the defender opposing his disposition and alleging he was not obliged to instruct by writ, but offered to prove by the parties' oaths contained in the disposition the sums truly paid to them; to which it was answered by your procurator that the defender behoved to instruct the onerous cause by writ, and the creditors' oaths were not sufficient, and if such probations should be sustained it were most dangerous; and as in law, witnesses could not prove one sum of money above 100 lib., so the depositions of any party whatsoever could not fortify any disposition granted by a father to his son of greater sums, and not only this, but many other grounds were alleged for you. And notwithstanding of all, the Lords *in presentia*, sustained the disposition, the defender proving by the creditors' oaths the sums truly paid by him; and as to the payment clause ordered him to instruct by writ. The most part of the lawyers were not satisfied with this interlocquitor, whereupon my Mr. spoke to my Lord President and told him it was hard to sustain the disposition, unless the defender would instruct the onerous clause be writ. His answer was that it was to no purpose to make any further application, for if the creditors were persons of good repute and fame, the Lords would sustain the probation by their oaths. But if you have any relevant objection against them, I think the Lords will hear you thereupon, and if the lands disponed be no more worth than the sums contained in the disposition, or what he can instruct upon his mother's contract of marriage, which his agents here affirm to be 5 or 6000 merks, then you must consider what objections you have and send it by the first post. Till it come to my hand with your answer, nothing more can be done in the business. As for Alex. Rose right, you cannot overtake him, upon the Act of 1621, as being a confident and conjunct person, and therefore you must send me information upon what grounds you intend to reduce his right. Sir, these things cannot be done without money, and therefore I expect it with the next occasion both the compts I sent. I have consulted as to this last dispute, and when it comes to be debated again I must consult, not only advocates who must have money, but also clerks. This is all at present from your affectionate friend and servant, (Signed) HEN. SINCLAIR.

Addressed—"For Mr. William Robertsone of Inshes."

No. LVIII. Anno 1673.

BAILIE WILLIAM MACBEAN OF INVERNESS.

THE annexed sensible letter from one of the merchants of Inverness to the Laird of Inshes at Edinburgh details a somewhat harsh proceeding against the writer's brother. Mr. Macbean, who could only sign his initials, was equal to the occasion, as is seen by the step he took for his brother's relief. Some of the expressions are quaint, for instance, "you know what for a man he is."

The Macbeans have been long established in Inverness, and, though not numerous, have held good positions.

I have long had an address or ode in very faded ink to General Wade, both in Latin and English, which I thought was the production of the Rev. Alexander Macbean of Inverness. Upon referring to it lately, I see the heading in Latin is "In thema, D. McBane."

The last four lines are thus :—

"When therefore he is dead and gone,
Let this be writ upon his stone :
He never liked the narrow road,
But ran the king's highway to God."

Follows the letter referred to :—

Inverness, July 4th, 1673.

Much honoured friend,—I question not but your cousin, James

Robertson, has informed you with this bearer of the debate which has fallen out betwixt him and me, being occasioned by himself, for I need not tell you for you know what for a man he is. Lauchlan Macbean, my brother, being resting four score pounds, Scots money, payable at Whitsunday last, and the young man not being provided at the peremptor time, and could not keep the day, he has registered his bond, and when the ten days expired, thereafter he yokes two officers to him, and has put him in prison, being upon the headreap of his voyage for Leith, and the bark which he had charge of being laden with malt ready to loose, which I take it to be done through evil will than any mister (?) he had for money. I being loath to let him lie in prison, and being scarce of money at the meantime to relieve him with payment of the sum craved, I did register your bond wherein he is cautioner, and has charged him to make payment within ten days, all being done not through ill will to you or him, but to get my brother relieved. I know he has desired you to get out a suspension for this debt; if you please you need not put yourself to that charges, for I would be commanded by you in any lawful way, and would not be so brusk as to put at him in your absence, unless he deserved himself at my hands. For fear that you would be mistaken in the matter, I have written these lines to let you know the mystery thereof. No further at present, but that I am, sir, your affectionate servant to serve you,

(Initialed) W. McB.

Addressed—"To his much honoured friend, Mr. William Robertson of Inshes. These."

Memorandum on fold of paper—

This letter should be carried by William Kealdach, but missed the occasion, wherefore I was forced to send it by this bearer.

No. LIX. Anno 1674.

MR. J. MACKINTOSH, FROM THE CASTLE OF MOY.

THE annexed straightforward and well-written letter derives much of its interest from having been written within the ancient stronghold of the Mackintoshes, in the island of Loch-Moy. Letters written from castles and houses which have long ceased to exist, or be inhabited, are peculiarly interesting. There are the remains of two castles or fortresses within a short distance of Inverness, with regard to which I have no letter or document. I mean Castle Leathers, and the fortress of Glack, overhanging the burn of Holme. If any one possesses a document referring exclusively to those two places, I shall esteem it a favour their communicating with me. The castle in Loch-Moy was not finally quitted until early in the eighteenth century. The writer of the letter was of the Balnespick family, and it will be gratifying to know that, through the intervention of the Laird of Mackintosh, the writer's request for a tack of part of the lands of "Kinrara of the Woods" was granted.

Follows the letter referred to :—

Isle of Moy, 26th May, 1674.

Honoured and worthy cousin,—I have written oft'times to you, but received no answer as yet, concerning that land which I spoke ong since for, for the Laird did show me that he got a letter from you to be directed for me, but that it went by his hand at Dalcross, so that he could not come by it. But he shows me that what was written in your letter is that you would not give me that land without a cautioner for the duty. Sir, I hope you may be, with the Lord's assistance, deceived of your opinion of me, for it seems to me that you think me the worst debtor in Badenoch, when you would seek from me that which no man in Badenoch has given, neither was it sought by any superior. If that be the way you intend to put me off, I will not longer look after it, and will search for myself, else go. But if you have a mind to deal with me as I expected, and as you ought to do, being a true kinsman, I shall, with the Lord's assistance, prove dutiful and pay you honestly. I do expect your uttermost answer herein within eight days at furthest. I have referred my mind to the Laird, who will show you fully my intention. This being all at present from him who is, sir, your assured cousin to serve you.   (Signed)   J. MACKINTOSH.

Endorsed—" These for my honoured and worthy cousin, Lachlan Mackintosh of Kinrara."

No. LX. ANNO 1675.
SIR GEORGE MACKENZIE OF ROSEHAUGH.

THE annexed letter from the famous lawyer and scholar is not in itself of much interest. It is addressed to the Laird of Inshes, who had studied abroad along with Sir George, and appears to have lent him money. Sir George Mackenzie has been accused of getting obnoxious persons punished, in order to get their escheats, and certainly many grants of exorbitant fines in his favour are to be found. The present Rosehaugh, in the parish of Avoch, has no connection with the Rosehaugh in Rosemarkie, which belonged to Sir George. At his death Sir George left considerable estates, of which little now belongs, it is understood, to his representative, Lord Wharncliffe. Sir George Mackenzie's character is open to hostile criticism in several respects, but his connection with literature, and the foundation of the Advocates' Library, gives him an honourable position in history.

Follows the letter referred to :—

Sir,—I am your debtor, and expected a favourable creditor in you. My being here this last year may in some manner excuse me from ready money, till by another year I recover it at home, and then since I see you so pressing, I shall endeavour to pay you, but this year it is impossible for me, though you may distress me. I am to meet with Orchany, and I shall endeavour to transact, but I cannot promise success. However, it shall be endeavoured seriously by your assured friend to serve you.

(Signed) GEO. MACKENZIE.

London, 14 Oct., 1675.

Addressed—"For my much respected Mr. William Robertson of Inshes. These."

No. LXI. Anno 1676.
ALEXANDER MACKINTOSH OF CONNAGE.

THIS family enjoyed in a marked degree the favour of the Earls of Moray. Alexander, second of the race, the writer of the letter after given, was much mixed up in the affairs of the period, and is accused of not acting fairly by his Chiefs in the troubles and struggles of the latter with the Camerons, in reference to the lands of Glenlui and Loch Arkaig. Alexander had a deputation under the Earl of Moray, Heritable Sheriff of Inverness-shire, and was commonly known as "The Sheriff Bàn." He died much in debt, and after his death his estates were adjudged. The representation of Connage devolved upon Mackintosh of Culclachie, now known as Nairnside. Hugh Mackintosh, who made good his claim to the estate on the death of his distant cousin, Sir Duncan Mackintosh, who held a high appointment in the Canary Islands, and was the last in the direct line of Culclachie, sold the estate to Robert Macbean, a native of Strathdearn, commonly called of Tortola. Mr. Macbean, who married Margaret, daughter of Dalmigavie, was at one time in good circumstances, but the fluctuations and precarious nature of West India commerce were such that, upon his sudden death, Culclachie, re-named by Mr. Macbean "Nairnside," had to be sold early in this century. It was purchased by the late Raigmore, and remains in his family. If there be any male descendants of Connage, they must be in a very humble position.

Mrs. James Dunbar must have been a clever woman, like the first Mrs. Duncan Forbes, able and willing to carry on her husband's extensive business.

Follows the letter referred to:—

Mistress,—My being unwell all this while, has both kept me from home and from looking after my affairs; but now, if the Lord spare health, I shall take care to answer your desire, so far as I

can, with all possible convenience. Though I cannot promise all, yet a part I hope when I come to your town shall be performed, that so I may as I am able answer your husband's expectation of me, who am, your affectionate cousin.
                    (Signed)   ALEX. MACKINTOSH.
27 May, 1676.
Addressed—"For my affectionate cousin, Janet Dunbar, spouse of James Dunbar, Merchant Burgess of Inverness. These."

No. LXII. ANNO 1677.

CULLODEN AND HIS CO-PROPRIETORS OF THE KINGSMILNS.

THE annexed sensible and decided letter from the second Culloden, to his co-owners of the Kingsmilns, is interesting. The mantle of his clever parents fell upon John Forbes, but, whilst they lived and throve by being on friendly terms with the Burgh, he, with the other larger vassals of the town, combined against what they held to be the usurpations of the Burgh, outwith their own charters.

Inverness was for centuries in trouble with its neighbours. About the middle of the sixteenth century, the Council passed an Act against the encroachments of neighbouring clans, and the marriage of widows with property, with any other than resident burgesses. This was to guard against danger from without. About the end of that century, thinking to strengthen its position and at same time to oblige influential burgesses, the Burgh commenced the system of feuing, which was continued with great activity from 1590 until 1650. Within that period, the Coble Fishings, the Kingsmilns, the Forest of Drakies (including the greater part of Inshes and Castlehill), Carnlaw to Culloden, the Glack of Drumdivan to Holme, etc., were all feued out. The terms of these charters are pretty stringent, and were intended to include, for town stents and other burgage taxes, lands extra burghal, but holding of the town. It was ultimately decided that these extra burghal lands were not liable for purely burghal taxes. As, therefore, the feu duties were but trifling, and the only benefit derived, it followed that the feuing tended to the permanent impoverishment of the Burgh.

The Burgh, by this extensive feuing, was hit in another form.

As time rolled on, the reclamation of land was begun, necessarily involving enclosures.

I have copy of a piteous complaint given in about 1726 by a large number of the community to the Magistrates of Inverness, stating that, in consequence of Castlehill having lately enclosed several large parks for the purpose of cultivation, they had been deprived of their old rights of carting of stones for their biggings, and of heather for thatch and use in their malt barns, and praying for demolition of the enclosures. Some further particulars in relation to this curious proceeding may hereafter be given.

Follows the letter referred to :—

Gentlemen,—As I said to you befor (in my oppinion) such ane good offer as this ought not to be slighted, wherfor I intreat you close with the honest man according to your condiscendance, ffor I did see the tack yesterday, and ffor my owne pairt I see nothing to be eiked or paired in it. Iff I had not some friends with me and am obligded this day to wait upon my Lord Murray, I should have been with you, but if you scrouple anything upon the accompt of my absence, to remove any obstacle you may have in that, these shall oblidge me, like as by the tenour heirof I oblidge myself, to subscribe the tack whenever it is presented to that effect, so that I think you do not well to dreich tyme or postpone the business any longer. So to your consideration I remain your loving friend and servant.

(Signed)   Jo. FORBES.

Cullo., 26th January. 1677.

I pray you to excuse my absence, for, if it were possible, I had waited upon you.

Addressed—" These. For Provost Rose, Castlehill, Inshes, Alexander Paterson, or either of them at Inverness."

No. LXIII. ANNO 1678.

KENNETH MOR, THIRD EARL OF SEAFORTH.

FOR several generations the family of Seaforth had their chief abode at Chanonry, not a stone of it however, remaining, though the name of "castle" attaches to certain localities. Kenneth, the third Earl is recorded to have died in the month of December, 1678. The letter after given, dated 14th November of that year, gives no indication of his being at that time ill, or an invalid. It is interesting chiefly as showing that the nobility and gentry of that period were as fond of sport as they now are, though it is known sport was followed in a different fashion from what it is now. Then the big drives, beats, and meets were attended gladly by all and sundry, the results being a large distribution of game among the people, festivity and mirth going on for days, and numerous animals, destructive of domestic fowls, corn, and pasture, destroyed. The writer of the letter was born in 1635, and thus only forty-three at his death, many of his years being spent in confinement, on account of his attachment to Charles the second. His marriage with Isobel, sister of the first Earl of Cromarty, must be deemed a most unhappy one for the house of Seaforth, for it was she, left in charge of the estates during her husband's temporary absence in Paris, who put the Brahan Seer to death, under circumstances well known in the Highlands. These have been carefully put together by Mr. Alexander Mackenzie in his *Prophecies*. She, unhappily, was not the only woman who, in the North, brought ruin on her husband's house and family. Well would it have been for her, had this Countess followed the example of the prior Countess Barbara (her husband's mother), who lived a godly life, and dying at a great age, left some lands in mortification for the poor of Chanonry, which mortification and dole is still in useful and active existence.

Follows the letter referred to :—

Chanonry, 14th November, 1678.

Sir,—I have received your dog, of whom I shall have a care, and shall restore him with thanks when he is called for. I have also sent a second order for the gun to Stranaver, and whenever I have received her she shall be sent to you. This, with my service to your lady, is all from your faithful friend and servant.

(Signed)   SEAFORT.

Addressed—" For Master William Robertson of Inshes. These."

The quaint misapplication of pronouns by the Earl, when describing the dog and gun, is not a little amusing, being exactly what uneducated Highlanders of the present day are accused of.

No. LXIV. ANNO 1679.

THE MARQUIS OF HUNTLY AND THE GOODWIFE OF DOCHGARROCH.

THE ancient family of Maclean of Dochgarroch, friends and adherents of the Clan Chattan, well known as Clan Tearlaich, though they parted with the last of their lands some fifty years since, have preserved many of their titles and papers, selections from which, full of interest and local significance, would fill an ordinary club volume.

The lands of Dochgarroch were part of the Castle lands of Inverness, and paid feu to the family of Huntly. These feus were frequently wadsetted, and amongst other wadsetters of the Castle lands were one Thomas Fraser, generally styled of Haughs, and Katharine Gordon, his spouse, who survived him. I infer that Katharine was connected with Huntly by a bar sinster. For some reason the Marquis wished to withdraw his grant, and wrote Mrs. Agnes Fraser, daughter of Struy, and liferent possessor of Dochgarroch, the following letter, which, with a notorial copy, is extant among the Dochgarroch papers. As is well known, "The Bog" was the old name for Gordon Castle :—

Bouge, 1st March, 1679.

Mistress,—Some years ago I gave orders that you should pay your feu duties to Katherine Gordoune, but since I am informed that she does not make such uses thereof as I expected, I do hereby desyre that you doe soe no more, but that you retain them in your own hands, till you shall see my orders to some person else to require them, and this shall be your warrand from your affectionat friend. (Sic. Sub.) HUNTLY.

This is the just and true double of the above written letter or order, nothing added thereto, nor diminished therefrom, but agreeing word by word with the principal, is attested by us Nottars Public under subscribing at Inverness the 24th day of April, 1679 years.

(Signed) W. CUMING, Notarius Publicus.
(„) D. CUMING, Notarius Publicus.

The goodlady of Dochgarroch must have been well pleased to retain the considerable feu in her own hands, but Katharine Gordon was equal to the occasion. Agnes Fraser or Maclean, who had, prior to the Marquis' letter, been decerned against, pursued a reduction in regard to the feu duties of Dochgarroch, saying the Marquis of Huntly had stopped her from paying the same to Katharine Gordon. Agnes compeared by James Grant (the first Baronet of Dalvey), and Katharine by Rorie Mackenzie, both advocates. The Marquis of Huntly, not appearing, the Lords preferred Katharine Gordon, by decreet, dated 8th January, 1680. It would seem that the Marquis had been "squared," to use a common expression, after the granting of his letter.

In connection with this matter a curious protest, by the energetic Katharine in person, termed on the back, " Protestation and Instrument—Kathrin Gordoun agt. Davoch Garrioch, 1684," has been preserved, and is here given :—

At the Castell Door of Inverness, the 29th day of March, 1684, and of his Majesty's reign the 36th year—That day in presence of me, Notary Public under subscribing and witnesses after mentioned, compeared personally Kathrin Gordon, relict of the deceased Mr. Thomas Fraser of Hauches, liferentrix of the feu farm duties of Davochgarrioch and Davochnalurgin, and passed with me to the said Castle door of Inverness, as being only place appointed for paying and delivering all the said feu farm duties of the said lands yearly betwixt Candlemas and Pasche conform to the Marquis of Huntly his original rights thereof, and the said deceased Mr. Thomas Fraser and Kathrin Gordon, her liferent right following thereupon; and there required of John Maclean, now of Davochgarrioch, the foresaid feu farm duties, being two chalders good and sufficient victual—half bear, half meal—and in respect the said John Maclean of Dochgarroch, nor no other person or persons in his behalf, came not as yet to pay any part of the said victual of the foresaid farm duties of crop 1683 years; Therefore protested that the said John Maclean of Dochgarroch should be liable in payment to her for the highest price for each boll thereof; conform to the Lords of Council and Session their prices and modification of the same, or otherways, according as any other boll of victual, of the quality foresaid, either in Town or Parish of Inverness, should happen to give or pay betwixt the date of these presents and the term of Martinmas next to come; and for all other cost, skaith, expences, and charges to be incurred and sustained by her thereby; and for remeid of law, upon all and sundry the premises, the said Kathrin Gordon, life-rentrix aforesaid, asked and required instruments of me, Notary Public subscribing. These things were done betwixt five and six in the afternoon, day, year, month reign, and place foresaid, in presence of William and David Fraser, shoemaker burgesses of Inverness, and Andrew Mackenzie, shoemaker, there, witnesses called and required to the premises.

    (Signed) H. FRASER, Notarius Publicus.

No. LXV. Anno 1680.

MR. A. ARNELL.

IN another letter, I state that the Laird of Inshes was craved to pay the funeral expenses of his brother-in-law. son of the Honourable Thomas Mackenzie of Pluscardine. The Laird is here asked to pay a bill incurred in France by the same ill-fated impecuniate. He was rather unfortunate in family connections, for, besides these calls by a brother-in-law who had hardly any claim, he appears to have been obliged to support on many occasions his son-in-law, Duncan Robertson, brother of the well-known Alexander Robertson of Strowan.

The letter seems to have been from some one in an humble position, as he gives the address of another, perhaps the writer's master.

The alley which I decipher to be "Steivens" Alley, off King Street, Westminster, of course no longer exists. King Street itself is now not much of a street, though the Blue Boar's Head Inn still remains. In King Street, once the principal street of Westminster, died in poverty the Poet Spenser, 1599, as also Sir Thomas Knevett, who seized Guy Fawkes. For many years Oliver Cromwell had his residence in the same street.

Follows the letter referred to :—

London, 1st June, 1680.

Sir,—I suppose you have received a letter from Mr. Andrew Forster which will give you an account of your good-brothers drawing a bill on him for six pounds sterling, which he owed me in France, for which I had his bond. He wrote to Mr. Forster that you would not fail to pay him upon his account, but Mr Forster will not answer his bill—but, Sir, I believe if you would return the money, and cause take up your brother's bond, he would think himself very much obliged to you, for it is known to most of the officers in the regiment what necessity he was in when I served him with a horse. Sir, I pray let me know by the first post whether or not you will return the money, and you will very much oblige, Sir, your very humble servant.

(Signed) ALEXR. ARNILL.

Direct yours to Captain Colt, in Steivens (?) Alley in King Street, Westminster.

No. LXVI. Anno 1681.

ALEXANDER CHISHOLM, SHERIFF-DEPUTE OF INVERNESS-SHIRE.

THE annexed flowery letter from the acting Sheriff of the County to the Provost of Inverness, is couched in terms which would hardly be used by modern holders of these offices.

Mr. Chisholm long held the office, and from documents extant, must have been generally in straitened circumstances. His expression that the prisoner would not trouble the jail of the burgh long, as it was intended that he be "despatched," is significant. As the paper docquets MacRorie a "notorious thief and murderer," his evil reputation seems to have been universal.

Objection to the admissibility of witnesses were carried of old to an absurd length, greatly defeating the ends of justice. For instance, in the case of the Burgh against Culloden and others in 1673, Alexander Mackintosh of Connage, and Alexander Chisholm, both Sheriff-Deputes of Inverness, were objected to as habile witnesses for Culloden, by the Burgh. "As to Connage, he is brother-in-law to Culloden, having married his sister," and "as to Alexander Chisholm, he is a moveable tenant to Culloden." The Court of Session refused the evidence of both. So bitter were the Burgh authorities in this case, that the simple certificate of a single fact, attested by Borlum and Kyllochie, two of the Justices of the Peace for Inverness-shire, was objected to, because the one Justice had married Culloden's *wife's sister*, and the other Culloden's *sister's daughter!*

Follows the letter referred to :—

Moniack, 25th Nov., 1681.

My Honourable Lord Provost,—I send herewith a famous person, Duncan vic Rorie, famous for his actions, that in my time none exceeded him. Nor can I compare him to any except to him that burnt the Temple of Diana, for with him he had a sympathy. So that I hope you will command that he be watched and kept with care, for he is exceeding shifty. The bearer can give you any further account of him. I shall endeavour he be despatched that he be not long troublesome to your jail, which is all at this distance, only my humble and hearty respects offered to you and the rest of your Magistrates, and please to believe when I say that I am, my very honourable, your most faithful and affectionate friend to serve you.

(Signed) ALEX. CHISHOLM.

Addressed—"For the Honble. Lord Provost of Inverness."

Endorsed—"Alex. Chisholm, Sheriff-Depute, his letter anent Duncan Mac Rorie, a notorious thief and murderer."

No. LXVII. Anno 1682.
CAPTAIN ROSS AND HIS THIEVING RECRUITS.

The letter after given, addressed to the Laird of Inshes, refers to a horse lifting by the recruits of Captain Ross, on their way southwards from Ross-shire. The gallant Captain seems to have considered the stealing but trifling, whereas the beating and wounding by Inshes' people of the thieves was a serious affair.

The name of Blair, from whence the letter emanated, reminds me of the battle of Killiecrankie, and of Lord Dundee, as to whom I have been reading with the greatest interest the recent volume issued by the Scottish History Society called "The Grameid," by James Philip, an actor in the events. It unfortunately ceases in the very early days of July, 1689, although there is hope that the conclusion may yet be discovered. All Lord Dundee's movements during 1689 are graphically given, Badenoch and Lochaber being frequently traversed and what occurred detailed.

People of old, before Wade's time, going south, chiefly passed by Glen Tromie through the Minigaig passes and hills to Athole, but there is abundant evidence in this work, that oftener than once Dundee had gone out of Badenoch into Rannoch, and of consequence by the pass of Drumochter.

The battle of Killiecrankie was fought in the afternoon of Saturday, the 27th July, 1689, and it is not a little singular that perhaps the last paper signed by Dundee was a bond for six hundred and fifty-nine merks, in favour of Duncan Macpherson of Cluny, which, by an assignation of it in my possession, shows that the bond was dated *at Breakachie,* on the 26th of July. Dundee had a considerable force at the battle, and it would be interesting to know whether his whole forces were at Breakackie on the day preceding, and how they marched.

Lord Dundee's alleged letter to James VII., announcing the victory, has been pronounced a fable, he having fallen early. It is clear that Cluny, by accepting Lord Dundee's obligation, did not fulfil what Mackay wrote of him to the Duke of Hamilton, under date, Elgin, 27th June, 1689—"The enclosed I got from Cluny Macpherson, Chief of that Clan, which I send your Grace. I believe that he is not ill inclined, and will come to his duty, though fear made them stand off hitherto."

The Grameid is a magnificent panegyric in Latin on Lord Dundee. The town of Inverness has good reason to honour his name for his intervention in saving it from Keppoch; and in spite of the obloquy cast upon him, Highlanders generally do not and will not forget as worthy of their admiration "Ian-dubh-nan-Cath."

Follows the letter referred to :—

Blair, 13th May, 1682.

Sir,—As I was following my men from Inverness, I had an account from Angus MacAllan of an horse of yours that was taken away, and a discord betwixt some of your men and mine. Sir, I know not whom to blame for the abuses committed on both sides, but I judge that your men were a little too hot for a trifle, that four of them should design to murder ane man, yours being well armed, but him on the other, not armed, and all but of his being one countryman. The man was mightily abused, beat down by stones, and cut most desperately in two or three places, so that I am forced to hire for him all the way. There is nothing of this I impute to be done by your knowledge or direction, and being sensible of your civility and kindness made me return your horse, how soon I did overtake the company. Only I entreat you, sir, if such an occurrence fall due hereafter, ye be pleased to order your tenants and servants not to run in arms against the King's soldiers of design to murder them, so long as they know there is an officer to command them, and especially the soldiers being but raw recruits, who are ignorant of discipline. However, sir, I am very sorry the like should fall out on your lands, and if I were able to serve I would be most willing while I am, sir, your humble servant.

(Signed)   ALEX. ROSS.

No. LXVIII. ANNO 1683.

SIR DAVID FORBES, ADVOCATE.

WHEN one is dealing with the seventeenth and preceding centuries, letters preserved are generally found to relate to business. The gossipping ones only came in about the time of Queen Anne. It is necessary, therefore, to take such as can be found, and, though I give several letters from Sir David Forbes, still his are so precise, particular, and at same time so intelligible, even to ordinary readers, that I have selected them.

There is an amusing reference to one Matthew Murray, who so disturbed Sir David's equanimity that he is set down as being subject to "lunaticisme." Further, and apparently for personally annoying and threatening Sir David, Murray had been put in prison and otherwise censured.

As if he had not been sufficiently careful, Sir David adds a postscript of some length to his previous long letter.

Follows the letter referred to :—

Edinburgh, 27 April, 1683.

Sir,—I received yours of the 16th instant, but admire ye are not more positive with me anent what I wrote to you in my last anent the proving of the tenor of that minute, without which, at the long run, your cause must lose. And, therefore, consider my last letter again, and tell me what length ye can go in order to the proving of each particular article—videlicet, how near your memory can serve you to write a paper of the tenor of the minute, for that is the paper that must be proven to have been the tenor, and ye need not care whether it be long or short if it mention the substantial heads, though it were the better it condescended upon other circumstances. And ye must mind that. it be in form of a minute bearing in the narrative the true date as near as ye can, and the agreement of parties, etc. Next, ye are to ask your witnesses insert of what they remember of the same, and your cautioners, and such as trysted the affair for you, as also the witnesses that saw it cancelled and innovate by the disposition, to see what they know in reference to the said minute, or could depone thereanent, and specially if there be any writ extant that anyways relates thereto. I say that I expect by the first occasion that ye will give me a positive account of all this, that, according to the account ye give me, I may advise you whether ye may do any good in this affair or not. And though the vacation be long, yet ye ought not to lose the benefit of it, nor can I advise you whether to cite witnesses upon the summons or not till first I know what they will be able to say; for, if they could say well, I might get a citation upon the summons itself, against the sixth or eighth of November instanced for taking the depositions to lie *in retentis*. But your method in this must be as I told you in my last, immediately to cause execute against the representatives for the first diet to the first of November. And thereafter return me the summons with an account of what the witnesses can say, and the other particulars above-mentioned, that I may instantly find out Henderson wherever he be, up and down the country, for executing it likewise against him to the first of Novr. too, and immediately thereafter I shall return you the summons duly execute for the 2d diet against the said representatives to the 8th or 10th of Novr., and likewise send you my thoughts according as ye give me information whether it be fit to cite witnesses or not upon the summons, because, regularly, witnesses upon points of probation should be by a diligence after litis-contestation in the cause. I am the more concerned to have your affair go right that this pitifull fellow, Matthew Murray, out of his resentment of the stop that was put to his decreet absolvitor, and the ordinance and appointment for your being heard again, he has become exceedingly insolent, and, I think, must be subject to lunaticisme, for I have been necessitated to get him put in prison and otherwise censured for his misbehaviour towards me anent this affair. Your adjudication against David Fowler is extracted and given in to be allowed. I have spoken to Mr. John Lauder, to whom I gave in your summons and charge against Daviot to be rectified by the writer who did raise it, and this is all at present from, Sir, your assured friend and servant. (Signed) DA. FORBES.

The adducing of witnesses for proving the tenor of your minute will not subsist nor be allowed in this process of reduction against Henderson, but the tenor of the minute must be proven in a separate and distinct action, upon which, if it come to a close before Henderson can get this action of reduction to an end, we may repeat as proven, by producing the decreet of proving the tenor, and if the tenor come not timeously to a close, we may repeat the same if once tabled, and get it brought in by way of reply in our reduction.

Addressed—" For the Laird of Insches, Inverness. These."

No. LXIX. ANNO 1684.

SIR DAVID FORBES, ADVOCATE.

THE annexed letter from Sir David Forbes of Newhall, deals in a very clear manner with the law as regards provisions in marriage contracts. The law has always been positive, but has often given rise to disagreeable questions between very near relatives. When a couple were contracted and the portion to the lady fixed, there could be no doubt that as a rule this portion or tocher was meant by her relatives and understood by her intended, to be in full of the lady's fortune. Unless, however, this was expressly stated in the contract—and half educated practitioners frequently omitted the clause— at the death of the father, the husband and the lady could claim a share of his estates.

This seems to have occurred in the case of Marjory, only sister of William Robertson of Inshes, referred to in Mr. Forbes' letter after given. She married as her first husband, Angus Mackintosh of Daviot, and secondly, Colin Mackenzie of Redcastle.

A striking illustration of the inequality arising from a defect in a marriage contract occurred within this century in the Breadalbane family—one sister only securing a few thousands under a strict marriage contract—the spendthrift husband of another getting enormous sums which might have been as well dropped into the sea.

Follows the letter referred to :—

> Sir,— I have considered your sister's contract of marriage and find the want of the clause of accepting the tocher, and discharging all further pretentions, to be a great omission, which all the arguments you touch will have enough ado to supply. But I shall do the best I can, though I cannot promise you anything positively in respect of the Lords *Nobile officium*, by virtue whereof they find things beyond expectation, etc. In the meantime I shall crave a commission by a bill for examining your witnesses, insert for proving

the tenor of your minute, to lie *in retentis* till the cause come to be advised by the Lords, who called it before themselves to be debated *in presentiae*. I wonder you send not over your charters, and other titles for insisting against Davie (Daviot) as I wrote to you by my last. And this is all at present from your most obliged and humble servant,

(Signed) DA. FORBES.

Ed., 26th February, 1684.

Addressed—"For Mr. William Robertson of Inshes. These."

No. LXX. Anno 1685.
WILLIAM BAILLIE, COMMISSARY OF INVERNESS.

THE name of Baillie was at one time common in the town and parish of Inverness.

Upwards of 300 years ago William Baillie, who succeeded to the estate of Dunain, on the death of his elder brother without issue, was Provost of Inverness. His issue and their descendants took firm hold in the burgh as merchants and professional men. Provost William's eldest son, Alexander Baillie of Dunain, in the year 1620, was obliged to take legal steps to protect himself against the hostility of his brothers David and William.

Alexander narrates, by way of complaint—"That whereas David and William Baillies, burgesses of Inverness, the said complainers unkind and unnatural brethren, having conceived a deadly hatred and malice against him without any just cause of offence, or injury done by him to them, but only because he took a writ from our trusty cousin and counsellor—George, Lord Gordon, of the room called Dochnacraig, whereunto they could nor can pretend no right title nor kindness, they, for that only cause, resolved in the malice and cruelty, of their hearts to have his life, and to slay and murder him. Under trust and friendship, and for this effect, being informed that upon the 10th day of April, 1629 years, John Baillie, his the said

Alexander's servitor, was going out of the Burgh of Inverness to have met with his master, they made choice of that time to put their barbarous and unnatural purpose in execution, and came to the said John, and pretending great shows and tokens of love and friendship to his master, their brother, they desired to accompany the said John that they might meet with his said master, whereupon the said John simply yielded, being noways privy to the treachery of their hearts, and coming on the way, perceiving that the said Alexander had not kept tryst, seeing God who is the protector of innocents, had drawn him another way, they then quarrelled the said John, and with drawn swords invaded and pursued him of his life, struck him through the arm and wounded him in sundry parts of his body, to the great effusion of his blood and peril of his life, and there left him lying upon the ground for dead."

It is to be hoped that even so far back as 1620, it was unusual and uncommon for two burgesses of Inverness to take the road between Inverness and Dochgarroch, armed with swords, with the object of murdering a brother.

Commissary Baillie was a cadet of Dunain, and one of his daughters became second wife of the Laird. He appears to have farmed Torbreck, a part of the Dunain estates, as is seen by the letter after given.

Amongst the ancient names of Torbreck now in desuetude are those of Fingoulan—a sheiling—and Coille-vor-na-Skiach, corrupted as far back, I observe, as 1590 into Killivorskie. In a case of disputed marches 'twixt Bunachton and Wester Gask on the one side, and Culduthel and Torbreck on the other upwards of a century ago, it was stated that Killivorskie was originally a forest, extending from Dalcross to Achnabat, on the ridge betwixt the vallies of the Ness and the Nairn. At a later date a dispute arose 'twixt Culduthel and Torbreck as to their hill marches, which, in consequence of the unscrupulousness of one of the arbiters, resulted in the almost entire loss of the Torbreck grounds. The little remaining of these hill grounds beyond the Aultmore dropped quite recently into the absorbing Culduthel and Wester Leys grasp.

Follows the letter referred to, addressed to James Dunbar, merchant, Inverness :—

I am so busy at my books that I cannot go to town, and so scarce of money that I cannot pay my feu duty. Therefore I pray you give the bearer 8 lb. 8 sh. Scots, and receive a receipt from William Duff, late treasurer and collector of Inverness. I got the last week his demand, so as I am not master of so much money, I hope you will not refuse this request from your loving gossip to serve you.

(Signed) WM. BAILLIE.

Torbreck, 23rd Sep., 1685.

I, William Duff, Treasurer of the Burgh of Inverness, grant me to have received from William Baillie, Commissar of Inverness, the sum of eight pounds eight shillings Scots, as one year feu duty of his fishing coble on the river Ness, from Whitsunday, 1684, to Whitsunday, 1685. Witness my hand at Inverness this, the 22nd day of September, 1685 years.

(Signed) WM. DUFF.

No. LXXI. Anno 1686.

THE MAGISTRATES OF INVERNESS AND THE ARMS ON THE STONE BRIDGE.

THOUGH the Arms of Inverness varied at different periods, I had believed, from the information supplied by the late Mr. James Suter, they were formally matriculated about the year 1681. No record is found in the Lyon Office, nor in the Town Records, but many of the Lyon Office records were destroyed by fire during last century. Such being the position, it is fortunate that some evidence remains of the views of the Burgh Authorities in the years 1685 and 1686, on the point.

There is given the letter of instructions from the Provost and Magistrates, dated 7th October, 1685, to Mr. James Smith, master mason, of Edinburgh, who, with his father, appears to have erected the bridge. The letter is very interesting, but in itself gives no special instructions as to the Town's Arms, although there were such instructions. Mr. Smith, on 28th May, 1686, writing to Inverness, says, "Altho' I have cut the Town Arms likewise according to our communing, yet your line by George Duncan puts me to a stand, for after I had cut our Saviour upon the Cross, supported by a dromedarie on the dexter, and an elephant upon the sinister, with the words above upon a scroll, Fidelitas et Concordia, with the word Inverness and the year of God below, I find by your letter it is your will I should cutt the dromedarie for the Arms supported by two elephants with the words above."

The above intended alteration is not very clear, but it indicates doubt on the part of the authorities as to the correctness of their original instructions. However, Mr. Smith declined to make the new cutting under an additional payment of £5 sterling, and it was not done. The Arms were boxed, and a minute bill of the cost of putting it on board a ship at Leith exists, including 14s. Scots for "aile to ye men." Whether this was too strong for their heads or too weak for their tastes, the boxing and packing was ill done, and when the Arms arrived at Inverness, a protest was taken upon the 17th July, 1686, that "the King's Arms are broken in many parts, and the most fine parts spoiled." A payment to Smith of £30 sterling was made, which presumably included the £10 for Mrs. Smith's gown, a really handsome present in those days.

Follows the letter referred to :—

Mr. James Smith.

Sir,—The under subscribers, as Magistrates of Inverness, do hereby commissionate and employ you to cutt and work four Coats of Arms, to wit, the King's, the Burgh of Inverness, the Laird of Macleod's, and Provost Dunbar's. The King's Coat of Arms to be one fourth part better than the other, the Town's Arms to be one fifth part better than the other two, and Macleod's and Provost Dunbar's to be alike good work, and all of them to be cut on the finest free stones can be had; and the arm stones be well cut. A fifth stone whereon there is to be an inscription, and to be placed above the Town Arms, to bear the year of God when the Bridge was founded, the Magistrates' names then in charge, the year of God when the bridge was finished, and the Magistrates' names then in charge, and your father's and your own names, master of the work, and the foresaid Coats of Arms, and the stone with the inscription to be wrought betwixt this and the first day of April next, and when done to be boxed and carried to Leith and shipped on our charges. For doing whereof we, as Magistrates, oblige us and our successors in office to pay you the sum of four hundred merks Scots money, at the term of Whitsunday next. And also we oblige us and our successors in office to pay you the sum of ten pound sterling money at the foresaid term of Whitsunday, as a token of the Burgh's and our respects to you, for buying ane gown to your wyfe. And it is hereby understood that the boxing and charges of shipping of the foresaid stones is to be on our charges, by and attour the four hundred merks. We entreat that all may be as well done as possible for the money, and fail not to have them ready again the day above mentioned, and we remain your affectionate friend,

(Signed)   JO : CUTHBERT, Provost.
Inverness, 7 October, 1685.

No. LXXII. ANNO 1687.

WILLIAM ROBERTSON OF INSHES AND HIS STOLEN CATTLE.

THE annexed graphic letter from the Laird of Inshes to his cousin Balnespick, in reference to a serious lifting of cattle from the Inshes fields on a Sunday, probably during divine service, has been preserved.

The letter is dated 3rd September, and the theft having taken place on the 25th of August, Inshes seems to have made good use of the interval in acquiring precise information as to the thieves, their route and destination.

The system would never have prevailed so long were it not that it was a formidable weapon used quietly but effectively by landowners owing personal or clan grudges against each other. Were the cattle lifters not protected in this way on their return, the game would not have been worth the candle.

Thus, Sir Ewen Cameron of Lochiel, when a complaint was made by Gordonstoun of a serious theft off his lands, does not condemn the practice—" Moray was fair prey "— but merely expresses his regret that the cattle were taken from a friend, and on that score promises restitution or compensation.

Follows the letter referred to :—

Inshes, 3d September, 1687.

Sir and Loving Cousin,—These are showing you that upon Sabbath was eight days, the 25th of August last, there was stolen out of my field seven head of cattle, of which there was one gotten back that straggled from the thieves, which my men took home, who were in pursuit of them. The other six, I am informed, were carried to Badenoch, to the Davoch of Laggan. There was but three in company, as I am informed, took them away, viz., two men and one boy. The men's names, as I am informed, were Sorle-Dow-vic Fiulay-Vic Allister, in Laggan, John Dow-vic-Sorle-vic-Ian-Mor, the boy's name I got not. These men dined in Altanaslanach on Sabbath day with Mackintosh, his bowman, and the said Sabbath by ten o'clock at night, as I am informed, carried away the said oxen and cows. Their colours and marks are as follows, viz., one dun ox and one dun bull, one black ox, and one brown young ox, with a white ball in his forehead, one gaird or sprainged cow, red and black, and her horns little and cross, and one large black. I entreat you make all the search ye can, to know if they came to Badenoch, and acquaint me thereof, how soon ye can, and send me your advice what to do thereanent, which is all at present from, sir, your affectionate cousin and servant.

. (Signed) W. ROBERTSON.

Let this present my service to your bedfellow and children.

Addressed—" For his much respected and affectionate cousin, Lachlan Mackintosh of Balnespick. These."

No. LXXIII. ANNO 1688.

THE REV. ANGUS MACBEAN OF INVERNESS.

THE name of this worthy and sorely-tried clergyman is held in the North with great respect. He was younger son of the Laird of Kinchyle, an honourable family of good standing, of which was the gallant Gillies Macbean, who distinguished himself at the battle of Culloden.

Mr. Angus Macbean was admitted to Inverness in 1683. It is said he entered with hesitation, being dissatisfied with the then Establishment, and demitted office in 1687.

The letter after given shows the tyrannical and inquisitorial course pursued by the Privy Council of Scotland. The letter is from the Magistrates of Inverness, and as they are reported to have entertained strong prelatical views, perhaps they were not unwilling to inform. It seems curious, however, that they appear to have been set in motion by Duncan Forbes, third of Culloden.

The letter bore fruit. In course of the very month of January in which it was written, Mr. Angus was, according to Shaw, carried a prisoner to Edinburgh, and on 27th February deposed by the Archbishop of St. Andrews. Being committed to prison, bail, though offered to a large amount by Gordonstown and Culloden, was refused. In ill health he languished in prison until December, 1688, when the Revolution opened the doors of his prison. He died within two months thereafter, in the thirty-third year of his age.

Follows the letter referred to :—

Inverness, 10th January, 1688.

Right Worshipful,—In obedience to an Act of His Majesty's Honourable Privy Council, commanding all Magistrates of Burghs to give an account of all Presbyterian meetings and preachings within their jurisdictions once every month to their Lordships or their Clerk, we have written this line to inform you that Mr. Angus Macbean, lately minister of this place, did preach in his own house within this burgh, upon Sunday, being the eighteenth day of December last, and in a meeting-house taken for that purpose, every Sunday since, whereof intimation was made to us by Duncan Forbes of Killoden, by way of instrument; and the said Mr. Angus has continued his preaching in the aforesaid meeting-house, in the forenoon and afternoon every Lord's Day. We add nothing else save that we are, Right Worshipful, your Worship's very humble servants.

No. LXXIV. Anno 1689.

JOHN GRAHAM OF CLAVERHOUSE, VISCOUNT DUNDEE.

THE Laird of Mackintosh, not getting much support from the Crown, but rather the reverse, in his serious questions with the Duke of Gordon, and Keppoch, was not inclined to bestir himself for James the Seventh, when his Crown was endangered in the year 1688. James's most devoted and powerful adherent in Scotland was Lord Dundee, who exerted himself in every way. His death at Killiecrankie was fatal to King James. The annexed appealing letter to Mackintosh has been preserved, but not the one referred to as having been written a few days prior. Mackintosh did not take arms; but the Macphersons seem to have cordially acted with Dundee. During his sojournings in Badenoch, Lord Dundee was on several occasions at Presmuckerach, described by Phillip as a "lowly place," honoured by his hero's visits. Dundee was really the guest of Malcolm Macpherson, then of Breakachie, who is designed as "forester" in Badenoch to the Gordon family. He possessed the farms of Breakachie, Crubinmore, and Presmuckerach at a rent of 370 merks, being allowed to deduct therefrom 40 merks for his "forestrie fee."

Follows the letter referred to :—

Kokstoun, Apl. 24.

Sir,—I wrote to you the day before yesterday, concerning the present state of affairs, yet having the occasion of this bearer, I am so concerned that you make no wrong step to the prejudice of your family, or to your own dishonour, I would not forbear to mind you of the just cause the King has, or the objections you have to him, and the happy occasion you have now by declaring for the King to oblige him and all honest men in such manner. As you will be sure to be established in all your ancient rights, and rewarded according to your deservings, you may assure yourself ever of all the good offices and services lays in the power of, sir, your affectionate cousin and most humble servant,

(Signed)   DUNDIE.

Addressed—" For the Laird of Mackintosh."

It will be noticed Lord Dundee calls Mackintosh his cousin, and truly, the Laird's mother having been Miss Magdalen Graham of Edzell. It is to be feared when Dundee speaks of establishing Mackintosh in his ancient rights, that he promised more than he could fulfil. These ancient rights must have meant the Lochaber estates of Glenlui and Loch Arkaig, but which, being then in possession of Sir Ewen Cameron of Lochiel, a powerful and enthusiastic supporter, could hardly be restored.

As is well known, Mackintosh's only son came out with all his strength in 1715 on behalf of the Stuarts.

No. LXXV.   ANNO 1690.

LIEUTENANT R. INNES AND THE PLUSCARDINES.

THE annexed letter is without date or place, but I make it out as having been written in 1690, and probably from abroad, where the writer would be in active service under Lord Douglas.

James Lord Douglas, Earl of Angus, fell at Steinkirk in 1692 in the flower of his age.

The representation of the Seaforth family, on the death of the last Seaforth, would have devolved upon the heir male of the body of Thomas Mackenzie of Pluscardine, third son of the first Lord Kintail by his second marriage. As it turned out, Mackenzie of Allangrange was able to establish that all the nearest males to Seaforth, before the descendants of his predecessors, Simon, the fourth son of the first Lord of Kintail, had failed.

Thomas Mackenzie of Pluscardine made a considerable

figure in his day, and in the wars of Charles the First and Second.

He had at least two sons, Colin and Thomas. Colin was served heir to his father in the month of May, 1687, and his issue, if any, are extinct. Thomas, the second son, is the person referred to in the annexed letter as having died 16th November. The address of the letter would indicate its having come from abroad, and that the writer and Thomas Mackenzie were brother-officers. On the other hand, the expression used of "sending up money" to defray the deceased's debts would almost infer that the letter was written from England. The writer, when referring to the two northerners who joined him in having the deceased interred, does not refer to them as having army rank.

William Robertson of Inshes married, as his second wife, Sibilla Mackenzie, daughter of Thomas of Pluscardine, and the Robertsons in consequence claimed to be the representatives of Pluscardine, as heirs of line.

Follows the letter referred to:—

Sir,—I have written to your mother-in-law and brother in order to your brother, Thomas Mackenzie his death, which happened upon the sixteen of November, which is extremely here regretted by all that knew him. And by the judgment of all knowing persons that was about him, it was supposed that grief was the occasion of his distemper that resolved in his death. I shall not add many words, but from this let you know that there is a necessity that ye must fall upon speedy course for the sending up money for defraying the debts of the defunct, conform to this list I have sent herein enclosed, for which sum Murdo Mackenzie, George Graham, and myself was forced to engage before his corpse could be interred. I hope ye will tender so much your own credit as not to suffer his name to be questioned for so small a matter, and his friends to suffer for their kindness, but that ye will cause the money contained in this list to be sent up by bill to Mr. Forrester, who will make speedy delivery of it to every person's satisfaction. Their receipts ye shall receive for your further clearing. Hoping ye will show the memory of your dear brother (who had very much confidence in you) that kindness of despatch that the world have no

occasion to complain of your unkindness. This is all at present from, sir, your humble servant.
(Signed) ROBERT INNES.
Leftenan in Lord Douglas Regmentt.

Addressed—" For the Laird of Inchess, in the Sherefdome of Innernes, Mouraye."

Had the list of debts been preserved, it would have made clear what is now obscure.

No. LXXVI.   ANNO 1691.

WILLIAM HAY, LAST BISHOP OF MORAY.

IN the ecclesiastical history of Scotland, the party in power is always to be found persecuting its opponents. The oppression of Episcopalians after the Revolution of 1688 has never been exhaustively and authentically written. Many clergymen no doubt conformed, but the feeling in the dioceses of Moray and Ross was strong against Presbyterianism, so that not until after the death of Queen Anne did it become supreme and exacting. The annexed letter is an interesting contribution to the literature of the period in connection with the hardships and sufferings of non-jurants and outed clergymen. Most of the gentry about Inverness were staunch Churchmen, as were the Municipal authorities.

Bishop Hay, of the family of Dalgetty, was born in 1647. First inducted to Kilconquhar, he was afterwards translated to Perth, having the degree of Doctor conferred upon him by Archbishop Sharp. A Royal warrant for inducting him into the See of Moray passed on 4th February, 1688, so that he enjoyed the See for a very short time. According to Keith, he suffered the common fate of his order, and died at the house of his son-in-law, John Cuthbert of Castlehill, on 17th March, 1707. There used to be at the house of Millburn, a very handsome marble tablet to the memory of the Bishop, by the above mentioned John Cuthbert, doubtless intended to be erected in some church. It may possibly have been in the old High Church of Inverness, replaced in 1770 by the present building.

Mr. Hector Mackenzie, who had been for some time minister of Kingussie, was translated to Inverness in 1688, and conformed. His late superior, however, does not scruple to request his aid in the painful circumstances detailed, which was doubtless freely given.

Follows the letter referred to :—

"Inv., 31 January, 1691.

"Revd. and Much Honoured,—Having received advice from the Archbishops and Bishops who are at Edinburgh of the extreme necessity which hundreds of our clergy (to the great scandal of religion) are now brought to, and that the prospect of it does not affect persons of all ranks who have any sense of religion, or bowels of humanity, that they show great forwardness for the relief of those of such a sacred character, and in so sad a distress, and therefore and for the more effectual and orderly carrying on of that design, those of our Order are advised to write to some ministers and gentlemen of integrity in each Presbytery within our respective dioceses, to collect from persons of quality and others whose hearts God shall open, to bestow such allowances as they think fit, that it may be remitted to Edinburgh, with all convenience, to Doctor Gavin and Doctor John Cockburn, who are condescended upon to be the public receivers of that charity. Gentlemen, the deserved reputation you are all under, and the influence you may have upon others, obliges me to solicit your labour in that affair, and I shall not doubt but you shall condescend to take upon you (as many other worthy gentlemen do) the charitable though troublesome employment of collecting within your parish, and employing your interest with noblemen, gentlemen, and others within that district for obtaining their charity towards the persons and purposes foresaid. And lest a suspicion of an undue and unequal application of that money may discourage gentlemen from contributing so liberally as otherwise they would, you may assure them that all possible care is taken for preventing that inconvenience. For lists are now gathering of all the suffering clergy within the Kingdom, with an account of their merit and sufferings, and there are appointed six or seven churchmen of undoubted reputation, besides some ingenious gentlemen, lawyers, physicians, and burgesses, who are to make impartial distribution at the sight and approbation of the Archbishops and Bishops that may be upon the place. Gentlemen, I am hopeful there needs no apology for giving you this trouble, when you consider the sigular sufferings and sad circumstances of so many worthy and distressed churchmen; and I am pursuaded that your sympathy with them shall not only overcome any disinclination you may have to undergo it, but also shall engage you to great diligence and care about them, which, as it is work worthy of true Christian gentlemen, so it cannot miss to be rewarded by God, thankfully acknowledged by all concerned therein, and shall be received by none more dutifully than by, much honoured and very reverend, your humble servant.

(Signed) WILL. MORAVIEN.

Gentlemen, Master David Polson of Kinmylies having consented to receive what shall be sent to him, and to remit it accordingly, it is desired you may consider that the seasonableness of this good work will add much to the esteem and value of it.

Brother, be careful that an account of the names of those who contribute, with the sum of their contribution, be sent in to Edinburgh, that the Bishops at Edinburgh may know how to adjust accounts with the general receivers.

Addressed—"For Master Hector Mackenzie, minister at Inverness, to be communicated to Duncan, Inshes, Commissary Baillie, and the rest of the gentlemen of that parish."

No. LXXVII. ANNO 1692.

HEW FRASER OF BALNAIN.

THE family of Farraline threw off several off-shoots, one of the principal being Fraser of Erchite. Erchite again sent off Balnain towards the close of the seventeenth century. Alexander of Erchite's second son, by his second wife, was Hugh Fraser, first of Balnain, the writer of the letter after given. He married a daughter of The Chisholm, by whom he left one son, Alexander Fraser, second of Balnain. Alexander was twice married, and had a large family. His first wife was Jane Fraser, daughter of Foyers, by whom he had, with other children, Hugh, who was shot in an encounter with the Customs' officers in a boat in the Moray Firth in 1735, and William Fraser, Writer to the Signet, who acquired the lands of Aldourie and others from the Barbours; and from his eldest daughter are the present

Fraser-Tytlers of Aldourie. By his second wife, Jean, daughter of Angus Mackintosh of Kyllachie, Alexander Fraser of Balnain had, with other children, Thomas Fraser, of Antigua, father of Doctor William, father of Colonel Thomas, father of Captain John, the present Fraser of Balnain.

In the last half of the eighteenth century the law was strongly represented in Stratherrick. Besides Simon Fraser of Farraline, advocate, Sheriff of the County of Inverness, there were practising in Edinburgh William Fraser of Balnain, James Fraser of Gorthlick, and John Fraser, brother to Simon Fraser of Ness Castle. William Fraser was a writer in Inverness, Charles Fraser, Commissary there, and others. Alexander Fraser, of Lincoln's Inn, of the Leadclune family, was also a man of great note in his day, extending for the long period from 1786, when he lived in Staples Inn, to 1830, and later.

Follows the letter referred to :—

Bellnayne, ye 11 Appryle, 1692.

Honored Cozen,—I received yours as your messenger went up the country. I hear they met Donald Raitt at Foyers. However, I have come under bail to answer my Lord Lowat's Court, where you may be assured to have justice of him, or any other you are concerned with in these parts. For Vic Aonas, I can say he is not ane dollar's worth in the world, otherwise I would cause secure it. Wherein I can serve you, you can freely command me as your affectionate cousin and servant,

(Signed) HEW FRASER.

Addressed—"For the much-honored Mr. William Robertson of Inshes. These."

No. LXXVIII. ANNO 1693.
THE LAIRD OF GORDONSTOUN'S STOLEN CATTLE. STRATHSPEY, BADENOCH, AND LOCHABER MEN.

THE annexed letter, from the Clerk of Badenoch to the Laird of Gordonstoun, contains an interesting and full, though confused, account of a theft by Keppoch's men. It would appear that the upper Strathspey watchers pursued the Lochaber men, not for restoration, but to have "their own proportion, which was the oxen."

Colonel Hill, referred to, was governor of Fort-William at the time of the massacre of Glencoe. Mention is made of three Keppoch men as residing on the Dulnan River side, in Badenoch. The locality was Easter Lynvuilg, over which William Mackintosh, the third Borlum, held a wadset. It is described in the letter as a "brae room." It is long since people ceased to dwell on Dulnan side in Badenoch; and of late the uppermost farm of Eile, in Strathspey, has been cleared. The upper Dulnan is very inaccessible, but well worthy of a visit. Behind the Lynvuilgs, Alvie, Kincraig, Dunachton, Raitts, and Ardbrylach, the river flows pleasantly, its green rich banks covered with luxuriant juniper. The mountain of Knock Frangaich is a prominent object. The top of the valley closes abruptly with precipices, reminding one, though on a small scale, of the famous "posts" of Corrarder, in the parish of Laggan.

It will be noticed that the Keppoch men upon Dulnan side above alluded to, are gingerly described as "soldiers for their own benefit"—the cautious scribe not caring to give their real or chief calling.

It is well known that all the cattle stolen from Moray passed to Lochaber by the Dulnan as the quickest route. John Beg Macandrew, the terror of Lochaber thieves, lived at Delnahatnich, on Dulnan. Sir Robert Gordon, to whom the letter is addressed, the third Baronet, was reputed a wizard, and many curious tales are recorded of his eccentricities. Doubtless, as Borlum's daughter, Jean, had married Lewis Gordon, Sir Robert's brother, Borlum would have exerted himself, and procured satisfaction.

Follows the letter referred to:—

Right Honourable,—I received yours, and as for the Strathspey men, it is questionless that Ranald's son-in-law, James Grant, who is Inverlaidnan's second son, and stays still with Ranald, and commands the Watch under him, was the man that ount hunded (?) the Lochaber men, and sent with them to take up the goods; two off the Watch, one Frazer, and ane other called Mack-Gowe vic Loyde, and after their return to Strathspey the Watch took their own proportion, quhich was the oxen. And as I told you before (they) sent them afterwards to Lochaber, when they saw the rest go home, and knew that they could not get them keeped. All this the thieves confessed when I was at Lochaber, and likewise that John Frazer in Tomurke was the man (who) shew them, and let them know your tenants' goods among all the goods that grassed in the hill, and gave them meat and drink to maintain them. Keppoch will be the onlie man (who) will oblige his own men to come and prove this, which I am sure he will be somewhat suire to do, only for fear of Ranald's loss. But a line from the Duke, with a protection to the witnesses, will be the onlie thing will make Keppoch do this, which I am sure your Ho/ may soon get with the first post. I am informed he has the last week settled with Colonel Hill, so that he will be the easier met with at any occasion. I am confident, at least, he will not stand to send his men to prove against Frazer. I am likeways lastly informed there are three of his same countrymen who lives upon the Duke's land under Borlum, in ane brae room upon the water Tullnan, very near marching with Strathspey, who has a hand in the Strathspey Watch, as soldiers for their own benefit. Write to Borlum and let them be called, and I am misinformed if they do not much to the proving of the matter. I have written to Craigmill to send up two or three of the tenants to be at my house again the 8 or 9 of October, to bring home their oxen, for no sooner I would not appoint with them, for we will not get our business done at Lochaber sooner than five or six days' time. As for the tenant your Ho/ writes, you know it was Phineas Nicol, to whom you wrote your letter, that I spoke for. I should be glad he were dwelling there. However, he promises that he will go down along with me to see your Honour once in the next month of October, and then we shall see to it. I have sent you both the Lochaber men and this countryman's names that is to prove the matter in a paper apart, and so I rest, Right Honourable, your verie assured friend and servt. to power,

(Signed) J. GORDON.

Addressed—" For the Laird off Gordonstoun. These."

No. LXXIX. Anno 1694.

THE GOODMAN OF CUTTLEBRAY AND BORLUM CASTLE.

The ancient barony of Cardell, one of the possessions of Randolph, Earl of Moray, included what was afterwards known as the barony of Durris. This barony remained for a considerable period in the possession of a branch of the Dunbar family, in whose time the Castle of Borlum was erected. The barony was acquired early in the seventeenth century by the family of Cawdor, who, very shortly afterwards, feued it out in various portions, retaining the superiorities until the beginning of this century, when they were sold. Shaw describes Borlum as having been in itself a barony, but in the titles, for centuries, it is described as lying within the barony of Durris. William Mackintosh, first of Borlum, feued the lands now commonly called Ness Castle, with the exception of Kinchyle, about the year 1610, and the Castle of Borlum continued to be the chief residence of the family until about 1760. I do not happen to possess a single letter written in the Castle, with the exception of the insignificant one after given, although in possession of many deeds signed within its walls. At the date of the letter, the proprietor was William, the third in descent, father of Brigadier Mackintosh. There is a place called Cuttlebray, in Banffshire, and the writer, whom I term the goodman of Cuttlebray, was probably sent by the Duke of Gordon to transact some business with Borlum, who represented the Duke in and about Inverness. The Castle must have been a place of some strength. Simon Lord Lovat mentions that he had strongly fortified it, and it is referred to by the Rev. Robert Baillie of Inverness, on the 6th April, 1716, thus:—" Wednesday the army marched from Badenoch towards the head of Strathspey, and yester night encamped at Moy, and this night are to encamp at Borlum. . . . I hear that to-morrow or Monday the troops in this town will march to the camp at Borlum." If one going towards Lochend, after passing the fourth mile-stone below Dochgarroch, looks across the river, he will see a few very old trees here and there, denoting the park as it existed in the time of the Borlums, and there is a tradition that these, and one ancient sycamore at the present garden, were planted by the Brigadier, who is known to have been a great improver. After the sale of Borlum about 1760, Mr. S. Fraser, the purchaser, changed the name to Ness Castle, then heard of for the first time. A farm house was erected near the Castle which henceforth came to be named Ness Castle Mains, while Mr. Fraser himself, when occasionaly living in the North, erected for himself a house near the river, and laid out a handsome garden, which still remains. This house was called Ness Cottage, and, being accidently burnt about fifty years ago, in the time of Marjory, Lady Saltoun, she, instead of re-building, bought from Torbreck's creditors the place formerly called The Darroch, and transferred to it the name of Ness Castle, which it now bears, and is the property of Mr. F. Walker.

After the erection of the new farm-house the old Castle fell into decay. It was partly used by servants of the tacksman, and partly as a barn, and in the year 1780, some of the straw having been set on fire, the Castle was set in flames, and became a complete ruin. The last person born within it was John Macdonald, commonly called "Ian Bàn Lochunagan," father of the brothers Macdonald, one of whom is now light-house keeper at Bona, and two others live at Bona Ferry. John Macdonald, when the place took fire, was carried out in a blanket, being but a few weeks old.

The walls and remains began to be removed by those who wanted stones, which caused Mr. John Fraser, the new proprietor's brother, on the 18th July, 1785, to issue these instructions—"I have written the Captain (Capt.

Thos. Fraser of Leadclune, then tenant of Ness Castle Mains) that he is not to meddle with or carry off the lime or rubbish of any of the old Castle—old or new." Not a stone of the Castle now remains, but a careful observer will recognise the spot, now under cultivation, from the quantity of burnt white lime in the soil. Many respectable tenants occupied the Mains of Ness Castle, and when it fell into the late Mr. Alexander Mactavish's occupancy, he called it Ness Park. Under the Baillies, to whom Borlum now belongs, the original has been revived.

Follows the letter referred to :—

Borlume, 31 Dec., '94.

Much hond. sir,—Tho' I presume too far on the first introduction of our acquaintance to burden you with letters from my Lord Huntly, yet I am in hopes you will pardon such freedom, and retaliate with me when occasion offers that I can serve you, and if this book packet cannot go conveniently to your company, to send it back with the bearer. In case you have carriage, be pleased to deliver it to George Duffus, tewdor to my lord Duke of Gordon. Either of the ways you will oblige, your very humble servant,

(Signed) CUTTLEBRAY.

Addressed—" For Baiylie Dunbar, at Inverness."

No. LXXX. Anno 1695.

PROFESSOR HUTCHESON OF EDINBURGH.

In No. LXXXI. I give a translation of a letter in Latin addressed by a Collegian in Edinburgh to his father, wanting supplies.

I here give a letter from the youth's professor, in reply to one from the father, which is not without interest.

The father appears to have complained of the extravagance of his son in clothes, and the reply was that burghers' sons in Edinburgh, who were students, "go very neat in their apparel." Other complaints were made by the father, and the curious answer was made, that "the *origo mali* flows from his want of the Latin tongue."

I have always understood that considerable prominence was given to the study of Latin in former times in Scotland, but have seldom seen it in so exaggerated a form as here, where want of it is gravely put forward as accounting for any folly or extravagance in which a youthful Collegian might indulge.

Follows the letter referred to :—

Sir,—I received yours dated the last of October, and I am very sorry for the bad character some have branded your son with : for my part I confess I am absolutely a stranger to his conversation before he came to my house, and since I find "nothing in him blameworthy." I look upon him as the soberest of all the students at this college. What might be his miscarriage in buying of more clothes than was necessary I think may be rationally concluded an innocent question with his condisciples, especially considering the burghers sons go very neat here in their apparel who are students. If I find his good nature abused by any extravagance, I give you assurance I shall neither conceal it from him nor you. But I hope better things of him; he is painful enough, but I find the *origi mali* flows from his want of the Latin tongue, which, although he is beginning to advance in it, yet hath much hindered his progress in philosophy. Sir, his first entry with me was the 1st of October, and so the quarter is past, and by the date of this you will see it is thirteen days more. The custom is, you know, to pay per advance; things here are dear, and the times have been sufficiently troublesome to me; for Castlehill, he is not yet here nor any word from him. The rest of your commands as to Mr. Kennedy, or to assist your son in any thing wherein I can be helpful to him, shall be obeyed by your obedient friend and servant,

        (Signed) W. J. HUTCHESON.

Edin., 13th January, 1695.

No. LXXXI. Anno 1696.
A COLLEGIAN TO HIS FATHER FOR SUPPLIES.

THE annexed letter, couched in fair Latin, it is to be hoped, produced the needful supply. The same story ever holds—the impecuniousness of youth at Universities

The writer of the letter did not turn out very well, hence his name is suppressed, but the letter itself shows a good spirit, and an affectionate disposition.

Most of the youths from the Highlands attended the Universities at Aberdeen, a few going to St. Andrews, and some to Edinburgh. Those from the West Mainland and Islands of Argyleshire, attended at Glasgow.

The law of Scotland being much founded on the civil law, it followed that Latin was the prime and favourite language taught at Scottish Universities and other schools in Scotland for centuries.

Follows the letter referred to, translated almost literally :—

Edinburgh, January 9th, 1696.

Most Loving Father,—I received thy letters dated the 18th of November, by which thou promised to send both money and letters by the Laird of Castlehill, whom I have not seen, and of whom I have heard nothing up to this time, which has so grievously troubled me that forthwith amazement and trembling seized upon me by the consideration that (which God forbid) thou hast utterly consigned me to oblivion. I have as yet given very little money, nor have I to give, to my most careful host and my Regent. So greatly am I straitened that I know not whither to turn me. I beseech thee most loving father to be mindful of me, and as soon as possible relieve me from the miseries by which I am oppressed, by sending me as much money as is needful for my necessities. And I faithfully promise that I shall never, by my prodigality, abuse thy munificence. But I humbly beg that thou mayest exceed the ordinary limit for this occasion, less I become beggared by debt. The very best of health I wish to thee, and also to my dearest mother, and to my brothers, sisters, and all my cousins.—I am, thy most devoted servant and most submissive son.

(Signed)   R. J.

No. LXXXII. Anno 1697.

LORD SALTOUN, AND BRODIE, ANENT THE DOWAGER LADY LOVAT.

The plot, by the family of Athole, to ruin the male branches of the House of Lovat, through the instrumentality of the Frasers of Saltoun, is well known. The circumstances occurred in the year 1697. In Lord Lovat's own memoirs the transaction is thus referred to:—"While this was transacting, the Master of Lovat, little suspecting the machinations which the Lords Athole and Tullibardine were preparing against him, was employed in disposing of his noble prisoners. For some time he detained them in custody, and threatened to hang them for having intruded into his inheritance and sought to deprive him of his lawful and hereditary rights. At length, however, by the intercession of certain barons of the low country, who came to solicit the liberty of Lord Saltoun, Lord Mungo Murray, and their attendants, he dismissed them." The letter after quoted is not quite consistent with Lord Lovat's account, for it would appear Lord Saltoun was first liber-. ated, while Lord Mungo Murray was detained at Castle Downie.

The Saltouns got such a fright that they withdrew from the engagements for an alliance with the heiress of Lovat. She was afterwards married to Mackenzie, younger of Prestonhall.

It may be mentioned that when the Dowager Lady Lovat was allowed to go south and join her relatives in Perthshire, she stayed the first night of her journey, and the best part of a day, at the house of Inshes. William Robertson, the then laird, greatly exerted himself on the lady's behalf.

Follows the letter referred to:—

Gentlemen,—The circumstances which my Lady Dowager of Lovat and her brother, Lord Mungo Murray, are in at Castle Downie, occasions us to intreat you will be pleased to go there and do what lies in your power for their liberation, and for this end we entreat you do what you can to convince Captain Fraser that his setting them instantly at liberty is the best way for him to take for preventing further hazard and the public taking notice of it. We are, gentlemen, your humble servants,

(Signed) SALTOUNE.
(„) J. BRODIE.

Inverness, 15th October, 1697.

Addressed—" For the Laird of Inshes and Dr. Mackenzie."

No. LXXXIII. Anno 1698.

JOHN ROBERTSON OF LUDE.

THE great possessions in Perthshire of the Clan Robertson have been much curtailed. The once important family of Lude has ceased to appear on the roll of landowners. The annexed letter from the laird in 1698 speaks for itself, and is kindly, sensible, and friendly.

Mr. Duncan Robertson, younger son of Struan, wished to marry his namesake, the Laird of Inshes' daughter, and prevailed on some friends to accompany him to Inshes, to settle matters, and become his cautioners.

All went on agreeably, and Mr. Duncan departed with his friends and engaged man.

When the draft contract afterwards came to be adjusted, the friends drew back, much to the young gentleman's discomposure. He wisely applied himself to Lude, and got him to write Inshes the letter referred to.

The marriage did take place, and the parties lived as happily as broken fortunes, on the part of Mr. D. Robertson, permitted. His letters to his father-in-law and other connections are well couched, and whether from France, where he was attached to the exiled Court for some time, or from London, where he appears to have been at a low ebb, his letters are those of a gentleman.

Follows the letter referred to :—

Lude, March 21st, 1698.

Sir,—I received yours the 17th of this instant, and went alongst with Mr. Duncan, Struan's son, to Logieraitt, and brought my brother, Mr. Patrick, also there, where we trysted with the gentlemen that are mentioned as cautioners in the draught of the contract. I know not what conditions and promises passed betwixt you and the said gentlemen when they were with you at Inverness, but upon Saturday last, when the paper was presented and read to them, they denied to subscribe the same, for which the young gentleman is very much concerned. I am very sorry to see him so much vexed, but in the meantime it lies in your own hand to help that for the young gentleman is very ingenuous, and will give you his own security any way ye please to frame it, which security is beyond all exception. I do not doubt but my Lady Struan will warrant you in corroboration of any security he can give. Sir, I hope you will mind your promise to me when I was kindly entertained at your house, which was, that you would take your hazard of the young gentleman's own security as the Laird of Struan's son, and you told me also that if he were Laird of Struan, you would bestow ten thousand merks upon him. But I find the young gentleman will take conform to your last condescendence, he is so forward in the business. Seeing that I have the good fortune of your discreet lady her acquaintance, and your own likewise, I presume therefore to give both of you my humble advice, which is as above written, viz.—To take Mr. Duncan's own security, for if it were my own case, I would do it myself, considering the prospects he hath. I do not enlarge farther, save only my humble service to your discreet Lady, and to all your family, and that I am, sir, your affectionate cousin, and most humble servant.

(Signed) Jo. ROBERTSON.

Addressed—"To the Laird of Inshes att Inverness."

No. LXXXIV. Anno 1699.

SIR DAVID FORBES, ADVOCATE.

JOHN FORBES, second of Culloden, by his wife, Anna Dunbar of Grange, had five sons, whereof the second, David, became an advocate. According to the late Mr. Duff of Muirtown, in his account of the genealogy of Forbes, Sir David Forbes of Newhall, Mid-Lothian, was a very eminent lawyer and man of letters, and ancestor of the family of Rae of Eskgrove; Sir William Rae, Lord Advocate, being descended from a daughter of Sir David Forbes. The men of letters in Edinburgh long found Sir David's seat a very agreeable retirement; here his nephew, Duncan Forbes, afterwards Lord President, passed much of his early life, amidst scenes devoted to learning and the muses.

Mr. Duff's book was published at Inverness, at the *Journal* Office, in 1819; and it is rather singular that, though seventy years has elapsed, one of the subscribers still flourishes in Inverness, viz,, "Evan Baillie Fraser, Esq., younger of Inchcoulter."

In the letter, after quoted, to the Laird of Dunain, Sir David calls him his cousin, in respect that Elizabeth, aunt of Sir David, had married William Baillie of Dunain.

The proprietors of Dunain were much oppressed and harried by the Grants, Macdonalds, Camerons, and other Western clans, as the old high road from Inverness to the West ran through the hill lands of Dunain, Dochgarroch, and Dochnacraig. The letter after quoted refers to a serious claim, made good by the Laird of Dunain against Grant of Conachan, tutor for Glenmoriston.

Follows the letter referred to :—

Edinburgh, 5th Dec., 1699.

Loving cousin,—I received yours of 21st November last, with a decreet before the Commissioners of Justiciary, at the instance of Charles Baillie, your cedent, against Glenmoriston, for £4800, as the price of cattle plundered by his men from your father. And your question seems to be if your being creditor to Glenmoriston by the said decreet at the date thereof, viz., the 7th April, 1699, may not thereby have such a ground of compensation against Glenmoriston as to extinguish anything you're owing him; so as upon the 20th May, 1699, when his creditors arrested in your hand, ye owed him nothing, and might be free so to depone in the furthcoming. And you insinuate something about my having written to you formerly about this matter; but you have not sent me up a double of my letter, nor any particular account of the matter, so that I am left to my divination for finding out what I might have written to you. However, in the first place, your decreet ought to have mentioned the names of the Commissioners who made up the quorum at that time. 2ndly. Your decreet ought to have carried the depositions of the witnesses in the becaus (?) thereof; at least you should have sent me the double of those depositions that I might have considered how the *corpus delicti*, or depredations by these Glenmoriston men, was proven, as well as how the penalties and prices were liquidate. If your probation as to these points be full, your decreet seems to be a good ground of compensation, whereon you may be assoilzied in the furthcoming. But you must mention your ground of compensation, by way of quality, on your oath, and therewith produce your decreet. I shall enquire unto anything more against you in the Session, and am, your affectionate cousin and humble servant,

(Signed) DA. FORBES.

Addressed—"To William Baillie of Duncan. These."

No. LXXXV. ANNO 1700.

LADY MACDONELL AND AROS.

ANGUS MACDONELL of Glengarry, a great Royalist, was raised to the Peerage by Charles II., in 1660, by the title of Lord Macdonell and Aros. This ambitious man strove hard to get himself acknowledged as Chief of all the Macdonalds—a position not at all likely to be accorded him by the Macdonalds of Sleat and Clanranald, of at least equal standing with himself. He and his clan entertained a great antipathy to the Town of Inverness, and were the cause of much trouble and expense to the Corporation. One of his demands was that the town should renounce all claim to the superiority of Drakies, of which he was proprietor. We have seen several deeds to which Lord Macdonell was a party, and they are signed at Kingsmilns. From the letter after quoted, written by his widow, and dated at Inverness, it would seem that the widow's connection with the town and its neighbourhood lasted long after his death, in 1682.

The writer was Margaret, daughter of Sir Donald Macdonald, first baronet of Sleat, who survived her husband many years. They had no issue, but the widow must have had some lands or jointure off the Glengarry estate. The money did not appear to be punctually paid, and the lady being pressed by a creditor, is most anxious that her honour and good name should be kept clear.

Follows the letter, the old spelling not being observed :—

Hond. Sir,—You have had an ill opinion of my conscience when you thought I would not give annual rent out of any man's money that I would get in time of need. I know very well that little thing you had of mine had been but useless for you, and that it was out of respect to me, you was pleased to give your money, so that I am willing to give you presently my ticket, carrying annual rent. And since I am in extreme necessity for the present, I hope you will do me the favour to send me a little, which you will have, how soon I have got any from the Highlands, which I expect to be shortly; for I will assure you if I had not been disappointed by others, I would have paid your money with annual rent long ere now. Expecting this little favour from you, I remain, your very loving friend.

(Signed) M. MACDONELL.

Inverness, the 26th of January, 1700.

Addressed—"To The Much Honoured Hugh Robertson, late Provost of Inverness."

No. LXXXVI. Anno 1701.

THE EARL OF PORTMORE.

IN a former letter (No. LXXXIII.) I referred to Mr. Duncan Robertson, younger son of Strowan, who married the Laird of Inshes' daughter. The marriage was apparently a happy one, but the young couple were always in pecuniary straits. Duncan being sent to Paris, complains that he has not a day's health since he arrived, that he has spent most of his money, and earnestly begs that Inshes will send money to take him to London, and he asks that his letters be sent to the care "of Mr. John Shaw, of the White Lion Tavern in the Strand, second door to the Exeter Exchange."

I have no information as to the result of the expedition referred to in the annexed letter.

The first of the Colyear family enobled, was the writer, who was created Lord in 1699, and Earl of Portmore in 1703. The title is extinct.

Follows the letter referred to :—

London, ye 30th of March, 1701.

Sir,—Being a wellwisher and servant of the family of Strowan, my inclinations naturally lead me to show any kindness I am capable of, to your son-in-law Mr. Duncan Robertson. Being a younger brother without any employment, his intentions are to try his fortune in an expedition I am to be engaged in with the Duke of Ormond. I hope you will approve of it, and help to set him out as a gentleman, and as I make no doubt, but there will be occasions happen, I shall lose none in which I can serve him, or give you any demonstration of my being, sir, your most humble servant.

(Signed) PORTMORE.

No. LXXXVII. ANNO 1702.

THE LAIRD OF LETHEN.

DISPUTES regarding marches have been for upwards of two hundred years a source of trouble and expense, particularly to Highland landlords. I know of one family whose first march dispute extant goes back to 1584. The annexed letter, from the Laird of Lethen to the Laird of Calder, the two chief proprietors in Nairnshire, relates to their hill marches. The letter is a very courteous and proper letter in the circumstances. Yet the writer abates nothing when he asks that the corn be divided.

When the Cawdor family acquired a hold in Wales and sold Muckcairn, it was under contemplation to sell the northern estates as well, which were at the time almost eaten up by wadsets. This excited not only remonstrance but consternation, and the "Hawthorn Tree" being invoked by the relatives in the North, the design was abandoned.

Follows the letter referred to :—

Very Honourable,—I have met with many clamours and complaints from my tenants concerned, and next adjacent to some of your Brae lands—to witt, Capernoch, Flinismor, Auchnatine, and Both—complaining that some of your tenants there, particularly one Leitch, alias McClerk, in Boath, who has taken in my tenants cattle and put them in folds, and taken poinds from them feeding upon the commontie betwixt your tenants and mine, which they have been perpetually in use and wont to do, both yours and mine upon the commontie. And besides this, several of your tenants have riven in and made burntland upon the commontie, and has their cornes growing on it, which belongs to you and me equally. Sir, you know this unequal dealing by your tenants in appropriating the commontie to themselves, to which I have just and equal right for my tenants there, is intolerable. I went up this day to see whether it was so bad ; finding it true, as I have narrated, I thought I was concerned to take instrument, and from the honour and respect I bear to you, wherein I shall never willingly be wanting, in the first place to have recourse to you to acquaint you thereanent, nor questioning but what is done is without your warrant. Therefore, sir, if you do see it fit to give your commands that no such encroachment be made in time coming, and that the corns growing upon the commontie may be by sight of indifferent persons divided, it will put an end to any further debate thereanent. And if not, I hope you will pardon me as concerned for the time without giving you offence, to do what is incumbent for me. I entreat for your answer hereanent, and when I may be of use to do you service, you may always assuredly command.—Very Honourable, your truly affectionate, most humble servant,

(Signed) D. BRODIE.

Lethan, 22nd July, 1702.

Addressed (seal entire)—" For the Very Honble. The Laird of Calder. These."

No. LXXXVIII. ANNO 1703.

AN INDIGNANT FATHER TO HIS SON.

As the family referred to in the annexed letter exists, it is not thought advisable to give names.

The case in question was not of an ordinary character. The eldest son of an embarrassed family made a good marriage as regards blood, coupled with fair fortune. Naturally, the lady's friends were somewhat exacting as to settlements, and the nature of securities to be granted. The son and his brother seem to have been pushing the father rather severely to do more than he either felt inclined, or, indeed, was able to do. Matters, however, ultimately turned out better than might have been expected. This eldest son died young, without doing very much harm, and his wife, as mother of the next succeeding heir, a spendthrift, did much to keep the family together.

She was in part rewarded by living to see her grandson act a prudent and wise course, doing all he could, and with success, to re-establish the family.

Follows the letter referred to :—

Edr., 24th Oct., 1703.

Loving Son,—I was no more out of humour yester night than I am now after my prayers, but your stubborness, cold heartedness, and what I am ashamed to name towards the ruin of the family wherein you had your breath and education, put me both in grief and consternation. What method you propose in your letter is a cure worse than the disease. As for you going abroad, it is not the first time I could heartily wish you had God's blessing and your father's alongst with you. To give you any title of what you pretend to, to your wife, or any one else, is but a shifting of the question, and however it may take with me, as you may be sure it cannot take well, yet I am afraid it may be bitterness in the end to both. I offered all that was in my power, and much more than ever I thought both you or your brother should demand, but I hope was justified in that before God and man, which is the faith and true sentiment of your heart-broken father.

(Signed)   R. W.

No. LXXXIX. ANNO 1704.

KENNETH MOR MACKENZIE, FIRST OF DUNDONELL.

By the close of the seventeenth century, the cadets of Seaforth had spread all over Ross. The letter after given was written by the first Dundonell, to his nephew Allangrange. The original name was Achadonell, and the family lived in comfort on their estate, of great extent but of little rental, till the beginning of this century. The present family of Dundonell is the Ardross branch. Allangrange, to whom the letter was addressed, was an author and man of note in his day, and had acquired the Barony of Allan through his marriage. There are some magnificent trees near the old house of Allangrange, part of which is over two hundred years old, by the date above the door. I have several of Allangrange's letters, one of which may be hereafter given. In one without date, addressed to his brother-in-law, the laird of Kincraig, he says, "My uncle Dundonell and his sister, the Mistress of Fairburn, is here. I have some diverting prints sent me, if Coul has not already given them to you." He was a keen politician, and under date 16th December, 1709, writes in a postscript to his uncle Dundonell, "For news, Tarbat is Secretary, Ogilvie, Chancellor, and Preston Hall expects to be Treasurer-Depute and so forth. We are big here too with expectations of the Sheriffship. My Isabel has her love to you and to Sibilla and the bairns, and we expect you here to your goose at Christmas. The English hath got a very great victory over the French and Spaniards, with a great deal of plate and money. The Union between this kingdom and England is going on very well I hear."

Follows the letter referred to :—

Loving Nephew,—I received a line from Thomas Mackenzie, who served Seaforth once, showing me that he had my lady's order to receive the feu duty of Achaydonill, and that he had her discharge thereof to be given me when I paid the money. I believe you have the disposition, and if you have it, would be much pleased that ye might pay the amount at this time, for I have been six weeks from home, and now our harvest is on hand, and like ill being from home. If Thomas would leave the discharge with some trusty friend to Hallowmas, I would see it paid then, or if you could get as much money as would pay the feu duty to him at this term, I would thankfully pay it again. If ye can get me kept at home at this time, and pay the feu duty, it would singularly oblige me. If it cannot be done without my going, acquaint me by the bearer, and I shall wait of Thomas Mackenzie as I promised in my letter to him. This all at present. I rest yours to serve you.

(Signed) K. McKenzie.

Achaydonill, the 28 of August, 1704.

Addressed—"For Mr. Simon Mackenzie of Allangrange. These."

No. XC. ANNO 1705.
PRINCIPAL WILLIAM CARSTARES.

THE writer of the annexed letter was a man of great note in his day. After many sufferings, he acquired such power and influence in Scotland under William the III. and Queen Anne as to be styled "Cardinal" Carstares. He was principal of the Edinburgh University, Moderator of the Assembly, and Chaplain for Scotland, with the revenue of a Bishoprick. He died on 28th December, 1715, leaving many papers, valuable and very interesting. The letter is addressed to Sir Hugh Campbell of Calder, who busied himself in his old age with the composition of papers on religious subjects. His works and those of his son, Sir Archibald, were, "Collection of Letters, etc., and Essay on the Lord's Prayer, 1704" (the work referred to in the letter), and " Middle State, Edinburgh, 1721." But they are now almost entirely unknown, like the singular and rare compositions of Mr. Rose, of Nairn, and Mackenzie of Allangrange. Sir Hugh was very troublesome to the clergy, keeping up constantly a correspondence, which, from the answers of several, were not altogether appreciated.

Follows the letter referred to :—

Edr., May 11th, 1705.

Honourable Sir,—Nothing but a crowd of business would have caused me to make so late an acknowledgment of the honour you were pleased to do me in presenting me with your treatise. I shall not, sir, presume to trouble you with my thoughts of the design and scope of it. The things in which we agree as to the chief subject of it, do, in my humble opinion, bring what we differ on within so small a compass, as I persuade myself, sir, that you do not think that either of us should cool our love to one another, or hinder our communion in divine worship. We all heartily acknowledge that it is an excellent and incomparable pattern, and we bless our Redeemer, the great Apostle and High Priest of our Profession, that He hath left it upon record in His Scriptures for our instruction and conduct in the great duty of prayer, and we hope we desire and endeavour to improve it for these ends, and we have not the least doubt that it may be lawfully used in the very terms in which it is expressed. But I think it is also my duty, Honourable Sir, to let you know that I received two letters from you directed to the Moderator of the late Assembly; the first had your treatise enclosed, and I did in what you recommended in that matter all that in my circumstances I did judge was proper for me to do. And I doubt not, sir, that you have heard that this last Assembly hath recommended to all the ministers of this Church to have a particular regard to the Directionist for worship in all their holy administrations, that we are obliged by a Divine command in all public prayers to use the very words and syllables of that holy pattern, and that successively, too, without the intervening even of such paraphrases upon the several parts of it as, sir, you yourself give in your Book, is that which, I must confess, I have not yet seen a cojent reason to persuade my belief of it, and this is all, sir, that I shall take the liberty either now or hereafter to trouble you with upon this head. The other letter about the Paroch of Ardersier, was read in the Assembly, and was referred to the Commission, where, sir, you shall have all the assistance in what you desire, and what is in the power of, Honourable Sir, your most faithful and most humble servant.

(Signed) W. CARSTARES.

No. XCI. ANNO 1706.

AN INVERNESS WATCHMAKER.

THE following letter, from an Inverness watchmaker, in the beginning of last century is amusing. Twenty years before, there would appear to have been no watchmaker in Inverness, seeing that the authorities had to negotiate with one Kennedy, then in Aberdeen, to regulate the town clock. The name of the writer of this letter would point to his being a native of the East country, and he was evidently a man of some reading. So far as I have observed, the Inverness watchmakers were generally of foreign extraction, with one noted exception, however, in the person of John Macdonald, who flourished 100 years ago, and had a great reputation all over the North.

Clocks and watches are objects of great interest to the

young, and no more welcome visitor entered the house of Dochnalurg than old Watters, a native, I believe, of Caithness, when on his semi-annual rounds. Watters' business was, I think, taken up by Maclennan, who must have been well known to many readers. The letter is addressed to Dr Forbes, younger son of the third Culloden, and brother to the Lord President. Follows the letter referred to :—

Inverness, 12th July, 1706.

Much honoured,—This day I have your discreet letter, with the inclosed, on receipt of your watch, which, I am hopeful, will please you; and as for the shaking of the crystal, I am getting home some from Edinburgh within eight or ten days at furthest, and I shall change it then, when you please, to your satisfaction. The contrivance for making her go fast and slow is only a nice concept, which few workmen can discover (without taking down the watch), but I assure you does no prejudice to the axle of the barrel; and as for your thinking her plainer than ordinary, particularly than Mr. Bailie's, there is a very good reason for the plainness you mean. You fancied she wants some curiosities or cut work there (which other watches has), but its as true that the silver plate with its figure that makes her go fast, etc., lies beside the cock, and has some cut work about it in other watches, but your watch has that upon her dial plate; and so cannot have it on both sides. I have, on observation of famous Tompious' watches, that they are the plainest ever I did see, and I have, and others, observed of many watches, that where there is most carvings and cuttings, there is little good action where it is most essential. The chief properties of a watch (after being rightly calculated), is to have a well-cut tooth and pinions, and small pivots of strong pillars, and if your watch have not all these, I am much mistaken. I designed when I got her to try her eight days, but considering she went so well the night I had her, and that you wanted her too long, I ventured to send her. I am very certain she has a good and regular pulse, and if she go a little fast or slow, you can cure it yourself, as I taught you in my last.

This, with my respects, besides saluting you, and returning you the beggar's benison, with all the comforts of this life is all from, Sir, your most humble and most affectionate servant,

(Signed) THO. KILGOURIE.

Addressed—" For the Much Honoured Doctor Forbes, at his Lodgings in Elgin."

No. XCII. Anno 1707.

SIR DONALD GORME OF SLEAT.

WITH Sir Donald Gorme, fourth baronet of Sleat, who succeeded in 1695, and died in 1718, the race of warriors truly so termed, of the Sleat family, may be said to have terminated. The annexed letter from Duntulm is interesting, Sir Donald being the last occupant of the castle. This grand old ruin we had the pleasure of inspecting quite recently, and the place where captives were summarily sent through, falling hundreds of feet into the sea, is still complete. We were told that a child of the family, and nurse, accidentally fell through, and this caused the castle to be abandoned early in the last century. It is to be regretted that so many of the stones have been taken to form dykes round the adjoining lands. The letter is addressed by Sir Donald to the Laird of Mackintosh, and written with his own hand. Keppoch had been so obstinate in refusing all compromise with Mackintosh, that the latter had to invoke the full strength of the law, and it would have fared hard with the former unless he had obtained the influence of Sir Donald, who, coming to the assistance of Keppoch, effected a settlement about the year 1700, and agreed to become his cautioner in a new tack. Coll of Keppoch, however, never had any money, or he was indisposed to pay Mackintosh, so, seven years after, the latter was obliged to complain to the cautioner.

Carefully tied up with this letter is a singular bond of caution by Sir Donald Gorme, dated at Duntulm, 3rd August, 1700, and witnessed by Lieutenant Charles Mackinnon, late of Colonel Mackgill's regiment, and James Macdonald of Oronsay. The principals are John Macdonald of Castletown, yr., and Mr. Eneas Macqueen, late minister of Sleat, now in Knock, who were accused of harbouring, and refusing to give up to justice, Angus

Macdonald, brother german to Keppoch, and Angus Macglasserich, accused of mortally wounding Rory Mackinnon in Sulomis; all being taken bound to keep the peace, under a penalty of one thousand Scots.

Follows the letter referred to :—

Duntulm, 15th May, 1707.

Sir,—I had the favour of yours of the 24th past, by Alex. Clerk, and was surprised to find Keppoch so remiss in paying you his tack duty, for which I am bound as a cautioner. I cannot think what has been the occasion of his falling short, but will write to him pressingly of it in two or three days, and if he give not satisfaction, I have as much concern to press him with diligence as any man can have in my case, but till I may have time to hear from him, I hope you will delay diligences, which will be very obliging upon, sir, your most humble servant,

(Signed)   D. MACKDONALD.

My wife gives her service to you and your lady, to whom you will please to present mine, and also of Drummuir.

No. XCIII. ANNO 1708.
COLL MACDONELL OF KEPPOCH.

AFTER a struggle with Mackintosh, lasting over twenty years, Coll of Keppoch settled down quietly, ultimately becoming his pensioner. For many years during the first half of the eighteenth century, Cluny and Keppoch regularly received a sum of one hundred merks per annum from Mackintosh, the receipts for which bear to be in name of "gratuity" on the part of the grantee. Coll was always behind with his rent, and letter XCII. shows that Sir Donald Gorme of Sleat, the cautioner, had to be applied to. The letter of excuse after quoted is of importance, as showing the entanglements and embarrassments into which Keppoch had become involved during his early stormy career. A comprehensive genealogical account of the family of Keppoch was contributed to the *Celtic Magazine*, some years ago, by the late lamented Mr. D. Macpherson, a native of the Braes, and it is stated that some old papers connected with this interesting family will shortly be published.*

Follows the letter referred to :—

         Keappoch, 8th Oct., 1708.

 Sir,—Being instantly going to Edinburgh to relieve my English baill, I have left this for you to assure you that it is impossible for me to pay any of Mackintosh's rent this year, having been obliged to spend three thousand merks by my imprisonment at Edinburgh, journey to and from London, my stay there, and my ten weeks' sickness at Edinburgh. However, I shall strive, God willing, to pay two years' rent the next year, so that I am hopeful Mackintosh will have me excused this year, because of the misfortunes I trysted with. In the meantime, I am, sir, your most humble servant,
      (Signed) COLL MACDONELL.

Addressed—"To Paul Macphail, Chamberlain to the Laird of Mackintosh," and endorsed " Keppoch's letter, promising to pay his rent, due 1707 and 1708, at once in the year 1709."

 Coll's request was agreed to. He died at Keppoch at an advanced age.

No. XCIV. Anno 1709.

SIR HARRIE INNES, BARONET.

THE family of Innes is, undoubtedly, of great antiquity, although many will not be disposed to accept the Flandersian origin.

It is to be regretted that a family which was so long prominent in the north-east of Scotland should have become entirely dissevered from their ancient habitation.

Not the least unfortunate event in the history of the family, and its branches, was the case of the predecessor of the late lamented Sheriff Cosmo Innes. He had purchased from the Gordon family the fine Barony of Durris, and laid out a deal of money upon its improvement. Some time after, the title was challenged successfully,

---

* These have been published but do not come up to anticipation.

resulting not only in the loss of Durris but also of the old patrimonial estate.

Sir Harrie Innes, of Innes, the writer of the letter after quoted, was the fourth Baronet, and died in 1721. His mother was Lady Margaret Ker, third daughter of the first Earl of Roxburgh. Sir Harrie's grandson, Sir James, the sixth Baronet, succeeded to the Dukedom of Roxburgh early in this century, the family name being now Innes-Ker.

The letter after quoted shows Sir Harrie to have been a kindly, jovial person. His writing is not very distinct, and I have some doubts as to the word which I have made "Rabletts." Possibly rabbits were intended, but the spelling is as given. The letter is of some interest as connected with a family long resident in the East country, and indicative of the friendly intercourse prevailing at the time 'twixt one gentleman and another.

Follows the letter referred to :—

Dear Sir Archibald,—According to my promise, I send you that Litle Bitch, which, you say, is of the Mar. of Lothian's brood. I also send you one of her puppies; the other I designed ffor you, which was a dog, was stole. I can assure you they are the fynest Halking spannils I ever saw in this country.

John Macpherson says you wantt a pair of rabletts, when ever you send ffor them you shall command what I have.

I offer my kind service to Sir Hugh, to your Lady, and be assured as none wishes the ffamilie better so none minds the old Commaradship more affectionately nor can be more, dear goodman of Blyth, your oblidged and most humble servantt,

(Signed) HARRIE INNES.

Innes, June 10, 1709.
To Sir Archibald Campbell of Clunies.

No. XCV. ANNO 1710.

GEORGE, FIRST EARL OF CROMARTIE.

DURING his long and somewhat chequered career, this Earl had only one leading and fixed principle, viz., the aggrandisement of his family. He owed much to the Stuarts, having the chief management of Scottish affairs during the latter years of the reign of Charles II., and the whole of that of James II., but he was ready enough to acknowledge the new dynasty. He was born in 1630, and died in 1714, a few years after the date of the letter hereinafter quoted. Created Viscount Tarbat in 1685, and Earl of Cromartie in 1703, he had the great influence to procure his lands, situated in various parts of Ross-shire, incorporated into and within the county of Cromarty, these lands being of greater area than the original county.

The letter is addressed to his son, Sir Kenneth Mackenzie, and chiefly relates—though there are ominous Parliamentary references—to a debt owing to the Laird of Inshes.

The male descendants of the Earl are extinct. Like his namesake, Sir George Mackenzie of Rosehaugh, the Earl was an accomplished scholar and elegant writer. His versatile character was notorious, giving rise to the following severe couplet :—

> A few describe him true as steel,
> The many, slippery as an eel.

Follows the letter referred to :—

10th November, 1710.

Dear Son,—After I shall have the honour to wait on the Queen, I shall write in answer to yours better than I now can ; as to my own business, I am just as you left me. I had this letter three days ago from Mr. Robertson, son to Inshes. I do blame you for my being in this trouble. Your civility and mine to Dachmal : (Mackenzie of Dochmaluag) is not well requited. I would expect that, though I had not put provision so long since in your hand, yet having given you some effects, and having effects also in your own hands due to me ; I say, I hoped you would satisfy that debt, whereof I write so often to you.

The Parliament is to be prorogued (as I hear surely) for 10 or 12 days longer. The greatest affairs will be in at the very entry ; and very great ones too. Adieu.

Addressed—"To Sir Kenneth Mackenzie, sonne to The Earle

of Cromartie, to the care of the Postmaster at Fortrose." (Seal entire.)

I have several interesting papers connected with Sir Kenneth Mackenzie, and select the following as a specimen, being Bond of Relief by the Earl of Argyll, and Viscount Tarbat, relative to Sir Kenneth's cautionary obligation for Allan Muidartach, Captain of Clanranald, 1697—

Be it kend to all men by these present letters, us Archibald, Earl of Argyll, and George, Viscount of Tarbat, Forasmeikle as upon the 21st day of July last bye past, Kenneth Mackenzie of Cromartie became cautioner and surety to the Lords of His Majesty's Privy Council for the peaceable and good behaviour of Allan Macdonald of Moydart, under this present Government, and that he should present the said Allan Macdonald to the Lords of Privy Council when required thereto, and that under the penalty of five hundred pounds sterling money, as the same bond of the date foresaid more fully bears. And the said Archibald, Earl of Argyll, and George, Viscount of Tarbat, considering that the said Kenneth Mackenzie should sustain no loss, trouble, nor prejudice through his said cautionary and for the kindness and favour we have and bear towards the said Allan Macdonald. Therefore, witt ye us to be bound and obliged, likeas we by these presents bind and oblige us, conjunctly and severally, our heirs and successors to free and relieve the said Kenneth Mackenzie of Cromartie, his heirs and successors, of all cost, skaith, and damage, interest, charges, and expenses that he or his foresaids shall happen to sustain or incur through his being cautioner for the said Allan Macdonald in any manner of way. Likeas I, the said Allan Macdonald of Moydart, by these presents, bind and oblige me, my heirs, and successors whatsoever, to warrant, force, relieve, harmless and skaithless, keep the said Archibald, Earl of Argyll, and George, Viscount of Tarbat, and their foresaids, of all cost, skaith, damage, trouble, or inconvenience they or their foresaids shall happen to sustain or incur through their foresaid obligation in any manner of way. And for the more security we are content and consents that these presents be insert and registered in the Books of Council and Session, or any judges' books competent within this kingdom. That letters of Horning and other executorialls needful may pass hereon in form as effeirs, and to that effect we constitute over Procurators, etc. In witness whereof we have subscribed these presents, written by Kenneth Mackenzie, writer in Edinburgh, at Edinburgh, the fifth day of August, in the year sixteen hundred and ninety-seven years, before these witnesses, Mr. James Mackenzie,

one of the Clerks of Exchequer, and the said Kenneth Mackenzie.
(Signed) ALL. MACDONALD.
(„) ARGYLL.
(„) TARBAT.
JA. MACKENZIE, Witness.
KEN. MACKENZIE, Witness.

No. XCVI. ANNO 1711.
BRIGADIER WILLIAM MACKINTOSH OF BORLUM.

THE only letter belonging to me of my distinguished relative is given in the sequel. It is written in a very firm bold style of writing. The reputation of this gallant soldier is not falling off—his name is even yet popular in the county Palatine, and songs in his praise are sung by real Lancastrians. Some of his direct descendants in the female line live at Newtonmore. The heir male of the Borlums may be found in the United States, the descendant of Lachlan Mackintosh of Knocknagail, Bailie of Badenoch, to whom the letter was addressed, but being an alien, the male representation may be truly said to rest in Mackintosh of Raigmore.

The Brigadier's writings show him to have been a man of high education and extensive reading. Three years before his death, a prisoner in the Castle of Edinburgh, his name is found among the subscribers to the new edition of Major's Latin History, published in 1740, wherein he is styled "The Honourable Brigadier General William Mackintosh of Borlum." There is a fine piece of pipe music, never published, called "William of Borlum's Salute," noted in part of Angus Mackay's Manuscript Collections, now in possession of the Duke of Hamilton, and a contemporary piece of poetry of some merit by a female admirer, has been recently published. The letter after given in itself is of little value, but it may be connected with memorials of the Brigadier, still to be seen in the Park of Raitts. Writing in 1835, the then minister of Alvie, for the new Statistical Account of Scotland, says :—"The lawn in front of the house is adorned with upwards of one hundred trees of hard wood, and a fine row of elms along the old military road, planted by Brigadier Mackintosh in 1715." It is doubtful if he had time to think of planting in that year, but he was busy in 1711, and it is not improbable that some of the trees then ordered are amongst those still standing.

Follows the letter referred to :—

Reats. May 17, 1711.

Loving Brother,—I wish you joy of your bargain, and if it was much greater, and my credit or interest sufficient, you might depend of them. I have signed the three bonds, and am hopeful my friends, the creditors, will not stickle at the formality of a manual delivery, which ceremony (was I present) I would as cheerfully do as sign them.—I am, your loving brother,

(Signed)   WILL MACKINTOSH.

Forget not to get me a bag full of ashe and siccomore seeds, which I believe hang yet on the trees ; also, an ounce of spinnage, and half an ounce of garden cresses seeds.

Addressed on the back thus in another hand—"For Lachlan M'antoch, Bealie, in Beadenoch."

Endorsed in different writing—"Borlum's bonds within this letter, 1711."

No. XCVII. Anno 1712.

DR. ARCHIBALD PITCAIRN, THE SCOT.

IN another letter I make some reference to this distinguished physician and Latin scholar, some of whose unpublished poems I have the good fortune to possess.

Dr. Pitcairn, who was born in 1652, came of an ancient Fifeshire family. He first studied divinity, then law, and finally medicine, having passed in 1680 as M.D. at Rheims. He was afterwards professor at Leyden, but finally settled in Edinburgh in 1693 on his marriage with Miss Stevenson. He became the first medical practitioner in Edinburgh, and was frequently called to London. He was a man of convivial habits and quick temper, involving him in constant disputations. As an instance of his convivial nature, he notes, I observe, on one of his poems sent to a friend, "This was the club on Christmas Day last. George Drummond, keeper of our Tolbooth, fills the glass to the top always. Barclay of Tough is a check on George, who seldom drinks out his glass. Robin Clare, surgeon, makes us laugh. Thomas Kinkaid is a Latin poet, an honest fellow, and lately made an honorarie surgeon, though neither he or I know anything of the trade." Wodrow, an unreliable authority, says of Pitcairn, "Drunk twice a day."

The Doctor was also an eminent mathematician. His disputes with the clergy, he being somewhat of a free thinker, a Jacobite, and Episcopalian, were constant and protracted. He satirised the clergy; they on the other hand styled him infidel. An amusing anecdote on this point has been handed down, and is noticed by Chambers. One of the cleverest of the Doctor's reverend opponents said he would make him acknowledge this character out of his own mouth. Two associates sallied out, accompanied by a stranger in Edinburgh who was taught his part. Dr. Pitcairn was watched, until observed going along in a great hurry, as if to a critical case. The stranger went behind the Doctor, and tapping him unexpectedly on the shoulder, asked if he were "Dr. Pitcairn, the Atheist." Taken unawares, the Doctor, only considering the first part of the query, turning round answered "Yes," not discovering that a trap had been successfully laid for him, until he saw the two reverend gentlemen near at hand laughing heartily.

Dr. Pitcairn's works have been published in several forms. Perhaps the best known are the selections from his poems, published by Freebairn, at Edinburgh, in 1728.

His elegy on the death of Lord Dundee is much admired, and far superior to the English translation, although the work of the illustrious Dryden.

From the unpublished poems, which are printed in fine

type on half sheets of paper, I select the following as a fair specimen. Now-a-days such a thing would hardly be attempted even by an Unitarian :—

AD
JESHUM CHRISTUM
Dei Filium.
ARCHIBALDUS PITCARNIUS Scotus.

Natali vestro, lacrymis jejunia pascunt
Discipuli *Cnoxi*, quos *Usinulca dedit.

Quippe *Pharisaci* mutata voce fuere,
Adventumque Tuum, maxime *Christe*, timent.

Ne monstraretis, parendum Regibus esse,
Antque juberetis reddere cuique suum.

Nunc postquam terras placuit tibi linquere, gaudent
Esse sibi festum fas agitare diem.

Et ridere Deum, qui nobis talia suasit.
Qualia *Cnoxiacis* esse nefasta placet.

Andream nobis Tu *Jacobum*que remitte,
Qui Te, *Cnoxiacis*, auspice, verba dabunt.

The following is a capital rendering by Mr. Allan Macdonald, LL.B., who worthily upholds the Latinity of the Inverness Bar, in which, during the last hundred years, it has held no mean repute :—

Metrical Translation.

Knox's diciples, following Calvin's way,
With tears and fasting mark thy natal day.
For they're but Pharisees, styled differently,
And fear Thine advent, O Thou Christ most high
Lest Thou should'st teach them kings must be obeyed
And order that to each his dues be paid.
But they rejoice now Thou'st abandoned earth
I' th' right to spend their days in feast and mirth
And mock at God, who recommends to man,
What Knoxites choose to place beneath their ban.
Oh send back James and Andrew in Thy name
To put these Knoxites, Lord, to utter shame.

In transmitting an ode, Archimedis Carmen ad Regem

*Calvinus.

Gelonem ex Graeco versum, et Albae Graecoe repertum, Anno 1688," Dr. Pitcairn writes to Dr. Forbes of Elgin thus :—

Doctor, I send you the last edition of Archimedes to King Gaelo. Another shall appear shortly, which shall be sent. Mr. Duncan, my worthy friend, will tell who Issachar is.—Yours,
(Signed) A. PITCAIRN.
9th Augt., 1712.

The Duncan here referred to was President Forbes.

Most of the odes have manuscript alterations in the Doctor's own handwriting. The last I have in date is 29 May, 1713, to "Margarita, Regina et Diva Scotorum," and he died at Edinburgh on the 23rd October of that year.

A son who took a prominent part in the Rising of 1715 was pardoned through the intervention of a friend who had been indebted to Dr. Pitcairn. The Doctor's valuable library is said to have been purchased by Peter the Great of Russia.

No. XCVIII. ANNO 1713.

ALEXANDER, MARQUIS OF HUNTLY, AFTERWARDS SECOND DUKE OF GORDON.

THE annexed anxious letter, from the second Duke of Gordon, while Marquis of Huntly, will be read with sympathy. The first Duke would not have written such a letter, for his wife had left him and taken refuge in a convent in Flanders; he, on the other hand, raising a process of adherence against her. The writer of the letter was the last Catholic, his children and their descendants being Protestants. The sick lady, married in 1706, was Lady Henrietta Mordaunt, daughter of the famous Earl of Peterborough. Much of the Peterborough property fell ultimately to his great grandson, Alexander, fourth Duke of Gordon.

The letter is addressed to Dr. Forbes, of Elgin, a practitioner of high standing, an accomplished scholar, who, with his professional brother, Dr Stuart, were friends and correspondents of the well-known doctor, Archibald Pitcairn. Dr. Pitcairn, who styled himself THE SCOT, one of the finest Latin scholars Scotland has produced, used to print his odes on little slips of paper for circulation, newspapers being then almost unknown as a means of publicity in this respect.

Follows the letter referred to :—

Sir,—Just now I saw your obliging letter to Mr. Irvine. I must and shall acknowledge my gratitude for your willingness to do my wife the favour of a visit, now you are so indisposed ; but that must not hinder my endeavours for your care. I have, therefore, sent my chariot to wait on you. Three or four days past, my wife complained of a violent headache, and sickness in her stomach, and of a soreness all over in her bones, and, night before last night, some little pimples began to appear over her body. Yesterday, more came out, some pretty big, and many in her face very little. What makes her apprehend most danger is . . . . which makes her fear her illness very dangerous. However, I hope the best, with your good advice and Dr. Stuart's, who was sent for yesterday about three in the afternoon. I hear to-day she is fuller than last night ; her sickness and soreness still continues, but more moderate than before the out-striking. She has slept a little, but both of us are very impatient for your coming. Pray bring with you what you think necessary. You shall be taken good care of, as if at home, and extremely welcome to your most affectionate unknown friend and humble servant,

(Signed)   HUNTLY.

Gordon Castle, 8 in the morning.
Addressed—" For Dr. Forbes, at Elgin."

After his succession, Alexander appears to have looked well into his affairs, and transacted a good deal of business in person. Here follows a good example of the holograph letter of a clear-headed person, thoroughly cognizant of what he was doing :—

Sir,—I have transacted your bond, granted to my father with your son-in-law, and have given him a discharge of the same. There is another bond of yours granted to John Macpherson of Corronach, my father's Chamberlain, for two hundred and eight pounds Scots, as some byegone feu-duties resting by you. The bond is now of a pretty old date, and I think it your interest to order the payment of it, without putting me to the trouble of doing diligence on it, since, notwithstanding thereof, my father, at my desire, gave you an entry without taking notice of it.—I am your affectionate friend,

(Signed)   GORDON.

G : Castle, 20th October, 1721.
Addressed—" For William Baillie of Dunzean."

No. XCIX. ANNO 1714.

THE DEBATES ON THE SUCCESSION.

THE following letter from John Forbes of Culloden, an actor in the important discussion on the Protestant Succession, is of great interest. John Forbes, 4th of Culloden, the writer, commonly called "Bumper John" sat in Parliament before his brother the Lord President—the family of Culloden being zealous Protestants. The letter is addressed to Culloden's connection, Dr Stuart of Elgin, and was sent open under cover to the President, who adds, as will be seen, a valuable P.S. of his own.

It is well known that Queen Anne in her latter years inclined to favour the claims of her brother, the Chevalier St. George, and had she lived a couple of years longer, it is supposed that the Act of Settlement passed in the reign of William and Mary would have been repealed. The Queen's death in August, 1714, a few months after the date of this letter, was sudden, and left the Jacobites unprepared; but, notwithstanding, the strength and influence of those who declared for the Chevalier were so great, that had a General with the military talents and social rank of Montrose or Dundee appeared, the result of the Rising of 1715 would have been different.

The period of history in question, does not present a pleasant retrospect. Public morality and spirit were very low, and the abominable life led by the Elector of Hanover is well known. The extraordinary liberties and interferences in English affairs, taken by M. de Schŭtz, this petty potentate's emissary, leading at one time to his withdrawal from the kingdom, seem incredible. The letter, which is given in the original orthography, is as follows:—

Sir,—Since my last ther hes been very hott work in both houses of Parliament, about ten dayes agoe. The Lords were on the affair of the poor Catalans, as you'll perceave by the address sent you fformerly. They have last week been upon the state of the nation with relation to the Protestant Succession in the House of Hanover, and the Courte after a long and very warm debeate, carried by a vote, That the succession was not in danger under the Queen's administration, by a majority of 13 only. The Whigs, endeavour'd all they could to distinguish betwixt the Queen and the administration, by putting the question, that the succession was in danger from the actings of the ministrie, but could not help themselves, and the vote passed as above, yett tho' they lost that vote, they think they have gain'd a great deall, because my Lords Angilsie, Abbinton, and a great many more, are come over to the Whigs, and have openly declared themselves ffor the protestant succession, to that degree, and with that warmth, that my Lord Angilsiea said in the debeate, that if he could lett himself believe there was any in the house of Lords, that did oppose the succession by ffavouring the pretender he would not only ffirmly oppose, but also most heartily convoy him to a gibbett, to have justice executed upon any such vilanous trateur, if any such was, after this vote was past. The Whigs took the Treasurer in task for giveing money to the Clans, but the majority that carried the former vote, reckoned the giveing that money good service done the Q. and government. and thanked his Lordship therefor.

By the address herewith sent you, you'll perceave that tho' the Whigs by force of numbers voted the succession was secure, yett they did not belive it so, and would have some better security for it than a vote, by having a pryce put on the Pretender's head. The debeate ran in the house to have him brought in dead or alive, but the Whigs passed from that and came in to the termes of the address, when they gott the Q.'s answer. It put them almost mad, and Teuesday last they mett on it, wher the debeats runn so very high, on that words of her majestie's answer (industriously promoted that they were to address the Q. of new), and back it with such reasons as would convince her majesty and the world that ther ffears and jalousies were too weell grounded, and rather universally belived then industriously promotted, and after a long debeate on this subject, in which they tore the ministrie and the peace with Ffrance and Spain to pieces, as pernicious and destructive to this nation, in its sacred and civill concerns, and particularly as tending to the subversion of the protestant succession, I say after a long debeate, they came to a division, and divyded 61 to 61—only the Court carried it by two proxis. But the Lords present were equall and had not some of the Whigs been absent, and on or two seek, they had, as is believed by many, certainly carried the point, and are still in hopes to dee it, God grant them success. However, tho' they have lost this heat also, yett the Court are greatly affraid, and nothing the less that Barron Shŭts the Envoy of Hanover, hes last day by express order from his master demanded from the Lord Chancelour of Brittan, the Duke Cambridge's writte to sitt in parliament. The report is, that when this demand was made, the Chancelour was so stunn'd, that he knew not what answer to make, but after being sylent for some· tyme, and being again press't, by Barron Shŭtts for an answer, he told him that he belived a writte could not be issued to any that was not in Brittain. The Barron desyred to know, if he should give that answer to his master, to which the Chancelour replyed, by no means, that he only spoke this as his own oppinion, but that before he could answer his demand, he behooved him to acquaint her majesty. I hear now the Barron has gott the writte, but the Court are so allarmed with the Duke of Cambridge's comeing, that ther are as is said two expresses sent within these two dayes, to stop him.

The Lords mett again on Wednesday last, the 13th instant, to consider of her Majestie's answer to ther address of the eight instant, and it was then that the debeate above narrated about the word industriously promotted occasioned the division of sixty-on to sixty-on. The Lords displeased with the answer made the Q. a second address, which is also hierwith sent, as a reply to her answer, in which, because they could not keep out that word indoustriously which the majority forced on them they pamed in the word universally which showes the Whigs' dislyke to the present measures, and how barbarously the nation is used by this torie ministrie. Yesterday they mett again upon the state of the nation with respect to the peace with France and Spain. They satt very late, but in spyte of all the Whigs could do, the Court by a majority of over sixteen peers carried ane address of thanks to her majestie ffor the safe, honourable, and advantageous peace, as the call it, she hes so gloriously obtain'd ffor her kingdoms. This address was sent this day to the Comons ffor ther concurrance, and it was greatly pressed by the Court that we should instanter close with the Lords in the address, but after a very long and warm debeate, we have defferred giveing answer to the Lords till Thurs-day nixt, and in the meantyme addressed her majesty to lay the severall treatties with Ffrance, Spain, and the Trety of Commerce, also all the directions and instructions given her ministers ffor the makeing these effectuall before the Commons. That when we have examined them weell, so as to understand them, we may, ffrom a true sence of the great advantages we have from these treatties, be in condition to thank her majesty with a better grace than now we can doe when intyrely ignorant of them. I need not make this letter longer by telling you what the Commons are doeing. I reffer you ffor that to the votes, only this I doe say, that on Thursday last when we were on the Succession, our Speaker, Sir Thomas Hanmer, acted a very honest handsome pairt, lyke a man of honour, and a brave patriot, who would not be beat from his reason by numbers, or menascliles (menaces) as he told them in his speech, but boldly declared for the protestant succession, and gave unanswerable reasons for his believing it to be in danger from the present administration, and to his immortall honour be it spock, he did this in face of the Court, and in defiance of all the prefernments they did offer. The house was never so ffull as att this division. The Whigs were 208 and the Court 256. Ther is ane other piece of news I had almost forgott to tell you. The place Bill for restricting the number of officers to sit in Parliament cam to appear in the house of Lords, and had not on of our Lords been lockt out when the question was putt, it had certainly passed. But now it is thrown out. Dear Doctor, lett this long letter serve as appologie for my long sylence, when any thing occurs worth whyle, and that I dare adventer to write, you shall hier ffrom me. If you want any such glasses as you wanted to divert you send a memorandum of such as you want, and I shall be carefull of it, mynd me to all ffriends, and belive me to be ever yours.

London, 17th Apryle, 1714.

Please communicate this to Innes, because I am so wearied that I can write no more this post.

Inverness, 27 Aprile, 1714.

Sir,—As I have transmitted you this Letter of my Brother's, I thought it not amiss to acquaint you that the private letters which we have in town import, that the Bishop of London, the Bishop of Bristol, and our Scots Earl of Loudon are come over to the Whiggs upon the last division of the house of Lords, as weel as, Anglesey, Abingdon, Cartwright, Ashburnham, Jersey, and the Arch-bishop of York did upon the former, its written likeways from London that Mr. Hanmer, besides language used which will make him irreconcileable with the Court, brought over 50 members of the October Club that was once thought so dangerous, and its believed that more will soon follow. If you think my conjecture worth the noticing it is, that the Treasurer, not expecting to succeed in a parliamentary indemnity tho' proposed, hes underhand raised this stir against himself that he might be approven of at least by resolves of parliament, but when once that design is smoakt, its ten to one he have as many to oppose him in the one course as in the other.—Yours

(Signed)   DUN. FORBES.

No. C. ANNO 1715.
MR. JONATHAN FORBES, MARINER, SON OF DR. FORBES, OF ELGIN.

THE following letter from a nephew of President Forbes to his father is amusing. He must have been a well brought up youth, unaccustomed to the strong language of sailors of modern times, who, if placed in a similar situation, would doubtless have indulged in several expletives.

Now-a-days there would seem to be on the part of certain members of Parliament a longing for exclusive privileges, enabling them to say and do what they like in regard to others. These people should have lived in 1715, when they could not only denounce others with safety but swindle them as well.

The writing is bad, as is also the spelling, some words being very funny. "Eleven" is written "A leven," voyage is written "voag," and so on.

Follows the letter referred :—

London, July the 2nd, 1715.

Dear Sir,—This is to let you know that on the 27th of June last I came safe to London, and has been some time ago in England, but had not the opportunity of getting this length no sooner, which was the occasion you heard not from me before this time. I have been very unhealthy on the coast of Guinea, but, thanks be to God, recovered it, and am now in perfect health, and hope yourself and my mother are in the same.

My friend, Mr. Urquhart, told me that you have been very unhealthy yourself, for which I am heartily sorry, but blessed be God

Almighty you had somewhat recovered it, as he tells me, of which I am heartily glad.

Our ship was discharged at Bristol, and I was obliged to travel up to London. We made a very good voyage for our owners, though they paid us our wages but rogueishly, obliging us to take eight months' pay when we had eleven due to us. Our head owner is supposed to be broke, and is likewise a Parliament man, so that we could not make him do it by force, because there is no such thing as troubling any member of the House upon any such account. Therefore, we was obliged to take what they pleased to give us; otherwise we might have wanted it these seven years to come. I alone was not so used, but likewise all the ship's company from the captain to the cook boy. I have seen no friend as yet, but Mr. Urquhart and Dr. Innes, who both give their respects to you. This is all at present, only my duty to yourself and my mother, and prays God may keep you both long in the way to give your good advice to myself and the rest of the children, which ought to be the daily prayers of us all towards such dutiful and loving parents as you are, and it shall be the prayers and wishes of, dear sir, your most humble servant and dutiful son until death,

(Signed)   JNO. FORBES.

If pleasing to let me hear of your well-being, it will be very gratifying to me. I lodge at Mr. Urquhart's, as formerly, and the directions of your letter may be the same. I am looking out for another voyage with all diligence possible.

NO. CI. ANNO 1716.

SIR HUGH CAMPBELL OF CALDER.

THE affectionate letter after given was not despatched. There is marked on the back "Coppie of a letter desynd to be subscrived and sent by Sir Hugh Campbell of Calder, to his grandchild, now Laird of Calder, the week before his death, 1716." No doubt Sir Hugh had suddenly become past writing. He died on Sunday, 7th March.

The years of 1715-1716 were very critical to many a Scottish family.

While the Duke of Argyll was the most prominent supporter of the Hanoverian interest, Lord Breadalbane and several of the important Campbell families, including Calder, were in favour of King James.

Why Sir Hugh Campbell, who had occupied much of his time in the consideration of ecclesiastical matters, should almost on his death-bed order his men to take the field for the Stuarts does not appear. He was himself too old, his son, Sir Archibald Campbell of Clunes, was a Hanoverian, his grandson was young and resident in England, so the command was given to his grandson, Duncan, eldest son of Sir Archibald. This Duncan, who had married Katherine, daughter of Trotter of Morton Hall, left an only child, Elizabeth, born in Rome, 17th October, 1725, a lady of great beauty and highly accomplished, judging by her letters. She died unmarried in the year 1748. The accession of the Calder men to the Rising could not be denied, and it might have fared ill for the Calder family, had not Sir Hugh died so opportunely. As it turned out, influence was brought to bear in favour of the young laird not suffering for his grandfather, and the whole blame was put upon the unfortunate Duncan of Clunes, who for many years was an exile from Scotland.

Follows the letter referred to:—

My dear grandchild,—My last by Brigadier Grant, altho' some days sooner written, will not come to hand before this, and now the state of my health differs so much from that my last attempt, that I must tell you I am past hope of recovery and of seeing you in life; nor can I enlarge as I should wish, particularly of what concerns you. Therefore, I only wish the Great God direct you in all your ways and keep you to act a part in your day as may be pleasing in the sight of God, and agreeable to your friends.

I particularly recommend to you and to your uucle, my only son, to support, comfort, and love one another as becomes relations so nearly concerned. Your uncle has acted a part for the family in general, and for you and me in particular, as you upon trial will find, as I have done. Therefore, I require and expect your kindness to and care of his numerous family and particularly where he or his sons can serve, do not employ strangers. May Almighty God direct you, him, and all mine, in ways acceptable in His sight, and expecting your regard to this my last advice, at the same time desires heartfully to bless you in the name of the Lord, and am, my dear grandchild, your most affectionate grandfather.

No. CII. Anno 1717.
WILLIAM MACKINTOSH, AN INSURGENT OF 1715, LIEUTENANT IN BORLUM'S BATTALION.

THE unhappy position of those taken prisoners at Preston is painfully illustrated by the letter after quoted. That death which befell so many was more merciful than the lingering sufferings of those detained in confinement. Many were transported to the plantations, to a condition no better than that of slaves.

The detention of the Preston and other prisoners after a period of two years, became such a scandal that Government or the King had unwillingly to consent to their release, previously trying to screw as much out of their friends, themselves impoverished and well-nigh ruined, as possible.

The writer was a Lieutenant in Borlum's battalion, and the William Shaw referred to was quartermaster.

Follows the letter referred to:—

Prestoun, 17 January, 1717.

Loving Cusine,—I had yours only yesterday, whereby I need but have faint hopes of success to a possession, but if enquiry were made, Bailie Stuart, at Inverness, knows that some of those possessors are not old tenants, and that others of them are bad payers and very turbulent. However, do you what you can with all parties, which is all can be demanded or expected of you. Duncan-mac-Ian-du-vic-Ewen, is not at Lancaster, having been transported, but the other 4 are, and I went there of purpose a month ago to see them, and there is no doubt of their being discharged the first of March at the Lancaster Assize.

There is near 200 prisoners there as yet, all common people and servants, who, we believe, will all be discharged at same time. Letters from Newgate here signify that the condemned prisoners there expect their pardon at the king's arrival.

Your friends and countrymen here are all well. There is none at full liberty but William Shaw, Cameron, and I, nor have we got one fardine but the £20 received at London for our sustenance all this time. The rest have a good lodging and 16 pence p. day paid them, but are under guard, yet are allowed to go abroad as oft as they please, with a single sentry, and sometimes without any, so that I reckon they are better stated than we are. Being wearied out of all patience here, waiting a discharge that's too long a coming, and finding myself at full freedom, Will Shaw and I resolve, God willing, to take journey for London in a day or two to purchase our discharge if possible, rather than hang on here any longer, not knowing for what, or to what purpose. This journey being without any call or order, will leave us very poor, but better finger off than always bleeding, so that if you have any occasion to write anything to me, you will put a cover about my letter and direct it for John Dyoss, at the Black Periwig, in King Street, Westminster, London, which will always come to my hand. Your friends here give their service to you, which, with mine, and wishing you good success in your law suit, and a safe journey home, is all from, sir, your affectionat cusin and servt.

(Signed) WILL: MACKINTOSH.

As for Sutherland's bill, do in that as you list, for I know not what success it may have. These poor lads in Lancaster are much displeased at you and Dunmaglass for never minding them or writing to them. They have 4s. paid them daily, by which they live with the charity of some others. If you please to write to them, call them invalids in Lancaster Castle, to the care of Mrs. Gashat, in Lancaster, who is their good friend. Tordarroch and Kinchyle are discharged a month ago without on fardine to carry them home with, probably will be our fate too.

No. CIII. Anno 1718.
THE REV. LACHLAN SHAW, HISTORIAN.

THE annexed letter, written at an early period of Mr. Shaw's career, gives the name and address of his father, and of one of his brothers.

The land referred to forms part of the Barony of Dunachton; the letter indicating the care of the Chief, that the relict of a deceased crofter should not be disturbed, and which involved a journey by Mr. Shaw to Moy Hall. Mr. Shaw naturally refers, in his writings, in a kindly manner to the family of Mackintosh, whom he regarded as Chief. Mr. Shaw had access to the Kinrara MS., and corrects in his own way, in his own History (which is but little known), some errors, but none which are very material. He kept adding to his History up to the last, and some part at the end is written in a large shaky hand, very different from his ordinary hand, round, small, and well formed.

Northern antiquarians and others owe much to Mr. Shaw, who was most courteous and observant and thereby got access to many valuable deeds and papers at a time when these were jealously guarded. Certain deeds of the greatest importance to the family of Mackintosh disappeared during the disastrous guardianship of the Laird of Grant, 1622-1634. It was hoped Sir W. Fraser, when it was known he was examining the Grant papers, might have thrown some light upon the matter, if not actually discovered the lost documents. Whatever he may have found, if any, is not disclosed on the face of his three valuable volumes concerning the Grant family.

Follows the letter or obligation referred to :—

I, Mr. Lachlan Shaw, minister of the Gospel at Kingussie, do hereby, in the name of Donald Shaw, in Rothiemurchus, my father, and Duncan Shaw, my brother, oblige us that whereas the saids Donald and Duncan Shaws have the three aughten parts of Achnabechan in tack from the Honourable the Laird of Mackintosh; ——, relict to ——, and presently in possession of one half aughten part of the said land, shall be allowed to possess one half aughten part of the said land, during the said tack, and she always behaving dutifully. As witness my hand, at Moy Hall, the ninth day of November, seventeen hundred and eighteen years,

(Signed)   LACH : SHAW.

No. CIV. Anno 1719.

LADY ANNA STUART OR ROSS OF BALNAGOWN.

THE annexed curious letter from a lady, who did her best to destroy the House into which she had married, will, in its perusal, create mingled feelings. One who could quote Scripture so aptly, and who appears so resigned to death, might be supposed to have lived a fair, just, and honourable life, giving to all their due; robbing none.

But it was notoriously the reverse. Having no children by her husband, David Ross of Balnagown, heir male, and representative of the Earls of Ross, she first entered into an intrigue to have her younger brother, Francis Stuart, declared heir. In course of time, by deaths, Francis became heir to the Earldom of Moray, and such rights as were conceded in his favour, entirely voluntary, he was not above disposing of for money. Ross of Pitcalnie was next heir male, and nothing could be alleged against him openly, except that he was not a Presbyterian. Lady Anna was accused of being much under the control and influence of several clergymen of the Established Church. The story of the nefarious proceedings, first of Lord Ross, and afterwards of General Charles Ross, I have narrated elsewhere. The ultimate decision in the House of Lords was a great blow to the then Pitcalnie and his friends and supporters. I observe that Mr. Colquhoun Grant, Writer to the Signet, the agent in Edinburgh, who had in his youthful days served as a volunteer with Prince Charles, writing to a relative of Pitcalnie's, says, of date 31st May, 1776, "I know that you will be concerned for the fate of your friend Pitcalnie. It is the more grievous that I had certain information of the Lord Chancellor having formed an opinion upon the case for reversing the judgment here, and for reducing all the deeds. But another great Law Lord was finally of another opinion, and of consequence we have failed of success." The title of Lord Ross has long been extinct, and just lately their fine place of Hawkhead, in Renfrewshire, has been sold, after being, either in the male or female line, for five hundred years in the possession of the family. General Ross has left no descendants in the male line. These two brothers, though named Ross, were nowise related to Balnagown, nor to the old Earls of Ross; and since the death of the late Pitcalnie, it is doubtful if any heir male of the Ross Earls of Ross exists.

There is a memorandum on the back of the letter in these words:—"The above paper was written by Lady Anne Stuart of Balnagown, a very few days before she was taken ill of that sickness whereof she died. She being in the most heavenly frame, delivered the same to her chaplain, Mr. William Miln, as a pure evidence of the Lord's distinguishing goodness to her, and of the great advantage of real and solid godliness, especially in the time of sharp affliction."

Follows the letter referred to:—

I can say it is matter of grief and lamentation to me that when I had my health and strength I did not improve them as I ought to have done to the glory of God; much pains has the blessed Lord been at with me, but alas! I have ground to mourn in dust and ashes that I have been barren and fruitless, but glory, glory to His great name that there is a fountain opened for sin and uncleanness; the blood of Christ cleanseth from all sin, and it is to his precious blood my soul desires to betake myself alone for salvation; for there is none other name under heaven given among men whereby we must be saved: I know in whom I have believed, and I am persuaded He is able to keep to me that which I have committed unto Him against that day. I desire to say with holy Job, though He slay me, yet will I trust in Him. I have been now a long time under the Lord's afflicting hand; yet adored for ever be His great name that ever he bestowed a rod upon me; the wonderful way that I have been helped up is a clear evidence to me that it is in love and not in wrath, and that which encourages me the more to think so, is the many sweet scriptures the Lord was pleased to bear in with power upon my spirit in my great distress. I cannot now set them down here. When I had my speech, I told Mr. Miln and others about what sweet cordials I got: O that all the world would help me to praise the Lord; never was there a poor worm more indebted to free grace than I am. The righteous Judge of heaven and earth is my witness that He keeped me breathing to heaven that I might be delivered from sin, from hard thoughts of God, and from murmuring under His hand; as all my mercies come from free grace, so I acknowledge this was the Lord's doing, and wonderful in mine eyes. Since the latter end of May was a year, and this is the last of July, 1719, I have been in a sad case night and day, except some blinks now and then the blessed Lord was pleased to give me. The faithful ministers of the Lord have been very sympathising with me, not only by myself in prayer, but, I am informed, they were earnest with the Lord in my behalf in their churches, tho' I was not named; their Great Master bless their labour and reward their sympathy to poor unworthy me; I have not cause to complain of the Lord's dealing with me. I have ground of praise and adoration to the Lord that He cast me not headlong into hell as my sins deserved. The enemy is many times casting temptations in my way; but, glory to Christ who suffered being tempted, He is able to succour those that are tempted. Precious Christ undertake for me, for if the Son make me free I shall be free indeed.

Oh! I am grieved that I cannot praise him.

No. CV. Anno 1720.

ALEXANDER, SECOND DUKE OF GORDON.

In a former letter (No. XCVIII.), I gave a specimen of this nobleman's composition. The letter now given is published as being perhaps almost the only friendly letter received by the Mackintoshes during the four hundred years they stood as vassals of Huntly. The Chiefs of Mackintosh were vassals of both the Earls of Huntly and Moray, and, in consequence of the protracted rivalries of those Earls, frequently placed in a difficult position.

Although, without any cause that I can see, the Mackintoshes rather inclined to the Earls of Moray the latter made an ill-return.

Those great Lords in Scotland had extravagant powers

and privileges, which were frequently rigorously enforced, yet, as a rule, it is found that they were nearly always greatly embarassed in their pecuniary affairs.

Follows the letter referred to :—

Sir,—Yesternight at my return from Strathbogie, I had your letter. You know it was not my fault we did not agree much sooner, which would have been better and cheaper for us both. Friendship is what I wish for with all mankind, and I shall never resist it on my part. I have not yet seen Westhall since my return from London, therefore, as yet, cannot appoint a time for our meeting. I shall speak to him ere long, and shall then advise you of time and place of our meeting. Pray think who you will put in our submission of marches instead of Kyllachie, who, I am told, is dead. All disputes ought to be cleared at same time, since you have had, and probably have, pretended friends about you, who have not been for our agreeing, and will always occasion disputes if in their power. You know them, and I have some guess of them also. But I hope all such will be disappointed, if you prove to me, as I shall to you, an affectionate friend to oblige you, (Signed)   GORDON.

My wife and I return your Lady our humble service and thanks, and so do my child.

Gordon Castle, 13th April, 1720.

Addressed—" For the Much Hond., the Laird of Mackintosh."

The marches referred to in the letter were those between the Parishes of Laggan, Kingussie, and Alvie, in Lower Badenoch, and the Braes of Strathdearn, in the Parish of Dunlichity; and were fixed by Gordon of Glenbucket for the Duke of Gordon, and Cuthbert of Castlehill for Mackintosh, in the year 1721.

No. CVI. Anno 1721.

SIR ARCHIBALD CAMPBELL OF CLUNES, AND JOHN CUTHBERT OF CASTLEHILL.

AFTER a long career, the Cuthberts of Castlehill went down, upon the death of George Cuthbert, who filled the office of Sheriff-Depute, and died in 1749. The story goes that a curse fell upon the house, in consequence of the Sheriff erroneously pronouncing doom upon two poor women against whom he had a grudge, and who were burnt for witchcraft at the foot of Alt Murnack, where it joined the Millburn, a few yards from the sea. In a process in which George Cuthbert was concerned, in the year 1745, Margaret Cuthbert, daughter of the deceased John Cuthbert of Plaids, which John was eldest son of John Cuthbert, Town Clerk, and grandson of Provost Alexander Cuthbert of Inverness (and thus a cousin of Castlehill), with consent of James Rutherfurd, meal-maker in Edinburgh, her husband, accuses her cousin, the Sheriff, and his father, John, that old Castlehill got her father to allow him become a trustee, that he sold and took conveyances not to her father, but to himself, and that the process of adjudication, at the Sheriff's instance, is taken "in hopes, as the representer is in very mean and indigent circumstances, to establish a right to her father's estate, without any opposition, or giving her any value or acknowledgment for the same." Although the Sheriff died in such embarrassed circumstances that the creditors took possession, and his family were scattered over the world, the father, John, must have been in affluent circumstances, for I find the Laird of Inshes alone owes him nearly four thousand merks. The ranking and sale of the estate lay in the Court of Session for about thirty years, and until 1779, when it was purchased by Robert Jamieson, W.S., for about £14,000, on behalf of some members of the family, who had done well in the New World. As showing how things had scattered and disappeared, the only title prior to the decreet of sale in 1779 was one single document, a retour of date 1624. The first Cuthbert taking up a title was Joseph Cuthbert of Drakies, in the State of Georgia, who got a disposition from Jamieson in 1786, but immediately disponed to George Cuthbert, Provost Marshal of Jamaica. The acting and moving spirit in this re-establishment of the family was Lewis Cuthbert, brother of George, who was in Britain in 1785, if not earlier, and made the acquaintance of his relations and the friends of the family. The estate was almost lost at the outset; George Cuthbert died embarrassed on 17th June, 1790, and his brother and heir, Lewis, in 1792, writing to a friend, says—" My mind is at length made up not to part with the estate of my ancestors, and I have the pleasure to tell you that matters are likely to be on such a footing soon that there will be no necessity for bringing the estate to sale at all ; but should any unforeseen circumstance thwart my present negotiations with my late brother's creditors, and a sale thereby become unavoidable, I am in that case determined to bid even beyond the utmost value of the subject rather than lose it." In another letter, from Bath the same year, after mentioning that he had just returned from visiting his brother, the Bishop of Rodez, at Paris, Mr. Cuthbert says—" I am much obliged to you for your desire that I may continue the proprietor of the estate of my ancestors. It is an object of my greatest ambition, as may naturally enough be supposed. I am sorry to say that, through the improvident conduct of my deceased brother, that object can be accomplished by me in no other way than by paying its full value to his creditors." Mr. Lewis Cuthbert settled with the creditors, and spent a few years in the North, living at Cradlehall, in good style, and, when he travelled, carried six horses and two men servants. By 1796 he began to get into difficulties and returned to Jamaica, dying about 1802. He had granted a conveyance of his estates to Abram Roberts, banker in London, and a director of the East India Company, who began to sell off in 1804. Lands of the value of £60,000 were sold, so enormous had been the rise in value since 1779. The affairs again got into the Court of Session, and proceedings were going on as late as the year 1834. Now there are no Cuthberts in Inverness, and the gallant attempt of Mr.

L. Cuthbert failed disastrously. The Barony of Auld Castlehill extended, I fancy, at an early period to the Millburn, the Kirk Session lands forming a part. There was a Court and Barony jurisdiction at Lochgorm, and the mill referred to in the titles was doubtless that now known as Midmills. Part of the Barony lay north and west of the high road, including the present mansion-house and some of the lands of Millburn. It was in the time of the Hon. Archibald Fraser of Lovat that Auld Castlehill came to be called "The Crown;" and the estate of Castlehill, as now belonging to Raigmore, was feued by the Cuthberts from the town in part, and Muckovie from the Lords Lovat. The Cuthberts of Drakies, an offshoot of Castlehill, long held a good portion.

Follows the letter referred to :—

Sir,—I have, as you say, at last received the papers you wrote of, particularly my brother's holograph obligation to your uncle David for five hundred merks Scots money, and interest thereof, since the sixteenth September, sixteen hundred and eighty-six. Item an assignation thereof from the said David to his son William, and a translation of the same from the said William in your favours, with the general charge of entering heir, inhibition and decreet before the Lords, raised at the instance of the said David against Gilbert Campbell, eldest son to the said Sir Alexander, and your discharge of the debt and whole diligences to the Laird of Calder. And now after my son Hugh and I have gone through the papers, and considered the whole, its truly my opinion you should ask no expenses, and that for several reasons, obvious I doubt not to yourself, and that I will mind you of at meeting.

And, therefore, except you forbid me, I will certainly offer them to the Laird of Calder for the neat principal sum and current annual rents if he be pleased to accept of them; but whether he does or not, I do hereby promise to hold compt to you for the contents of the papers, as said is, in case they be not returned upon demand.

The advice I offer to you is certainly what I would go in to if I was Castlehill, and you the Laird of Calder, and think him kind, as well as just, in so doing.—I am, dear Gossip, your affecate, Gossip to serve you. (Signed) ARCH. CAMPBELL.

Calder, 15th Nov., 1721.

Your expenses is but a trifle, and I think you can make no

better of it than to let the Laird of Calder see you resolve to deal friendly by him, and pass the expenses as a thing not to be mentioned by you to a person you value so much as the head and representative of the family of Calder.

Castlehill took nine years to think what he should do, and finally, in a cramped and tremorous hand, he writes at the end of the foregoing letter, as follows :—

At Calder, this 15th of April, 1730, the contents of the above and within letter is satisfied and paid to me.

(Signed) JOHN CUTHBERT.

He died in March, 1733, survived by his wife, Mrs. Jean Hay, only child of William, Bishop of Moray.

No. CVII. ANNO 1722.

THE REV. LACHLAN SHAW, HISTORIAN OF MORAY.

I AM in possession of many letters from Mr. Shaw, but unfortunately nearly all of little general interest. Mr. Shaw was born in the year 1692, appointed minister of Kingussie from 1716 to 1719, of Calder from 1719 to 1734, and of Elgin from 1734 to 1774. In the year 1774 he demitted his charge, and died in 1777, in the 85th year of his age, and 61st of his ministry. There is no address upon the letter, but I infer that it was addressed to Sir Archibald Campbell of Clunes, absent for the time in Edinburgh or London on his own or the Cawdor affairs. Mr. Shaw, whose writing is beautifully round and distinct, had a kindly, sympathetic, and benevolent temper, as is well seen in the letter after given. His name will ever be held in honour in the North.

Follows the letter referred to :—

Honourable sir,—You have so full and particular ane account of our countrey news by your friends who have gone from here last week, that it were impertinent in me to make a repetition of them, and therefore I refer you entirely to them, and to my Lady Drummuir's letter by this bearer.

My Lady Clunes continues very tender; she is so extenuate that she can't use the proper means either for present case or for recovery; and I must use the freedom to acquaint you (seeing I know you expect I should impart my thoughts of her trouble with all ingenuity, and I could not forgive myself if I did it not) that I have greater fears about her than I have had in any sickness I ever saw her in. A shortness of breath, frequent trembling, of which she is insensible, and a more than ordinary swelling, are symptoms which to me are discouraging.

If it is not proper to trouble you with such ane account at this juncture, you'll pardon my freedom, and allow my good intention to atone in some measure for my faults. All the rest of the family are in health, and this day young Archie pay'd a visit to his grandmamma.

My Lady Drummuir informs you how your directions are execute with respect to the house and other particulars, and, as far as I can understand, your business without doors is going on very well. We all long to hear of the event of the process, and I shall say that if prayers and good wishes can any way contribute to your success, and the disappointment of your adversaries, you have a large share of them. I hope that the blessing entailed upon the peacemakers shall be your and your friends' allowance, and if peacemakers shall be called the children of God, I wish the disturbers of our peace may seriously lay it to heart whose children they are and whose interest they promote.

You'll do me the honour to offer my best respects and compliments to Mr. Hugh and Colin, to Kilravock, the Clerk, etc.

Wishing you much of the conduct of the unerring spirit, to direct, guide, and succeed you in your affairs, and a safe return hither, that we may rejoice together.—I am, with great respect, H. S., Your honourable's most obliged and most humble servant,

(Signed)　LACH. SHAW.

Calder, Feby. 26th, 1722.

P.S.—All I shall say at this time of your honourable's care in my affair, is that I can't enough thank or reward you.

I am at a loss by your absence at this time, when I'm busy with my garden, and want much your direction and assistance, as I doe also in settling a tenant in the possession, which I cannot labour without great loss.

No. CVIII. ANNO 1723.

THE MAGISTRATES OF INVERNESS AND THEIR CRIMINAL JURISDICTION.

IN No. 25 of *Antiquarian Notes* there is an account of a petition and complaint by the Magistrates of Inverness, in reference to their being summoned to appear in the High Court of Justiciary, for alleged excess of jurisdictive criminal powers. It is stated in the article that it had been communicated to me by the late Mr Dempster of Skibo, who informed me that the paper had been found among the papers of Dundas of Arniston, then Lord Advocate.

By accident I discovered the copy letter after given, which, doubtless, refers to the same case. The particulars of the crime not being given in the letter, I quote from the statement for the Magistrates, of date 23rd Oct., 1723— "That on 11th June, James Miller, tidewaiter, and Richard Barlow and Francis Powell, soldiers, before it was daylight in the morning, having called to a boat which was rowing about one hundred yards distance from them on the river, to come to the shore, and, the boat not having readily answered, the tidesman ordered the soldiers to fire, and three shots were accordingly fired, whereof one pierced the boat, and another killed one of the boatmen."

Being taken red-hand, the Magistrates considered they had power to try for murder, but they restricted the libel, and the punishment was that " The prisoners who all were accessory to the death of the man, be whipped in place of further punishment ; and they ordered the tidewaiter to pay £33 6s. 8d. sterling as assythment or reparation to the widow and children of the deceased for the loss they sustained."

The whipping of so important a Government official

as the Inverness tidewaiter probably caused the proceedings in the Justiciary Court.

It will be observed that a curious expression occurs in the letter. The Magistrates say, "having brought the criminals to tryall before us, within three suns."

Follows the copy letter referred to, endorsed thus :—

Copie letter to the Mags. of Perth, 4 Nov., 1723, anent a Murder.

A murder having, some months ago, been committed within the liberties of this burgh, the criminals were immediately seized and imprisoned. And the private persons injured, with concourse of our fiscal, having brought the criminals to tryall before us within three suns, we proceeded in virtue of the powers vested in us by the rights of our burgh, and pronounced doom therein regularly and agreeable to the laws of our country, as we hope. Notwithstanding whereof our actings have been so far misconstructed that a criminal prosecution is intented agt. us before the Court of Justiciary, and tho' we are not at all solicitous anent the event of that prosecution with respect to ourselves personally, yet we will, with the utmost zeal, assert the privilege of our Burrow, which was struck at by it. And therefore it is that we give you the trouble of this by Mr. Baillie, our Town-Clerk, intreating you'l be pleased to communicate to him the manner in which the right of sheriffship within your Burgh is conveyed to you by your charters; because we have bein many times told that the rights of your Burrow and that of ours are the same with respect to the said jurisdiction; and we shall likeways intreat you'l be pleased to recommend to your Clerk to communicate to Mr. Baillie if your Baillies are virtually Sheriffs, if they are so named at your annual elections, or if they or any others are only chosen Sheriffs when any emergency happens. We are told by our lawyer that the knowledge of these facts will be of great use to our cause, and therefore, as we would with most cheerful hearts contribute whatever lay in our power towards the supporting of the rights, honour, and dignity of the ancient and good town of Perth, we persuade ourselves ye will not deny this request of

THE MAGISTRATES OF INVERNESS.

4th Nov., 1723.

No. CIX. ANNO 1724.

MACKINTOSH AND "NISBET'S HERALDRY."

THAT Chief of the Mackintoshes commonly called "Laird Lachlan," after his escape from the consequences of being out in the '15, set himself vigorously to the work of consolidating his influence as Chief of Clan Chattan, and the improvement of his estates. He kept up considerable state, and appears to have been very fond of music, there being still extant numerous receipts for young men in his employment receiving instruction in various branches of music. The Laird was evidently much disturbed by what appeared in *Nisbet's Heraldry*, as may be gathered in the letter from his clansman and agent in Edinburgh, after quoted. About the beginning of last century, the nobility and gentry began to be anxious about their pedigrees, whence arose a deal of falsehood and exaggeration, which it required upwards of a century to remove. Indeed, it may be said that much of the falsehood then put into circulation still remains. Nisbet's book is still considered a good authority. The name of the well-known Thomas Ruddiman, it will be observed, is mentioned in the letter.

Follows the letter :—

Edr., 10th Jany., 1724.

Honble, Sir,—My last went by John Ross, the former post, in answer to yours, about the debt due by the late Sir Donald, to which I refer. By this bearer, McGregor post, I have yours of the 3rd, wherein you complain of the injustice done your family by a wrong recital of facts in Mr. Nisbet's "Heraldry," etc. According to your order, Mr. Duff and I waited Mr. Ruddiman, but he was so busied that he put off the meeting till Monday next. We are resolved to have Mr. Nisbet with us if he can be had, and, whatever the result is, you shall be informed. You need be in no manner of pains for want of time to do your family justice, if you resolve it, because the appendix which Mr. Nisbet is to publish will not probably be very soon out, seeing he has to be encouraged by subscription, to which, no doubt, you will be assisting. In the meantime, your store ought to be gathered to the full, that, if possible, there may be amends made for former faults and omissions, which are almost unpardonable. Mr. Ruddiman shall not be idle here, and (without a previous bargain) might be rewarded, according to his pains, tho' he succeed not, according to wish. I wish my assistance could be of use, since I am, honble. sir, your very affect. humble servt.,

(Signed) ALEX. MACKINTOSH.

Addressed on the back—"The Honble. the Laird of Mackintosh, at Moyhall."

No. CX. ANNO 1725.

MR. ARCHIBALD CAMPBELL, WRITER, EDINBURGH, ON BUSINESS OF THE LAIRD OF CALDER.

THE annexed lengthy letter shows the care and minuteness of a lawyer of the early part of last century in dealing with his constituent's affairs.

The letter is all about business, and though for a moment in the postcript the writer deals in gossip, he soon falls back to business.

Sir Archibald lived more than twenty years after the date of this letter, and the wadset of Budzett continued in his family for a considerable period.

Sir Archibald was succeeded in Budzett, an old possession of the Dallas family, by his son, Dr. Colin Campbell; the latter by his son Archibald, and he by his only child, Mrs. Colonel Baillie of Dunain. In her time the wadset, the last of those remaining on the Cawdor estate, was redeemed, and about the year 1830.

Before the death of Lady Anne Ross of Balnagown, she had deposited with Sir Archibald Campbell a number of valuable papers.

They were exhibited by Sir Archibald's grandson, Archibald above-named, fifty years afterwards, in the great process regarding the right to the Balnagown estate.

Follows the letter referred to:—

Edinburgh, 17th June, 1725.

Sir,—Yours of the 8th current I received by Thomas Ross, with ten pounds sterling, and the rental for the year 1724, which was so late acoming, though I timeously and frequently wrote for it. that now it won't answer the design. So whatever be the consequence to Calder, I am not to blame for it, having sufficiently exonered myself. I wish you were more expeditious, particularly in matters requiring it. You have wrote me of no business at all, nor sent me by so good an occasion as Thomas Ross the papers I sent for, but you refer me to him, and he can say no more than you are pressing my going north, as to which I wrote you before. I have spoken of it to the Commissioners, who have directed me to desire you will immediately send up a particular memorial of all the debts you think proper should be cleared, especially Drummuir's and other lucrative wadsets, and how money, and on what terms, may be better advantage than by the present wadsets, be raised from different hands instead of having too considerable a debt owing to any one creditor; together with a particular state of all the marches controverted by the neighbouring heritors, the whole wadsets of the family, and other papers I wrote for. And in your memorial take notice of the Commissioners granting you a wadset of Budzet, you having advanced the money. They likewise desire you will instantly transmit your account of charge and discharge for all the years since you computed last with Calder, including the crop 1724, and the particular rentals for every year; and take credit for whatever is due and in arrear either by feuars or tenants, or by merchants to whom you sold the victual, and keeping every year distinct and separate by itself. In your memorial mind to notice every particular affair proper to be considered, which may render one of us going north next vacation necessary, and write to the Commissioners yourself. Upon your transmitting me all those things, they will give particular directions about them, and intend to clear your accounts, and will consider how far my going north is necessary. You may likewise write to Calder about it; he, by this time, I believe, is gone to Wales. You may likewise propose to have your several claims settled, you being now so valetudinary.

It were very proper you disposed your affairs with respect to your children, as no differences or confusion might happen after it pleased God to call you, and keep what papers you sign lying by you, sealed, with a letter on the top of the bundle directed to any particular person in whom you can put confidence, empowering them to unseal your papers. Mind to write to me about Mr. Charles Ross' affair. Expecting a full and speedy return to this and my former letters unanswered, and wishing you perfect recovery, I am, with usual respects to your good lady and self, sir, your most affectionate cousin to serve you,

(Signed)   ARCH. CAMPBELL.

Colonel Munro's Commission is come down, as Sheriff of Ross, and General Ross', lieutenant of that county, and General Wade is come. Cavers Douglas is postmaster, in place of Sir John Inglis. Being settling with Captain Alex. Campbell the debt due to Dr. Weem's heirs, I see you paid a debt to one Ensign Robert Rutherfurd, some time one of the gentlemen of the Troop of Guards, but the assignation thereof, which you took in the Lady Calder's name, does not bear the particular sum you paid. The principal sum was 650 merks, due by the doctor and his son's bond, there was a precept drawn on you for £474, which you did not accept, and there was a decreet of furthcoming obtained against your father, yourself, and nephew Sir Gilbert. Please look over your accounts with the lady and Mr. James Anderson, and any other papers passed betwixt you, and see how much you paid, vizt., principal sum, how much annual rent, and how much expence, and send me a particular note thereof by the very first. There was another Robert Rutherfurd (now of Fairnalee), then General Receiver, who was a creditor of the Doctor, and to whom you paid, £111 of principal and £4 of interest. So don't mistake the one Rutherfurd for the other. Their designations will distinguish them. Pray hasten your answer to this particular.

Addressed—" Sir Archibald Campbell, Clunies at Calder, to the care and despatch of William Mackintosh, merchant in Inverness."

No. CXI. Anno 1726.

DANIEL BARBOUR OF ALDOURIE.

THE name of Barbour was long prominent among the higher burghal families of Inverness. Bailie John Barbour, father of the writer of the letter after given, had acquired the lands of Aldourie. He left several handsome daughters, one, Mrs. Colonel Delane, another, Mrs. Mackintosh of Kyllochie, another, Mrs. Mackay, mother of Mrs. Colonel Fraser of Culduthel, and another Sibella, the unfortunate heroine of the celebrated Moray marriage case in 1730-1732.

The lands of Aldourie, a part of the barony of Durris, were for a long period owned by the Mackintoshes. The first Alexander Mackintosh is understood to have built the house of Aldourie on its present site, and following examples not uncommon, he built on the very extremity of his property to the north. The lands next adjacent belonged to the Macbeans of Kinchyle, and as early as 1632, the proximity of Aldourie house to the march was so inconvenient, that an agreement for alteration was come to. The march west of the road by Dores to Foyers, was the burn of Dourack. Its course is now much straitened and altered, but of old it ran within a few feet to the north of the house of Aldourie, and when in spate endangered the building. Ever since 1632 it has been a struggle with Aldourie to increase its area northward of the burn. Time after time it has been increased, but at great loss of hill ground and heavy feus, until at length within the last few years, the north march of Aldourie from Loch Ness is the road leading to Bona Ferry.

Sir James Mackintosh was born in the house of Aldourie, though the estate had for some time passed out of the Kyllochie family. His mother, Mrs. John Mackintosh, who had been a Miss Macgillivray, of the Clune family, and connected with the Balnains, was, in consequence of a fire at the house of Clune, temporarily moved to Aldourie, and there gave birth to Sir James.

The letter after given is addressed to Mr. George Mackintosh, a careless youth, son of Mr. John Mackintosh, advocate, who had been out in 1715. The transaction referred to, arose out of a combination betwixt Bailie John Mackintosh, of Inverness, grandfather of George, Bailie Watson, of Inverness, and the Barbours, all men of wealth, to buy up the debts affecting the last of the estates of the Hays of Lochloy. They wished to purchase these estates, Inshoch and others, but Calder and Brodie went beyond them, and were the successful bidders, but under burden of the debts and adjudications.

The name of Barbour does not now exist in Inverness, and can only be found with such contemporaries as Cuthberts and Vauses, in the monuments in the Chapel Yard of Inverness.

Follows the letter referred to, addressed "To Mr. George Mackintosh at Inverness":—

Sir,—Some time agoe your mother gave me her obligation for £25 0s. 6d. sterling, payable out of the first and readiest of what money Calder owed, being the half of my expenses in getting that ravelled business to a settled balance, and seeing I am to pay some money to Mr. Archibald Campbell, I hope your mother and you will not scruple to draw bill upon him, and write him a letter with the bill, desiring that he pay it to me in part of what the Laird of Calder owes you, for he cares not to take the obligation in the shape that it is now. Mr. Watson and I are under submission in all matters betwixt us, and I have entered my claim to the arbiters, for a third of my expenses in carrying on our joint interest with Calder, soe that it is to be referred to his oath, and whatever I recover upon that head from him, I, by these, promise and declair that I shall pay to your mother or you, or to you both, the just and equal half of it. I have ordered my wife to give up the note, and to gett the bill and letter, for I have nothing else to keep me here, being obliged to pay money to Mr. Campbell, soe hope you will give me no hinder. Pray offer my humble respects to your mother, to the collector and his ladie, to William and his, and I sincerlie am, dear sir, your most affectionate humble servant.

(Signed)   DANIEL BARBOUR.

Edin., February 25th, 1726.

No. CXII. Anno 1727.

DAVID ROSE OF HOLM.

THE family of Rose has been settled for upwards of 300 years on their small but beautiful estate of Holme. It is an offshoot of Kilravock, and of the numerous heritors of the name, at one time in the counties of Inverness and Nairn, they alone survive.

William Robertson of Inshes had married, as his second

wife, Sybella Mackenzie, daughter of the Honourable Thos. Mackenzie of Pluscardine, and there was a subsequent marriage with the Inshes and Holme families.

The late Colonel Sir John Rose of Holme was an ardent Liberal. At the passing of the Reform Bill in 1832, tradition records he was not much of a scholar, a circumstance commemorated in a highly popular, and well-known electioneering rhyme, of the time of the Grant and Macleod contests, giving the various peculiarities of the Whig magnates in Inverness-shire, etc.

> " Kilcoy swore he was a sinner
> If he worked without his dinner,
> And the Colonel at school
> Could never learn, learn, learn."

The supposed lady authoress' nearest male relative had more than one call for satisfaction from the indignant satirized.

Follows the letter referred to :—

Sir,—When I was last with you, you said you would draw precept for my behoof on Paterson, tacksman of the Kingsmilns, to answer me four bolls good and sufficient grinded malt. And though there be severals that I owe trifles to at Inverness, and that would agreeably take pennie worth in meal, malt, or bear for their payment, yet as my wife has use for the malt, it will mightily oblige me that you draw, and at the same time cause your tacksman accept the precept you mention, which, when so done, may be sent me with notice from the miller when I shall send for the whole, or the half of the malt. Four bolls at ten merks per boll amounts to £2 4s. sterling, the sum you are due me. Excuse this trouble, and I am, Sir, your affectionate grandchild and obedient humble servant, (Signed) DA. ROSE.

Holm, 7th Sept., 1727.

My wife and I give our grandmother our kind service.

No. CXIII. Anno 1728.
JAMES BRODIE OF INSHOCH.

THE letter after given is in itself of little value, deriving its interest from the place where it was written. When we see castles long in ruin, or visit the sites of those where now not a stone exists, one's thoughts naturally revert to the whilom occupants, wondering what kind of people they were. Hence letters from such places bring up the writers vividly before us, and we can trace in them very frequently their character and disposition.

Every railway traveller is familiar with the old castle of Inshoch, situated near the railway, betwixt Nairn and Brodie Stations. Shaw thus refers to it:—" In the lower part of the parish of Auldearn, towards the Firth, is the barony of Inshoch, with a large old house, the seat of the Hays of Loch Loy and Park. This was a very ancient branch of the house of Errol, and were lairds of Park about 400 years. By their declining, the lands of Inshoch and Park came into the family of Brodie about the beginning of the eighteenth century." The ruins are most interesting, and, alas, like so many of our ancient castles, kept in a mean state. In the times of Wallace and Bruce, the Hays of Loch Loy were prominent figures, gallant soldiers—worthy of their descent. The castle is said to have been occupied until towards the end of last century, when, being partially destroyed by fire, it was deserted.

We are not certain who the writer was, who had just lost his wife, but presume he was James Brodie, commonly termed of Whitehill (brother of George Brodie of that ilk, who died in 1716), whose grandson, James, succeeded to the headship of the family and estates, on the death of his second cousin, Alexander Brodie of Brodie, in 1749.

The writer speaks of Sir Archibald Campbell of Clunes, to whom the letter was addressed, as a relation, but the only connection we are aware of—somewhat remote—was the marriage of Sophia Campbell, Sir Archibald's sister, and Alexander Brodie of Lethen, cadet of Brodie.

Follows the letter referred to :—

Sir,—This is to acquaint you that it has pleased God Almighty to remove my dearest wife, and that I intend, God willing, she

should be buried on Tuesday next, the eighth of this month. Therefore, if it consists with your conveniency, I will expect you here, as a relation, a little sooner than the ordinary time.—I am, sir, your most humble servant,
(Signed) JA : BRODIE.
Inchoch, Oct. 2nd, 1728.
Addressed—"To the Honble. Sir Archibald Campbell of Clunes, Sheriff-Principal of the Shire of Nairn, Calder."

No. CXIV. ANNO 1729.

LACHLAN MACKINTOSH OF KYLLACHY.

SUCH of the Mackintoshes as had no lands in the lower parts of the county were compelled to hire lands, for the purpose of raising the needful supplies of corn. The Chief raised his corn at Dalcross, and Kyllachie, after the sale of Aldourie, rented lands in the parish of Ardersier.

At the Rising of 1715, the Laird of Kyllachie was well advanced in years, but still took the field, together with his eldest son Lachlan, the writer of the letter after given. The elder Kyllachie was taken prisoner at Preston, the younger having escaped. At this period many Campbells were favourable to the Stuarts, the Earl of Breadalbane being actually in the field, although he contrived to escape forfeiture. In the north Sir Hugh Campbell of Calder, then an old man, was so favourable, that one of his grandsons, Duncan Campbell, younger of Clunes, by his desire, took arms, with many adherents. Sir Hugh died early in 1716, before any proceedings were taken, and the estate was thus saved. John Campbell, the succeeding Laird of Calder, who had settled in Wales, was, naturally interested in the fate of his cousin, the younger Clunes, and others connected with his family and estate. Amongst others, the Laird befriended old Kyllachie, tenant of his grandfather Sir Hugh, and made him the promise when in prison in London, that neither he nor his posterity should be disturbed in their possession.

The Laird's uncle, Sir Archibald Campbell of Clunes,

had a large family, and their was some intention or rumour as to his settling one of the sons in Ardersier, which he had the power of doing, as the factor and representative of Calder. Hence the correspondence which is now given, displaying firmness and straightforwardness on the part of Kyllachie, who had, by this time, become head of his family, with conciliation on the part of Sir Archibald, who, I notice in several letters, speaks of "Honest Kyllachie."

Lachlan having died young, unmarried, was succeeded by his next brother, Alexander, who had settled in business in London as a merchant. He continued in business, only visiting the north occasionally, Ardersier being given up. Alexander, who had married one of the Barbours of Aldourie, died, without issue, about 1770, when he was succeeded by his brother James, who lived at Connage. His eldest son, Captain Angus Mackintosh, was killed in the American wars being in turn succeeded by his brother, Captain John, who was father of Dr. James, afterwards Sir James Mackintosh. Within a period of fifteen years there were four Lairds of Kyllachie.

Follows the letter referred to :—

Honble. Sir,—Being informed by the sub-tenant in this place that you have ordered them to give their usual dues to you, I have thought fit to advertise you of a letter I had from the Laird of Calder, wherein he allows me to possess and compt for all my father and I ever possessed in this place upon account of ane promise given to my father, when prisoner at London, never to remove his children after him as long as they did duty. I know not what you will make of this; but in case I be not reponed to the sub-tenants, as your son has reponed me to what he possessed, you'l excuse me to represent the matter to Calder to have his plan mandate to you to the above effect. I am not intending the least to trouble the Laird if you do me justice, but excuse me to let him know by the first post your hinderance of me in my possession, unless by homologating to what is above written. Return me an answer, and I am, your most humbe servant,

(Signed)   LA: MACKINTOSH.

Arderseir, 22nd May, 1729.

If you please, consult Calder's letter to your son; it will say as much as what's above.

Calder, May 23rd, 1729.

Sir,—I do not understand what you mean by your letters, for I have seen Calder's letter to my son, and both of us agree to your possession of that farm of Ardersier to the same extent you had it before his entry, without troubling sub-tenants or any. other person living under you, except to require your doing duty, as your honest father did before you; and if Calder has, by his letter to your self, allowed more, so shall I, but if you consider my friendship to yourself, all along, particularly in giving you down a third or fourth part of the sum you were justly due me, you will rather accuse your self of ingratitude than me of inclining less or more to do the least injustice to any person upon earth, therefore, for our mutual satisfaction, I want to see Calder's commands and yourself, which will oblige, sir, your hble. servt.,

(Signed) ARCHD. CAMPBELL.

You need not suspect my son Charles's inclining to take any other possession in the Parroch of Arderseer.

NO. CXV. ANNO 1730.
LACHLAN MACKINTOSH OF THAT ILK.

AFTER his escape from the perils of taking up arms in the 1715, which step his widow, Mrs. Anne Duff, and Dowager Lady Matheson, in her Memoirs, laid upon the shoulders of Brigadier Mackintosh, Lachlan Mackintosh set himself to clear off debts and consolidate his estates.

Another leading feature in the character of this Laird, known by tradition as "Laird Lachlan" pre-eminently, though there were many other Lachlans Lairds of Mackintosh, was his desire to unite and consolidate the Clan Chattan ; and, under altered circumstances, to form the Clan anew, an *imperium in imperio*. The numerous bonds, agreements, and obligations which he caused be entered into throw much light on the views and aims of a great Highland Chief in the transition period, betwixt the years 1715 and 1745.

The fine estates of Gellovie and Aberarder in Laggan were sacrificed about 1726 for the above objects, and the putting an end to any questions about the headship. The estate of Bochruben was also given to Dunmaglass for his service in bringing about the Macpherson solution, and at a later period, arising out of the same transaction, the estate of Clune, with its extensive grazings in Glenballoch and Tullichero, had to be parted with, but all to no effect as regarded Laird Lachlan's intentions and objects. The estate of Dalcross, as now known, is but a small part of the original Barony of Dalcross, appertaining to the family of Lovat. As mentioned in former letters, the Mackintoshes, particularly after they lost Culloden, were ill off for corn lands, and so fancied Dalcross. It had been adjudicated by creditors from the Lords Lovat, and ultimately purchased by Lachlan Mackintosh of Tor Castle, father of the writer of the letter after given, who lived latterly at, and died in, Dalcross Castle. It was not known that the Laird of Mackintosh had taken the precaution, by payment of a small sum, of purchasing the equity of redemption from Fraserdale, and the disposition did not happen to be recorded. Happily it was preserved, for General Fraser's doers, about 1778, after the restoration of the Lovat estates, and nearly a hundred years after the first possession by the Mackintoshes, intimated a claim. They were able, it would appear, to plead with success, that neither the long negative, nor positive prescriptions had run, in respect of minorities, Crown possession, etc., intervening, and offered to pay the debt. This unexpected demand after so long a possession of a subject essential to the Mackintoshes, and from lapse of time of very much more value than the debt, some £600 stg., caused much trepidation. The Laird, afterwards Sir Eneas Mackintosh, was serving in America, but the zeal of a devoted clansman, Mr. Charles Mackintosh, Clerk to the Signet, discovered the disposition, which was at once put on record, and the Lovat claim was abandoned. It was not connected with the Lovat claims that Mr. Baillie of Leys had written to the Laird of Mackintosh the letter to which the following is a reply :—

Sir,—I have received yours, and cannot complain of your civility

in this affair, though, in the meantime, I thought to hear no more of this old story. I shall acquaint you before you leave the country what further I can get myself informed in the affair, which is all from, sir, your assured friend and humble servant,
(Signed)   LA : MACKINTOSHE.
Moyhall, October 2nd, 1730.
Addressed—" To Mr. John Baillie, Writer at Edinburgh, for the present at Inverness."

No. CXVI. ANNO 1731.

ALEXANDER MACKINTOSH OF KYLLOCHY.

THE annexed letter is the first of a series extending over about sixty years, which passed betwixt Alexander Mackintosh of Kyllochy and his widow, commonly called Lady Kyllochy, on the one hand, and Mr. John Mackintosh, merchant, in Inverness, and his son, Provost John Mackintosh of Aberarder, on the other hand. Angus, the father, and Lachlan, the elder brother of Alexander, had been both out in the 'Fifteen. Alexander, being the second son, betook himself to commercial pursuits, and settled in London, from whence he never returned, notwithstanding his accession to the estates upon the death of Lachlan. He was a keen man of business, and clannish to a degree. He died in or about 1770, leaving to his wife, one of the Barbours of Aldourie, the life-rent of the estate and all his other means. Lady Kyllochy, as she was termed, lived for some years in London, in considerable style, but latterly returned to Inverness. She died about 1790, at a great age, in a house, part of the property in Church Street belonging to her, and afterwards to three generations of Suters.

The eldest cadet of the house of Mackintosh was that of Rothiemurchus, and the second, Kyllochy. From Kyllochy springs Holme, Farr, and Dalmigavie. The next is Balnespick ; and of the others—Borlum, Aberarder, Corrybrough—are descended of younger sons of Lachlan Mor

Mackintosh of Mackintosh, who died in 1606. Raigmore, Drummond, and Geddes are cadets of Borlum.

During most of Alexander of Kyllochy's time, John, the son of his neighbour Captain Donald Mackintosh of Dalmigavie, was in business in London; as also Mr. Charles Mackintosh, uncle of Provost John Mackintosh; and the well-known saddler of the Haymarket, Mr. Alexander Mackintosh, uncle of Mr. Alexander Mackintosh, last of Phoppachie. During this time, also, there were in active service in the army, Captain, afterwards Sir Eneas Mackintosh; Captains Angus and John Mackintosh, nephews of Kyllochy; Captain John Mackintosh, of Corrybrough Mor; Colonel William, Captains George and Lachlan Mackintosh of Balnespick; Captain Eneas Mackintosh, of Raigmore; Captain Donald Macqueen, of Corrybrough; and members of the families of Macbean of Kinchyle and of Faillie, of Macphail of Inverairnie, of Macgillivray of Dunmaglass, of Shaw of Tordarroch, etc., showing that in the latter half of the last century the Clan Chattan were as well to the front abroad as they were powerful in Inverness. The invoice is hardly worth copying, being for cloth and other goods. The amount came to £35 3s 1½d, from which, curiously, though twelve months' credit is given, a discount of five per cent. is allowed.

Follows the letter referred to:—

London, 27th May, 1731.

Sir,—I had yours, and, in compliance, above is bill of invoice for a parcel sent on your account on board the "Wheat Sheaf," John Irving, master. You may depend no man in London can or will serve you on more reasonable terms than myself, and am obliged to you for trying. I have drawn on you for the amount, which please to accept. It is at 12 months after date. I cannot say I have the good fortune to be acquainted with you, but your spouse I well remember, to whom please give my services, as also to your and my relatives about you. Please to apply to my cousin, John Shaw, for receipt of shipping, and accept the bill in his hands for the value, and you will oblige D.C., your humble servant,

(Signed)   ALEXANDER MACKINTOSH.

Addressed—"For Mr. John Mackintosh, merchant in Inverness."

No. CXVII. ANNO 1732.

ALEXANDER BAILLIE, WRITER IN EDINBURGH.

THE writer of the annexed letter was of the family of Dunain, and long filled the office of Procurator-Fiscal of Inverness. He lived to a great age, and is found as late as the year 1782.

At the period in question he was a jovial youth, ostensibly pursuing his legal studies, but enjoying the pleasures and amusements of the Metropolis, as so many of his class have done for ages. The letter is quoted on account of certain allusions in it. First, there may be noticed the allusion to Colonel John Roy Stuart, one of the many adherents of the Royal House, whose memory has long been surrounded with the halo of romance. He had been for several years in the Hanoverian service, also, if he did not actually serve in France, was a frequent visitor, and mixed up with the Scottish exiles and Jacobite adherents.

Upwards of thirty years ago there appeared a long and most interesting paper in the *Inverness Courier*, concerning certain proceedings which took place about 1730, in the Consistorial Court of Edinburgh, to establish a marriage between Miss Sibilla Barbour of Aldourie, and Mr. John Stuart, nephew of Charles, fifth Earl of Moray. The proceedings are minutely detailed in the *Courier's* account—how Mr. Stuart came to Inverness on a visit to John Forbes of Culloden—how he became mixed up with all the gaieties of Inverness, his introduction to Miss Barbour, and the heavy drinkings and card-playings indulged in by Shaw Mackintosh of Borlum and other bloods in the neighbourhood. Mr. Stuart paid marked attention to Miss Barbour, and they were ultimately married by the well-known Mr. Morrison, of Contin, who afterwards, under the influence of fear, cut but a sorry plight in his character of an important witness. There does not seem to have been any stain on the character of the lady, but the gentleman and his friends having disputed the existence of a valid marriage, Miss Barbour had to take proceedings against him, in which, after a desperate struggle, she was successful. In the *Courier* report, it is said that of Sibilla Barbour's future history nothing was known, and the writer seems to have been unaware that a child had been born. That this was the case, however, is seen by the letter after given. Mr. Stuart, in 1730, had no great position, nor was the lady's position at all incompatible; but the whole circumstances connected with Mr. Stuart's brief sojourn at Inverness, and his doings there, were far from being creditable to any of those concerned. In 1735, upon the death of Earl Charles, the succession opened to Earl Francis, who was father of James, ninth Earl of Moray, and of Mr. John Stuart. Mr. Stuart was, in 1741, elected member of Parliament for the Fife Burghs, and afterwards became a Colonel in the service of the States General. It is probable that Sibilla Barbour and her child did not long survive, but whether or not, in *Douglas's Peerage*, published in 1764, Mr. Stuart is not credited with wife or child. Mr. Baillie uses an expression, now obsolete, viz., "peuthering," in anticipation of a Parliamentary election, but neither is the meaning doubtful, nor was the practice.

Follows the letter referred to:—

Honourable Sir,—I was honoured with yours, dated August 29th, which I only received the night before Mr. Shaw left this place. I met him accidentally at the Laigh Coffee House, where I got your letter from him; he in a moment vanished out of my sight, and never could get any more notice of him till I sent to Drumuir's lodging, and got notice to my great surprise was off for the north. I must own I have been very much out of my duty in not writing you much sooner, and for reasons I can't pretend to give, only during the session I always expected to have the pleasure of seeing you here, and since vacation came on, I'm so much among the K—— that they have turned my head so that I can think of nothing else but themselves, and you

know, sir, they are very bewitching creatures. But let them alone;
I expect to play them a turn by making some of their Southland
rigs some time or other make amends for the many idle hours
I have spent with them.

I have not forgotten what you were pleased to recommend to
me at parting. I have it always in remembrance, notwithstanding
of my rambles, and particularly in looking out for a good K——
for my dear Duncan. I have a great many in view, but one
particular person—a good acquaintance of mine—would be a very
fit person for his purpose, who by name is Miss M——, worth
two thousand pounds sterling, but I'm afraid my friend when he
would see her would call her Miss Clumsy—that is the only fault
I see about her; her other qualifications are very good. She has
a great many Lowland lairds about her, but now and then I tell
her she must be a Highland lady; she smiles and laughs and
sometimes tips one with her fair fingers along the mouth (but in
the meantime I wish I could bring it about in earnest). I'm over-
joyed to understand that you are perfectly recovered, and that my
lady and the two young ladies are in good health. Sir, you will
be so kind as give my most humble duty to them, and I swear
had Woodspurs half Doctor. Faustus art, he would pass several
of the winter nights in their good company, and now and then
take a Highland trip, and sometimes a minuet with Miss M'Kil-
lican, but since I have not that magic art as to bring me in a
night's time, I must defer till next vacation again, which time I
purpose to have the pleasure of seeing you all at C——, that is to
say, if my peace be made up with my lady for not sending her
things sooner, and really it was not my fault, let her blame her
cousin, John Roy Steuart, for he would have them to carry north,
and has had them these two months in his custody expecting every
day to go north, but now is called to the Regiment, and I have
taken them from him, which you will please receive herewith. You
have here enclosed a note from the jeweller to me of the weight
of the gold sent by my lady and the balance due for the locket.
The pocket-book cost 4s. sterling, mending and putting in glass
to the spectacles was 18 pence, which is in all one pound, six
shillings, and four pence. I shall be glad to know how the locket
pleases my lady with the other things. For news, I can send you
none, only that my friend, Mrs. Barbour, is like to gain her point,
but I fear she will not make a plack of her babie. Mr. Steuart is
received very well by my Lord and Lady Murray, and likewise
by his father and mother, it being the only point he had to gain.
Commissary Steuart is just now north with a commission to take
a great many people's oaths in that affair; and to be of as much
use as he can to Mr. James Steuart in peuthering for the ensuing

election of Parliament for shire of Murray; he also sets up for the shire of Fife here; if both do, Mr. John will represent the one.

I wrote Duncan ten days ago. I shall be glad to hear from him, and am, honourable sir, your slave and servant, while
(Signed) ALEXR. BAILLIE.
Edinr., Septr. 24th, 1732.

Pray excuse this confused letter, I being on extraordinary great haste at writing of it, and hardly know what I say.

Note.—The Decreet of Declarator of Marriage at the instance of Sibilla Barbour, a volume of several hundred pages, has come into my possession.

No. CXVIII. ANNO 1733.

JOHN FORBES, FOURTH OF CULLODEN.

THE following letter, from John Forbes, fourth of Culloden, shows the extraordinary difference in the hour of dining at the present time compared to what it was a century and a half ago. This laird is best known from his hospitality and convivial habits; but, judging from several letters, he must have been a man of equal ability with others of his distinguished family. Being extremely popular and peacefully minded, his services were continually sought and cheerfully given in the settlement, at a disturbed epoch, of family quarrels and neighbours' disputes. With reference to the dinner mentioned in the letter, it can be imagined with what delight "Bumper" John, ever hospitable, must have received intimation of the Laird of Macleod's visit. It may also be left to imagination how, after a good dinner, potations deep, and toasts many, the Laird of Inshes was able to ride home safely in a dark night. Culloden died in 1734, without issue.

Follows the letter referred to:—

Dear Sir,—I expect the Laird of Macleod and two or three friends to dine with me to-morrow, the 2nd inst.

If you will be so good as to favour us with your company, it

will be very obliging, dear Inshes, to your affectionate faithfu
friend, and most humble servant,
(Signed)   Jo: FORBES
Coll, 1st Novr., 1733.

P.S.—We will wait for you till two o'clock.

No. CXIX. Anno 1734.

JOHN CAMPBELL OF CAWDOR.

THE family of Cawdor, as is well-known, acquired their chief properties, both in Scotland and Wales, through marriage with heiresses.

John Campbell, writer of the letter after given, who used the old spelling of "Calder," had married Mary Pryce, the last of these heiresses, and, being much in debt, mostly inherited, sold not only the grand estates of Islay and Muckairn, but had the mind of selling his northern estates also. This John Campbell of Calder was succeeded by his grandson, also called John, who, long in the House of Commons, was raised to the Peerage by the title of Baron Cawdor in 1796.

A curious circumstance in connection with the courtship and marriage of the first Lord Cawdor, who, in his choice, did not follow the example of at least three of his predecessors, is given in *Anecdotes, Reports, Truths, and Falsities for the year* 1788. *Passages from the Diary of Lord Robert Seymour.* Lord Robert, who was born in 1748 and died in 1831, being at one time member for Carmarthenshire, had good opportunities of knowing the circumstances connected with the following anecdote :—" 1788, May. Lady Caroline Howard married to Mr. Campbell. His acquaintance with Lady C. arose from waiting in Grosvenor Place one morning for a sale beginning at Tattersall's. Walking up and down in the street, he saw the beautiful Lady C. at the window. In vain Mr. T. sent him word that the sale was begun ;

Mr. C. would not desist walking still in the street to gratify himself in looking at the beautiful Lady C. He enquired of Mr. Tattersall the name of the lady whose beauty had made so deep an impression on him. Mr. T. informed him that she was Lord Carlisle's daughter —a very poor and distressed nobleman. This encouraging Mr. C. in the hopes of his addresses being accepted, he prevailed upon a friend to introduce him next day, and very soon after his acquaintance he offered a carte blanche to Lord Carlisle, who desired £500 pin money, and a jointure of £2000, the match to take place very soon. Mr. C. is a descendant of the famous house of Cordor (sic), his estate in Wales being very considerable."

This was an apparently real case of "love at first sight' on the part of the gentleman.

Before parting with Lord Robert, I extract a paragraph regarding the Prince of Wales and the Countess, afterwards Duchess, of Sutherland.—" 20th March, 1788.— The Prince of Wales has taken such a violent antipathy to the amiable Lady Sutherland, that he takes every opportunity of affronting her, which he did so effectually last week, after supper at Cumberland House, that she fainted in her chair. The Duchess (of Cumberland) had the effrontery to laugh at what he said."

Follows the letter referred to, in as fine hand-writing as could be wished, flowing, but large and distinct :—

> Sir,—I believe I could not do anything more agreeable to you than sending your son, Hugh, a factory to manage my Scots estate. I had a long tryal of his integrity here, and I believe I could hardly have found one in your country who understood country business so well as he does. I suppose you will judge it proper to give him possession of the Mesnes of Calder immediately. I am sure he will put you to no inconvenience. My humble service waits on your fireside, and I am, sir, your very humble servant and nephew,
>
> (Signed)   J. CAMPBELL.
>
> Stackpole, Sept. 15th, 1734.
>
> Addressed—" To Sr. Archibald Campbell at Calder, near Nairne, by Edinburgh. London. Free J. Campbell."

No. CXX. ANNO 1735.
JOHN POLSON, ADVOCATE, LATE OF KINMYLIES.

THE family of Polsons were numerous and influential in Inverness during the seventeenth century. They possessed burgage property largely, and one of them acquired a quarter of Merkinch. They came originally from the north, where the name is still common. A gentleman interested in the name gave me a table showing that they had a great hold in Jamaica in the last half of the eighteenth and beginning of this century. When the Frasers of Kinnairies were descending in the scale, the Polsons were in the ascendant, and their rise culminated with the purchase of the western portion of the Barony of Kinmylies, and what is now termed Kinmylies. This occurred about 1685, David Polson, who long held the position of Sheriff-Depute of Inverness, being the purchaser. But he either had not sufficient means, or ran very shortly into debt. Between 1700 and 1710 debt accumulated fast, and at his death, leaving a large family, nothing remained but a sale.

Alexander Fraser of Fairfield, who had married Inverallochy's sister, had incurred the high displeasure of Lord Lovat, as may be seen by his letter to Inverallochy saying that were it not for his lordship, the clan would have cut him off. Fairfield was in a worse pecuniary position than Sheriff Polson. He was foolish enough to purchase Kinmylies, but had to sell it shortly to the army agent, Ross. From Ross it was purchased by Alexander Baillie of Dochfour, and is still the property of Baillie of Dochfour.

Mr. John Polson, younger of Kinmylies, became an advocate, and for years he was engaged in realising his father's scattered property.

Having sold a portion to Mr. Duncan Fraser, merchant

in Inverness, brother to Simon Fraser, first of Ness Castle, he addressed the following letter to Mr. Robert Scheviz of Muirtown :—

Sir,—Having sold my claim upon the tenements in Inverness, and salmond fishing belonging to Alexander Maclean, to Duncan Fraser, merchant in Inverness, and Alexander Maclean having wrote me that he has likewise sold his right to said Duncan Fraser, this serves to intreat you will deliver Mr. Fraser all writings whatsomever concerning those subjects now in your hands. Dear sir, your most obedient humble servant,
(Signed) JON. POLSON,
Edinburgh, January 20th, 1735.

Folded up with Mr. Polson's letter is the following one from Alexander Maclean, brother to Dochgarroch, who possessed the subjects through his wife.

Dear Sir,—You will please give all the papers in your custody, relating to Kinmylies' claim against me, to Duncan Fraser, merchant in Inverness. I mean the rights or other papers upon that heritage disponed to Duncan Fraser by me. With my respects is all from, dear sir, your most obliged humble servant,
(Signed) ALEX. MACLEANE.
Inverness, 22 Sept., 1735.

Both letters are addressed to Robert Scheviz of Muirtown. Scheviz of Muirtown was witness against Lord Lovat, and his Lordship in his defence made very free with his character and mean fortune.

No. CXXI. ANNO 1736.

SIMON LORD LOVAT.

LORD LOVAT'S letters never fail in interest. Whether it be "High Politics," or the most trifling personal concerns, the style is perfect. From the letter after given, I gather that he had apartments in Edinburgh from a Mrs Macleod, and objected to certain charges. In any case, he inveighs handsomely, calling her "jade" and "witch," the whole Clan Macleod apparently falling within his censure.

It can be imagined that one who knew so well how to put man against man, also knew how to invoke clan feuds and antipathies.

In this case, and at this time, he was all against the Macleods, and, as is known, had long been in strict alliance with the Grants. The day was not far off, however, when the Macleods were everything, when he erected a most complimentary memorial in Kilmorie of Duirinish, supported heartily and successfully Macleod's candidature for the county representation, and might be heard in his convivial moods singing "ow ow uileag iad," and other songs, the reverse of complimentary to the Strathspey Grants.

Lord Lovat met his fate with the greatest fortitude, and very properly was anxious as to his reputation.

As to the former he writes as follows to his agent, Mr. William Fraser, under date "Friday evening, 8 o'clock, 8 Apl, '47. Most dear Cousin—The fatal hour is come at last. The Major was here within this half hour, and told me that he was sorry to be the messenger of bad news—that he had orders to tell me that the dead warrant was signed against me, and that I am to be executed on Thursday next. I do assure you, dear William, that it does not at all discompose me."

As to the second point, I give the following letter from a copy in my possession, not knowing whether it may not have been already published. The memoirs were not published until 1797, and must be accepted as the authentic exposition of Lord Lovat's own views. No indication to this effect is given on the title page or in the preface, but it is known that the Memoirs were issued by the Honourable Archibald Fraser of Lovat. The letter runs thus:—

Dear Cousin William,—I wrote a letter in September or October last to Mr. Donald Fraser, minister, desiring him to deliver up to you my memoirs, now in his keeping in trust for my behoof. But, as he has not complied with my said letter, I by these authorise you of new to call for my memoirs, and in case he refuse to deliver them up to you, to be disposed of as directed this day by me in presence of my cousin, Mr. James Fraser, apothecary, in Craven Street, and witness to this letter; you are to take such steps for recovering my said memoirs as you shall be advised. But I hope Mr. Fraser will prevent you any trouble on that head by comply with this my request, and deliver you my memoirs. I am, dear William, your affectionate, humble servant,

(Signed)   LOVAT.

Tower of London, 4 April, 1747.   James Fraser, witness.

Lord Lovat at the trial denied that the patent of a Dukedom had been sent him, or ever existed.

Follows the letter referred to, the address being wanting :—

Dear Cousin Thom,—I received your letter by the last post, and I give you my sincere and hearty thanks for your care of my affairs at Edinburgh. I find that Thomas Brodie is very often out of town, and that it is very unsafe for me to trust my letters under his cover; I therefore beg that you may excuse the trouble that I give you to send them under yours, till I have the pleasure to see you, because (Lewie) Houston is likewise very often out of town, and you are the only person that stays constantly in the town of my friends, and one that I can entirely trust, and I will endeavour to have a grateful sense of your services.

As to that old witch, Mrs. Macleod, I do assure you that she will never make so much of it as you offered to her, for, though I was at Edinburgh to-morrow, I will not give her one single farthing more at the solicitation of any Macleod at Edinburgh, but since she is a clamorous old jade, I rather you should agree with her than otherwise.

I send the bearer who was there before, Simon William Oig's son, for my cloathing to Mr. Waugh; I have written to Lewie Houston to do me the favour to see them packed up, but in case he be not in town, I hope you will take that trouble, and great care must be taken that the horse's back be not spoiled, for he cost me 20 pounds sterling, and what I have sent for of clothing, will be but a light burden for him. I would not for the value of the clothing hurt him; I beg you deliver out of your own hand my letters, because they carry essential business for Mr. Drummond and the Laird of Luss, as well as to Mr. Macfarlan and Mr. Brodie, about my law affairs, and be so good as to send me their answers. If Captain Fraser be in town, I entreat you will give him my most humble service, and tell him that I will write to him fully by the next. I intend,

God willing, to go to my Company in nine or ten days, and I hope to be at Edinburgh towards the last days of this month. I will send you an express from Taymouth, to intreat of you to take some lodgings for me, but you will hear from me first by the post, and I ever am, very affectionately, dear cousin, your most obdt. humble servant,

(Signed)   LOVAT.
Beaufort, 7th June, 1736.

No. CXXII. ANNO 1737.
JOHN MACKINTOSH OF THE HOLME FAMILY.

THE respectable family of Holme are the second oldest heritors in the parish of Inverness, being an offshoot of Kyllachie, dating from about 1610—that of Mackintosh, of Essich, dating from 1568.

John Mackintosh—a prudent, careful man—lived during the first half of last century, having married Elizabeth Baillie of the Dunain family.

His eldest son and successor, William Mackintosh, was for some time a writer in Edinburgh; and a younger son (John), the writer of the annexed letter, finding no opening at Inverness, joined the large band from the Highlands, under General Oglethorpe, which sailed for the recently-formed State of Georgia. To help him in starting in the New World, his relative, Mr. John Mackintosh, father of Provost John Mackintosh, assisted him, three years being the period within which it was thought the money could be repaid.

This document was thereupon granted :—

Inverness, 8th October, 1735.
Sir,—Three year after this date pay to me, John Mackintosh, senior, merchant in Inverness, or order at my shop six pounds fourteen shillings sterlin money value given you by
(Signed)   JO : MACKINTOSH, Senr.
To John Mackintosh, son to John Mackintosh of Holm.
Accepts.   (Signed)   JOHN MACKINTOSH.

The young emigrant did not forget his benefactor

he seems to have thriven, and does not forget to ask after old friends and relatives. The William and Angus, Lynvuilg's sons, referred to in the letter annexed, were the founders of the families of Ballifeary and Drummond. Follows the letter referred to:—

Dear Cos.,—I am not forgetful of the many favours you conferred upon me, particularly your act of benevolence at my departure from your place, and hopes, through Divine assistance, to be in a condition of making you an acknowledgment. I am ready to consign your money as you advise. I refer you to Sandy for description of this part of the world, and hopes you will use your interest with his father, for servants and necessaries, since he is resolved to settle here. You will remember my kind service to your wife, your uncle Angus, and William and Angus, Lynvuilg's sons.—Dear sir, your affect. cousin to serve you while
(Signed) JOHN MACKINTOSH.
Darien, in Georgia, 3rd December, 1737.

No. CXXIII. Anno. 1738.
MRS. SYBILLA ROBERTSON, CARIE.

THE annexed curious letter from a lady in regard to her husband, is interesting. I am uncertain as to her identity. The place from whence it is written (Carie) may mean either the place of that name in Glencannich, long in desuetude, but which was of old tenanted by people of good standing, or the jointure house in Perthshire of the Dowagers of Strowan, the last word in the P.S. being indistinct. The letter is addressed to "Mr. John Taylor att Inverness," but I forget how it came into my possession. It shows that, as early as the year 1738, tea was in common use in the north among the better classes. The name Sybilla was not uncommon among the ladies of the Inshes family after the time of Sybilla Mackenzie, second wife of William Robertson of Inshes. It is also found among the Barbours of Aldourie:—

Carie, January 31st, 1738.
Dear Sir,—This is to let you know that we are going to renew

our correspondence again. I really thought that you and others would have satisfied my creditors in what you promised them, but if there has been anything wanting on our side to make it good, it shall be so no more. In the meantime, I hope you'll be so kind as to get for my husband a suit of black clothes, not too coarse nor too fine, and what things he may want for his mother, which need not be extravagant, since she does not dress. Give my service to my dear cousin, your wife, and tell her I think myself much obliged to her for the care she had for my husband when last at her house, and I hope she will have the same just now ; make him take his tea every morning, and broth for his dinner, for drinking does not agree with him. Please make offer of my service to her, and believe me to be, dear sir, your most humble servant,

(Signed)   SYBILLA ROBERTSON.

P.S.—When you or any other friend writes to me, direct for Mrs. Robertson at Camgran (?).

No. CXXIV. Anno 1739.

SHAW MACKINTOSH, SIXTH OF BORLUM.

IN the distressed state of the family of Borlum, after the attainder of Brigadier Mackintosh in 1716, and the death of the elder Borlum at a great age in 1717, the Brigadier's eldest son, Lachlan, fifth of Borlum, found it necessary, when quite a youth, to go abroad and seek his fortune. He landed in New England, and was hospitably entertained and put in the way of business as a mariner, by his grand uncle, Henry, younger son of the second Borlum, who had been long in the New World, and established a high position in Rhode Island. In the Registers of Bristol City, in Rhode Island, under date 15th August, 1721, there is proclaimed an intention of marriage 'twixt Mr. Lachlan Mackintosh, of North Britain, but then of Bristol, and Mrs. Elizabeth Mackintosh of that town. Also, that Elizabeth, daughter to Lachlan Mackintosh and Elizabeth his wife, and grand-daughter to Colonel Henry Mackintosh, was born 13th September, 1722, and Mary Mackintosh, daughter to Lachlan

Mackintosh and Elizabeth his wife, and grand-daughter to Colonel Henry Mackintosh, was born 22nd August, 1723. In the month of June, 1723, Lachlan Mackintosh of Borlum was "cast away at sea" on a voyage home to Bristol two months before his youngest daughter, Mary, was born.

The old Borlum, no doubt in concert with his eldest son, Brigadier Mackintosh, who must have even then been preparing for the rising, had executed, in the month of January, 1715, a disposition of Borlum in favour of his grandson, the before-mentioned Lachlan, then in minority. The destination was to heirs male, and accordingly, upon the death of Lachlan, his immediate younger brother, Shaw, succeeded. The Badenoch estates of Raitts and others were not destined to heirs male, so that Shaw, who took possession, had his nieces as probable claimants. Shaw was brought up in a loose way, and was generally found in the revellings and junkettings of the day. He had considerable natural parts and a knowledge of business, as is seen in this letter to his brother-in-law, Mr. Jonathan Forbes, merchant in Inverness, asking to get himself defended from a process at the instance of the minister of Alvie, afterwards of Petty :—

Reatts, 1st Augt., 1739.

Dear Sir,—I got the enclosed summons to-day unsigned—two great informalities ; no subscription, and one false day, the execution of it bearing yesterday. I wrote to Chapman an answer to his letter, to let alone calling it this session. If he does not wait the days of citation, May, and after you give this as defences, if not sustained, which, I am sure, they will, as I offer to prove my allegation, what the summons itself does not, crave a day for me to answer the charge and oblige. Engage a procurator to take my defences if I must go to law. Pray deliver Tam Fraser Gortuleg's letter.—Yours,

(Signed)   SHAW MACKINTOSH.

His character, drawn by no friendly hand a few years before, is annexed. Shaw, who had married Jean Menzies of Woodend, did not go out in the '45, but his Jacobite proclivities are seen in the no doubt profusely highly coloured account of Prince Charles's strength approaching Corryyaraick, conveyed to Cope, who, in consequence, changed his course, and quickened his movements to Inverness.

We now go back to New England, and in the year 1736 find that Lachlan's children must have lost their mother, and were being brought up by a Mrs. Lewis in Boston, no doubt a near connection. Mrs. Lewis was by birth a Miss Palmer, and there was living in the house also her brother, Thomas Palmer, junior, the writer of the letter after given. Shaw Mackintosh, anxious about his right to Raitts, and knowing his nieces were well off in Boston, through their mother and grandfather had resolved to bring them home so as to be under his control. What occurred is graphically told in Mr. Palmer's letter, herewith given. Though the ladies were very young—14 and 13—and only "skweaked" in place of "screamed" when seized, yet Shaw's notion that the youth had matrimonial designs, was correct, as may be seen in the sequel. The ladies did not get Raitts, but their descendants established certain claims, some sixty years later, when the estate was judicially sold.

Follows the letter referred to:—

I had some difficulty as to the word "Kim" in the second line, but it appears that the person addressed was named "Eliakim" Palmer.

Boston, Nov. 30th, 1736.

Dear Kim,—I received yours of the 27th Sept. by Capt. Bennett, and note Mr. Hopkin's bill is accepted, and your observations of the orders in the disposal thereof when received.

As to Mr. Mackintosh, the errand he came upon, was, as you observe, to persuade his nieces to go with him to Scotland. They being very much averse to it, has occassioned a very odd scene in the family, which no doubt you have seen in our Prints of his attempting to carry them away contrary to their inclinations, after a very extraordinary manner which I ought to have acquainted you with ere now, which I hope you will excuse, the particulars of which I shall relate. When he arrived here, he came to Mr. Lewis, without any letters of recommendation to him or properly attested credentials to prove he was related to the said ladies, but was treated by Mr. Lewis as their uncle, and seemed to be very well pleased his nieces were so well situated, but being resolved to prosecute the design of his coming, after a while he began to work upon the ladies' affections, to induce them to go with him by presents and insinuations, and all the sophistry he was master of, which was considerable, which had no effect upon them. He then applied to the Governour, where he met with a very strong repulse; and afterwards he went to work with his lawyers without effect. But was determined to carry them off by force, which he attempted in a very violent manner. He invited Mr. Lewis and his wife and the two ladies to dine with him, and coming home between nine and ten in the evening, he had posted ten or a dozen blood-thirsty men like himself in the pasture, which took up the ladies when he gave the sign, and hurried them away. He then laid aside the polite gentleman, and acted the ruffian, with sword and pistol, which he did to the life, and was resolved to carry them off at the risk of his own life and them that opposed him, as he said upon his examination. I happened to be at home at the time, heard a skweeking, ran out, and followed them, and laid hold of one of the ladies, and endeavoured to rescue her, but was prevented by my receiving a wound in my right arm from Mr. Mackintosh. I immediately went to Mr. Lyde's, and called him to assistance, but it was too late, the boat was put off, and gone down to Nantaskett. I went directly to the Governour, and got a warrant to apprehend him, which I gave to an officer, and went down to Nantaskett with eight or ten men, armed, on board Captain Dunster, bound to London, where we found my gentleman walking the quarter deck at break of day, with sword and pistols, and swore by his Maker nobody should come on board. I told the officer to do his duty, which accordingly he did. He then was obliged to surrender, whom we brought up, together with the young ladies, to the great joy and satisfaction of the whole town. There never happening an affair of this nature in this part of the world before, occassioned the town being in an uproar all night. The people were so incensed against him that, as soon as he came ashore, it being Sunday morning about church time, a considerable number of people being gathered together, the mob laid hold of him, and would have done him justice had not some means been taken to prevent it. He was carried before the Justices, examined, and committed to jail, and was bound over to the next Superior Court to have his trial; but the ladies being afraid he would make a second attempt afterwards, consented to his request that Mr. Lewis should drop his prosecution upon his giving a bond for £2000 with two sureities that he never would molest them again, which he accordingly did, so there was an end to that affair.

He is now going upon another scheme to get them out of Mr. Lewis family, upon the account of my having an opportunity of gaining their affections before they are capable of choosing for themselves. He has petitioned the Judge of Probates, which petition the judge took no notice of, but confirmed Mr. Lewis as guardian to the eldest, she being of age to choose for herself. He has appealed to the Governour and Council, and is to have a hearing this week. It is thought he will have interest at home to get them removed; therefore, I desire you would be industrious to get intelligence some way or other of what he is like to do, and watch his proceedings, if possibly you can, and whether he is likely to come back and when, and write me from time to time as you get intelligence, and in time, that we may act accordingly here. He designs for London, either in Morris or one of the first ships, which you will hear of when he arrives with you. He will be very expeditious, the youngest being of age next August to choose a guardian. If ever he falls in your way, I beg you will take no notice of him, for he has used the family very scrubby, after all the civility shown him here, not only in that villainous attempt, but in saying many scandalous things of Mr. Lewis, and his wife, and I.

It would surprise you to know what provision he made for the ladies' voyage, being nothing but six shifts, four caps, and two homespun petticoats, all ordinary and very much wore, and needle and thread packed up with them, to employ the ladies upon the passage as pastime. This usage of them when on board, twitting them of not minding what he said, after such a manner, as if he designed to return it. What he designed to do with them, the Lord knows, he being next heir to their estates concludes this Topick. My father has now as severe a fit of the gout as he had this twenty year, but is something better. I know no other reason for his alter ng his way of living than my mother's being ill a long time before she died, and not being able to provide for him as usual, he came into it insensibly, and has continued in it ever since. He found no disadvantage by it, for he was as hearty as ever he was in his life before the last fit. He joins with me and sister Lewis in our best respect to all the family. My father desires you would tell my uncle Henry he will answer his letter by some of the next ships.

Sister Lewis was in danger of being carried off by Mackintosh —the fellows taking her up by mistake instead of one of the ladies Your compliance with my request in this long epistle will very much oblige me, and if any charge attends your strict enquiries about the affair, you will please to charge it to account of your affecte. brother and humble servant.

(Signed)   THOMAS PALMER, Junior.

You'll receive handkerchiefs from Capt. Morris you sent to be made up.

Readers may wish to know something further with regard to those mentioned in the foregoing interesting letter. How shocked the Puritans of Boston must have been on that memorable Sunday!

Mary Mackintosh, the youngest of Borlum's daughters, married the foregoing Thomas Palmer, junior, and died 8th October, 1742, in the twentieth year of her age, leaving a son (Thomas, the third Thomas Palmer in succession, a child of two years, who died unmarried. Elizabeth Mackintosh, the eldest, married the Honourable Isaac Royal, of Melford, near Boston. Mr. Royal, in the year 1747, presented to the Church of St. Michael's, Bristol, two silver tankards and an alms basin, which are still in use, and his memory is held in honour. Mr. and Mrs. Royal had two daughters—Mary Mackintosh Royal and Elizabeth Royal. Elizabeth Royal married William Sparhauk, grandson in the female line of the famous Sir William Pepperill, who, after Sir William's death, succeeded to the baronetcy, taking his name and great wealth, the greatest in America, and was the second Sir William Pepperill. Lady Pepperill died at Halifax, 8th October, 1775. Sir William, like his grandfather, was a great Loyalist, and was ultimately deprived by the new Government of all his estates. He retired to England, and had a pension from the English Government. He was much respected, and one of the founders of the British and Foreign Bible Society.

We hear a great deal of boycotting in these days. The system is old. Before the Independence of the States this is how Sir William Pepperill was treated by a resolution passed for York County, at Wells, 16th Nov., 1774 :—"It is therefore resolved that he hath forfeited the confidence and friendship of all true friends of American liberty, and with other pretended counsellors holding their seats in like manner, ought to be detested by all good men ; and it is hereby recommended to the good people of this county that, as soon as the present leases made to any of them by him are expired, they immediately withdraw all connection, commerce, and dealings from him; and that they take no further lease or conveyance of his farms and mills until he shall resign his seat, pretendedly occupied by Mandamus. And, if any person shall remain or become his tenants after the expiration of their present leases, we recommend to the good people of this county, not only to withdraw all connection and commercial intercourse with them, but to treat them in the manner provided by the third resolve of this Congress." Thus no family in America suffered so severely for their loyalty as the descendants of Brigadier Mackintosh, against whom an act of attainder still remains a blot on the Statute-book.

Sir William's only son (William) died without issue. Of his three daughters, the eldest, Elizabeth Royal Pepperill, married the Rev. Henry Hutton, and there are numerous descendants; the second, Mary Hirst Mackintosh Pepperill, married Mr. Congreve, and died without issue. Harriott, the third, married Sir Charles Thomas Palmer of Wanlip Hall, Leicestershire, Baronet, of whom there are many descendants, including the present Baronet. The Huttons and Palmers are the co-heirs of line of Borlum.

No. CXXV. ANNO 1740.

EWAN MACPHERSON OF CLUNY, THE YOUNGER.

THE letter after given refers to a curious matter, fully detailed in the memorial for Macpherson of Banchor, also quoted. The legal proceedings were referred to arbitration, Mr. Hugh Campbell of Clunes being appointed on the part of Banchor, and Robert Urquhart of Burdsyards, on the part of the travelling merchant or chapman, Urquhart. The incidents show the manner of transacting business in the middle of last century, and the difficulty of changing a ten pound note. Urquhart's story was that he could not read, and that the note had been tendered to and in the hands of several, in particular, a soldier at Ruthven Barracks, and it is very likely that he was the real culprit, as it would not suit one in the position of Urquhart, dependent to a great extent on his character, to indulge in so dangerous a game. As late as 1749 there were soldiers at Ruthven, the names of "Jonathan Collier and Francis Jennings, soldiers in General Barrel's Regiment, lying at Ruthven," being attached to a legal document of date 24th July, in that year.

Young Cluny was attainted under the name of "Evan," but he maintained that his name was "Ewan." The letter after given distinctly bears to be signed "Ev:," and I have looked at other signatures, all identical, showing the letter "v" small, with two dots after, all enclosed in a flourish surrounding the letter E. Cluny acted most energetically in this affair for his friend and clansman; indeed, if the affair were his own, he could not have been more active. He had a good knowledge of business, as is shown by his letters, and did not disdain to add to his income by acting as Captain of a watch. The following shows the business way those matters were conducted :—

Forres, June 15th, 1745.

Received from Sir Robert Gordon of Gordonstoun, the sum of £4 16s. 3d. sterling, and that as his whole proportion of the watch money paid to Ewen Macpherson of Cluny, at the rate of half-a-crown out of the hundred pound of his valued rent to me.

(Signed)   JOHN DUFF, Junr.

Follows the memorial referred to :—

Memorial anent the Grounds of Process 'twixt John Macpherson of Banchor and James Urquhart, merchant.

Banchor was bound to pay 12 pounds sterling, or thereby, to John Mackintosh of Lynwilge at the term of Martinmas, 1738, for a certain subject delivered to him by the said John Mackintosh to that availe sometime in September preceding, of which same Banchor agreed to give five pounds at making of the bargain preadvance, if he had but a ten-pound note then in his custody changed; but, having done his utmost, could not get that done in the country. Notwithstanding that, Lynwilge still pressed for the five pounds; at last Lynwilge, immediately after a September market in Ruthven, came to Banchor's house, and, presuming that the ten-pound note might be changed at Ruthven the day after the market, prevailed with Banchor to go there for that purpose. But, having employed a young gentleman merchant there to get account if the note could be changed in the town or by the officers residing in that place, found it could not be got done; upon which Banchor fell in with this Urquhart a travelling chapman who told him he could not do it himself, but would search once more town and barracks in order to get it done.

When Banchor, he, the former young man, and several others, and Lynwilge particularly, went into a public-house in Ruthven, and in presence of the whole company Banchor took the ten-pound note out of his pocket-book, read it in their audience, as did also Lynwilge, and Banchor delivered it in their presence to Urquhart, who immediately went out with it, in order to change, but, returning in less than one half-hour, told it had defied him, and gave a note folded up to Banchor, which he, suspecting no fraud, without looking to, put up in his pocket-book, where it remained in his pocket for upwards of a month, till that Banchor had occasion to be paying money to a certain gentleman in presence of other two men, and taking out his pocket-book gave the note as a ten-pound one to the gentleman, upon receipt, opened and looked at, and said, "Sir, you have only given me a five-pound note, in place of the ten," which, to his surprise upon looking at it, Banchor found to be fact, nor was it a wonder, as he had no other note in his possession, but (as he was sure) the ten-pound one.

No doubt he lost his temper partly at the time about the thing; but that minute condescended upon Urquhart as the only person had opportunity to play the trick, having never as much as looked to, or handled, his note, since the time he met with him. Banchor was silent about it for a considerable time thereafter, till that Urquhart chanced to come to the country, and then insisted for a warrant from the Bailie of the regality of seizing of his person, unless he found bail to answer before him, against a certain day, for what Banchor had to say against him, and his reason for so doing was that this chapman had no settled place of residence, whereout of he might be cited to any judicator. Urquhart in the Bailie's presence, the warrant not obtained, voluntarily agreed to compear before him against a court day at Ruthven, and found bail for that effect. He was allowed the day suited his conveniency best, whether short or long, and he chose a very short day, about eight or ten days after that, against which time, indeed, the spark had an advocation and tabled it.

It lay over thus to last November; then he insisted in a process of injuries and large damages, sustained through aledged confinement, before the Lords, against Banchor. He libels maltreatment and several other stories quite false in fact. The Lord-Ordinary, after some pleading on both sides, has ordained both parties to prove the several facts condescended on, but refused a commission to examine witnesses in the country.

Follows the letter from Cluny the younger to Mr. Hugh Campbell :—

Dear Cousine,—I assure you I'm much surprised how this sudden appointment came about, unless it was contrived, 'twixt Urquhart and his advisers, that there should be a march stollen on Banchor, seeing the fellow as well as several others, that take a particular concern in his affairs, known well, that Banchor could not attend this diet, upon account of his being in the South. I write you these not knowing but you'll judge it necessary to send my other letter to Burdsyairds, seconded strongly by one from yourself. I hope the plan will be altered upon Mr. Forbes his account, and pitching on the time, will be suspended till you hear from me after Banchor's arrival home, you'll desire Burdsyairds acquaint Achynany of what I have wrote; meantime have sent the submission that you may take the trouble of accepting it, as also desire Birdsyairds do the same; pray acquaint Birdsyairds not to detain the express any time.—I am, with my compliments to Mrs. Jean, and my good friend Mr. Duncan, dear cousine, yours most affectionately, while
(Signed)   Ev. MACPHERSON.
Cluny, 3rd July, ten at night.

P.S.—The express is appointed come to Calder with Birdsyairds return.

Addressed—"To Mr. Hugh Campbell, factor to the Laird of Calder."

No. CXXVI. Anno 1741.
JOHN BAILLIE OF LEYS, CLERK TO THE SIGNET.

WILLIAM BAILLIE, Commissary of Inverness, grandson of Dunain, acquired the lands of Mid Leys about the end of the seventeenth century, and founded the family of Leys. His son, John Baillie, who became a Clerk to the Signet, with an extensive business, was the writer of the letter after given. He was succeeded by his son, Dr. George Baillie. Colonel John Baillie, some time member of Parliament for the Inverness Burghs, younger son of George, ultimately became possessor of Leys and other lands. Leys Castle is situated on an eminence, whereon there formerly existed a keep or stronghold, going back to the time when the three divisions, Wester, Mid, and Easter Leys, formed part of the Barony of Dalcross and Lordship of Lovat.

The letter, addressed to Mr. John Mackintosh, merchant, and then town treasurer of Inverness, is interesting, inasmuch as it brings before us the name of William Maitland, a painstaking and industrious historian. His works were "The History of Edinburgh from its foundation to the present time, also the ancient and present state of Leith, and a perambulation of diverse miles round the City. Edinburgh, 1753." "The History and Antiquities of Scotland, from the earliest account of time to the death of James the First, Anno 1437. And from that period to the accession of James VI. to the Crown of England, Anno 1603, by another hand. London, 1757." (This is the work referred to in the letter.) "The History of London from its foundation to the present time, continued to the year 1772," By the Rev. John Entick, M.A., London, 1772.

Follows the letter referred to :—

Edinburgh, 30th June, 1741.

Sir,—I sent you last post a receipe for the missive dues of your town, and now, according to my promise, I return you the town's eques, by which the £170 Scots remitted is exhausted and some shillings over, these eques having cost, 'twixt burrow mails and office dues, £5 5s. 8d., and the missive dues, you know, come to £9 1s. 0d. There is this night gone to the Burrows in the Moray Firth a protection for all the men to be employed in the herring fishing, as there is to the Firths of Fife and Clyde; so that I hope, if it please God to send the fishing, they shall be protected ;

and the getting this from the Admiralty has been one of the best acts of the Convention of Burrows. I forgot to acquaint the Magistrates that there is a gentleman, one Wm. Maitland, of approved reputation in what he undertakes, who has petitioned the Burrows for what will be very honourable for themselves, to have their assistance only in giving an account of the foundation, antiquities, and constitution of the several Burrows in Scotland, and which he is to apply for by proper queries to be sent. I reckon it my duty to acquaint you, as I would not trouble the Magistrates with much writing, to entreat that they would be pleased to look into their oldest charters, and make exact copies of them to set forth their own antiquity, etc., when the gentleman demands it, it having been the general opinion of the whole Burrows that he should be so assisted.—I am, sir, your most humble servant,

JON. BAILLIE.

Addressed—"To Mr. John Mackintosh, Town Treasurer of Inverness."

No. CXXVII. ANNO 1742.

PROVOST HOSSACK OF INVERNESS.

FOR many years prior, and some years after the battle of Culloden, the name of Provost Hossack stands out conspicuously in connection with the town of Inverness and the surrounding districts. He was head of the great mercantile firm of John Hossack & Company, and his business, and it may be said his legal habits and social position, are well brought out in the letter after quoted, which has been selected from numerous others of his still extant. Provost Hossack's father (Thomas) was in business in Inverness, as a merchant, prior to 1685, for in that year he gets decree of adjudication of a rood of land in Bridge Street, Inverness, against James Forbes, lawful son to the deceased, Alexander Forbes, some time merchant in the Burgh. Thomas Hossack was also possessor of, and transmitted to his son, the lands (where now the *Courier* Office stands) and old Bank of Scotland Buildings. The description, from an old writ, of these, as being at one time the Burgh School, may he quoted—"All and haill *ane* particale of burgh bigged land, with the old house built thereupon called the School House, and timber house built thereafter therein, with cellars, lofts, chambers, close before and behind, parts and pendicles of the same lying within the Burgh of Inverness, and sheriffdom of same, near the water of Ness, and on the east side of the same, bounded by the lands some time pertaining to the deceased Robert Rose at the east, the said waters of Ness at west, the lands some time pertaining to John Forbes, and now to those dividing right from him at the south, and the common vennel of old, called the School Vennel, at the north parts respective."

When the Bank of Scotland came to be at the foot, and afterwards the National Bank at the top of the School Vennel, the name of Bank Lane took its rise. The street called Fraser Street, leading to the river, was previously described as a common vennel, its present name being comparatively modern.

Provost Hossack was also proprietor of the lands on which the National Bank stands. The Provost left two daughters. One married the Rev. Murdoch Mackenzie, of Inverness, of excellent memory, to whom, reserving his liferent, he disponed his Bridge Street property in the year 1749. The other (Barbara) was married to Provost Phineas Mackintosh of Drummond, but left no issue. There are numerous descendants of Mrs. Mackenzie, amongst others the family of the late Hugh Miller, now possessors of the old house of Drummond, and some lands adjoining.

The Provost's letter is interesting, and refers to several people of note—President Forbes, Lord Lovat, the Laird and Lady Mackintosh, and the Robertsons of Inshes.

Regarding Lord Lovat, it is matter of tradition that he was ostentatious in his equipages; and the story goes that it being confined to royalty to drive eight horses, Simon occasionally drove seven horses and a bullock, to put himself in numbers on an equality with royalty, without breaking the law. In any case, he drove Lady Mackintosh from and into the town with six horses, and even this appeared to be somewhat unusual, as it attracted the special attention of the douce and steady-going Provost.

Lady Mackintosh, after her husband's death, lived at Leith, and is interred in North Leith church-yard, where the family of Invercauld had a burial place.

Follows the letter referred to :—

Inverness, 9th January, 1742.

Dear Sir,—Your favour of the 1st curt. gave me great comfort. May God preserve my Lord-President in good health and spirits for many years, for the comfort of his country. His overseer (Johnson) was buried yesterday; he died of three days' illness.

The spirit of opposition which prevails may produce effects that will influence the affairs of Europe and America. I hope gentlemen who are honoured by their country with great approbation of their conduct will endeavour to preserve the merit of it—a person who halts betwixt sides, has no regard paid him from either.

I send you, enclosed, answers to your queries in the best manner I can at present. I have not seen either of the Inches's; when I do, I will converse upon some of the queries.

I was honoured last night with a visit from the Laird and Lady Mackintosh, otherwise I would have sent by this post to your cousin, Mr. Wm. Forbes, the copy of the rental by which we raised a year's rent, also a current account thereon; you may by next call for them from him, and take such assistance as they can give you.

Your friends here are all well, and remember you frequently in a glass of punch. Dr. Fraser was here with Lady Mackintosh. They had come on the Thursday evening from Lord Lovat's, where they were for three nights. His lordship sent coach and six for them, and returned them to town in that manner, and with a great retinue. All health and happiness to you.—I am, most affectionately.

(Signed)   JOHN HOSSACK.

Addressed—"To Mr. Wm. Forbes, writer, at his House in the Lawn Market, Edinburgh."

No. CXXVIII. Anno 1743.
LADY ANN MACKINTOSH OF MACKINTOSH.

CAPTAIN ENEAS MACKINTOSH OF MACKINTOSH, afterwards Sir Eneas Mackintosh, in announcing to a clansman the death of Lady Anne on the 2nd March, 1784, writes that "this occurred after an illness of five months, she preserving the use of her reason to the last, and dying without a sigh. From your connection with my family, I have taken the earliest opportunity to inform you of this event. You, I, and the whole Clan, have lost in Lady Mackintosh a steady and sincere friend, and I fear it will be difficult to find her like." This tribute by her husband's nephew and successor was not over-rated. · Retaining, as her letters show, a strong natural affection for the House and Clan Farquharson, she, at same time, threw herself, after her marriage, heart and soul into everything tending to the honour and prosperity of Mackintosh, and the haill Clan Chattan. Two letters are given, one, written when, young and in early married life, she was amusing herself at Moyhall, the other in declining years, from Bath, showing her still active in what concerned her late husband's family, and concluding with the statement that she should ever remember Inverness and her friends there with the greatest affection.

Follows the letter referred to :—

Lady Mackintosh's compliments to Lady Dunain. Was glad to hear from Miss Nellie Baillie that Dunain and his lady has kept out pretty well this season. There is two Muscovia ducks at Moyhall. The drake was killed by accident. Miss Baillie says there is a drake and no duck at Dunain. If the drake is sent by the bearer, it will be very obliging, and they shall have a pair in return.

Addressed—" To Lady Dunain."

The other letter, addressed to Provost John Mackintosh, is as follows :—

Bath, June 5th, 1778.

Dear Sir,—It is a great while since I had the pleasure of hearing from you, but I hope you and all your concerns are well, as I had a line from Mrs. Mackintosh, Kyllochy, lately, who said nothing to the contrary. I leave this next week, and goes the way of London for Scotland. As I will be some weeks at Captain Oliver's at Greenwich, has sent you a frank enclosed for that place. Enclosed is a letter for Mr. Andrew Monro, and an order in it for you to pay him six guineas, which his cousin, Miss Monro, wished the favour of me to cause pay him at Inverness, and so I beg you will send Mr. Monro it, out of the money from Dalcromby, when you receive it, which I shall allow him at acquittance.

Mackintosh got a company in the Duke of Gordon's Fencible men. I wrote your brother all about it, and I thought it right to accept of it, but I can be no judge of those matters at such a distance, but wrote his Grace that I left it to be determined by Mr. Lachlan Mackintosh, to consult it with the rest of the name, as Mackintosh was not at home.

News I never write, and, indeed, we have none certain, but what you will see in the public papers. I have the pleasure to tell you that Lady Sinclair is better. They go for Bristol for a few weeks, and after that I hope she will be so well as to return to Scotland. I beg my best compliments to your family, and all my friends in Inverness. I shall ever remember the place and them with the greatest affection, and I am, dear sir, your obedient humble servant,

(Signed)   A. MACKINTOSH.

No. CXXIX. ANNO 1744.

JOHN BAILLIE OF LEYS AND LORD LOVAT.

THE following letter, giving a full account of certain processes betwixt Simon Lord Lovat and his neighbours, The Chisholm and Struy, is interesting in respect of the very distinct references to undue favour or influence upon the Courts of Law.

That the Scottish Tribunals were long corrupt is well

known. In the time of the Stuarts the Kings openly wrote letters in favour of litigants, and at a latter period the undue influence of great nobles, who might have procured the appointment of judges, was frequently exercised. Possibly Lord Lovat might have been boasting of his influences with the Argyll family, and he certainly was never tired of extolling their praises. The Duke of Argyll referred to by Mr. Baillie was Archibald the third, better known as the Earl of Isla, and there can be no doubt Lord Lovat stood high in favour of both the brothers.

Follows the letter referred to :—

Edin., 21st Decr., 1744.

Sir,—I received your letter by this post, and another from The Chisholm, both showing what rejoicings there were at Castledowny upon the victory obtained by my Lord Lovat against you both, which cannot be helped. I am conscious to myself I omitted nothing that could be said or done for you in this cause.

The last letter I sent you I thought would have reached you a week sooner than it did, which was the reason I desired you send an express with the answer, but as you did not get it in time, it was needless to send an express with the answer. But as I would loose no opportunity to serve you all in my power, I would draw a reclaiming bill for you, revised by all the lawyers, and drawn by Mr. Harry Home, which contained some expressions against my Lord's character that the judges took offence at, and desired Mr. Home to amend. The gentleman told the judges that he had no personal quarrel with Lord Lovat, nor did he desire to affront him, on the contrary, he was of my Lord's particular acquaintance. This occasioned a new petition to be drawn and given in for you, of which I send you a copy enclosed, which is appointed to be seen and answered against the third of January.

And now, my dear friend, if any terms of agreement betwixt Lovat and you could be brought about, so as you might get a part of the contents of the bond and your expenses of process, I should be well pleased, and this would be a good time as long as we have any hopes. I dare not mention in a letter what lords were for you or against; in this case you had but 5 of 14 for you. The new Lord Tinwall and Elchies spoke against you. The chief lord, in particular, was for you, and when your new petition came in there was a majority of the lords voted to have it seen and answered, and my Lord Arniston said he was against the judgment given against you, for he was not in the house at the time. This is all I can say in writing. The design of the new summons of reduction, etc., given you all is to bring you to take charters from Lord Lovat as your superior. Please inform me to what purpose your papers were put into my hands, and upon what occasion, that I may look for them, if it was to produce in any process they will be found there, but at present it has escaped my memory.

The expenses of an appeal will be £100 sterling, besides, if yourself or any other were going to London to manage it, the personal charges might come at, I reckon, to £50 more. I am not fit to advise you in this case.

I think you have got hard justice if it stands, yet I am not a man of resolution to press you to appeal. My reason is that I fear the Duke of Argyle will be against you, who has a vast interest in the House of Lords, and this I guess from what I saw here. The letter from my lord to the clan, which Castleleathers gave in to the process, from which we expected good, I fear did us harm, because it conjures the clan to be faithful to the Duke of Argyle and his brother, the present Duke, forever. I know not so good an agent, if you was to appeal, as Castleleathers, if he be able to go to London, as he has an ear, I hear, with the Duke. I will send you my account from first to last when I have time to do it. Meantime, this last brush cost more than twenty guineas.—I am, your cousin and servant,

(Signed) JON. BAILLIE.

Addressed—"To Thomas Fraser of Struie, Esq., by Inverness."

No. CXXX. ANNO 1745.

JOHN, SECOND EARL OF BREADALBANE.

GENERAL STEWART of Garth, writing of the Black Watch, says—" Early in the year 1745, three new companies were raised and added to the regiment. The command of these was given to the gentlemen who recruited the men—the Laird of Mackintosh, Sir Patrick Murray of Ochtertyre, and Campbell of Inverawe. The subalterns were James Farquharson, the younger of Invercauld; John Campbell, the younger of Glenlyon; and Dugald Campbell; and ensigns, Allan Grant, son of Glenmoriston; John Campbell, son of Glenfalloch; and Allan Campbell, son of Barcaldine."

The letter after quoted from Lord Breadalbane to Mackintosh shows the interest taken by the Earl in the two new companies. The old Laird of Glenlyon, who had been out for the Stuarts in 1715, was still living, and retained his attachment to them so strongly that he never forgave his son for joining the Government, and refused to see him in his last illness, in the year 1746. A younger son of Glenlyon, Archibald, was out in 1745, and escaped. Some years afterwards Archibald took service in Fraser's Highlanders, and was shot through the body at the Battle of Quebec.

The letter, in a very shaky hand, was written from Holyrood Abbey, where, until the present reign, the Breadalbane family had an official residence. And though the year is not given, there is no doubt it was 1745. The "Curse of Glenlyon" is a well-known tale.

Follows the letter referred to :—

Abbey, Edr., 5th March, 1745.

Cousin,—Having this opportunity of the bearer, the young Laird of Glenlyon, a Lieutenant in the new-raised Highland Companies, and Allan Campbell, a son of Barcaldine, an Ensign in them, I congratulate and wish you joy of having a Highland Company. No family in the Highlands more proper; your interest in Lochaber and about Inverness making it so. I also wish you joy of your marriage, so that the old Clan Chattan may be united in you, which I have seen in your grandfather's time. The bearer can tell you Lord Sempill's new instructions, and I recommend these gentlemen to your care, and I wish your family well, and am, sir, your faithful cousin and servant,

(Signed)   BREADALBANE.

No. CXXXI. ANNO 1746.

LORD H—— TO HIS SISTER IN FRANCE.
PRINCE CHARLES AND HIS LADY
SUPPORTERS AT INVERNESS.

THERE is just over a hundred years since the death of Prince Charles Edward. Services in his memory in England, on occasion of the centenary of his death, were said to have been forbidden by a high Catholic dignitary. If, by so doing, it was thought or intended that Prince Charlie is, or should be forgotten, never was there a greater mistake. His memory is now, and will continue to be, dear to true Highlanders in all time.

I think this a good time to publish the annexed letter, which, though without date, would be written in March, 1746. In a rare collection of original broadsides, prints of letters, accounts, poems, etc., all in the French language, bearing on the Stuarts, which Mr. Noble managed to secure for me, there is bound up with other very interesting matter, the letter after given. It bears to be dated from "Kennochan," a locality with which I am unacquainted, the nearest approach to it being Conachan of Glenmoriston. The partisans of the Stuarts were most active in circulating news in France. I should infer that the letter was printed in Paris for distribution in France, Spain, and Italy, in order to keep up the spirits of the party, and evoke support, and I, upon careful consideration, consider the letter fictitious, and invented for the above purposes in Paris. Lord H. refers to Oliphant of Gask, and undoubtedly the writer was well acquainted with what was going on. I give the letter as a great curiosity connected with Inverness; and the translation may, without being strictly literal, be taken as conveying the writer's exact meaning. I shall be glad if any light can be thrown upon the letter:—

Letter from Lord H—— to his sister, Lady ——

You are no doubt aware that our retreat from Stirling was caused by the absence of our brave Highlanders, over 4000 of whom, having taken a considerable spoil in England and at the battle of Falkirk, asked permission to carry it home, promising to return in a fortnight. If this mischance obliged us to withdraw the siege of Stirling, which we had begun before the battle, the Prince Regent was well recompensed for it to-day, by the conquest he made of the hearts of all the northern people of Scotland and the islands who had never seen him before; they came in crowds beseeching him with tears in their eyes to accomplish their deliverance.

His entry into Inverness resembled in some respects that of our Saviour into Jerusalem, the day being Palm Sunday, and the crowds of people who followed crying, "Great Prince, deliver us." Our Highlanders have returned in greater numbers, and more zealous than ever, so that far from our dear Prince's affairs being worse, they were never in a better condition. We are in a country which is inaccessible to the enemy, unless they wish to expose themselves to perish in detail as they have proved each time they tried to penetrate. The whole nation has taken arms to defend their mountains and cliffs; the women of this part of Scotland, who dress so like men one can hardly distinguish them, have formed a company of 112 women, of whom the eldest is not over forty. This troop of modern Amazons is led by a girl between 27 and 30, who has plenty of spirit and sufficient beauty to attract an honest man; her secretary is a girl about 25 years of age, apparently her sister, to whom she dictates letters, giving orders and receiving visits the while. She presented herself at the head of her company to the Prince with a military appearance that many of our officers have not. I declare had I not been informed they were women, I should have been deceived. They wear a cap instead of the head dress, and are dressed something liks a running footman, except that the petticoat is longer, and they wear a half riding hood which comes down to the knees, instead of a cloak. They are armed with axes and swords, only fifty (those who are at the head) having guns and bayonettes. The heroine made a speech to the Prince, which was remarkable, and shows her to be an educated girl. This is the translation given me by the Chevalier de Gask to send you:—

"Illustrious Prince, the wisdom and moderation which constitutes great men, accompanied by the valour which makes them heroes, causes us to recognise you to-day as our deliverer and king. In our deserted state we have for a long time vainly wished to see our legitimate kings again placed on the most ancient throne in Europe, formerly occupied by Fergus, to the time of Alexander. The Elector of Hanover, under malign influences, has shut out light and tied our arms and our tongues; but God, who punishes all sin, has put an end to this cruel slavery. This sin of our fathers must be expiated, after a certain time, as shown in the decree of His mercies. Our punishment is no doubt at an end, since God has given us your arm to deliver us. Like another of Ismel's judges, it has been reserved for you to effect this work. What happiness for us to add to our love a brilliant reward; we have never deserved your kindness. Victim of our infidelity, you are yet anxious to be the restorer; generous in all respects, virtuous beauty will no longer fear to appear in our towns; instead of being an attraction to licentiousness, it will serve as an ornament to decency and virtue. Under your wise and virtuous reign, our feeble sex will be honoured and respected like our neighbours. It is with these hopes that we have taken up arms to advance your reign, for your glory and our own happiness These arms, which, as you see, rust has spared, will never be laid down by us until we have crowned you in one of our churches, in default of the celebrated stone carried away by Edward I.

"The whole of my company declare they will never forsake you, but defend you under the greatest dangers, and shame those men who, born your subjects, serve against you with that cruel prince who has threatened (condemnè) your life. For ourselves, illustrious Prince, we have no engagement other than to serve you. Men are nothing to us; we are free and at your service from this moment, persuaded that God will protect you whom he has sent to be re-established on the ancient throne of your fathers. Our wishes will be more than accomplished if we can show by their effects how deeply we are attached to you."

After this speech the heroine approached the Prince, who made a movement to embrace her, but this noble girl threw herself on her knees and kissed his hand, despite the Prince's resistance and the promptitude with which he raised her up. She has twice supped with the Prince, soberly, drinking no wine. Except when at the head of her company, she has not a military air; on the contrary she is a sweet, modest-looking girl, who exercises great regularity. She is tall and well made, and has a very pretty hand. She does not at all resemble the French beauties, who cover their pale cheeks with rouge; her complexion, though somewhat dark, is clear and rosy, and to nature alone she owes her charms. She speaks her own language with great facility, and even Latin, from which she pertinently quotes passages. Her origin is not as yet known, and all the company are very reserved on that subject. She has great influence over them all, which she well deserves, judging by the attention and care she takes of each military girl. Their standard is round and plaited, and about the size of a parasol. It is made of pale blue linen, on which is embroidered in the vulgar tongue these words, "For the deliverance of Scotland." It shuts up like a fan when there is much wind.

The example shown by this girl has made a great impression in the towns and country. In the West of Scotland the highest ladies declare themselves openly in favour of the Prince; they feel themselves justified in so doing in consequence of the bad treatment shown by the Hanoverians to their sex (even those of the highest rank) in the Edinburgh prisons. Four have come forward as a reproach to their husbands, who are dragging their chains in the enemy's army, to join the Prince with arms and baggage ; three of these ladies have orderd out their vassals themselves, and have each formed a company consisting of 130 men, half Highlanders ; they have officers to lead and discipline them. The Prince received them with every mark of consideration and respect ; they assured him that all the Scottish ladies were determined to follow their example, and that many of the English were not far from doing likewise, several of these having assured them that though they were not free to prove their attachment and zeal by coming forward, they would club together to furnish supplies. I am not at all surprised at this attempt on the part of the English ladies, for independently of the interest they take in the restoration of the Royal House of Stuart, for whom they have always declared themselves partisans, even under the tyranny of Cromwell, they are treated in London with contempt. The King of Rome's son has gauged their heart by his power believing their taste to be more sensible than delicate, which, to the fair sex, is an unpardonable crime. They will exercise their vengeance, and we shall await the result. All is fair in war ; provided they furnish us with money they may amuse themselves.

Our successes continue. We have destroyed or dispersed all the Argyll militia, 200 of the men having come over to us. Within the last month we have defeated ten detachments, taken nearly 1200 prisoners, hardly a day passes that we do not gain some victory.

Since the taking of Inverness and Fort-George, which we have overthrown, to show to the nation we are trying to deliver it, we have taken possession of Fort-Augustus, which is an important step ; the new fortifications they are adding will make it as formidable as the King of Sardinia's " Brunette " (sic.) After defeating a detachment of Hessians, Lord George Murray on his side has taken Blair-Athole Castle. The people are devoted to the Prince, and he is now levying fresh troops in the country.

Although there will probably be some difficulty, we hope to take possession of Fort-William this week.

I have just heard that our troops have cut in pieces two battalions of Hessians who came with a larger corps to raise the siege ; the Highlanders showed them no quarter ; two pickets of our French troops, who were at the siege, have only spared two out of 300, and are now bringing them into Fort-Augustus as prisoners. In fine, my dear sister, provided France and Spain do not sign a Treaty of Peace and withdraw, we are certain to succeed this year, for all Scotland is resolved to fight against the enemy who have forced them to take up arms. Things have now come to such a pitch that it must be decided in our favour.

Our dear Prince is much better, so am I, so do not be uneasy about us any longer. The misery we endured in the winter is now past, and the patience with which the Prince bore it helped to make it less trying for us, but I will not enter into details lest I bring the tears to your eyes. As the weather improves we shall march towards the enemy, whom we do not in the least fear. I will write later more particularly, and will certainly apprise you of the great events which are now within reach.—I am, etc.*

No. CXXXII. Anno 1747.

LIEUTENANT NORMAN MACLEOD OF RAASAY.

RECRUITING for foreign service was kept up in the Highlands until the British Government saw the error of its ways, and encouraged the people to enter its own forces. So late as 1748, we find recruiting for the service of the States General.

It is recorded that the Laird of Raasay, of the '45, had two sons—John, who did not rise, but who materially assisted Prince Charles in his straits, although the family was strongly Jacobite, and Norman, who is referred to in the annexed letter, and to whom it was addressed, and is noticed as having been an officer in the service of the States General.

The documents remained in the possession of the representatives of Mr. John Mackintosh, merchant in Inverness, who also acted as a banker, or negotiator of bills (home and foreign), and paid the amount to Macleod.

Follows the letter and bill :—

Dear Normand,—Colonel Marjoribanks orders me to acquaint you that you are to draw on Solicitor Daunenberg for five hundred guilders as levy money for the recruits you are ordered to make, and one hundred and twenty guilders more when you embark them, for paying their freight over.

The King's beating order has not yet come down ; how soon

---

* See Appendix No. 3 for further particulars.

it comes shall be sure to send you a copy of it. I shall be glad to hear from you, and wishing you success, ever am, Dr. Normand, your most obedient humble servant,
(Signed)   CHARLES LYON.
Dundee, Dec. 10th, 1747.

Address for me to the care of the Postmaster, Dundee.

Addressed on the back thus—"To Lieut. Normand Macleod, of Marjoribanks' Regiment, care of Mr. John Mackintosh, merchant in Inverness."

Docquetted by Mr. Mackintosh, thus, "Captain Lyon's letter and Lieutenant Macleod's bill for G. 480, January 23rd, 1748."

Follows the bill referred to :—

Rasay, January, 23rd O.S., 1748.

Sir,—At three days' sight, pay this, my second bill, the first of this date not paid, four hundred and eighty guilders, Holland's money, to John Mackintosh, merchant of Inverness, in order value received of him, and place the same to recruiting account for Colonel Marjoribanks' Regiment, without furder advice from, Sir, your most humble servant,
(Signed)   NORMAN MACLEOD.
To Quirinuis Danenberg, Solicitor at The Hague.

Indorsed—"Pay the within contents to Mr. Hugh Inglis, on order value received by
JO : MACKINTOSH."

No. CXXXIII. ANNO 1748.

WILLIAM MACKENZIE OF GRUINARD AND PROHIBITION OF THE HIGHLAND DRESS.

THE annexed letter, addressed to Bailie John Mackintosh, of Inverness, is not of much interest except as regards the references to the Act prohibiting the use of the Highland dress, etc. This atrocious proceeding was not, as is often alleged, a dead letter, but frequently put in force. An unfortunate person named Mackay, from Sutherland, was seized in the streets of Inverness, and brought up before the Court, charged with wearing the Highland dress. His defence was that he had no other, and was not aware of the law. But, without sending for a tailor to refit him, or subscribing to pay for the poor man a pair of breeks, he was sentenced to six months' imprisonment *de plano*—barely a couple of hours elapsing from the apprehension to the sentence.

Such a proviso should never have been passed, or at least a movement for its repeal should instantly have been set about. The blood of Highland soldiers was spilt like water in many a foolish expedition on behalf of the British Crown before the repeal. In one sense the statute did good, because it gave rise to and originated the formation of societies and clubs exclusively connected with the Highlands, the people, and their language, which have tended so much to foster the ancient spirit.

The writer of the letter, member of a respectable Ross-shire family, seems to have taken matters coolly. He had sworn, and was ready to swear again, to the powers that were, and apparently cared for peace merely as it would bring a market for his salmon.

As arms could no longer be carried, swords were at a discount and sent to dealers. In the year 1748, the well-known Dougall Ged, of Edinburgh, writes, in regard to a sword sent him from Inverness for sale—" I have not yet got a chap for it, but have made it up for sale the best way I could get it. There was a piece broke out of the steel, which made it not so easy to mend." It may be gathered that this sword had seen service, and that the poor owner wished to be out of temptation.

Follows the letter referred to :—

Dear Sir,—I shall be glad how soon we may have the certainty of a solid and generall peace, and hopes you'll acquaint me by the first occasion, how soon you'll get an offer for my salmon. I have one last cask at Dingwall, and expects another from you again the end of this month, to pack what fish I have on hand; this year's fishing is not begun with me yet. Att your desire I have forwarded Achiltie's letter. I'll be fond to have from you the Disarming Act for the Highland dress with amendments lately made by Parliamt., how soon it comes to hand. Please give the bearer three yards and a half of good blew cloth for a great coat, with furniture. Do not forget to send good buttons, and as much coarse cloth as will make another to cover me when I attend the fishing, with furniture, two quair of paper, six bottles of white wine, four of sherry, and two of canary. As I'm a qualified man and ready to qualify again if there is occasion for it, I think you are safe enough to send me my small cask full of powder with two pound of small, and as many pounds of large shot as the bearer can conveniently carry.

As we cannot appear in our country habit any more, may send me some swatches of your cloths and fresees, and acquaint the prices, and am, Dr. Sir, your very affectionate humble servt.,

(Signed)   WILL MACKENZIE.

Udrigill, June 10th, 1748.

My wife desires you send her five yards of Inglish Tickin, one pound of hop, and two dram glasses, with two ounces sinamon, and some ribbons, one pound casteell soap.

No. CXXXIV. ANNO 1749.

BAILIE JOHN STEWART, INVERNESS, OF THE FAMILY OF KINCARDINE.

IN Mr. Duncan Stewart's History of the Royal Family of Scotland, published in 1739, he gives the descent of the family of Kincardine through Alexander, Earl of Buchan, whose son, Sir Walter Stewart, first of Kincardine, got a charter of the lands of Kincardine from Robert III. in the tenth year of his reign. The genealogy then is shown from Walter, for succeeding generations, down to John Roy Stewart, who is described the twelfth Baron, and "now an officer in the army." The historian, Shaw, narrates that about the year 1683 John Roy, the last Baron (a silly, ignorant man), was in a manner cheated out of his estate by his brother-in-law, Alexander Mackintosh, called the Sheriff Bàn, who made him sell it to the Marquis of Huntly for a very trifle; and the family, he says, is extinct. It is too true that the Stewarts lost their fine Barony of Kincardine in the manner mentioned; but it is not true that the family is extinct, for many representatives, both male and female, are now living, and some of them have lately come well to the front. It is very gratifying to Highlanders that, in the old burial-place, a fitting memorial of the Barons has now been erected. Mr. Duncan Smith records that Robert, third son of Walter, ninth of the genealogy, had a son, Robert Og Stewart, who was father of Alexander, which Alexander was "father to Bailie Stewart in Inverness." Bailie John Stewart was a prominent merchant in Inverness for many years. He was an ardent Royalist, and a keen Episcopalian. His name will be found among those calling Mr. James Hay as their pastor in the year 1734. He was concerned in the rising of 1715, and unhappily risked almost his whole estate in the '45. The letter after given, written in 1749, shows to what straits he was reduced. It is gratifying to be able to state that his request was not refused. It is a pity we have no information as to the person "in power and place" who so shamefully used the old man. As any information regarding the Barons of Kincardine is not without interest at the present moment, the following memoranda are here given :—

1. On the 12th of November, 1619, John Stewart of Kincardine, for himself and Elspeth his daughter, spouse to Mr. Angus Mackintosh, discharges part of her tocher.

2. On the 5th and 7th of November, 1634, Mr Angus Mackintosh, parson of Kingussie, and Elspeth Stewart, his spouse, grant a renunciation and redemption to John Stewart of Kincardine for 2400 merks Scots, part of the lady's tocher secured over the lands of Clachglassick and others. Among the witnesses are John Shaw in Auchnahatnich, Walter Stewart, son to the Baron of Kincardine, and William Cumming in Kincurdy.

3. On the 5th November, 1634, John Stewart of Kincardine grants bond for 4400 merks to Alex. Cumming, burgess of Inverness.

4. By 1642 John is dead, and proceedings are taken upon the bond for 4400 merks against Duncan Stewart, eldest son and heir of John.

Though not of great extent for a Highland estate, Kincardine, of old Kincairne, and now commonly called Glenmore, is a gem. Mountain, wood, lake, and river abound, but unhappily man, now and for many years, has been estranged from its bounds.

Follows the letter referred to :—

> Dear Sir,—It is great necessity makes me renew my address to you for your help at present. I am in pain and ashamed at the too frequent trouble I give you, but now I must desire you to let me have a little as you can spare, and make out a bill for what you send me now, and the thirtie shillings I formerly gott, payable in a month, again which time I hope I'll be able to pay it thankfully. I should not have needed to trouble you nor anie friend at present, but that a certain gentleman now in power and place has failed to pay me some money justly due me contrar to his oath and promises repeated times; this, and my son, John, his not being yet returned to England that I know, occasions my being greatly straitened. I give my best wishes to my cousin, your spouse, and beg pardon for my too great freedom, and I am, dear sir, your verrie affectionate cousin and obliged servant,
>
> (Signed)   JOHN STEWART.
> Inverness, 6th June, 1749.

Addressed—" Mr. John Mackintosh, merchant in Inverness."

No. CXXXV. Anno 1750.

THE REV. ÆNEAS SAGE OF LOCHCARRON.

MANY stories are related of this worthy clergyman, who, appointed in 1726, lived so uncomfortably with his turbulent and unruly parishioners as to pray the Synod in 1734 for his transportation to a quieter parish, alleging that his life was not safe. The Synod refused the application, but Mr. Sage, agreeing with the people, lived on to 1774, when he died in the 81st year of his age.

After settling with his people his principal troubles appears to have been connected with his heritors, who were very slack in payment, as may be seen from the letter after given. It is not unsatisfactory to think that in 1750, different from these degenerate days, it was chamberlains and factors who were hunted by minions of the law. Upon this matter of non-payment of stipends, I find a letter from Mr. Macaulay of Applecross. As executor of his father, the late minister of Bracadale, he, on 2nd October, 1749, writes from Kishorn giving the most peremptory instructions to take legal steps against Macleod and Mackinnon for large amounts of stipends due. The details are fully contained in the body of the letter, but, as if he had not said enough, he added in a P.S.—" I never got a penny from the laird." Of this Mr. Macaulay it is recorded that he was ordered by the Synod of Glenelg in 1759 "not to preach above the capacity of his hearers." Whether this task was impossible cannot be said, but he died the following year.

Mrs. Sage, who adds the postscript, was Margaret Mackay, daughter of the minister of Lairg, and married in the year 1728.

Follows the letter referred to :—

Dr. Sr.,—I wrote you some months ago that I expected your account, resting by me, would be paid before now. And indeed Fernaig promised payment of our stipends by his letter to myself from beginning of Febry. last. We have been necessitate to pursue Seaforth's factors with captions, but they have found means to escape several times, when search was made for them by messengers, so that we have no prospect to have a shilling till othe means be used to operate our payments.

You'll send me two quires writing paper, and some powder to make ink.—I am, dr. sr., your humble servt.

(Signed)   ÆNEAS SAGE.

Lochcarron, 19th April, 1750.

In Mrs. Sage's hand-writing—

"*P.S.*—Send a double of my account pr. bearer. Send a pd. good hops."

No. CXXXVI. ANNO 1751.
JOHN MACKENZIE OF DELVIN, C.S., AND ROSS OF KINMYLIES.

MR. MACKENZIE OF DELVIN, Clerk of the Signet, seldom or ever, in such of his letters as I have pursued, indulged in depreciatory remarks about people. On the contrary they are always kindly and of a friendly character. The letter after given would indicate that he had no great opinion of Mr. George Ross of Pitkerrie. This person was born about 1700, and was an army agent on an extensive scale in the reign of George II. He made a great fortune, purchasing the greater part of the Barony of Kinmylies, and afterwards, in 1772, the estate of Cromarty. Mr. Ross, very considerably improved the estate of Kinmylies, and planted what is now known as the Leachkin. The lands did not remain long in the family of Ross, having been purchased more than one hundred years ago by Alexander Baillie of Dochfour. Mr. George Ross, whose family of Pitkerrie was an offshot of Balnagown, died without surviving issue. His successors in the army agency, who continued the extensive connection of their predecessor with the North, unfortunately became bankrupt, thereby involving great loss to many in the Highlands and elsewhere.

Follows the letter referred to :—

Dear John,—You are at last like to receive your share of the price of unhappy Fairfield's estate, from the wise and great, and by just consequence, the rich George Ross of Pitkerrie, Esqre.

For this purpose the enclosed disposition in his favour, drawn by his Doer, is sent for your subscription, which do, at the sight of any writer who will fill up the date, and return it to your son or me.

There is a clause in it which is a little unusuall, as it supposes a possibility of their re-demanding from you some part of the sum now to be received in case of a shortcoming; but, as there is little

or rather no hazard in that, it was not worth contesting, and you may safely sign it as it stands. I continue, dear sir, your most humble servant. (Signed) Jo : MACKENZIE.
Edin., 2nd May, 1751.

No. CXXXVII. ANNO 1752.
MRS. NAOMI ROSS OF PITCALNIE.

THE annexed clever letter from Mrs. Ross of Pitcalnie refers to the great case of the Balnagown succession. In the annals of Scotland there is, perhaps, no greater case of fraud and wrong than the unscrupulous but ultimately successful attempts of Lord Ross and General Charles Ross, strangers to the family, to possess themselves of the estates of Balnagown. The leading and moving spirit in the extraordinary exertions made by the heirs male of David Ross of Balnagown to make good their claims to the estates was the writer of the letter after given. The claim of the heir male was founded upon two grounds : 1st, That David Ross, the last of the old Balnagown family, possessed under letters of entail; and 2nd, That he was so weak-minded as to have been susceptible of undue influence. Mrs. Ross was the daughter of John Dunbar of Burgie, and the third wife of Alexander Ross of Pitcalnie. The litigation continued after Alex. Ross's death, and was not ended until a considerable period after the succession of his son Mungo. In 1778 the said Mungo Ross formally claimed to be Earl of Ross; but he was unable from the embarrassments arising from the great litigation connected with the Balnagown estate to pursue the claim. As the families of Pitcalnie and Shandwick are understood to be extinct in the male line, it would probably be very difficult for anyone now to prove himself heir male and chief of the Clan Ross.

Follows the letter referred to :—

Dear Sir,—The enclosed for Dr. Mackenzie forward with all

speed; I leave it open for your perusal, to serve as an apology for not answering your letter sooner; the turn your friend has taken in his health, join'd to the many letters I have had to write relative to his grand affair at this momentous time (for I think I formerly told you the appeal comes on this month to be heard), has so hurried and perplexed me that I could not write you sooner. From what I say to the Doctor about his demand for meal, you'll observe I have none to dispose of, otherwise you two would be preferred to any others, but ready money was so much wanted that we sold all at 15s. per boll—bear and meal; the giving it to you both was the same as the money, had you bespoke it in time; however, your affectionate friend desires me say he has been so much obliged to you at all times that it vexes him you are come too late, therefore if a couple of bolls of meal can do you service he will send it up first boat goes from this out of our own provision, and the balance of your account; if not, let us know, that the full of your account may be sent per next post. I shall soon write Dr. Munro, as advised by you, under your cover. Pitcalnie offers his earnest wishes for your better health, and prosperity to your family, in which I join, being, dear sir, most sincerely yours,

(Signed) NAOMI ROSS.

Arboll, 13th April, 1752.

Keep Pitcalnie's bad state of health to yourself. I still trust he will be preserved.

No. CXXXVIII. ANNO 1753.

ALEXANDER BAILLIE OF DOCHFOUR.

THE present family of Dochfour sprung from that of Dunain, in the time of Alexander Baillie, seventh of Dunain. In the year 1657, David Baillie, designed as second lawful son of Alexander Baillie of Dunain, receives from his father the lands of Easter and Wester Dochcairns. These lands of Dochcairn formed the Wester and larger portion of what is now commonly called Dochfour, lying betwixt the Burns of Dochfour and Lochend. Prior to that date, David Baillie had acquired a redeemable right to Dochfour; having doubtless transacted with his relatives, the old Wadsetters. We find Alexander

Baillie in 1619, and William Baillie his son, in 1634, both described as of Dochfour. It was not until the time of Alexander Baillie, the writer of the letter after given, that the Baillies acquired an irredeemable right from the Gordons to that pendicle of land forming the original Dochfour. The house of Dochfour stands on Easter Dochcairn. The account of the Baillies in the *Landed Gentry* is meagre and incorrect. For instance, it states that David Baillie married Margaret, fourth daughter of Lord Lovat, by whom he had his son and successor, Alexander second of Dochfour. In fact, David's wife's name was Janet, and she and her son, Alexander, are infeft in Dochcairns in 1659. The account goes on to state that Alexander, the second, married in 1709 Hannah, daughter of Reelig, and left four sons, Hugh, third of Dochfour, William of Rosehall, Evan of Abriachan, and David, ignoring the facts that Alexander had been prior to 1689 married to Mary Grant, daughter of Alexander Grant, in Milltown of Ballacastell, and Catherine Ogilvie, by whom he had a son, William. Alexander had also another son, Alexander, by Hannah Fraser, infeft in 1709, and he lived to extreme old age, a witness in 1792, who had been his herd in 1732, describing him as being blind from age. The elder sons of Alexander having predeceased, the succession opened to his son Hugh, who became third of Dochfour. Alexander Baillie, the writer of the letter, and fourth of Dochfour, served an apprenticeship to his uncle, Evan Baillie of Abriachan, a wise and prudent writer, in Inverness. By his own industry and prudence, Alexander laid the foundations of that great and continuous good fortune which has fallen to the Dochfour family. In this he was assisted by his brothers, James and Evan, but the primary cause of fortune arose from the large sum left to Alexander by his illegitimate uncle, Ian Dubh Baillie, long successful in London as an upholsterer.

Dochfour's ideas as to trading 'twixt Inverness and the West Indies were not carried out, but it must be admitted

they look feasible, if French and other foreign privateers did not capture the trading ships. Alexander died, it may be said, broken hearted, in consequence of the death in 1796 of his only son, Colonel J. S. Baillie in the flower of his age. The Colonel's death is commemorated by a primitive monument in the ancient Clach-Uradain.
Follows the letter referred to :—

St. Christopher's, May 26th, 1753.

Dear Sir,—It is now upwards of a twelvemonth since I wrote you last from Nevis, to which I never had any answer, tho' I can honestly say that few people have a greater interest in the welfare of your family than I have by the many kindnesses you have all along shown myself, as well as the regard you have testified for my father's family.

I doubt not but my mother would have acquainted you with the contents of several letters I wrote her since I came to reside in this island, so that I have nothing new to say of myself, nor indeed of anything in this island, as I arrived only last night from Sambeero and the Anegado Sound, where I have been above a month as supercargo of a vessel belonging to Messrs Smith & Lambert of this place, laden with beef, butter, and flour. I have been in the employment of the former of those gentlemen since I left Nevis, and I believe I shall go in a few months to Nevis again to settle in that place as his factor, as he drives on a great trade in that, as well as all the other islands. You'll perhaps think it false, but I can from my own knowledge, assure you that, from 10th November last to the last day of April, he never had less than three vessels discharging at a time, all consigned to him from North America, the Coast of Africa, or the Bay of Honduras. His other expenses may be imagined from his clerk's salaries, which at this time comes to £700 sterling a-year, exclusive of indented servants. It will always give me the greatest pleasure to hear from you, and to know that yourself and your family are well. I am sure I left none behind me but one who I so often think of, and it shall be my constant wish that fortune may put it in my power one time or other to make myself one in it. Prudence should teach me to draw a veil over such thoughts, as they conduce nothing to alleviating present misfortunes and disappointments.

I'll entreat you make my kind respects to Lady Duncan, Lady Campbell, Miss Annie, Willie, and all your family, and believe that I am, most sincerely, dear sir, your most affectionate cousin and servant, (Signed) ALEX. BAILLIE.

P.S.—We have for several months had continual tracts of dry weather, which has raised the price of water to 1s. 6d. a gallon this week. I can, at same time, get very good rum at 2s. and it is expected it will fall.

The first money I can get I shall purchase a small vessel to use the trade from hence to Inverness. I am sure when rum is bought here at 2s. (which is equal but to 1s 1½d sterling, the difference of exchange being 75 per cent.) and sold there for 6s. or 7s. sterling, and sugar bought here at 2d. per lb., sold with you at 6d., there must be a good deal got by it; and, on the other hand, the oats that I fancy may be bought there at 40s. per hhd. at most, always sells here at £7 ; and beans, pease, oats, and oatmeal in proportion, In short, I see so many chances in a man's making money in that way to one against him, and such a benefit arising to the country by having their superfluities taken away, and their foreign goods bought cheap, which they now pay freight from, and extravagant prices at Glasgow for, that I'm resolved, whenever God puts it in my power, to have a small vessel, and try that trade in person.

If you favour me with a letter, direct for me at the house of James Smith, Esq., to be left in Lloyd's Coffee House, London.

Addressed—" Alexander Baillie, Esq. of Dunzean, near Inverness, N. Britain."

No. CXXXIX. Anno 1754.
J. M. ON HIS MATRIMONIAL DISAPPOINTMENT, ETC.

THE annexed letter from an annonymous correspondent in London, relating his disappointment and grievances, is amusing. The gentleman is full in his details, and, as it is written in a very correct, well-formed hand, bearing no signs of haste or want of consideration, it must be taken as his genuine views. Doubtless he consoled himself elsewhere. There is a good deal of gossip relating to Inverness youths in London. He particularly praises the boy, Lewis Cuthbert, afterwards of Castlehill. (See letter No. 106.) The letter is long but it will repay perusal. It is addressed to a lady well-known in Inverness about the middle of last century, viz., Miss Peggy Mackintosh, milliner. C. P. means

Cousin Peggy. I have many letters written to and by her, and they all show an admirable character. Bailie John Mackintosh was a well-to-do merchant in Inverness, from 1670 to 1710, who had married Marjory, one of two sisters named Cowie, considerable heiresses. Their eldest son, John, received an excellent education, and passed as advocate in 1702. He was appointed in 1715 an additional standing counsel for the town, in conjunction with Mr Robert Fraser. He had a fair practice, and married Mary Winram, daughter of Colonel John Winram, who, I infer, was Deputy-Governor of Edinburgh Castle, under the Duke of Gordon, in 1689. Unfortunately, and after he had arrived at mature age, John Mackintosh joined Brigadier Mackintosh in 1715, and acted as one of his lieutenants. The following is among his papers, "I, Mr. John Mackintosh, advocate, promise to pay to Major Ninian Boyd or order ten guineas, on demand. Witness my hand at Newgate this 9th of August, 1716. (Signed) JO: MACKINTOSH." He was ultimately discharged from prison, but, debarred from practising, his affairs became involved, and he died greatly in debt about the year 1722. He left, besides his widow, three children—Margaret, Henrietta, and George. The latter did not turn out very well. In 1731, in the Barbour-Stuart trial, George Mackintosh states that the ordinary business of himself and a few others was "talking, dancing, playing at cards, and drinking."

It was under all these depressing circumstances that the honourable character of Margaret Mackintosh, afterwards known as "Miss Peggy," displayed itself. She had been educated and brought up as a lady, but to support herself and the family, and in especial to pay her father's debts, she became a milliner and dressmaker in Inverness. It was nearly twenty-five years after her father's death before she paid off the last of his debts, and in some cases where the creditors stood out, she actually paid interest—one hard-hearted shopkeeper receiving a little more than double his debt. Some further particulars, in connection with a letter from the honourable Mrs. Gascoigne to Miss Mackintosh, will be given hereafter.

Follows the letter referred to:—

London, August 8th, 1754.

The gentle reproof in my dear C.P.'s last letter, only saying that I am one in her debt, makes me more angry with myself for having given occasion to it than the severest things she could have urged against me. But you are all goodness and affection, and your forgiving temper I am no stranger to. God forever bless you, my dear cousin, and for Heaven's sake never entertain a thought that I can be indifferent or ever alter in regard to you. Indeed, I never shall, and it would distract me to think that you suspected me capable of it. But I know you do not, shall therefore say no more on the subject. So you have heard? I don't doubt it; a great many besides you have, and I know how. But they have all talked prematurely, for you may believe, and might with reason expect, that I should make you amongst the first in the world acquainted with a thing of that nature was it likely to happen. As a proof of this, I'll tell you in few words all the affair, but it must be to yourself only, and I know it will be so, since I desire it. I was introduced by a youug gentleman, my most intimate friend, to a family of his relations. The eldest of his cousins—a lively, sensible, young lady—but neither very pretty nor handsome, but still agreeable, I saw, and loved; to you I need say no more. I had reason to believe that I was not disagreeable, or perhaps it was my vanity made me fancy so. In short, I proposed the affair, and received an extremely polite and obliging refusal. You'll perhaps think the last term odd; but obliging it was; for, after having thanked me in a very pretty manner for the regard I showed, and expressed her gratitude for my good opinion, she said that at present she had no thoughts of marriage, and desired I would never give myself a moment's uneasiness on her account, nor think more of the affair. I made another effort but with the same success, and I therefore determined to give it up. Little did I suspect then that a gentleman of £3000 a year was assiduous about her, and with a London lady every other qualification must give way to such a valuable consideration. I have not seen this lady since, nor know whether I ever shall, except by accident, or some favourable turn.

I know you will be glad to hear that I am become something of a philosopher in these matters, and that disappointments of every kind will sit much easier on me now than they would have done formerly, because why? I am older and ought to be wiser. I did not think to have wrote so much about myself, but I know you well, and shall not apologise for it. I shall have done with just saying that there are many agreeable women in London, if one looks out properly, and why may I not meet with one as well as others, who do so daily? One word in your ear. Had I a fortune of my own sufficient the d——l a one of them I would have. I know where I would look out for one, if I was matrimonially disposed, and in the condition I have just mentioned. When I first sat down to write, I intended to have made a short letter of this, as I had no frank, and would save a cover, but my good fortune has this minute provided me one. You shall therefore be obliged to turn a new leaf before you see "J.M.," or if you are already tired, reserve the remainder for a second dish, if you are not palled with the first, and faith, in my private opinion, both will require a good deal of seasoning to make them relish. However, I hope your indulgence will serve by way of sauce, and I shall go on with what I have further to say.

My brother and Jamie Porteous arrived here about ten days ago, after a very tedious passage. Lodie is at present in a fair way of getting the command of a sloop to Guinea, which he seems to like very well, as he will at least be more his own master than ever hitherto, and he has been on that coast before; but should this fail something else will cast up. He remembers you affectionately, and bids me tell you he'll not forget the snuff-box. (Not one word of the sugar till by-and-bye.) Jamie Porteous is a delightful lad, and received here with open arms by all his friends. He will be provided for presently. As to Jamie Gordon, I have great fears about him. He has always put a restraint on his behaviour in my company which imposed upon me; but my brother, before whom he has been more open, and off his guard, tells me he has passions which I highly disapprove and am greatly concerned for. Remonstrances with calmness, and as well-timed as I can, shall not be wanting, and while he continues here I'll have a watchfull eye on him. I wish he was settled abroad, where he cannot have the same number of temptations as here.

Lewie Cuthbert is one of the sweetest-tempered, sensible, promising young boys I ever knew. I love him much, and Dr. Hay continues to use him with the strongest affection, and is exerting himself to get him into the East India Service. Lewie cannot fail of doing well wherever he goes, and if he lives will do honour to all his concerns.

Now for dear Charlie—tho' last not least, and well does he deserve a paragraph for himself. I have had two letters from him since I wrote you last, in each of which you are remembered as you wish and deserve. He continues to keep his health, is idolized by those he is concerned with immediately, and beloved by all that know him. These joyfull accounts I have had from several hands, and they were all confirmed to me by one Captain Macmillan, who is lately arrived, and who was frequently with Charlie. He sent me a present of some rum by the captain. I shall write him by the first ship, and enclose your letter. Well I know he'll exert himself in your affair. God grant him success in it, and may everything prosper that can make my dr. C. P. easy and happy. Nothing but the strongest conviction of the sincerity of your regard for all your friends in general, and affection for some of them in particular, would have induced me to be so very minute, and to have spun out this letter to such an unconscionable length, and yet I have not done. In for a penny, in for a pound; all I think of is that it is to you I am writing, and I am not tired; I wish you be not. Captain Rogers will tell you that I fully intended sending the sugars by him, but they were not. I cannot give a good reason for it, shall therefore only say that you may certainly expect them by Captn. Bain.

As to the wig, if you can possibly fit yourself at Inverness, I am assured by those up in these matters that it will be much better, since it is hardly possible to send one by guess from here that would answer properly.

Now for my friends. How do Mrs. Mackintosh and her charming daughters do? My best wishes and most affectionate compliments ever attend them. May they be happy, thrice happy, and it will give me the sincerest pleasure and satisfaction. Lewie showed me a letter from his mother, wherein she is so good as remember me; I beg you'll return it in my name.

I'm vastly glad to hear that Mrs. Johnson is so happy; long, very long, may she continue so, and God grant that the rest of Lady Castlehill's children when they grow up, may promise as well, and be as lusty as those that are already abroad in the world. Pheine and his kind, agreeable wife shall ever preserve a large share of my esteem and affection. Happy may they both be, and if anything is wanted to compleat it, may that soon happen. I'll endeavour to write him along with this, and, indeed, I ought to have done it long ago. I am sensible of his regard for me, and if I don't write this time, shall soon. I beg you may remember me in the kindest manner to my old friend, Simon, and his wife, tho' unacquainted. Tell him nobody wishes him better than I do. Do you think I shall be hard put to it to fill up my paper? (for fill it I will since I have gone so far), indeed, I shall not, and could almost wish there was more of it. Lord, says you, what a wish was there. But you will soon be relieved in spite of me, for I can't make paper, tho' I can scribble on it.

Notwithstanding of some disagreeable things formerly, I was heartily concerned to hear of the loss Mrs. Walker has lately sustained by the death of her husband, and the more so as I don't know whether she is entitled to any pension. If a very sincere sympathy could be of any service to her, she has it from me. God grant her resolution to support herself, which, considering that I've been told she has had no great share of spirits for some time, will be a sufficient task. I have not room to tell you the principal design of the enclosed letter, only beg you'll deliver it, and Mr. Chisholm will tell you the purport. Now, the wished-for period is come. Adieu, then, my dr. C. P.

(Signed)   J. M.

P.S.—Remember me to your mother.

No. CXL. Anno 1755.
THE MAGISTRATES OF INVERNESS, AND IMPRESSING FOR THE NAVY.

THE annexed letters show how very humble the Magistrates of Inverness were to the war forces. Even the shameful press made by Lieut. Taff when the judges were in town, is not complained of, but merely used as an excuse for inability to perform what they would wish,

The name of "Kyd" is highly suggestive of a pirate and commander of a press gang. The pleasant way of dealing with unfortunates in prison may be contrasted with the present times. Perhaps Sheriffs in this age might not object to have much power, over, say, wretched rack-rented crofters. We read in novels and otherwise of the infamous doings by press gangs, but it is well to have actual cases before us, such as those referred to in the annexed letters.

Follows the letters referred to :—

21st April, 1755.

We have the favor of your letter of this date, with His Majesty's Royal Proclamation for encouraging able seamen and landsmen for entering voluntarily to serve His Majesty in the Royal Navy. This is placarded, and we have sent your publication through the town by a drummer and crier.

We had for promoting that service published a bounty to be

paid volunteers by our treasurer, and we have given bounty to one able seaman and three able men, who we apprehend are fit for sea service. We will give the Sheriff some men, who by order of the Lord-Justice-Clerk are to be delivered from our prison to any officers of the Navy having warrant from the Lords of the Admiralty to enlist or impress seamen into His Majesty's service. You will be soon acquainted with our resolutions and of the number that can in that time be had for sea service, for our county continues till the 15th May. We are, etc.

"To Captain James Kyde, commander of H.M. sloop 'Princess Anne.'"

13th June, 1755.

We have the favour of your letter of the 27th past. Our utmost endeavours came short of the success wherewith we wish to promote His Majesty's service, and the manning of the Royal Navy at this important season, a service inseparable from the interest of Gt. Britain.

We were provided with volunteers who received a bounty from us. When Lieut. Kidd came here, we delivered him the 26th April twenty men, and four men he got that were recruited for land service, but were under-sized. He paid them some subsistence from the date of the entry, which was the 5th April, and of the following entries, according to the list enclosed.

We thereafter, May 2nd, gave our bounty of 25s. to John Ross, an able seaman. Lieut. Taff got him in Cromarty when he arrived there, and kept him.

Lieut. Taff came here the 16th May. He acquainted the Provost with his powers, but that evening, without our being made known to it, when the Lords Commrs. of Justiciary had arrived in town, a violent press was begun, and that conduct rendered it less able to procure volunteers or others, for the rumour ran, and the town and neighbourhood for several miles were deserted by all such as imagined themselves fit for service; many of them have not yet returned to their employments. We received here on the 17th May, 15 men mentioned in the list enclosed. There are now some men in our prison whom we will deliver over for transportation. We wish you safety and success, and are.

"To Captain John Ferguson, Commander of H.M. ship 'Porcupine.'"

No. CXLI. Anno 1756.
THE PROVOST OF INVERNESS AND COAL DISCOVERIES.

IN the last I had occasion to comment on the obsequiousness, perhaps inevitable with a garrison near them, of the Magistrates of Inverness to the naval forces. The letters annexed are of a pleasing character, showing that the Magistrates were alive to the great benefits which might arise to the north if coal were discovered. I do not recollect to have heard of this matter until the letters came under notice. Of course, nothing came of the affair, and the Magistrates themselves seem to have entertained strong doubts. It is now well ascertained that there are no paying coal beds in the Highlands. Although coal has not been found, yet for a period long antecedent to the opening of railways, English coal, as a return cargo for pit props and wood, was cheap at Inverness.

Follows the letters referred to :—

Colonel Hamilton Lambert,
                            Inverness, 20th Nov., 1756.

Sir,—To favour the inhabiters of this town, and the people in a large district, I take the liberty to solicit you for leave of absence for such space as you think proper, to John Wright, engineer, a soldier of your regiment, and in the Colonel's company. He says he has discovered a coal to be near the town, and though our people have not entire confidence in his ingenuity or capacity, it were a reproach to neglect a matter that portends so much advantage to the Moray Firth. I know your disposition to promote a general good.—I am, with great esteem, yr's etc.

                            24th Novemr., 1766.

I have the favour of your letter of this date.

I am promoting John Wright's scheme for the discovery of coal ; it must be by a general subscription or contribution, the proprietors of the lands being at a distance, therefore I have not authority for ascertaining any premium to Mr. Wright for his finding coal ; but make free to say that if he finds a coal, so much the concern of the whole country, he merits, and a town and country will not use him ungratefully.

I am very thankful for the time you are to allow Mr. Wright to remain with us; but if there be any probable prospects of his progress (which is much doubted) you may expect following addresses :—
I am, etc.

No. CXLII. Anno 1757.

THE MAGISTRATES OF INVERNESS AND THEIR IMPROVEMENTS.

THE records of Council show all along a great regard for improvements. This becomes more prominent after 1745, and betwixt that period and the time of Provost Inglis, much was done. For many years the authorities were concerned with regard to the access to the stone bridge at the west. Houses were built up to the verge of the water, and the exit to the Aird and West was so narrow and tortuous as to be a positive obstruction when wheeled conveyances became common. There was no road along the river banks, and when, after much pertinacity on the part of the Magistrates, and standing out by Mr. John Fraser, Clerk to the Signet, the heritor, who at length consented to a considerable clearance; he stipulated that there should be a roadway towards what was known as the Little Green. About this period the Magistrates were engaged in forming Academy Street, long known as New Street, a term commonly in use in my early days. This street was made over the foul pool, and seems to have at first terminated opposite School Lane, as may be gathered from the letter after quoted. Mr. Hector Fraser, master of the Grammar School, to whom the letter is addressed, was a man of considerable knowledge, a good mathematician, and skilled in surveying and engineering. His family occupied a good position. The Magistrates deserve all credit for their adopting Mr.

Fraser's views, the street being really wide and handsome, considering its age. The work referred to would be that part of Academy Street from School Lane to Chapel Street, and much about this time the street at the foot of Church Street was partly lowered. On the point of the streets at Inverness, it may be mentioned that there were no foot pavements until 1795. I have the subscription list issued for this improvement, bearing that the funds of the burgh being inadequate a subscription was necessary. Provost Inglis, Culloden, and Provost Phineas Mackintosh each gave twenty guineas, but the subscription was not general.

Follows the letter referred to :—

24th August, 1757.

Mr. Hector Fraser, master of the Grammar School, Inverness, —The community is no less obliged to you than we are for your direction and application to New Street. We have judged it incumbent on us to extend the street below the run of the foul pool where it is very narrow—that is, from the Grammar School Lane northward. And to remove obstructions, we have even purchased from Robert Edwards, music-master, the enclosed ground west of the gable of his house, and we commit to you to order the dykes that enclose it to be pulled down, and that you order the same and the gate to be rebuilt in terms of the agreements made with him. Also that you cause take down the dyke at the foot of the hospital garden, and order it to be rebuilt in a line with the dyke of the garden ground, which belongs to the crofts on the other side of the Grammar School Lane ; that the same as well as the other may have their boundaries to an open, broad, High Street. The services you do to the community will be very memorable, and we are with particular regard,

Sir, your obdt. servts.

No. CXLIII. ANNO. 1758.

THE REV. JOHN CLARK OF STORNOWAY.

THE pleading letter of the clergyman of Stornoway to his father-in-law, Bailie John Mackintosh of Inverness, had not its desired effect.

Bailie John Mackintosh had much influence, but another, Mr. John Mackenzie of Delvin, Clerk to the Signet, had more. The Rev. John Morrison, who had, it is recorded, rare gifts, on one occasion gave Delvin a warning which saved his life. No wonder he used his great influence, and successfully, with Lord Moray in procuring Mr. Morrison's translation to Petty.

The strong Moderatism of Mr. Clark is shown by his putting his whole case on the securing of the favour of the patron. Mr. Clark seems, like other parish ministers in the Isles, to have been a large farmer, but withal does not appear to have been happy or comfortable in his position. He was ordained by the Presbytery of Inverness, having his first appointment as missionary in Strathglass. Whether he lost heart, by his want of success in being translated to Petty, is unknown, but he never left Stornoway, dying there in 1772, having been appointed in 1747.

Follows the letter referred to :—

Dear Sir,—Yours of the 27th March greatly refreshed us, as it acquainted us of your being in a fair way of recovery, and that your family is well. I wrote you some time ago news which I do not choose to resume here. As to the design of transporting Mr. Shaw to Forres, it would give your daughter and me great pleasure to be brought to Pettie. We are keenly bent to return to our native county, and there is no part of it we would prefer to live in before Pettie. The Earl of Moray, who is patron, and proprietor of the far greatest part of the parish, can settle in it whatever minister he please. The concurrence of the rest of the heritors, and of the elders and parishioners, would be very agreeable, but the Earl has the absolute disposal in his own hands. No stone ought to be left unturned to procure his presentation in my favours. This is the fundamental point; when this shall be obtained, the rest to be done are circumstances that may be easily managed. My living in this remote place debars me from contributing to prefer myself to any other. I hope you did and will exert yourself to the utmost to bring about my transportation from this place. I am persuaded that my friends, Mr. Mur. Mackenzie, Mr. Shaw, Pettie, and the minister of Croy, will readily give you their advice and assistance to do me service in the affair above-mentioned, or any other of that kind. The duties of my function in this extensive and populous parish, the daily application of sick persons to me from all quarters of this country, my residing at the distance of two miles from Stornoway, where I must go very frequently, altho' an arm of the sea and two rivers lie betwixt Tongue and it, and the great care and attendance which my large tack requires, together with some other circumstances, render my task almost unsupportable. May God be pleased to bring me to a more comfortable place.

I am sorry that any of the merchants here should give you any trouble on account of friendships betwixt them and me. They whose papers you sent enclosed are, indeed, my friends, but they never applied to me to recommend them to you. I wrote you on 29th April, but the packet lost a little time before my letter arrived. Your daughter and I will be mighty pleased to hear from you as soon as possible. We offer our best respects to you, Mrs. Mackintosh, the rest of your family, and other friends in your country, and we desire to offer our kind compliments to your son, William.—
I am, dear sir, your own, most affectionately,
(Signed) JOHN CLARK.
Tongue, 11th May, 1758.

No. CXLIV. ANNO 1759.

JAMES MACKINTOSH OF FARR.

THE respectable family of Mackintosh of Farr, sprung from Kyllochy, bore a good reputation in the County of Inverness for upwards of two hundred years. Unhappily, it has recently dropped out of the list of landholders. At the time of Culloden, Angus Mackintosh was the laird, and, holding the rank of Captain in the regiment of Clan Chattan, fell with the gallant leader Dunmaglass, Dallas of Cantray, and many other officers and men.

The position of his family was very low after 1746, but James, the eldest son, succeeded in getting into employment in Portugal, and, according to tradition, was one of those who escaped during the frightful earthquake in Lisbon, in the middle of last century.

In 1759, at the date of the letter after quoted, James

Mackintosh of Farr would have been under thirty years of age, at home apparently on his first visit. He, Dunmaglass, and Cantray, appear to have entirely forgotten, in the short period of thirteen years, the dreadful tragedy of Culloden, where their nearest relatives had been slaughtered, and were enjoying themselves to the full. The letter is gossippy and full of little interesting details. It is addressed to Mr. William Mackintosh, merchant, in London, brother of Provost John Mackintosh of Aberdeen, who died young in London. It is marked thus, "Came only to hand, 9th July."

Follows the letter :—

Farr, 22nd June, 1759.

Dear Cousin,—I received your kind favour, enclosing the newspapers, a letter from Mr. Parminter, and another from Lisbon. For your kindness in sending the first, and your care of forwarding the latter, I return you a great many thanks. I arrived at Findhorn about ten days ago, since which time, till this instant, I have not set pen to paper, nor has hardly had a moment's leisure, being so much taken up in the company of my friends, and in visits from one place to another, which has been the reason for your not hearing from me before now. Our passage down was really tedious and disagreeable—gales of wind, hail, rain, and fogs. We lost the convoy off the Skers, which place took us three days to weather. The morning before we arrived at Peterhead, there was a French privateer off, which gave us no small uneasiness going up the Firth, as it was said she steered that way. My friends at Earlsmill were very glad to see me; a finer family of children not in the two counties—the eldest is a perfect beauty, at least I think her so, and the second is little behind her. Your old acquaintance, Betty, still preserves her looks. She desired me remember her to you. Your aunt at Connadge was so ill that, notwithstanding I was two nights there, I could not get access to see her. Your other friends there are very well. Angus accompanied me to Inverness, and lay that night at your mother's, who was very well, as also the young ladies, your sisters. They were all extraordinary kind to me. Your father and brother were gone to Edinburgh. Angus accompanied me likeways to Moy, where we stayed two nights, and spent that time agreeably in company with the Laird and Lady, Cantra, Dunmaglass, and several others. The Laird desires my cousin may not forget to send down his chimney pieces by Capt. Johnson. I am now at

Farr, on my way to Flichity and Aberarder, and from thence I intend for Dalmigavie, and expects, before the latter end of July, to have all my little affairs settled and on my way for Edinburgh. The affair in dispute between Dalcrombie and me is not yet settled; he speaks high. However, I am resolved to have it settled some how or other before I leave the country, but I am afraid it will be a good deal of money out of my pocket. Should you have occasion to write me, may direct for me at Earlsmill, but need not trouble yourself to send me the papers, as my uncle has the Edinburgh, which is taken from the London Chronicle the night it arrives at Edinburgh. I shall write both you and my cousin soon, and am, with best respects to said gentleman, Mrs. Scott, Cousin Allan, and all friends, your most affect. Cousin and very humble servant,
(Signed)   JAMES MACKINTOSH.

P.S.—Miss Dallas of Cantra carries the bell of fine ladies. I I shall see her before I leave the country. There is a prospect of a fine crop over all the country. Two English drovers has been down and bought up 6 or 700 head of cattle and gone South with them. The importation of Irish cattle dampens their spirits much here.

No. CXLV. ANNO 1760.
JAMES BAILLIE, SON OF DOCHFOUR.

THE Baillies of Dochfour of the last century were a kindly and hospitable race, and well deserved their great prosperity.

James Baillie, the writer of the letter after given, was one of the younger sons of Hugh Baillie of Dochfour, and with his eldest brother, Alexander, greatly contributed to the prosperity of the family. Three brothers (Alexander, James, and Evan) all were extensively engaged in West Indian business, and it is curious to notice his expressing himself so strangely from the Island of St. Eustatius, then a foreign island, at the depredations of English ships of marque, describing them as pirates. Mr. Baillie afterwards commenced business in London, and was very forward in pushing the fortunes of young men from the North. He occasionally visited the North, and, writing to a friend in Inverness, of date 11th December, 1782, says:—"I have been flattering myself with the hopes of visiting the North a long time past, but every year or voyage I think brings its disappointment, and we still continue hoping on. I hope your puncheon of rum reached you safe to enjoy yourself and friends at this approaching season of festivity. We are almost at a stand here in business at present on account of the uncertainty of peace or war. I wish it was settled one way or other."

Mr. David Fraser, some time Judge at Gibralter, nephew of Simon Fraser of Ness Castle, writing to Inverness from London on 13th September, 1793, says:—"Before this reaches you, you will have heard of the much-lamented death of Mr. James Baillie, Dochfour's brother, of a dropsy."

Follows the letter referred to:—

Saint Eustatius, July 20th, 1761.

Dear Sir,—My last was by the fleet which sailed from Saint Christopher's in June, in which, I believe, I intimated my intention of going to England by the July fleet; but the times since have altered a little for the better, and I thought it a pity to leave this shop while there was anything adoing, and a prospect of trade improving in a more advantageous way than ever. I have therefore determined upon staying here, and God knows when I will think of leaving it again. We are still harrassed by the English privateers, but not so much as usual, owing to the activity of a few French men-of-war who have lately arrived at Martinico. and keep the seas pretty clear of these pirates. We are daily in expectation of important news from North America, having certain accounts that Admiral Boscawen has landed his troops on Cape Breton, and that they were likely to carry Louisbourg, which God grant may be the case. I was glad to hear from my brother Evan that you, the lady, and family are well, and give me leave to tell you that there is none wishes more ardently for the prosperity of your worthy family than me, and that if an opportunity of serving anyone belonging to it opens, I would most cheerfully embrace it, and serve them to the utmost of my abilities. I have, since my settlement here, done very well, and better than I expected when I set out from Inverness. However, Providence has been very kind, and to it only I am indebted for what I have. This goes by my cousin, Sandy Baillie, who has thought proper to return home after a very short stay here. I refer the particulars of what is new, to him, as he shall give you a more distinct account of these islands than I can possibly do with my pen. which is one of the worst. I beg my compliments to Mr. Duff's family, and am, dear sir, your affectionate cousin and obedient servant,

(Signed)   JAMS. BAILLIE.

No. CXLVI. ANNO 1761.

THE HONOURABLE MRS. GASCOIGNE.

THIS letter to Miss Peggy Mackintosh, her old schoolfellow and relative, from Mrs. Gascoigne, shows the latter lady to be well pleased with her relationship to the great. Many northern ladies married young officers stationed in Inverness, who afterwards rose to good rank. For instance, a sister of Sibella Barbour married Captain Delane, who is referred to in the trial of 1731, and I have a note that Lucy Barbour, relict of Lieut.-Col. Henry Delane, dying in 1768, leaves her sister, Elizabeth, commonly called Lady Kyllochy, sole legatee and executrix. In consequence of the death of the Duke, referred to in the letter, arose the famous Douglas cause betwixt the Duke of Hamilton and the nephew, or alleged nephew, of the Duke of Douglas. The nephew prevailed in the House of Lords, and after several changes, the great Douglas estates are now vested in the Countess of Home.

Miss Mackintosh, in her later years, received a small pension through Lord Auchinleck, and another only by favour from the Advocates. A connection, Mr. Aikman of Ross, writes to her, " I am convinced that a letter from you to Mr. Robert Macqueen will always procure you £5, though you stand not in the books for it. I know him a little. He has a great deal to say with Mr. Dundas, the King's Advocate, and present Dean of Faculty.

If your father's conduct in life as to politics was not too well known, there would be no great difficulty in getting you booked for a large annuity, but it would not be safe to bring that story into a meeting of the Faculty, for fear of a strong opposition." Alluding to the death of Mary Winram, Miss Mackintosh's mother, in 1758, Mr. Aikman says of the Winram family—"She was the last of the unfortunate family of her father, and indeed, so far as I know, the very last of the name, except our cousin, James, with whom that family, once opulent and creditable, and the very name of Winram will, to my great regret, probably extinguish." I should be glad of any information regarding the Winram family. Concerning Miss Mackintosh's sister, Henrietta, also a trouble to her, as was her brother, George, the Countess of Sutherland writes the following kind and sympathetic letter:—

Dunrobin, 3rd Nov.

Madam,—Your letter at any time needed no apology to me; but, on the contrary, it was very welcome when it was to inform me of poor Henny, whose situation I heartily regret I told her what I feared before she left this, but I would not have her friends be too much vexed at what cannot now be helped. You will see by my enclosed, which I desire you will forward (for fear of the curiosity of the family) what I would have her to do, and she may depend on all the assistance and friendship in the power of, Madam, your humble servant,

(Signed)   ELIZA SUTHERLAND.

P.S.—My service to your mother, and assure her I'll serve Henny to the utmost of my power. I believe I need not caution you not to send your letter to that place.

Miss Mackintosh lived in the Court in Church Street, Inverness, in James Dunbar's property, at the corner of Queensgate, and had continued to her the honourable seat in Church of the Patron of Bona, given to her father by the following, signed by the Dowager Duchess of Argyll on behalf of Strichen:—

Edr., 17 April, 1712.

These presents is to empower you, Mr. John Mackintosh, advocate, to possess a seat in the Kirk of Inverness, belonging to the

Laird of Strichen, and to discharge all others from sitting therein, and that during our pleasure allenarly. We have subscribed these presents, day and date, foresaid,

(Signed)   E. ARGYLL.

Besides paying her father's debts and supporting the family, Miss Peggy erected a handsome tomb-stone in memory of her parents in the Chapel Yard, Inverness. Though no tablet records her own death, this letter and No. 139 will keep her in honourable remembrance.

Follows the letter referred to :—

Edinburgh, July ye 22nd.

My Dear Miss Peggy,—The enclosed is of a very old date. My son, who I expected would have delivered it, was disappointed of that jaunt by his companion falling sick, and for all the quality frrends I have, I could not procure a frank sooner, though I am now the Duke of Argyll's cousin, and the Earl of Home's sister, by both in a sort allied to the great Earl of Bute.

Lady Lovat and Prim's compliments to you in the kindest manner. I durst not open the enclosed, least reading I should not send it, and I would rather expose any weakness as leave you to suppose I have entirely forgot you. I came here to have all I could of my son's company the 2nd of this month; he set out for England the 8th, and I heard from Leeds the 13th, when he had got very well on his way to Birmingham. This is his marriage day. I got the two franks; I mean, this, and the one I put on his letter to congratulate them on the occasion. I wish the King and Queen may find themselves as happy at the end of two years as they do.

The marriage and coronation engrossed every conversation till yesterday the Duke of Douglass departed this life. He has finished his last scene with great propriety as a real good Christian and a heroic Douglass. He has left the Duchess, his executrix, 40 thousand pounds, Lady Jean's son all his personal estate, £8000 a year. The people who expected to have got all this money 2 years ago have very long faces when that will was produced and declared to be void by his own hand before witnesses. This was immediately done on his being reconciled to the Duchess but not produced till after his death. How much good has that woman now in her power. She has done so far in her wedlock as getting him to provide for his nephew.

You see how stupidly and how hurriedly I write. What was once very easy to me is now become my aversion. I find my sight so much failed whenever I take a pen in my hand, but my regard to good people is unalterable. Whether you hear from me or not, be assured I am most affectionately yours,

(Signed)   G. GASCOIGNE.

Addressed—"Miss Peggy Mackintosh, in the Church Street, Inverness."

No. CXLVII. ANNO 1762.
GENERAL FRASER OF LOVAT.

THE following kindly letter from General Fraser is only one of many conceived in similar terms. He had certainly a deal in his power, but never spared any exertions to benefit a countryman, and particularly a clansman. Besides an easy and elegant diction the General at this time particularly wrote a beautiful hand. The person referred to got his appointment in due time.

Follows the letter referred to :—

Sir,—I delayed answering the letter I was favoured with from you about Lieutenant William Fraser, in hopes to be able to acquaint you that I had showed my regard for your recommendation by doing something essential for him, for at that time I was in expectation of having a second battalion added to my regiment, and in case that opportunity had taken place I certainly should have got some preferment for your brother-in-law. But as it has not, and there is no probability of new levys at present, the only thing in my power was to recommend him to Major Johnston, his commandant, which I have done in the strongest manner, and from the way in which I formerly lived with Major Johnston, I have reason to believe he will pay as great regard to my recommendation as to almost anybody's. I am just going to embark for Portugal, where I shall be glad to receive your commands, if I can be of any use to you or yours there or here, for I do assure you I am, with great regard, dear sir, your obedient and faithful servant,

(Signed)   S. FRASER.

The above letter had been carefully put aside by the receiver, who docquetted it, "Missive, General Fraser, 17th July, 1762," and it is now in beautiful preservation.

No. CXLVIII. ANNO 1763.

D. F. AND E. F.—TO MARRY OR NOT TO MARRY.

ALTHOUGH I am not aware that any of the descendants of those primarily concerned and referred to in the annexed letter exist, yet, as it is possible they may, it is better to withhold the names. I, however, indicate that both were named Fraser, and were connected with Stratherrick, as was the writer. The letter is addressed to a person in good position in London, brother of the lady, and whatever his reply, the marriage did not take place. The old fight of prudence and inclination is here well seen. All the lady's friends, male and female, are in favour, including "Lady Kilcoy;" yet the lady had her way, and the proposed marriage fell through. She afterwards made her choice, and it is to be hoped lived happily, though the chosen one was not a success financially.

Follows the letter referred to :—

Dear Sir,—I received your favours of the 8th ult., and shall observe to send the half-kitt salmon you order, how soon there is fish and that a vessel offers.

The cause of this is to cover the enclosed from —— by which you will find that he has been courting Betty for these several weeks. Your stepmother, my wife and I were early applied by him, and must own from the acquaintance we have had of him, and all we can learn of his character and circumstances, that it appears to us to be a very equal and agreeable affair; for the young man is only about two years older than her, has very good possessions, is worth two thousand pounds sterling (which is better than £3000 in this town), is sensible, good natured, and prudent in his own affairs. Yet Betty seems averse to him for no other reason than that she has had but little of his acquaintance, and that he had not that delicacy in address that she would choose in a man she would make her husband. As I am certain you can have no view in this or any such matter but her conveniency and happiness, I must say I would think it imprudent to miss such an offer, as they are not frequent in this corner. I presume none of her friends would be dissatisfied with it. I took the opportunity about eight days ago to acquaint Lady Kilcoy, by Mr. Hector Fraser, of it, and she told him she was not only satisfied with it but very fond of its success, which, I can assure you, would not have been the case with her, or others, had the former bargain, as to which you were twice wrote, taken place. She agreed last night that you should be writ to for your opinion.

On the whole, I beg you be so good as lose no time in making answer to the enclosed and this.—Your affte. friend,

(Signed)   D. FRASER.

Inverness, 2nd Oct., 1763.

No. CXLIX. ANNO 1764.

WILLIAM FRASER OF BALNAIN.

THIS family is one of the few of the Stratherrick Frasers which has been enabled to hold its ground on the east side of Loch Ness. The writer of the letter after given may be described as the real founder of the family, and his descendants clung for some time to the title, although another branch of the family had purchased the lands of Balnain and legitimately assumed the designation.

William Fraser was in much repute as an Edinburgh lawyer, and had a good deal to do with the affairs of Simon Lord Lovat. After his purchase of Aldourie, he came north every year and took great interest in the improvement of the place. It would appear from his letters that on his return journeys to Edinburgh he always travelled across Corryarraick, and in one letter there is an amusing account of the family's difficulties, from the breaking down of their chariot at the top of the pass in most inclement weather.

The letter after given is chiefly interesting as showing the great rise in prices of living in Edinburgh in Balnain's own experience, I think he went to Edinburgh about

1730, and it would appear that his board cost £10 a year, whereas in 1764 it would be £24.

The letter is addressed to Alexander Baillie of Dunain, whose eldest and unfortunate son, Colonel William Baillie, is referred to. The boy, proposed to be a lawyer, also became a soldier, and the person referred to as Charles was Balnain's brother, a well-known writer, and commissary of Inverness.

Follows the letter referred to :—

Edinburgh, 1 June, 1764.

Dr. Sir,—I had the favour of a letter from you some posts ago, and I am glad to know your family and you are well. I should have made you a return sooner, and in course, but that I have been a little engaged.

I observe what you write with respect to the two different meetings there was of the Commissioners of Supply. I should not at all be against Mr. Wm. Baillie's proposal, but I believe it would be necessary first to sound and have the approbation of some of the great dons of the county, who have larger properties in it than the generality of the Commissioners who ordinarily meet on the county matters. This first being had, I think the thing might be attempted, but it might give offence without that.

I am concerned extremely to think you are in any doubt about your son who is abroad. It would appear you have not heard from him by the late opportunities from that country. I hope Providence will favour him and you in your endeavours with respect to your son you have at home. If you have resolved to breed him to business in the way you say, and that he is himself inclined to it, I approve much of your beginning him in the country, and settling him with a proper person in a country place. The expense and education of a young man in this place is now become intolerable. When I came first to this place I was boarded for £10 a year, and your boy could not now be boarded under £6 a quarter; a nephew of mine, of much the same age with your boy, I pay this for. I take Inverness not to be an improper place to settle him in, and if Charles has accomodation for him the place is proper, because little temptation and few acquaintances, which is a great matter while a boy is young.

I beg my compliments to Lady Dunain and Miss Baillie.—I am, dear sir, your most obt. and very humble servt.,

(Signed) WILL. FRASER.

No. CL. Anno 1765.
MR. WILLIAM ROBERTSON, OF THE INSHES FAMILY.

As early as 1636 cadets of the house of Inshes had established themselves in Germany, and letters from them are extant. This movement abroad continued for over a hundred years, and in the interesting letter after given from Mr. William Robertson at the Chatellaine, Hague, it will be seen that there was a pleasant interchange between the head of the family and his cousin. The writer refers to his son, Colonel Peter Robertson, who, in another letter, is styled "Captain in Guarda's Dragoons, and Great Master of the Stables of the Governor-General of India, at Batavia." The writer's mode of expression and style of penmanship are both distinctly foreign.

Follows the letter referred to :—

Dear Sir,—I was favoured with your very agreeable letter dated Nov. 22nd. I was very glad to see that you and your dear sister are in good health, which I wish will continue for many years. I thank you for the good wishes done to me and my family, and that your attention is gone so far as to take care for me and my son, the Colonel, to be classed in the Baronage of Scotland, of which I will be very glad to receive a copy, and will return with great pleasure and satisfaction the charges you have been obliged to do, and whenever I am able to do you any service I will not fail. My two daughters will be very glad to be able to show their father's birth, as that would be sometimes of great consequence for them. So soon as I have received this copy, according to your promise, I shall pay the expence to the agent of Colonel Alex. Robertson, and desire him to remit the laid out money to you. If I was sure it would come safe to your hand, my daughters would send a small present for you and sister of their own work, but as they had once before sent to my nieces, the daughters of Mr. Fraser, my brother-in-law, my sister's children, by a Scots officer, and they never heard from them, they heartily doubt if it was delivered. There was two caps and flowers, and two pair bracelets, and two neckties, all of their own making, so that in case there was an occasion, would not fail another suit. Further, I must acquaint you that we have left off public business as we turn old, not being able for this affair, but have set up the linen merchandize, which, in case we should come to die, will be more honourable for my daughters, for they are brought up as ladys, and have an education as such, as my son the Colonel (Peter Robertson) had. And it was the reason of his fortune we had reason to expect by this time to have had letters from him, but the ship is cast away, so that it will not be before the month of June before we shall hear from him. But shall let him know what you have been pleased to do. And when you send this copy or book (I am afraid you cannot send it by the post but by some ship) you have only to direct it to be delivered to me, to Mr. J. Smith, factor, or Mr. Crawford, or Mr. Murdoch, at Rotterdam. Either of them will deliver it to me. Nothing more worthy your attention. I will leave off in wishing you and sister, my dear niece, all sorts of content, with the compliments of the season. My spouse and daughters are joining their compliments and recommending their and your friendship, and believe me to be, very respectfully, dear cousin, you most humble and affectionate cousin and obedient servant,

      (Signed) WILLIAM ROBERTSON.

Hague, the 12th Dec., 1765.

No. CLI. Anno 1766.

THOMAS FRASER OF GORTULEG.

WHILST some of the gentlemen of the clan whom Simon Lord Lovat styled "mean barons" turned against him, none stood more firmly by his Lordship than Fraser of Gortuleg. His name is frequently found in Lord Lovat's letters, and he seems to have been constantly at Castle Dounie.

When Prince Charles fled from Culloden, he crossed the Nairn at the Bridge of Faillie. He re-crossed a second time at Tordarroch Bridge, calling at the house, which happened to be closed. He then pursued his journey, dismounting at the house of Gortuleg, where he met Lord Lovat and had some refreshment. Continuing his flight, he arrived at Invergarry Castle about three o'clock the following morning. The Chevalier Johnstone followed a similar course as far as Fort-Augustus, and mentions that by changing horses he crossed Corryaraick, and was at Ruthven by two o'clock of the day succeeding the fight—an extraordinary feat.

A pathetic account of Charles' condition when at the house of Gortuleg has been handed down on undoubted authority. His visit was, of course, totally unexpected, and in hastily preparing an apartment for his refreshment, and conversation with Lord Lovat, the children, to be out of the way, were locked up in an adjoining closet, and told to be perfectly silent. Youth can not be long quiescent, and noises being heard by the Prince, he suspected treachery, and insisted on the door of the closet being opened. Upon seeing merely an agitated group of children he burst into tears, bewailing his unhappy state—that even the prattle of children should cause him alarm and suspicion.

The house which witnessed the above scene still stands and deserves a better fate than that to which it has been devoted. The house of Tordarroch also still stands. A writer whose views are entitled to weight, records that upon the 26th of August, 1745, after Prince Charles had passed Corryaraick, he was waited upon by Thomas Fraser of Gortuleg, in name of Lord Lovat, to assure him of his Lordship's services. Fraser advised him to march north, but this was over-ruled by Lord Tullibardine, and the general feeling in the army was to go south. Had Gortuleg's advice been followed, we have no doubt, the writer adds, "that formidable as the rebellion (?) was, it would have been more so. Besides the large increase of force which Charles would immediately receive, he would have secured the wavering fidelity of Lovat, a point of paramount importance. Lovat could, when in earnest, have sent upwards of 2000 men into the field, at a time when this reinforcement would have been invaluable, and several other clans would immediately join the insurgents when the cautious and powerful Chief of the Frasers had done so. Fortunately, however, for the Hanoverian dynasty, Charles marched to the south."

Gortuleg was especially exempted in the Act of Grace. He died at a very advanced age. The annexed letter, written in a cramped hand, betokening age, shows the writer, who was son of Lovat's ally, to have been of a kindly and neighbourly disposition. Alexander Baillie of Dunain desired the office of Collector of Cess, then vacant, and in the gift of the Commissioners of Supply, and the letter was in response to Dunain's application.

The family lost the estate about sixty years ago, but there are representatives, in good circumstances, in different parts of the Empire.

Follows the letter referred to :—

Dear Sir,—I have the pleasure of your letter of 22nd of this month, this moment.

I have not heard of any other candidate for the collection of supply in this county ; and I can scarce think of any, all things considered, has a better title to stand up for it. I shall always think of you and the concerns of your family, with honour and respect, and nothing but circumstances that have not yet occurred to me, and that I have not yet heard of, shall interfere with my suffrage in your favours.

When my son comes north, I am convinced he will soon be persuaded to pay his respects to Lady Dunain and to you, and to give his best advice and assistance in anything regards you and your family. My most respectful compliments to Lady Dunain, Miss Nellie, and to your young secretary, and give me leave to assure you that I am with a sincere esteem, dear sir, your most obdt. and humble servant,

(Signed)   THO. FRASER.

P.S.—Mrs. Fraser and Annie desire to be remembered in the most affectionate manner to you and family.

Dunain received the appointment, but did not survive many years to enjoy it.

No. CLII. Anno 1767.
THE REV. ÆNEAS SHAW OF FORRES.

Mr. Shaw, of the family of Tordarroch, was translated from Petty to Forres in 1759, and it is recorded to his credit that during the troubles in 1745-1746, he saved the lives of many by giving certificates of character to persons in his neighbourhood who had been engaged in the Rising. A singular case is reported, viz., that of his own servant, who had been seized by the Hanoverians while merely passing the road and hung on a tree, and was happily cut down by Mr. Shaw ere life was extinct.

The letter after quoted, addressed to Provost John Mackintosh, Inverness, is interesting in two points, as showing that a history or genealogy of the clan was in contemplation, and the name of Mr. Lachlan Shaw, who was of the Shaws of Dalnavert, is introduced. The other point concerns the great political contest which occurred in 1767, 'twixt the Duffs and the Grants—contests for supremacy which have continued to the present time. The Rev. Æneas Shaw died at Forres in 1773.

Follows the letter referred to :—

Forres, 28th Sepr., 1767.

Dr. Sir,—I have sent a horse for Miss Christy and taken the opportunity of sending a few potatoes to Mrs. Mackintosh, which I hope she'll accept. They have not been so early with us as ordinary, else I should have sent them sooner. I thought to have seen my friend, Charles, here about his genealogy of our clan, with such help as could be afforded him from Mr. Shaw of Elgin. I still insist on his coming. Pray let me have your opinion of Bob, how you think he may turn out, and give it impartially. My immediate concern is, his insignificance to you and the trouble he gives your house.

We are in a great stir and bustle about our county elections. Mr. Grant has given up the county in favour of his uncle, the Colonel. Against the Colonel have started two nephews, Sir James Innes, and Mr. Geo. Duff, brother to Earl Fife. Mr. Grant of

Grant's intention was only notified about 14 days past, and ever since there has been such whipping, spurring, and rattling of coaches, etc., back and for, that Sunday was no Sabbath day. There are seven nephews, all confederated to unhorse the Grants, but the probability is they will keep the saddle. Our kind compts. to all your family, and I am, with great truth, your affect. cousin, and much obliged servt.,

(Signed)   ÆNEAS SHAW.

My wife has sent her saddle, such as it is; if Miss can get a better, my wife's may be given to Smith, the saddler, to mend, if not, she may make shift to ride on it.

No. CLIII. ANNO 1768.

SIR ALEXANDER GRANT OF DALVEY, BARONET.

THE first Baronet of Dalvey was James Grant, King's Advocate, created in 1688, with remainder to heirs male whatsoever. Sir James Grant died in 1695, without issue, and the Baronetcy was dormant, though a brother survived a few years, until about 1751, when the writer of the annexed letter got his father, Peter Grant, designed of Inverlaidnan, chief of the sept "Donachie," then in his ninety-sixth year, to take steps for having himself served nearest heir male of his kinsman, Sir James Grant. Their being no opposition, the service was carried through, and Sir Peter enjoyed the honour for five years, dying in 1756, in his 101st year.

Sir Alexander Grant was engaged in foreign commerce, and possessed considerable lands near Fortrose. He purchased about 1740 the estate of Grangehall, near Forres, and as the family had lost Dalvey-upon-Spey, he changed the name of Grangehall to Dalvey. In 1761 he was elected member of Parliament for the Inverness District of Burghs, and in that year received a grant of arms from George the III., countersigned by the Earl of Bute. Sir Alexander only sat in one Parliament, being succeeded in

April, 1768, a few days after the date of the letter, by Sir Hector Munro of Novar. Sir Alexander was exceedingly useful in the way of pushing forward in the world young men from the North. My grandfather, Captain Mackintosh, got his first start in life in 1756 through him, he being, however, his cousin. When Colonel William Baillie of Dunain was on his way to India, he writes of the great attention and kindness shown to him in London by Sir Alexander. The foundations of a great fortune to the Oswalds of Auchincruive were laid when the founder was partner of Sir Alexander in the African trade. Misfortunes arose in business, and when Sir Alexander died, his brother and successor, Sir Ludovick Grant, had but a slender fortune. Notwithstanding, he had the good fortune of marrying two of his daughters to Highland chiefs of the first rank.

The Baronetcy of Dalvey remains, but the holder has no lands in Scotland.

Follows the letter referred to:—

Dalvey, 3rd April, 1768.

Sir,—I am ashamed to own the receipt of yours, dated the 12th March; but was unable to make proper reply thereto till I had wrote to London. A reply to my letter from London could not yet come—not by the very last post. I am informed in the general account of transactions that Captain Baillie, from the camp near Madras, has transmitted a bill for £80 sterling, drawn on Hugh Ross and Isaac Tolly, Esquires, to be received by me, if Robert Munro, chief mate of the "Pigot" should not be arrived, who had his power of Attorney to receive said bill or money. Mr. Munro has claimed and received the money, and will no doubt answer your bill for the same.—I am, with great regard, sir; your affectionate cousin and obedient servant,

(Signed) ALEX. GRANT.

I shall be in Inverness next Saturday, and will then show you what is wrote to me of this affair.

Addressed—"Alex. Baillie of Dunain, Esq."

No. CLIV. ANNO 1769.

THE CAMERONS IN AUCHINDAUL.

THE Aberarder in Laggan evictions occurred at an early period in the history of this detestable trade. I have recently fallen in with a case which began as far back as 1766, or four years earlier than that of Aberarder.

Auchindaul, pleasantly situated in the Lower Braes of Lochaber, was occupied by families bearing the dominant name of Cameron from time immemorial. At the time of the death of the third Duke of Gordon, the family was much embarrassed, and the augmentation of the rental closely looked after by the guardians of Alexander, the fourth Duke. Achindaul, with its grazings, was a large holding, standing classed as a six merk land. About 1759, a stranger named John Mitchell, fancied the place, and had the art to secure Achindaul on a five years tack, but upon condition that the old possessors were to be allowed one half thereof. This pernicious system of compulsory dividing and crowding by landlords had, in the case of Achindaul, the usual result. The old tenants got rather behind in their payment of rent, and probably questions of trespass also arose. In 1766 Mitchell attempted to remove the principal possessors, viz., Alexander Cameron, Duncan Cameron, Angus Cameron, John Cameron, Donald Cameron, senior; Donald Cameron, junior; and Elizabeth Dunbar; and the litigation ran on to 1769. Besides these seven crofters, there were at least four cottars, so that the population might be reckoned at the lowest as over fifty souls. The defences, as might be expected in such cases, could only be technical, but it may be stated that they were all well founded. First, Mitchell's tack had lapsed; he possessed under tacit relocation, and had not obtained the landlord's concurrence. Second, the witnesses to the service of the summonses were under fourteen years of age, and were not actually present at each service. Third, the officer's execution bore that the defenders had been personally served, but it was averred that only one had been ever seen by the officer. The officer was a Mr. John Ross, sheriff-officer in Fort-William, then called Maryburgh, and the boy witnesses were described as "Thomas Ross and Ewen Maclachlan, students in Maryburgh." Alexander Cameron of Glenevis, humanely came to the rescue of his namesakes, who, probably, were of the Sliochd Soirle, by giving a bond of caution for them. We hear a great deal nowa-days about what is called the "Plan of Campaign." But it seems not to have been unknown in Lochaber one hundred and twenty years ago. The pursuer, in a burst of indignation, in the year 1768, thus delivers himself in one of his pleadings—"Mr. Mitchell being laid under the necessity of convening before your Lordship these defenders in a process of removing, an uncommon spirit of litigation has appeared upon their parts, *and which they have nourished with the rents of their respective possessions;* for it must not be passed in silence that these defenders have not paid one fraction of rent for these two years past." Again, no doubt, referring to Glenevis, Mitchell says in another place "that it is well known that the aiders and supporters of the petitioners are persons of influence in the country."

Upon a proof, it was found that the witness described as "Thomas Ross, student," afterwards the well-known minister of Kilmonivaig, and son of John Ross, the sheriff-officer, was under fourteen; the other witness, Ewen Maclachlan, student, whom I first took to be the famous Latin scholar, could not be found, being described as a waif, who had accidentally strayed into Lochaber in the early part of 1766. The alleged personal service upon the defenders was proved erroneous. When the officer went to the first house there was a great disturbance, "the students" took to their heels, the officer was taken into a house after his alarm, and so well treated, that to the knowing outsiders, representing themselves as the defendants, who came to take the papers in order, as they said, to save him the trouble of going to their various houses, now that they discovered what a fine fellow he was, he handed them the documents, afterwards returning an execution of personal service, authenticated by the signatures of the "students."

The defence was successful, but, alas, only for a time; the poor Camerons disappeared, and for some period large farmers occupied Achindaul. As it would seem that at present the only house on the place is "vacant," according to the County Roll, it is well thus to recall, though but fleetingly, some memories of its ancient inhabitants.

Follows the letter of the crofters of Achindaul to their lawyers at Inverness, subscribed notarially, as the parties could not write:—

We, Donald Cameron, senior, and John, junior, Alexander, Duncan, Angus, and John Cameron, and Elizabeth Dunbar, tenants and possessors of part of the lands of Achindaul, do hereby empower William Fraser, Town-Clerk of Inverness, and Duncan Grant, writer there, our procurators in the Process of Removal pursued against us at the instance of John Mitchell, tacksman of the said lands of Auchinadaule, before the Sheriff-Depute. and his Substitute, at Inverness, and to propone an improbation of the execution against us, produced at his instance in the foresaid process against us, and to do everything thereanent that we might do ourselves if we were personally present.

No. CLV. Anno 1770.
LORD FORBES.

The Lords Forbes are Premier Barons of Scotland, the creation of the title going as far back as 1442.

Among the earliest bonds of man-rent, friendship, and others in the Mackintosh Charter Chest, is a bond of friendship betwixt William, Lord Forbes, and several of his clan; Duncan Mackintosh, Chief and Captain of Clan

Chattan, and his brothers, Allan and Lachlan; and Hugh Rose of Kilravock, dated at Forres, 9th August, 1467.

This ancient alliance, continued long thereafter; for three hundred and three years after the date of the bond we find the then Lord Forbes, upon the death of Eneas Mackintosh of Mackintosh, writing to his successor, Eneas, afterwards Sir Eneas Mackintosh, Baronet, the following friendly and sympathetic letter :—

Putachie, July 25th, 1770.

Dear Sir,—Last night I was favoured with your very kind letter, dated the 19th, giving me the melancholy accounts of my worthy friend and your valuable uncle's death. I think myself much obliged to you for your attention in writing me; and the family of Mackintosh may depend that I shall ever think it my honour, as it is my interest, to show them upon every occasion all the civility, friendship, and respect I am capable of. The valuable good qualities your uncle was possessed of I hope will be followed and prosecuted by his heirs; and I also hope what they owe to their aunt, good Lady Mackintosh, will be deeply impressed upon their minds. I beg my best and most respectful compliments to Lady Mackintosh, in which Lady Forbes joins me, to you and all your friends, and I am, and ever shall be to you and your family, with great truth and regard, dear sir, your faithful friend and most obedient humble servant,

(Signed) FORBES.

P.S.—Please tell Lady Mackintosh I shall write her soon, and be so good as excuse want of mourning paper in the house.

The death of this Laird of Mackintosh caused deep regret. Scores of letters like the above poured in; and from ladies that from the Countess of Moray bears the palm.

No. CLVI. Anno 1771.
THE REVEREND ROBERT MACPHERSON, IN LAGGAN.

MANY years ago, in the *Celtic Magazine*, I contributed a paper upon the depopulation of Aberarder, on the western side of the beautiful Loch Laggan. A bachelor half-pay chaplain, some time in a Highland regiment, was shown to have evicted, in the year 1770, eighty "honest" Highlanders, as they styled themselves, men of the ancient faith, cadets of the house of Keppoch. At the head of the dispossessed was Mr. Alexander Macdonald of Tullochcrom, referred to in the annexed letter. From it will be gathered some of the after proceedings arising out of the eviction. It may be as well to state here that the legal proceedings, which lasted for two years, ultimately ending in the House of Lords, were raised at the instance of the Forfeited Estates Commissioners and their factor, the notorious Butter. Aberarder was anciently divided into four ploughs of land, and it was from the three wester or south parts that the Macdonalds were evicted, the other plough being the property of a cousin of Tullochcrom, viz., Macdonald, commonly styled of Gellovie. Gellovie accommodated his cousin in his portion of Aberarder, and this thorn caused the proceedings after mentioned. The criminal summons narrates that Mr. Macpherson, having in the month of July, 1770, attained possession of his lands and farms of Aberarder and Tullochcrom, he found Alexander Macdonald in possession of and dwelling upon a small grazing called Innisnagaul, situated betwixt his two farms of Aberarder and Tullochcrom, and surrounded by his grass on all sides; that although this small grazing, paying no more rent than forty merks Scots, had never been inhabited but as a shealing for a few weeks in the summer, yet the said Alexander Macdonald thought proper to build houses and reside thereupon during the winter, although it was evident that the grounds of this small grazing were not sufficient for supporting one-third of his stocking of cattle. Poindings went merrily on, until matters came to a crisis, upon the 18th July, 1771, when several horses were poinded. Two of Alexander Macdonald's servants came for them, viz., Donald and John Macdonald, but were refused delivery, as they did not offer poind money. A watch was set by Mr. Macpherson, and about twelve at night on the 19th July, the above Donald and John Macdonald came, one armed with a gun, and desired Mr. Macpherson's two watchmen to let out the horses, or their brains would be blown out. One of the watchmen having gone for assistance and to give the alarm, the two Macdonalds leaped into the fold, and, with the assistance of a large grey hound, pulled the watchman to the ground, one of them holding him down, while the other, with the assistance of the grey hound, drove away the horses. When they had got away some distance, the watchman was released, but evidently much frightened, and though plenty assistance soon came up, the Macpherson party did not think it prudent to give chase. The horses, however, were seen on the morning of Saturday, 20th July, near the Bridge of Garvamore. The conclusions of the summons were for £30 damages, trespasses, assythment, and expenses; £20 to the Procurator-Fiscal of the Court for the public interest; and £15, forfeit under 1st and 2nd George I., for having, bearing, or using any arms or warlike weapon. It was in returning the draft to Inverness writers that Mr. Macpherson writes the letter fortunately preserved.

It may be here mentioned that General Stewart of Garth speaks highly of Mr. Macpherson when in the army; and though he affects ignorance of legal matters, his whole letter, and particularly his desire to keep free of the odium of being an informer in the matter of illegal carrying of arms, shows uncommon shrewdness. He added farm to farm, being at Dalchully in the year 1787, as a letter from him, titled on the back "Parson Robert Macpherson," bears. The Parson did manage to extirpate a good number of Catholic Macdonalds from Badenoch, but his own son, though he married a Macdonald, found no home there, and his honourable representatives, now of the fourth generation, are chiefly in foreign lands.

Follows the letter referred to:—

Gentlemen,—I had the favour of yours, enclosing the criminal summons. It is extremely well, nor have I the least doubt but every article in it will prove. I have two witnesses who will swear to the cattle being poinded upon my best grass, and I have other two who can depone as to the deforcement and the actors of it, with every circumstance mentioned on that head in the libel. I propose to summon two others with whom I have reason to believe the two deforcers were till they set out upon this midnight expedition. In my own opinion this will be sufficient to establish the fact without further evidence. The others formerly mentioned have, I find, very little to say, unless you think it material to prove that the horses were seen early next morning at Garvamore. But this, in my opinion, is a fact they will not attempt to deny, and I would be loth to call more witness than are thought necessary. There is one thing insisted on, in the libel, which, though it may be very proper, and you had all the reason in the world to include it, yet I am by no means fond of it, and that is your referring to the Disarming Acts and requiring Donald Macdonell to be found liable for the penalty of carrying arms. As all the facts and requisitions in that libel must be supposed to proceed from me, this particular one subjects me to the imputation of being an informer. I do not, anyhow, like it. That law is in thorough desuetude now in the Highlands, and though I am sorry for it, and think it a general misfortune to the country, yet the practice is too universal for a private individual to take any notice of it. I would have scored it out of the libel here, but I am so ignorant of law and its formalities that I thought it more prudent to send it to yourselves to receive this amendment. We have the Sacrament this week in this parish, which prevents my attending to any other business ; and it will take some time before the several copies can be made out. Will you mention in your next what day towards the middle or end of September your Court will sit, and most proper for me to get my business discussed. You will please also give me your real genuine opinion how far you think the defenders can be affected upon full proof of the facts, and whether Tullochcrom can be rendered in any measure liable. My situation would be far from pleasant if, after insisting in this process, I could make nothing of it. My neighbours would become more insolent and outrageous, and the law which helps to restrain them would be no longer a bugbear to them. Full copies of the libelled summons need only be given to the defenders. Common citation is enough for the witnesses. As this is the first process that ever I had to manage, and that my life has hitherto been in a very different line from the present one, and where I had no access to know legal forms, I must beg that you will be as particular, as possible in all your directions. I will certainly be with you at Inverness by the time of compearance.

But you will trouble none of my friends to attend me. We will do the best we can and stand on our bottoms. This goes by John Kennedy, a servant of mine; he and John Macpherson, one of my tenants, are summoned in a process at the instance of Angus Macpherson, Tirfadown. Lieut. John Macpherson tells me Mr. Bean has the direction of it. It will be obliging if he examine these men amongst the first, and dismiss them as soon as possible. I am, with regard and esteem, gentlemen, your most humble servant,

(Signed) ROBT. MACPHERSON.

Tullochcrom, 28 August, 1771.

In different places of the lybel, the defenders are summonsed to appear before the Sheriff or his Depute at Inverness, ought it not to be Substitute.

The witnesses for the prosecution were John Macpherson, student in Dalchurinbeg, John Kennedy and Donald Macpherson, tenants, Samuel Macdonell, tenant in Tullochcrom, Mor or Marion Stewart, his wife, Donald Macphilp, tenant in Moy, Elspet Macdonell, spouse to Donald Macdonell, tenant in Knock of Strathcruinachan, Archibald Macphilp, in Torgulbin, and John Macpherson, tenant in Garvamore.

Sixteen years later the affair had not closed. Mr. Robert Macpherson writes to a lawyer in Inverness to defend Angus Macphilp (son of the above Archibald), "from what he says was an unfounded charge, prompted by revenge for supposed injuries very foreign to the crime now alleged against him; and the resentment against Angus is owing to services his father and he had done me many years ago, or were supposed to have done to me."[*]

No. CLVII. Anno 1772.

LORD GEORGE GORDON, ETC.

It is not generally known that the hero of the Gordon Riots at one time represented the County of Inverness in Parliament. The annexed letter from his uncle to one

[*] See Appendix No. 4 as to a Gaelic poem in honour of Tullochcrom.

of the freeholders brings him before the public as a candidate for the first time. He did not continue long member, and some time subsequent to the lamented death of General Fraser of Lovat, another member of the Gordon family was brought forward in 1784, as may be seen by the Duke's letter of the 27th March, also given. Being upon electioneering matters in the county, I also give the letter of Lord Macdonald, a candidate in the year 1782. A vote in those days was of great value, the patronage of members being such as to enable them handsomely to requite services of support.

Follows the letter referred to :—

Preston Hall, Augt. 15th, 1772.

Sir,—I take the earliest opportunity to acquaint you that my nephew, Lord George Gordon, proposes to offer his services to the County of Inverness at the next general election, and to solicit the favour of your friendship and support to him on that occasion, which will confer a particular favour on the Duke and the family of Gordon. Lord George is now abroad on His Majesty's service, but as soon as he returns home, will wait on you in person.—I have the honour to be, sir, your very obt. and humble servant,

(Signed)   AD. GORDON.

Lord Adam Gordon was long at the head of the Military Forces in Scotland, and did much to extend the road system initiated by Wade.

London, March 27, 1784.

Sir,—The Parliament being dissolved, I take this opportunity of acquainting you that my brother, Lord William Gordon, intends to offer his services to the County of Inverness. Mr. Fraser of Lovat is to support him with his interest. May I beg leave to request the same favour of you, which will confer a particular obligation upon me.—I have the honour to be, sir, your most obt. and most humble servant,

(Signed)   GORDON.

The female descendants of the Duke of Gordon are very numerous, but on the death of the fifth Duke, some fifty years ago, the heir male was so remote as to be found in the descendant of a younger son of the first Marquis of Huntly, so created in 1599.

Lord Macdonald had been created a Peer of Ireland a few years prior to the date of the following letter :—

London, 18 February, 1782.

Dear Sir,—May I presume to address you upon the present occasion, which has so unexpectedly afforded me the opportunity, to honour me with your support, if such an interest shall declare in my favour as to give me hopes of succeeding our late worthy representative. I lament that my confidence in the ability of General Fraser and my improvidence in not extending my resources to the utmost, in case of so fatal a contingency, have thrown me off my guard. The electors will no doubt view me in the more favourable light that I am more a dependent on them for support, and my success will, of course, lay me under the greatest obligation. I am confident that there has not been in my own day a period when individuals have had so ample a field for speculation, and as my connection with Inverness-shire is well understood, I shall not fatigue you with arguments by way of arrogating to myself a preferable title.—I ever am, with the greatest regard, dear sir, your most faithful servant,

(Signed)   MACDONALD.

Lord Macdonald would seem to have been sorry he had not created as many freeholds as his estates could afford, and his vague references to the period no doubt meant the American War, then practically at an end.

No. CLVIII. ANNO 1773.

MR. WILLIAM MACKINTOSH, SON OF DALMIGAVIE.

THE old family of Dalmigavie sprung from Kyllachie, and held a respectable position in the County of Inverness. The lands, together with those of the Coigs, in the Braes of Strathdearn, are the only lands in the lordship of Stratherne not holding of the Earl of Moray. Captain Donald Mackintosh, father of the writer of the letter after given, was laird of Dalmigavie for upwards of sixty years. Writing of Strathdearn, it may be noticed that the heritor longest in possession of his paternal estates in Inverness-shire, belongs to that district, and has (1889) entered upon the seventy-second year of possession. Captain Donald's eldest son, John, engaged in business in London, first with his neighbour, Alexander Mackintosh of Kyllachie, and subsequently on his own account. For years he was successful and much thought of, and his letters show him to have been warm-hearted and clannish, but, unfortunately, his latter years were spent under a cloud. He married in England, and his son, William, who was a free mariner, succeeded his grandfather, Captain Donald Mackintosh.

The writer of the letter after given was also a mariner, and traded to the East Indies. He succeeded in the world, and died unmarried. The letter is given on account of the gossip it contains. The Colonel Fraser referred to was the famous General Simon Fraser, killed at Saratago in 1777. The letter is addressed to Bailie, afterwards Provost, John Mackintosh of Inverness.

Follows the letter referred to :—

London, February 24th, 1773.

Dear Cousin,—I am favoured with your very obliging letter of 21st November, accompanied by another to Colonel Munro in my behalf, for which I return you my most hearty thanks, and have the pleasure to acquaint you that your application has been attended to most respectfully by the Colonel, who has not only procured a second mate's station for me in one of the company ships against next season (having been too late for this), but behaved with the greatest politeness and civility to me on every occasion, since you did me the honour of introducing me to his acquaintance. He only obtained a certainty of this a few days ago, which, by his own desire, has been the cause of my not acknowledging sooner the receipt of your favour. He is certainly very much of a gentleman, and deserves every good opinion that you may have entertained for him, for I assure you he interested himself very much in this matter, which is a favour not easily to be obtained. I shall be happy to embrace every opportunity of showing you how sensible I am of the obligation, and hope you will do me that favour of giving me every opportunity that may offer to evince the same. I am extremely sorry to hear of your bad state of health, but glad to hear by our cousin John that you are on the recovery, and hope to have the confirmation of it from yourself. My poor brother John has been very ill, and in a dangerous way lately, but is now thoroughly recovered, and looks better than he has done for years past. He is going into another branch of business, the Bill way, but I do not understand what it is, and flatters himself he will do very well. He has in my opinion the most desirable emotion of the mind to know that he has the best wishes of all his friends for his welfare, as well as their commiseration for his misfortunes, which is the greatest comfort a depressed mind can be entertained with. My brother, Alexander, is at Bristol, and I fear is in as good a state of health as ever he will be, for I look upon his constitution to be past recovery, though he rather mends on it. All other friends and relations here are well.

Major Russell has been, I believe, married a few days ago to a West Indian widow, with a fortune of £1200 a year, and Charles Grant, of Bengal, by way of distinction, a Miss Fraser, a niece of Colonel Fraser. Both matches were made up in the Colonel's family, though, I understand, the latter not with his approbation, but this piece of intelligence, I presume, you would hear before now.

If I cannot employ myself before the Company takes up their ships in August, I will, if times and circumstances permit, do myself the pleasure of seeing you at Inverness how soon the season invites; as no person wishes more to see his friends and relations in that country than he who is with the greatest respect, dear sir, your affectionate cousin, and most obliged servant,

(Signed)   WM. MACKINTOSH.

No. CLIX. Anno 1774.

JOHN MACPHERSON OF BALLACHROAN (THE BLACK OFFICER).

THIS person made a considerable stir in Badenoch for the last thirty years of his life, but it was as nothing in comparison with the sensation caused by his death in Gaick in the first year of this century. He was a man of great ability, actively engaged in diverse business—constantly striving in the pursuit of gain. All came to nought, and years before his death he had become bankrupt. I have many of his letters, showing him servile to superiors, agreeable to equals when he chose, tyrannic to his inferiors. In the year 1767 he was living at Phoness, and is described as "Lieutenant John Macpherson of the Battalion of Highlanders, lately commanded by Major James Johnston," and had seen service abroad. His chief home military work was recruiting, carried on with extreme rigour and arbitrariness. He was constantly engaged in litigations of a severe and protracted nature, one process I have seen—that referred to in the annexed letter, with Lachlan Mackintosh at Shanvall, lasting over twenty years, which ultimately either fell asleep or terminated by Mackintosh's death. A specimen of his letters is hereafter given. The Ballachroan Macphersons were a respectable family, long in the place, as tenants or wadsetters. Some of his descendants in the female line are in good positions at home and in India. A lady still lives (1889) who was married so far back as 1818 at Ballachroan, while yet in the occupation of the Black Officer's family.

Follows the letter referred to:—

Sir,—I received your favour of the 28th ulto., covering a summons of wakening against Lachlan Mackintosh, which I hope by this time is returned to you with an execution thereon. I now send you the Act and commission for taking the oaths of Messrs. Young & Innes. The submission betwixt Lachlan Mackintosh and me lies still in the hands of the Clerk of Submission, who lives at some distance from the place, and cannot just now be sent. But I know there is no clause therein declaring that any proof taken by the arbiter shall be a legal evidence in any process except before himself, in which event, the submission, I presume, would be no manner of use in the present process. As I suppose the first thing you will think necessary will be letters of supplement from the Sheriff of Elgin, for bringing Messrs. Innes & Young before your court to be examined, if that is refused, a bill of advocation should be immediately presented to bring the case before the Lords. I know how much this defender trifled with us before, and occasioned dilatories for some years. I now entreat you would push the affair with the outmost vigour. As I have lain so long out of my money, I lost my patience about it. Mrs. Kenneth Macpherson will let you have what money is necessary for carrying through the process.—I am, sir, your most obt. servant,

(Signed) JOHN MACPHERSON.

Bellchroan, April 6th, 1774.

P.S.—There has been an expense of about £7 occasioned by

our submission, which I suppose you will think proper to add to our former claim, and I shall send you a particular account thereof by the next occasion.

No. CLX. ANNO 1775.

CAPTAIN ALEXANDER GODSMAN OF THE 89TH HIGHLANDERS.

AN entire stranger to Inverness, though long a resident, has, from a peculiarity in his daily life, identified his name in all time coming with the town. The annexed letter, though lengthy, is full of interest. It is addressed to the unfortunate Colonel William Baillie of Dunain, who died in captivity in Seringapatam in the year 1782. Colonel Baillie has endorsed it thus—" Lt. Godsman, dated Sept., 1775, received the 1st May, 1776, at Madras;" and it, with other papers, was delivered back by Tippoo Saib to the Colonel's brother and representative, Colonel John Baillie, father of the last Baillie of Dunain.

In the year 1759 the old 89th Highlanders was raised, under the influence of the family of Gordon, one of the lieutenants being Alexander Godsman, writer of the letter, and a native of Banffshire. The greater part of the short time the regiment was embodied (for it was reduced in 1765) was spent in India. After being reduced, Lieutenant, commonly called Captain Godsman, was appointed factor or local representative for the Castle lands by the Duke of Gordon. At the date of the letter, Godsman was living at Dochfour, but he afterwards removed to Crofterton of Altnaskiah, and farmed part of the Haugh lands, belonging to the Duke. In a picture of the old house of Drummond and surroundings, dated 1796, it is seen that there was not a single tree on the Haugh and Altnaskiah lands, east of the burn. Captain Godsman's house stood on Crofterton—a narrow strip on the south side of the Old Edinburgh Road as it starts off from what is now called the Culduthel Road. After his indoor work was over, and his early dinner, Godsman, invariably at the same hour—wet or dry—walked along the edge of the Haugh slopes as far as the descent to the burn, not only that he might see how things were getting on, but to enjoy his "constitutional" and the magnificent views all around. He was somewhat bent, and walked with his hands behind his back. Hence the place got, and will now ever retain, the name of "Godsman's Walk." When Provost Phineas Mackintosh built the old house of Drummond, he and his visitors frequently took the Godsman's Walk as a short cut, the Altnaskiah lands being open and in part muir, until Provost Robertson feued Altnaskiah from Cantray, who had succeeded the Duke of Gordon in the Haugh lands.

The lands of Dochfour referred to extend from the burn of that name to a small rivulet running past the present offices of Dochfour—those to the south of said rivulet being called Dochcairn. James Baillie referred to, was the real founder of the great prosperity which favoured the family. Dying without lawful issue, his estates went to his brother Alexander.

Captain Godsman's remarks about faggot votes and the American War are highly proper and in advance of his time, but it is not a little curious that he was himself made a faggot voter, and being with others struck off the Roll for Inverness-shire by the real freeholders, was very angry and presented a suspension of the vote of exclusion.

The doctor referred to was Dr. Alves of Shipland, maternal grandfather of Colonel Inglis of Kingsmills. Will the manner in which Colonel Hugh Grant of Moy, his cousin, C. Grant the elder, James Macpherson, and many other Highlanders during the eighteenth century made great fortunes in or by their connection with the East Indies ever be written?

Follows the letter referred to :—

Dochfour, 23d. Sept., 1775.

Dr. Sir,—I had the pleasure to receive your very agreeable letter, dated Elore, 1st Janry. last. How soon it reached, I showed it to your mother and nearest friends, who were all very happy to be informed of your and brother's welfare, and, I assure you, none more so than your humble servant. I was very glad to hear Frank was well, and wish he may be provided for before now. I could not help envying your happiness, when you told me that honest Sinclair and you was taking the "t'other nogg" during the holydays, and very anxiously wished I could have made one of the party, had it only been for one afternoon.

Your mother and all friends are perfectly well at present, nor has any material occurrence happened since I wrote you last. You are pleased to express yourself as very much obliged to us for the great attention we pay your affairs in this country; how far our conduct on the whole may be deserving of thanks I cannot pretend to say, but one thing I can aver with truth, that we mean well, and if the art of thinking right be wanting let it not be charged against us as a fault. We have got the Craig to the northward of the House of Dunain inclosed, and mean to have it planted directly with firs, and as some few places be fit to receive ash, beech, birch, elm, or any other kind of wood, we are to plant them accordingly where 'tis thought they'll grow.

The inclosure is a dyke or ditch very well execute, and measures 3184¼ Scotch ells @ 3d. per ell, which amounts to £39 16s. 0¾d. This is besides a little bit of an inclosure round Tomaluack, which is not yet finished. I imagine what ground is comprehended in the inclosure of the Craig will be considerably above 100 Scots acres. The acre generally plants about 5000 firs; planting and the price of plants will be about 2 shillings the thousand, so that the expense of planting a 100 acres with firs would be about £50, besides any utensils that may be necessary. I fancy the expense of this job will be about 100 guineas or something above it, but this is only my own conjecture at present. When this planting is grown up, it will be a most beautiful ornament to the place, as well as very useful. The spirit of planting has seized the neighbouring gentlemen to a high degree, and if your disposition should lead you that way on your homecoming you have plenty of subject to work upon.

Mr. Alexander Baillie, my predecessor in this place, upon an application to the Duke, has got a feu-right of it, upon paying £30 st. of yearly feu-duty; he has indeed paid the *Pretium Affectionis*, but as Dochcairn, his own property, lies contiguous, they will both make a commodious farm to him when joined together. He and I are on the best terms imaginable, and he thanks me for being instrumental in bringing about the bargain. I honestly assured him I had no interest in the matter, nor nothing to bestow but good wishes, which was not wanting.

He proposes to build a fine house and offices on the lands of Dochcairn, preferring a situation there to Dochfour, and proposes laying out 3 or £4000 on the improvement of them both, jointly. He is just now enclosing the hill above Dochcairn and Dochfour, and is to have it planted this month, or, I should have said, this autumn.

The time of my removal from Dochfour is not quite certain, whether at this Whitsunday first, or Whitsunday, 77. Mr. Baillie said, notwithstanding of his bargain with the Duke, I was as welcome as his brother to stay as long as I found it convenient. I would wish to give him entry to the place as soon as possible, that I may not retard the improvements he means to carry on. It is just now in agitation that I remove to Altnaskiah, a farm of the Duke's lands hard by the town of Inverness; and there is only wanting a house and some offices, which, I fancy, will be built for me at the Duke's expense. When your mother heard the news of this bargain she was much cast down on account of my leaving Dochfour till I convinced her that I would be within less than an hours' walk of Dunain from the place I designed to remove to.

If it please God you come home well to this country, Mr. Baillie's being so close in your neighbourhood will be a very great acquirement to your happiness, for he is a most desirable man, both for a friend and a neighbour. His brother James is very lately gone from here to London, where his lady is, and, I hear, he intends soon going out to the West Indies on business. The third brother, Evan, is settled at Bristol in a company trade, and Duncan, the youngest, is in the West Indies. Colonel Hugh Grant, who came home very lately from Bengal, has brought home an immense fortune, and is just now going through the neighbourhood pricing estates, for he is resolved to be a purchaser near this place.

I have little news worth pains of repeating, either domestic or political. Last session a Bill was brought into Parliament for abolishing the trade of splitting valued rents, by which means barons were created that had no real property, and often in such numbers that the gentlemen of fortune, who possess property and superiority both, found themselves of very little weight in the county. The Bill was allowed to be printed and sent down to Scotland that it might be considered of by the freeholders of the different counties in Scotland before it should pass into a law.

Those counties where there are a number of gentlemen of real property and superiority will vote for the Bill passing into law, but where the superiorities of a county are confined in the hands of a few great men, no doubt their artificial forces will be instructed to vote against it, but their vote will go for nothing. The matter will be strongly contested on both sides, and if the Bill pass, many great men in Scotland will lose—some five, ten, twenty, and some thirty thousand pounds spent in creating barons ; and Finlaison and Leith, who are barons in three counties, may make the last use of paper of their charters. The present contest 'twixt Britain and her North America Colonies engages the attention of all ranks and degrees ; whether Britain shall have power to tax them or not, or whether the most valuable blessing of a free people shall only belong to themselves.

The only recontre they have had with the King's troops worth pains of notice was on the 17th of June last ; and, although they were defeat, they discovered a far greater degree of courage and bravery than Britons believed them to be possessed of. There is a talk that some new regiments will be raised to send to New England, to assist the rest of the King's troops there to enforce obedience to the laws of the British Senate ; should this take place, I believe General Fraser will be pretty certain of getting the command of one of them, and will have the nomination of his own officers— he made an application to this purpose already, but matters had not come to that pitch to make reinforcements of that kind necessary, and hitherto have only augmented the companies at the rate of twenty rank and file.

The Americans think themselves capable to repell any force Britain can send against them, and this notion may inspire them to hold out much longer than people imagine, and oblige Britain to raise several new regiments before they can be brought to order. The British Senate have been all along a good deal divided about the measures thay ought to pursue, which has proved a stimulus to the courage of the Americans, and may serve to spun out the contest longer than otherwise there was any reason to expect. The Clan of Macgrigor have got their name restored by an act of the last Session, and they have likewise offered to raise a regiment to go against the Americans. Mr. Willox now takes the name of Macgrigor, and in case raising of regiment takes place, he has great reason to expect a company in the Macgrigor Regiment.

Mr. David Mitchell, your agent in London, took a good deal of trouble about recovering the things you was so kind as send us in compliment. We paid him the duties and all manner of charges, each according to the proportion charged us, and the Doctor remitted the whole to London, but Mr. Mitchell would make no charge for any trouble he had been put to about the matter, which, I think, is but doing him justice to mention. In a former letter I express'd my obligations to you for this mark of your affection and kindness.

Mrs. Margt. Baillie, upon receiving yr. draft on London was so struck with a sense of gratitude towards you that all power of expression seemed to be lost for a time. In your last to the

Doctor, you mentioned giving your nurse a year's rent; he observed that probably you did not advert that they at present rented the Mills, beside the possesion of land, and that both put together would be a very considerable sum—that it was probable you did advert to their having got something already, and that, therefore, it would be imprudent to make them any advance at present. I agreed with him in this, but observed that such a sum as they got formerly would do them a great service, nor did I think you would grudge it in the least. He said, when it appeared their necessity was very pressing, something might be bestowed, so in this position that matter stands.

Willie Ross, I believe, will get the full allowance you ordered him first, this year; as, poor man, he'll be at a loss for want of his stock of sheep, for they must be put away on account of the planting. You see we are economists even of your charity, for which, I'm afraid, we will not get great thanks. I have now taken up so much of your time that I daresay you'll forgive for concluding. Please remember me in the kindest manner to yr. brother and Frank, and my good friend, Dr. Sinclair, and believe me ever to remain with perfect sincerity and regard, my dr. sir, your very affte. and very Hum. servt.,

(Signed) ALEXR. GODSMAN.

P.S.—Your acquaintance and friend, Mr. Arthur Cuthbert, has not yet visited this part of the country since his return from India. Should he come this way, I would introduce him to your friends, and you may believe no civility in our power would be wanting. Upon the bargain being finished with the Duke for the place of Dochfour, your mother discovered an inclinaation for my taking Dunain-croy. I assured her I willingly would have completed with anything she seemed to place so much satisfaction upon, but that such a step would not be agreeable to some of her friends, and that, very probably, it would be the means of creating a misunderstanding 'twixt her and them, which, of all things in the world, I was most determined to avoid; that it would be highly deserving of reproach if I even suffered myself to be the innocent cause of breeding the most distant difference among connections. However, the lady (unknown to me) took an opportunity of mentioning such a thing, asking how it would do, but as no answer was made she was then convinced it would be disagreeable and did not press it farther. We all agree very well, and it shall be my study to do so still. The Lord pity the frailty of poor mankind, for I'm now convinced that there can be no business carried on under the sun without some sort of party work taking place or seeking a place in it; no transaction can be of so little consequence as exclude it, for it even descends to buying the street dung of Inverness. If you remember, you mentioned something to me in a letter about the Farm of Dunain in a postscript. I always show your letters to your mother and to the rest of your friends, when they contain nothing but fair generals. This letter was only shown to the lady after I had cut off the postscript. She asked if the paper was not whole, for there seemed to be some cut off. I readily told her that our intimate acquaintance, Mr. Sinclair (standing by you when you wrote me the letter), had got your leave to add a postscript to an old acquaintance of ours in the regiment, and that I had cut it off and sent it to him. This pleased her extremely well, for she was afraid that it might have contained some bad news about yr. brother. She is at present as well as can be expected; but one at her time of life cannot be expected to have great strength. She is, perhaps, one of the fondest parents in the universe, and all her wishes are to live to see you. I don't recollect if I wrote you since we took infeftment and sasine for you on the lands of Dunain. The Precept of *clare constat* cost £5 5s.; and a year's feu-duty @ 14s. pr. boll, £19 12s. I daresay the Doctor writes you punctually about your money matters, and will send you exact states from time to time how matters stand. I mentioned twice to the Dr. that I could get the Duke's bond for any money you might have to spare in this country, but, as he did not seem to take any notice of my proposal, I did not speak of it afterwards. I fancy he thought giving it to Torbreck might, perhaps, be laying a foundation for the estate. Adieu. A. G.

No. CLXI. Anno 1776.

JAMES BOSWELL OF AUCHINLECK.

THE letter after quoted shows the biographer of Dr. Johnson in a new character. Those familiar with his history are aware that he detested the Scottish bar, to which he was thirled by the imperative commands of his father. His diary, over and over, is full of bitterness at his fate, yet it is clear from this letter that he was well qualified to take a distinguished position at the bar. He entirely failed in making any figure at the English bar, to which he was also called, and, indeed, his habits were of such a

procrastinating and idle nature, that it is astonishing what he really managed to perform. By parties who did not desire the prosperity of either family, the Keppochs were, after Culloden, stirred up to several acts of unfriendliness against the Mackintoshes. Proceedings had to be adopted against them in 1776, as mentioned in the letter. These differences were got over for a time, but twenty years later matters terminated in a breach, the representative of Keppoch retiring to Ireland, and afterwards to America, some of the family getting refuge at Insh. For upwards of thirty years thereafter there was no Macdonells in Keppoch of the old race, and some ill-feeling arose at the time in the Braes, in consequence of another Macdonald (Alexander of Glencoe) becoming tenant. It will be seen that Boswell writes rather strongly in favour of landlord rights, but, in justice to his memory, I quote some admirable extracts from his last will and testament, written with his own hand, and dated the 28th day of May, 1785:—
"Lastly, as there are upon the estate of Auchinleck several tenants whose families have possessed their farms for many generations, I do by these presents, grant leases for nineteen years and their respective lifetimes of their present farms to John Templeton in Hopland, James Murdoch in Blacktown, commonly called the Raw, James Peden in Old Byre, William Samson in Mill of Auchinleck, John Hird in Hirdston, William Murdoch in Willockstown, and to any of the sons of the late James Caldow in Stevenston, whom the minister and elders of Auchinleck shall approve of, a lease of that farm on the above terms, the rents to be fixed by two men to be mutually chosen by the Laird of Auchinleck for the time, and each tenant. I also grant a lease in the like terms to Andrew Dalrymple in Mains of Auchinleck, my baron officer. And I do beseech all the succeeding heirs of entail to be kind to the tenants, and not to turn out old possessors to get a little more rent."

Follows the letter referred to:—

Sir,—I was sorry yesterday when I opened your packet to

observe a summons of removing, at the instance of the Laird of Mackintosh, against Macdonell of Keppoch, as I know well how indulgent the family of Mackintosh has ever been to their tenants. But your letter made me easy, as I saw from it that there is no severity on the Laird's part. Kindness must be reciprocal to be lasting; and if the tenants in Highland countries imagine that the laird is to retain the benevolence of old times, while they have the indifference and selfishness of this modern age, they must be undeceived. The summons, which I have attentively considered, appears to me to be unexceptionable, so that I have no alterations to suggest. I think there is no incompatibility in the different conclusions, as they are alternatives. You are quite right in lybelling upon the Act of Sederunt, 1755, as you are thereby set free from the statutory forms in a removal, which are so various and so nice that there are many chances for an informality happening. The only reason which you could have had for not lybelling upon the Act of Sederunt, would have been to avoid the alternative of caution, which you do not wish to do. And, indeed, I much doubt if the Court would have pronounced a rigid declarator of irritancy. I rather imagine that payment before sentence would have been held sufficient to prevent it, as in ordinary cases of feus and tacks. In every view, then, the summons is properly framed.

I shall be glad if caution is found, which, I daresay, will be the case, as the tacks are so advantageous to the tenants.—I am, sir, your most humble servant,

(Signed) JAMES BOSWELL.

James's Court, 26 Decr., 1776.

To Mr. Charles Mackintosh, Clerk to the Signet.

No. CLXII. Anno 1777.

JOHN MACKINTOSH OF CORRYBROUGH, CAPTAIN 42ND, ON THE AMERICAN WAR.

THERE are in Strathdearn two Corrybroughs, one of old termed Corrybrough Macqueen, the other Corrybrough Mackintosh. The latter is, and has been for the last hundred years, part of the heritage of the Mackintoshes of Balnespick. The writer of the letter after quoted was the last of the old Mackintosh family of Corrybrough, having sold the estate to Balnespick in the year 1791.

The letter is kindly, sensibly, and well put together. It details very clearly the difficulties with which the British army had to contend, and the hostility of the colonists. It also shows that the opening of letters was a common practice by those in authority. Thackeray, it may be recollected, found great fault with George III. for always referring to General Washington as "Mr." Washington, forgetting or ignoring what is well known to have been the universal rule in the army and otherwise. It will be noted that in the two references to his name in the letter after given, he is described as "Mr." Washington.

The Cousin Angus of the 71st referred to, who met with the accident, was Captain Angus Mackintosh of Kyllachy, who unfortunately died in America. The laird was Sir Ewen Mackintosh of Mackintosh, then Captain Mackintosh, who, some years afterwards, on his passage home was taken prisoner by the French and kept for a considerable time in captivity. The Mrs. Munro was sister-in-law of Provost John Mackintosh, to whom the letter is addressed, and daughter of Dr. Chisholm, Provost of Inverness. She accompanied her husband, Mr. Munro, of Granada, several times to the West Indies, was a lady of great beauty, and so attractive in manner as to be the toast and admiration of all who had the happiness of her acquaintance. The Charles Mackintosh was the Provost's brother, and Clerk to the Signet—the wise and confidential adviser of most of the influential gentry in the Highlands.

Follows the letter referred to :—

Camp near Philadelphia, 21st Dec., 1777.

My Dear Friend,—I did not expect to have been so long without hearing from you. Not one syllable since I left Scotland. Only from the knowledge I have of your worthy heart, and the confidence I have in that friendship and esteem which has so long and sincerely subsisted between us, I should be jealous and uneasy at your long silence. But on this occasion, I judge of your sentiments from my own—that is to say, that no distance of time or place will in the least diminish that friendship and affectionate regard which I hope will ever subsist betwixt us. You see, my dear friend, how easily we forgive those we esteem. As you must long ere now be sensible of the pleasure I receive from your friendly correspondence, I need not press you to write me, though I would not have you turn too lazy, from the indulgence and latitude I must always give you. Therefore, if not before you receive this, soon after I shall expect a long epistle from you. You will long ere now see the operations of last campaign from General Howe's letters, so that I will not trouble you with a repetition. The beginning of this month, General Howe marched his army towards Mr. Washington, who was strongly posted fifteen miles from this town, in order, if possible, to bring him to a general action. But though we drove in all his outposts, and marched up within half a mile of his lines, where General Howe waited three days, changing position and offering himself at different parts of the enemy's lines. But all to no purpose; they were determined not to quit their stronghold, and the General did not think it prudent to attack them in the strong position which they occupied, and which they had fortified with much labour and pains.

Had we attacked them, I make no doubt that we should have carried their works, but then we must have lost many men, and the season of the year was so advanced that we could make but very little use of a victory. We marched back to Philadelphia, and though we retired in the face of the enemy, they did not molest our rear. We have since remained peaceably within our lines here, and quarters are now preparing for us in town for the remainder of the winter. I heartily wish we were under some cover. Canvas is very poor shelter against the severe northwesters that prevail here at this time of the year. I am now writing you in a soldier's tent, which is all the cover I have had this campaign, and I am tired enough of it. I hope powerful reinforcements will be sent us in the spring. Some vigorous measures ought to be pursued, or give them up entirely. I am sorry to say that at home the war is not looked upon of that consequence which it deserves, though I hope the misfortunes of the last campaign will open the eyes of many. I can assure you, my friend, that this country is not so easily conquered as many believe. It is wide, almost without bounds, covered with woods, and abounding with large rivers; many parts of the country naturally so strong that it is extremely difficult to make advances with an army. Take along with this the numerous inhabitants of the country, who are rebels almost to a man—the few among them that are well-inclined to Government, or rather those that are tired of the tyranny of Congress, are kept in such awe by the militia, and even by their own neighbours, that they dare not declare their sentiments, but are obliged in their turn to take arms against us. Such, and much worse than I have described, being the situation of this unhappy country, judge what measures are necessary to reduce them. What gives me pain is the vast numbers of families that must be ruined, and even starved, before this unfortunate contest is over. The leaders of the rebellion being men of desperate fortunes, leaves but little hopes of an accommodation, but by reducing them by force of arms. As I am told our letters are generally opened, I shall add no more on this subject. This, I confess to you, prevents me from writing you often, as it deprives me of the pleasure I should have of giving you such information from this country as might entertain you a little. I had a letter from my sister some time ago, wherein she gratefully mentions your friendship and kindness to her. You cannot, my dear friend, oblige me more than by taking some notice of her. I hope she will deserve it, and some people flatter me by telling me that she is a very good and agreeable girl; and, as she is now my only charge, I own to you I am much interested in her, and would do everything in my power to make her comfortable and happy. My brother, Lachlan, is in a very good way in the Commissary Department at New York. In a letter I had from him the other day, he tells me he had a letter, dated in June last, from your pupil William, who, with Angus, he says, are well and in a fair way of making money. I hope you will see them some day or other return to their own country, and give you satisfaction for the friendship and protection you afforded them in their young and needy days. I saw Mr. and Mrs. Munro last April at New York. You may, perhaps, have seen them since at Inverness. If so, make my kind compliments to them, and tell Mrs. Munro had I known where to direct for her, she would have heard from me. As she promised to let me know, I hope she will keep her word.

The 71st Regiment went from this last week for New York, by which I lose the pleasure I should have with Cousin Angus this winter. Poor fellow had a narrow escape on our last expedition against Mr. Washington, but not from the enemy. He was overset by a waggon, and the wheel went over his leg. But, by a miracle the bone is safe, though the waggon was loaded. He got a severe bruise, but will soon be quite well. He is gone with the regiment, so that his friends need be under no anxiety on his account. The laird is well, as, indeed, is all your acquaintances in that corps. Be so kind as send the enclosed to my sister, and remember me most affectionately to your sisters and the rest of our friends. Tell

Cousin Charles I can only send him what he already possesses, that is, my sincere love and esteem. I am, though very cold outwardly, inwardly, warmly, sincerely, affectionately yours,
(Signed) JOHN MACKINTOSH.

Addressed—"To Mr. John Mackintosh, merchant, Inverness, Scotland."

No. CLXIII. ANNO 1778.
GENERAL SIMON FRASER OF LOVAT.

FROM all accounts no men could be more dissimilar in every respect than Simon Lord Lovat and his son, General Fraser. I have many letters written by the latter, and all show a straightforward, honourable, and independent disposition. His death, without issue, was a great loss to the country, his clan, and people. No act of harshness occurred in his time, nor in that of his trustees, but as to what occurred after the taking possession by the General's brother, the less said the better. The Frasers, as landowners, have in this century disappeared greatly in Inverness-shire, and there are few of the name who would fall under the class of old known as gentlemen tacksmen or farmers. The General had much influence deservedly, and many owed their success in life to his assistance. The annexed letter is a fair specimen of his style.

Follows the letter referred to :—

Dear Sir,—I received yesterday your letter of the 18th. Mr. Dundas is not in town, but whenever he comes you may depend on my losing no time in doing my utmost in regard to the business you recommend to me. The £40 pension that is fallen is the best to apply for immediately; they never give reversions of pensions; all that could be had as to the succession to the £60 pension would be a promise, and a promise of £400 is not near so good as £40 in possession. I had several applications about the company in the Duke of Gordon's Regiment before I received your letter on the subject, and had before then taken what appeared to me the only part I could take, upon the supposition of the Duke's allowing me to have any voice in the matter, for I thought, and cannot help still thinking, that I could not with propriety have interfered with the succession in the regiment upon any other ground but that of procuring for the men raised mostly on my estate a captain of the country in which they were raised.

I beg my best regards to Mrs. Robertson and your family, particularly my godson, in which Mrs. Fraser joins.—I am, with great regard, dear sir, your obedient and faithful servant,

(Signed) S. FRASER.

Downing Street, Dec. 31st, 1778.

No. CLXIV. ANNO 1779.

COLONEL WILLIAM BAILLIE OF DUNAIN.

THE annexed letter, from Colonel Baillie to the Nabob or Arcot, shows the position taken by the East India Company's superior officers to the native rulers. The letter is plainly candid, and Colonel Baillie, by the postscript, seemed to have entertained doubts as to whether he was courteous enough to satisfy an Oriental potentate.

Some years prior, Colonel Baillie was dissatisfied with his progress, and, writing home to a relative on 4th March, 1771, says:—"The Carnatick is at present in peace, promotion hardly to be expected, and the few places of profit filled up by those who chance to have interest with the Governor and Council of Madras. The little I have had has always been through the military men, and from them at present nothing is to be looked for. Letters to Mr. Hastings, second in Council, and soon to be Governor, would help me much, but the method by which these could be obtained, I can neither devise myself nor direct my friends. At any rate be assured I will not be long absent, for I am entirely of opinion that a man had better return in the flower of life with a small fortune wherewithal to make himself and his friends happy, than with millions when, perhaps, he has not the good luck to overtake them, or constitution to enjoy it himself."

Warren Hastings was favourable to Highlanders, and through the intervention of Sir Alexander Grant of Dalvey Colonel Baillie got promotion, but, unhappily, it was not fated that he should ever return.

Follows the letter referred to :—

*To His Highness The Nabob Ameer ul Omrah, Bahadur,
&c., &c., &c.*

Your Highness may probably be surprised at not hearing from me sooner, more especially considering the friendly injunction you laid me under when I had the honour to take my leave. The fact is, I had nothing that could be pleasing to you or your father to write. What you had so much at heart, and appeared so advantageous to the Company, I saw at once to be dubious, and, soon after, not with prudence to be effected. This I consider unlucky for myself, as well as for the public. Tatulla Chaan is here, and in good health; from him I have daily accounts of great preparations making to the southward and northward in the Deccan, but none of my own people have come in lately. I trust at them to do their utmost—I mean Hyder Alli and the Subah. The Company, with the assistance of the Nabob of the Carnatic, will always be overmatch for them. We have great resources, and must be strong indeed when the fleet arrives. This detachment is encamped at Macunda, waiting for further orders.

I will esteem it a particular favour if your Highness present my humble respects to the Nabob, and assure him I am perfectly sensible of the honours he conferred on me when at Madras. I beg also to be remembered to Chagie Assum Chaan. His young cousin I will give every attention and civility in my power to. I shall not forget to embrace what opportunities may offer of forwarding your Highness's interest in these districts of Gontoor, Condavier, or Macunda.—I am, with great respect, your Highness's most humble and obedient servant,

(Signed)   WM. BAILLIE.

Camp, 7th December, 1779.

If in my address, there should be any impropriety, I hope it will be imputed to ignorance and no other cause.

No. CLXV. Anno 1780.

CHARLES FRASER, OF THE BALNAIN FAMILY.

OF the tribe of Frasers in Stratherrick, called Sliochd-Ian-Vic-Allister, were the families of Farraline (the head), Erchite, Culduthel, Balnain, etc. Hugh, Lord Lovat, who succeeded in 1417, had by Janet Fenton of that ilk, Hugh, his successor, and Alexander, ancestor of Farraline. Alexander married Janet Hay of Lochloy, and left three sons, the eldest of whom, John, settled in Ross-shire about the year 1440. John's eldest son, Alexander, married a niece of the Laird of Balnagown, and his eldest son, John, was the first who settled in Stratherrick, of whom the tribe Vic-Ian-Vic-Allister.

From this John, who was killed at Kinlochlochy, 1545, sprung the families of Farraline, Erchite, and Culduthel.

Alexander, first of Erchite, by his second wife, had a son, Hugh, first of Balnain, father of Alexander of Balnain. This Alexander, by his first wife, Jane, daughter of William Fraser of Foyers, had, with other children, William, first of Aldourie, whose descendants in the female line, presently possess that estate.

By his second wife (Jean, daughter of Angus Mackintosh of Kyllachy), Alexander of Balnain had a son Thomas, who died in Antigua in 1760. Thomas Fraser of Antigua had, with other issue, William Fraser, father of Thomas Fraser, and grandfather of the present John Fraser of Balnain. *Thomas Fraser of Antigua was also father of the writer of the letter after given, and of the celebrated Brigadier-General Simon Fraser, killed at Saratoga in 1777.

The letter after given is in its earlier part uninteresting, but the references to the Gordon Riots and the disturbances in Dublin, etc., are valuable. It is much to be feared that Ireland is in a far worse state now than it was a century ago. She has now no Volunteers, and the co-operation of the Dublin Municipal Authorities with those of the Castle could not be looked for. The writer held a good position in Ireland under the military authorities. Follows the letter referred to :—

Dublin, 26 June, 1780.

My dear friend,—I received the favor of yours by last packet only, tho' dated so far back as the 17th of April, and am happy to find you have Mrs. Mackintosh at Gibraltar, the air of which, you say, has re-established her health. It is lucky for more reasons than one you took your rib with you, and I most sincerely hope you may both be as happy as I wish you.

With regard to the letter you mention to have wrote when you was leaving England, I assure you it never came to my hand.

I have had much anxiety of mind about Power's Bond, and pushed him very much, but the truth is, his father died in worse circumstance than was expected, and he was unable to pay the money, unless he sold out for the money which his men was supposed to have cost in raising. Under these circumstances, I closed in with a proposal of his brother-in-law, joining him in another bond, which was perfected the 26th of last month, and payable the 26th November, when I informed both they must have the money then ready at all events, or I must certainly proceed upon it. I have every reason to think they will be punctual. At the same time I thought it for your interest to get a person of property joined with Lieut. Power, and, upon enquiry, the brother-in-law is a good man. I have an order for £14 5s. 7½d. Irish interest from the day the first bond became due, till the date of the present, which I shall receive in the course of a week or so, and remit to Messrs. Bishop and Brummell on your account. In the whole of this transaction I have acted for the best, and I hope it will meet with your approbation, as it has of your friends, Bowyer and Haste, to whom I offered your best wishes as mentioned in your letter.

Mr. and Mrs. Duchesne had your compliments offered to them, and the whole desired me to return you their sincere good wishes for your welfare.

Before this comes to your hand you will have heard of the dreadful confusion in England, occasioned by that wild countryman of ours, Lord G. Gordon. What the result of the proceedings against him may be I cannot guess at. An attempt was made here to riot, but timely suppressed by the spirited conduct of Government here (the Magistrates of Dublin and the Volunteers), who really have great merit in the way they have conducted themselves hitherto.

I have not the smallest apprehension of Gibraltar falling but with the British Empire, and the late success at Charleston makes us hold up our heads, helped by the drubbing you gave the Dons. If we are so fortunate as to give the French a flogging at sea, or shut them up in their fort I have no doubt but America will come over.

All my family, who are in good health, join in most affectionate compliments, and believe me ever, my dear John, with the most sincere regard, your most faithful friend,

(Signed)   CHA. FRASER.

Addressed—"Capt. John Mackintosh, 73rd Regiment of Foot, Gibraltar."

No. CLXVI. ANNO 1781.

LORD CORNWALLIS AND THE REV. DR. ALEXANDER WEBSTER OF EDINBURGH.

THE annexed admirable letter from Lord Cornwallis will be read with interest. In the unhappy war with the States, many Scottish and Highland officers fell. The Rev. Dr. Webster, to whom the letter of condolence was addressed on the death of his son, was a man of great note in his day. He founded the Ministers' Widows Fund; and got up, in the year 1755, the first enumeration of the people of Scotland. This census is looked up to as comparatively complete and authentic; but there is no doubt that, as regards the Highlands and Islands, the numbers were, from imperfect organisation, greatly under-stated. It is recorded of Dr. Webster that he promoted agricultural improvement in the Highlands and Islands. With regard to his wife, Mary Erskine, of the family of Mar, a curious tradition has been preserved. Dr. Webster was the minister of Culross, in which parish Mary Erskine resided with her aunt, Lady Preston of Valleyfield. She was courted unsuccessfully by a young gentleman, a great friend of the Doctor's. In his straits, he asked Dr. Webster to plead his cause with Miss Erskine. This he did with great energy, and, though the lady listened patiently, she expressed a decided negative, adding, however, these words—"Had you spoken as well for yourself, I might have answered differently." He very properly took the hint, and, though her friends were opposed to the match—she having a considerable fortune—they were married in 1737. The marriage was a most happy one, and it is related that Dr. Webster was most energetically aided by his wife in all his works of benevolence. Mrs. Webster died in 1766, and Dr. Webster, who had long been minister of the Tolbooth Church, Edinburgh, died in 1784. The title of Cornwallis, a house which produced eminent soldiers and statesmen, is now extinct.

Follows the letter referred to :—

Wilmington, 23 Aprile, 1781.

Dear Sir,—It gives me great concern to undertake a task which is not only a bitter renewal of my own grief, but must be a violent shock to the feelings of an affectionate parent.

You have for your support the assistance of religion, good sense, and an experience of the uncertainty of all human happiness. You have for your satisfaction that your son fell nobly in the cause of his country, honoured and lamented by his fellow soldiers; that he led a life of honour and virtue, which must secure to him everlasting happiness.

When the keen sensibility of the passions begins a little to subside, these considerations will give you real comfort.

That the Almighty may give you fortitude to bear this severest of trials is the earnest wish of your companion in affliction and most faithful servant,

(Signed) CORNWALLIS.

To the Revd. Doctor Webster.

No. CLXVII. Anno 1782.

MR. DUNCAN MACKINTOSH OF CASTLELEATHERS.

UPON the death, in 1820, without issue, of Sir Eneas Mackintosh of Mackintosh, the representation of the family opened to Alexander Mackintosh, some time of Jamaica, eldest son of Mr. Duncan Mackintosh, writer of the letter after quoted, by his wife, Miss Dallas, of the ancient family of Cantray. Mr. Mackintosh was very kind and clannish, as is seen by his letter, and lived prudently and quietly, acting as factor for his proprietor, Culduthel, long absent in the military service. That he lived peacefully and attained great age, was the merest chance. It is well-known that the Clanchattan Regiment was commanded at Culloden by Alexander Macgillivray of Dunmaglass, who, with all the officers, except three, fell on that fatal day. Alexander crawled to a well, where he was found dead, the place being known to this day as "Dunmaglass Well." How it was that he, not very closely connected to the head of the Clan, was selected, is not generally, if at all, known in the present day. Just the other day I looked over a manuscript (in my possession for years but never perused) compiled by one well qualified, from his position and knowledge, to know what he was writing about. The lady, his informant, I recollect myself, and very well, though long since dead, because she was one of the only two ladies I recollect who snuffed and swore— I mean that her conversation was well interluded with what I may term "swears," which always came in without sequence or cause. Sir Walter Scott knew many such ladies, and it was quite common in the highest ranks last century. The writer of the manuscript says an intelligent lady obliged the author with the following details:—" When the Mackintoshes were mustering, Lady Mackintosh sent for Duncan Mackintosh, Esq. of Castle-leathers, at that time residing at Daviot, and informed him that he was appointed to lead the Clan Chattan at the fight. He was highly pleased at this mark of honour, but in the meantime Dunmaglass sent a message to her ladyship that the Macgillivrays would not follow her banner, unless the chief command was entrusted to him. The lady, fearful of losing so important an ally, made a polite excuse to her relative, Mr. Mackintosh, importing that she had been compelled to place Macgillivray over him. He, indignant at what he justly conceived an affront, retired to his own home, and vowed he would not take part with one side or the other. The night before the battle of Culloden an English officer and party came to his house, and, demanding admittance, expressed surprise at so young a man (he being then unmarried) remaining idle there, and asked Duncan why he did not either side with his countrymen or their opponents. Mr. Mackintosh replied he had his own reasons. The Englishman, who afterwards proved to be General Hawley, wished to repose a while, but, being apprehensive of treachery, he grasped his host's hand into his, and holding it fell asleep, while his men stood guard around. When the battle was over, Hawley again took up his quarters with Mr. Mackintosh, and, as a mark of gratitude, gave him a pass which enabled him to save the cattle and property of several of his neighbours from the infuriated soldiers by claiming them as his own. In doing these good offices, however, he ran imminent danger. He was fired at more than once, and a bamboo walking cane which he carrried and long preserved was notched in several places by the sabres of the military, it being the only weapon he durst use to protect himself. Mr. Mackintosh had a full Highland dress, which he wore on occasions of ceremony 'by way of braggadocio,' as he told my informant, his ordinary habit being the trews, with a dirk as his only weapon. This dress some of the soldiers, in searching his house for rebels, happened to light upon, as well as a wooden box containing some Spanish pieces and a pair of pistols. Holding these articles as clear proof of a rebellious spirit, Mr. Mackintosh was instantly marched off to Inverness, under an escort, as prisoner. General Hawley was dining with Provost Hossack when intelligence was brought him of a rebel captive. On seeing Mr. Mackintosh, he cried, 'How! my host, what means this?' and instantly enquired into the particulars. They were such as to warrant instant liberation and an order for the restoration of the property. The pistols Mr. Mackintosh presented to the General."

As the above was communicated by Castleleathers himself to the lady, who informed the writer of the manuscript, it is generally correct. While pleasant to hear of one good action by the detestable Hawley, he could not have been at Daviot the night before the battle, and in this particular the account must be deemed inaccurate.

It is thus seen how Castleleathers escaped being leader at Culloden, the chances being a thousand to one, had he been, he would have met with Dunmaglass's fate.

Follows the letter referred to :—

Castle Leathers, 18 July, 1782.

Dear Sir,—I had a letter by these lads (Mackintoshes from Glengarry's country), from Lachlan Macqueen, wherein he informs me that they are my namesakes, and very honest fellows, pursued for a tocher as they tell me, and want to be recommended to a writer to answer for them when cited. As they are to pay him for his trouble I thought proper to recommend them to you, and I beg that no advantage be taken of them, or they will blame me and you. And in so doing, you will oblige your humble servant,

(Signed) DUNCAN MACKINTOSH.

Addressed—" Mr. William Fraser, writer, Inverness."

No. CLXVIII. ANNO 1783.

SHERIFF FRASER OF FARRALINE AND THE YEAR OF SCARCITY.

THOUGH more than a century has elapsed, the year 1783 —the year of the white peas—and that of 1782, is still frequently spoken of, and, indeed, is a period of fixing dates, among Highlanders.

There is an old catechist still living (1886) in the parish of Bracadale, reckoned as 110 years of age. When examined before the Crofters' Commissioners in 1883, the old gentleman was unwilling to state his age. It was thought he might have been caught by asking if he recollected the year of the white pease, but he was too wide-awake, and merely replied vaguely, perhaps that he was not born then, although, if the idea of his neighbours is correct, he would have then been about 8 years old.

The letter after quoted, written by Sheriff Fraser to Captain John Mackintosh, father of Sir James Mackintosh of Kyllachy, is full of interest in detailing the measures then taken for the relief of the Highland districts. It is most painful to think that even a single boll of meal for the use of such a considerable estate as Kyllachy was eagerly taken advantage of. On the other hand, it would seem that the pressure was more severe in certain localities than others more favoured, and which last did not require to take up the proportion allocated to them.

Follows the letter referred to :—

Inverness, 11th December, 1783.

Dr. Sir,—The meal sent to this county, to be sold at the reduced price of 8s 8d., was distributed by the Barons of Exchequer among the several parishes of this town and county, the proportion of the Parish of Moy and Dalarossie thereof was originally 24 bolls, but as 820 bolls of the 2000 bolls which should have come to this port were sent to Fort-William and Portree, owing to those at Edinburgh, who settled the arrangement, only 16 bolls could, with justice, have been given your parish. My directions were to write the ministers of each parish, and as the minister of Moy was *ab Agendo*, I wrote the heritors and elders, and had an answer from Mr Macgillivray at Dalmagerry, mentioning their having met, and that he was directed to take the quantity destined for the whole parish, and, accordingly, upon finding that some of the parishes had taken less than the diminished proportion, I sent an express to Mr. Macgillivray offering him the whole 24 bolls, providing he sent for the same on a day fixed at the time (which, I think, was eight days after the date of my letter), and such orders as were then sent, and a few afterwards by Mr Macqueen, yr. of Corrybrough, were duly complied with; and had any of your servants called then, so far as I had a voice, they would not have been behind with any of their neighbours. After the lapse of some time, I, in tour of duty, wrote the Badenoch and Strathspey parishes offering them what remained, which would be about half their original proportion, and on the arrival of the last 200 bolls, it was divided among parishes in Ross-shire—included in my abstract—who got none before, and residue to make up some wanted by the Parishes of Alvie, Abernethy, and Cromdale, and till the middle of next week, which is the time fixed for exhausting these orders, I have it not in my power to give above a boll to any mortal. That boll I'll give to the bearer, at my risk, to oblige you, and if it shall turn out that the other parishes above mentioned will not in due time send for their quantity, I can spare more, and then I shall cheerfully comply with any such commands as you may impose on, dear sir, your sincere humble servant,

(Signed)   SIMON FRASER.

Addressed—"To Captain John Mackintosh of Kyllachy."

No. CLXIX. ANNO 1784.

GOVERNOR ALEXANDER SHAW OF TORDARROCH.

THE ancient tribe of the Shaws had their principal holdings in Badenoch, Rothiemurchus, Strathnairn, and the Isles of Inverness-shire. Their head was Shaw of Rothiemurchus, and the chief branch was Shaw of Tordarroch. Ay Mac-Bean vic-Robert signs on behalf of the clan Ay the bond of union among the haill kith and kin of the Clan Chattan, in 1609. The castle lands of Tordarroch were, with others, given by the Earl of Huntly in 1568 to Lachlan Mor Mackintosh, 16th of the house of Mackintosh, in assisthment of the murder of William Mackintosh, the 15th, in the year 1550. It is probable that, if not already established on the lands, Robert, the grandfather of Ay, of 1609, was put in possession of Tordarroch by Mackintosh in 1568 No more attached clansmen to their chief for upwards of 250 years existed on the great Mackintosh estates than the Shaws of Tordarroch. Angus Shaw acquired the lands of Wester Leys, part of the lordship of Lovat, and is entered as owner in 1644.

The old house of Wester Leys still stands, but a wreck,

and the only marks which denote that it was once the duchas of a gentleman are a few ornamental trees around what must have been at the time the garden. The situation is commanding, being the last cultivated land to the left as one ascends by the Strathnairn road to the water-shed separating the valley of the Ness and Nairn. The present house of Tordarroch is certainly old, and, if not the one existing when Prince Charles drew up for a moment on the afternoon of the day after the battle of Culloden, it stands on the same site. A quaint bridge, very narrow, and with pointed arch, erected by Wade, spans the Nairn just opposite to the house.

Alexander Shaw, who may be considered the last of the Tordarrochs—for he sold Wester Leys to Col. James Fraser of Culduthel, and the wadset of Tordarroch was redeemed from him by Sir Eneas Mackintosh—was educated at Inverness, and enjoyed the friendship of many of its distinguished citizens. He entered the army at a very early age, and was wounded at Quebec in 1759.

He was Governor of the Isle of Man from 1790 to 1804. The accompanying letter, addressed to Captain John Mackintosh, father of Sir James Mackintosh of Kyllachy, shows a kindly interest in the North, from which he was long estranged by the exigencies of his profession. He alludes to the results of the great scarcity in 1783. The Governor's brother, Eneas, settled in Canada, and his descendants are numerous and in good positions. The Governor was twice married, and his grandson, John Andrew Shaw-Mackenzie of Newhall, is the representative of the Shaws of Tordarroch. His great grandson, Alexander Mackintosh-Shaw, is the well-known historian of Clan Chattan.

Follows the letter referred to:—

My Dear Sir,—I do not recollect I ever had from you or any other any directions about your young herd's half pay, otherwise you may be very sure I would not have neglected it, nor would I anything in which you had a concern, even more remote than for a son. Herewith you will now receive a Power of Attorney for the young man to sign, as likewise certificates to be signed by him and a Magistrate. The half pay will probably be in course of payment by the time you return me these papers. I lament exceedingly the accounts you give of the misery of that poor country, but, still, I wish from all my heart I were once more an inhabitant of it. I hope times and seasons will change for the better, and that even the same season will restore the poor people to some degree of comfort. I have been a little gaunt lately, leaving my little woman and her brat with her mother near Bath—and the appearance of a crop of every kind was very favourable indeed, and I am told they are everywhere the same—south and north. God send a good harvest. The prize money going to Gibraltar I do not hear anything of; but the prize money *there* will, I believe, soon be in course of payment. The mode of dividend and the quantum to each rank are ascertained. A captain's share is somewhat about £40.

Remember me kindly to all our friends, and believe me to be, most sincerely, your affectionate and faithful servant,

(Signed) ALEX. SHAW.

Old Burlington Street, 16 July, 1784.

The Gibraltar prize money only awaits the King's warrant.

No. CLXX. ANNO 1785.
FRANCIS HUMBERSTON MACKENZIE OF SEAFORTH.

THE old title of Seaforth terminated with the forfeiture of William, fifth Earl, whose son, Kenneth, bore the title of Lord Fortrose. The title was revived in the person of Kenneth, Lord Fortrose's son, but he dying without male issue in 1781, the Earldom became extinct. The representation then devolved upon Thomas Frederick Mackenzie Humberston, eldest son of William Mackenzie, son of the Hon. Colonel Alexander Mackenzie, second son of Kenneth, fourth Earl of Seaforth. The English estates of Humberston were settled upon the said Thomas Frederick, the eldest son of William Mackenzie, but, he dying unmarried in 1783, was succeeded in the representation by his next brother, Francis Humberston Mackenzie, writer of the letter after mentioned. In his time, and chiefly, it is said, in consequence of his exertions to raise men for the service of the country, much of the vast Seaforth estates had to be disposed of. Francis Humberston Mackenzie was created Lord Seaforth towards the close of the century, but at his death the title again became extinct. He lived in great style, and the order given to the Wine Shop at Inverness would, if given in these degenerate days, be thought quite startling.

The reputation of the Wine Shop in the time of Fraser, Wilson, & Co., was almost world-wide. Being connected with "The Grocery" (alas, now closed!) and the Hemp Factory, the partners of Fraser, Wilson & Co. reigned supreme. What firm or individuals now-a-days engaged in business in Inverness would dream of giving a public dinner? Yet here is a card addressed to the accomplished Professor Macgregor of the Academy:—
"Mr. J. Fraser presents compliments to Mr. Macgregor, and requests the favour of his company to a dinner proposed to be given by Fraser, Wilson, & Co., to-morrow, at Fraser's Hotel. Dinner at 4. Friday ev'g."

The quantity, as well as the quality, of the wines were well attended to by the old Company. It is related that, after bottling a considerable quantity of wine for a customer, it was discovered that the bottles, just come in from the manufacturers, were rather small, and did not contain the full measure; whereupon every bottle was instantly reclaimed from the customer, and other and sufficient ones sent in their place.

Follows the letter referred to :—

Gentlemen,—I shall be obliged to you, on rect. of this, to send to Brahan wine as below, with directions not to unpack the crates till I arrive, which will be abt. 10 days after you get this.

I trust you will send no wines but the best; and if you have not good, rather send none. I am, gentlemen, your most obedient humble servant, (Signed) F. H. MACKENZIE.

Grafton Street, May 31st, 1785.

	Doz.
Claret	50
Port	30
Sherry	25

No. CLXXI. Anno 1786.

ARTHUR FORBES OF CULLODEN.

THE family of Culloden are, with the exception of the Mackintoshes óf Holme, the oldest vassals continuously of the town of Inverness. Duncan Forbes, 1st of Culloden, was proprietor of the lands of Bught before he became purchaser of Culloden, and his son John, second of Culloden, became the vassal of the town in those lands bordering the sea, which lie within the parish of Inverness, from the parish march at the east to the bounds of Raigmore's lands at the west. There has always been a close affinity and kindness betwixt the family and the town and its authorities. The Lord-President, for a considerable time, had a yearly salary as Doer for the town. The only time when an alienation of this kindly feeling prevailed was in the time of John, the second Culloden, before referred to. Culloden, Inshes, Castlehill, Dunain, and other landward heritors of the parish had a severe contest with the town, lasting upwards of ten years, in reference to certain duties claimed by the town for articles of country produce coming into the market. John Forbes of Culloden appears to have acted as convener of the heritors, and much ill-feeling prevailed. The letter after quoted, dated just a hundred and three years ago, from Arthur Forbes, then of Culloden, to Provost William Mackintosh of Inverness, is an instance of the kindly feeling referred to.

Follows the letter referred to :—

Culloden presents his most respectful compliments to the Provost and Magistrates of the town of Inverness, and begs leave to present them with a set of chandeliers for the Town Hall, which, he hopes, will prove acceptable. So soon as the room is ready, upon being made acquainted, Culloden's butler will attend and see them put up.

Culloden House, Wednesday, 18th July, 1786.

"To Provost William Mackintosh."

No. CLXXII. Anno 1787.

ANNE MACRA, THE "WISE WOMAN" OF BEAULY.

I DO not give the name of the person to whom the following letter was addressed, because I believe his descendants would be annoyed to think that a man in his position, and of his education, could have been so silly as to apply in his distress to a wise woman, passing over the clever and experienced Doctor Chisholm of Inverness. Persons who practised like Ann Macra were generally unable to write, and thus their prescriptions are not to be found in black and white. Ann, however, writes an excellent hand, though the spelling is not all that could be desired, such as "broaths," and it is fortunate that her letter, a rarity in its way, has been preserved. The rules laid down are excellent, and though the contents of the vial are not, and would not, be disclosed, that being the writer's secret and power, it may be conjectured that the mixture was a powerful combination of herbs, calculated to relieve the patient.

In former days, when communication was difficult, most women had that knowledge of medicine and herbs which enabled the expensive services of a doctor to be dispensed with, and it would be well, in the fancy for ambulance lectures now existing, that a knowledge of herbs and medicine generally, were part of female education.

Follows the letter referred to :—

> Directions for using my Universal Physic :—Fasting in the morning. Wash the mouth with cold water, then swallow half-a-gill in a dram glass of what the vial contains ; immediately after take a spoonful of cold water now and then till it settles on the stomach. The drink should be cock broth, or water gruel, to be taken at half-an-hour after taking the physick. To drink plentifully after every movement, keep warm, and take moderate exercise.

Allow two days betwixt each dose. Avoid taking fish or milk while using it. The vial contains only two dozes.

Sir,—I would recommend to you to rise early and take as much exercise as possible by walking or riding. Your diet should be light food, weak, fresh broths, and you may eat as much ripe fruits as you please. Keep your feet and stomach warm. By observing these directions and using the above medicine, I hope in a short time you will get better of your present complaint. I am, sir, your humble servant.

(Signed)   ANNE MACRA.

Beauly, 8th Sept., 1787.

No. CLXXIII. ANNO 1788.
MRS. MACDONELL OF GLENMEDDLE, AND EVICTIONS IN KNOYDART, ETC.

CAPTAIN JAMES MACDONELL, third son of John, the 19th Glengarry, had an only daughter, Amelia, who married Major Simon Macdonell of Morar. The lady was an heiress, and much sought after when living with her widowed mother, the writer of the letter after given, which is not dated, but endorsed "June 1788." The Major did not get very much encouragement, being rather eccentric. He on one visit tried to bring matters to a point, but failed, and could not in decency prolong an already somewhat lengthened visit. Unwilling to give it up, he fell upon a ruse, which turned out a success, viz., by upsetting, as was thought, accidentally, a kettle of boiling water over his legs and feet. Being severely scalded, he could not be removed for a long time, and, nursed by the lady with that pity akin to love, he made such advances that he left an engaged man. Mrs. Macdonald, writing to a friend at Inverness, refers to the dispossessed people of the country. Her letter is dated in 1788, but it would appear that a serious emigration occurred two years before, judging by the following letter, dated in March, 1786:—" Mr.—— has been at Greenock to engage a transport to carry the Knoydart people to Canada; there are already at least three hundred passengers engaged, and it is thought there will be many more. The vessel is to be at the Isle of Ornsay the beginning of June. These people, when once they settle in Canada, will encourage others, as they are now encouraged by some friends before them. They will form a chain of emigration. *It is thought the country will be converted into a sheep walk.* Should this grow general, and our gallant Highlanders desert us, I fear all the sheep that can be introduced and reared will form in their stead but a sorry defence against our ememies." The italics are mine. Knoydart is now verily a sheep walk, and I well recollect the last and worst of the Knoydart evictions. Mr. Knox, who visited the West Coast in 1786 and quotes the above letter, adds that the number of people who embarked amounted to 550.

Follows the letter referred to :—

Dear Sir,—I take the opportunity of the bearer to enquire of your Mrs. Macdonell and young son's health, which I hope are all well. We are well. Mrs. Macdonald (her daughter) is recovering, but not very strong as yet. You, no doubt, have heard we have got a young James (her grandson, afterwards Major James Macdonald of Morar, a gallant soldier), a fine child. May God bless and make him a good man, if He spares him. I daresay you know the most of the news of this country, which is none of the best for the poor people who are dispossessed. If you have the notes and papers you got here the time you wrote the contract, at hand, send them per bearer. I forgot when at Inverness, and be so good as direct the bearer to Miss Gordon's house, where I lodged, as I left my riding clothes there, and a gown Amelia (her daughter) wants Miss Bremner to make for her. Mr. Macdonald, her, and I make offer of our kindest compliments to you and Mrs. Macdonell, and I am, dear sir, your assured friend and humble servant,

(Signed) JEAN MACDONELL.

Best compliments to Mr. John Macdonell, wife, and family.

No. CLXXIV. ANNO 1789.
SIR JOHN MACPHERSON, BARONET, AND THE INVERNESS ACADEMY.

EXTRAORDINARY exertions were made by the authorities at Inverness towards the close of the last century to establish an Academy. The times were propitious, many Highlanders holding good positions in the East and West Indies. In Jamaica alone, in the year 1790, mainly through the exertions of Lewis Cuthbert, the last owner of Castlehill of the name, upwards of £500 were collected. Many of the letters which passed are most interesting. The Magistrates in their letters were complimentary, and pointed enough in their expectations, while the replies were friendly and couched in affectionate remembrances of their homes in the North. It has to be kept in view that letters to the East were a year on the way, and the answer occupied a like period. From the numerous letters on the subject of the Academy, I select the one annexed from Sir John Macpherson as being an eminently sensible one, suggesting the objects to be attained. Sir John Macpherson, younger son of the Rev. Dr. John Macpherson, after filling certain subordinate positions in the Indian Service, was appointed a member of the Supreme Council of Bengal in 1784. He was not appointed permanently, to his great mortification, and the letter shows that he had expected to return. He was created a baronet in 1786, and died unmarried at an advanced age in 1821.

The Academy having been satisfactorily started in the year 1793, the energies of the authorities were immediately turned to the founding of the Northern Infirmary, opened in 1803.

The letter is addressed to Provost Mackintosh, Inverness. Follows the letter referred to :—

Brompton, near London, 23rd March, 1789.
Sir,—Tho' I had the honour of receiving your letter of the 18th

November, 1787, in course of post, I did not reply to it at the time, for various reasons, however much I felt myself disposed to render all the service in my power to the very laudable undertaking of which you have been selected Chairman.

Your letter addressed to me in India, under date the 17th February, 1787, missed me, for I left India when you despatched it. I wished, before I replied to your last, to receive it back from India, with the opinion of my attorneys, who would communicate its contents to those naturally disposed in that country to favour the object recommended.

This pleasure I have not yet received; and it was uncertain, till very lately, whether it might not be thought necessary that I should return soon to India.

Had that event taken place, I was determined (having first informed myself of the practicability and fair intention of the institution proposed by your committee) to give your plan effectual aid and to recommend it to all my Highland friends in the East.

Tho' my wishes upon an extended scale, and with all the force of my influence, cannot now take effect to promote the scheme of an Academy at Inverness as they would have done had I returned to India, I am equally zealous in every matter that relates to the advantage of the Highlands and the Capital of our native county in particular. I have written to my agent at Edinburgh, Mr. William Macdonald, Writer to the Signet, to advance, in the first instance, fifty pounds sterling (£50) as a contribution to the plan, and if I see that it succeeds as I could wish, I will make further contributions to its success.

The principal objects to be recommended to the attention of the Academy should be, in my humble opinion, a grammatical knowledge of the English language, with a master to teach, not so much the English pronunciation as a proper discrimination between English and Scotch phrases and idioms, and the meaning of words as they are pronounced in both countries.

2ndly, To write correctly and fluently, so as to qualify the scholars to be good accountants and copiers, and secretaries to officers on public service at home and abroad.

3rdly, Navigation and French and Drawing! The great advantages of such an institution are to qualify gentlemen's sons who have no property to earn their bread by embarking in the world in lines in which persons who know themselves to be born of good families may work with the pen, the pencil, and the sword for support. In manual professions of less credit, Highland youth of good birth seldom succeed. The old Grammar School of Inverness was, I believe, a good one on its former establishment, and was sufficient to qualify young gentlemen for the Colleges of Aberdeen and St.

Andrews, for the first steps to the Kirk and Scots Law, and Physic. I have conversed with several gentlemen who have subscribed to the Inverness Academy, and given them my ideas as above. If it is attempted to make it a *half-College* and *half-Academy* Institution it will not succeed in either line. On the plan I have suggested a small capital will enable good masters to undertake the conduct of the Academy, and a concourse of scholars might, in small contributions from each scholar, make good appointments for the masters.

The Corporation of Inverness should take care to regulate the places and prices for boarding the scholars, and I think Government would aid in building an Academy, especially if the extent of the islands comprehended in the shire, and their distance from the county town, are considered and properly explained to the Administration. I am sure Sir Hector Munro will do all he can upon this head.—I have the honour to be, sir, your very humble servt.,

(Signed) JOHN MACPHERSON.

No. CLXXV. ANNO 1790.

CAPTAIN SIMON FRASER OF FANELLAN, ON THE BARONY OF DRUMCHARDINY, AIRD.

THE Barony of Drumchardiny was of old a part of the Lordship of Lovat, though for some time the property of Lachlan Mor Mackintosh of Mackintosh, who died in 1606, and his predecessors. The historian of the family of Mackintosh bewails the trickery by which Drumchardiny was lost to the Mackintoshes. Any one looking at the fine plantations and fences which ornament the contiguous estates of Newton and Lentran, and particularly the hill lands, will probably be surprised to know that less than a century ago these hill grounds were undivided. A Mr. Warrand having purchased the part of Drumchardiny to which Mr. Mackenzie of Delvin, W.S., a previous owner, had given the name of Lentran, after the property of that name in Ross, gave it the uneuphonious name of Warrandfield. From papers in my possession, he proved as troublesome a neighbour to Fraser of Dunballoch and to Relig as he possibly could. The subsequent owner re-assumed the name of Lentran, which the estate still bears. The leading name of old of Lentran estate was Rinduie. By the letter after quoted, addressed to his agent at Inverness, Fanellan, who was Dunballoch's (afterwards styled of Newton) brother, gives a very clear and well-written account of the Barony. The lands were subsequently divided formally. Lentran estate has changed hands frequently within the last century, but Newton still remains in the possession of one of Dunballoch's descendants.

Follows the letter referred to :—

Lovat, December 9th, 1790.

Sir,—Yesterday I got the enclosed copy, at Mr. Warrand's instance. I find he will not desist in giving Dunballoch unnecessary and illegal trouble, and I find it must ultimately end in the Supreme Courts. Of all the *outré* attempts, this is the most absurd; there is not an individual in the Aird but knows that the hills and muirs of both estates are undivided, and that for upwards of a century every Act of property was indiscriminately performed by each proprietor, from end to end of it, by improvement or otherwise. Mr. Warrand's estate and Dunballoch's were originally one under the denomination of the Barony of Drumchardiny; then the muirs belonged to one man. After the dismembering of it, Mr. Mackenzie of Delvin called his part of it Lentron, and they and their successors occupied the muirs as formerly—I may say by the *Broad Cast*, wherever one of them chose.

A consequence that corroborates this is that my father and Delvin joined in protecting the whole without any distinct part being allotted each of them ; and they jointly got a decreet of Declarator against the town of Inverness and neighbouring heritors to prevent them committing any acts of property on it.

Many writs and hundreds of evidences can be produced to confirm it.

Now, Mr. Warrand is certainly playing a dangerous game. There is now a legal still-house erected on the muir. By the interdict they will be considerable losers, and depend upon it he will be obliged to indemnify their losses, which will be considerable, if the interdict is not immediately taken off. I will be in town Wednesday, and no sooner, but this won't admit of delay.

I should think this is an affair of property, and I thought inferior Courts could not receive and determine such. You will take every necessary and quick step to prevent the men's being great sufferers—they have paid the Excise duty, and that, with other losses, will become heavy.—Your humble servant,

(Signed)   SIMON FRASER.

No. CLXXVI. ANNO 1791.
SIR JAMES MACKINTOSH AND THE "VIN-
DICIAE GALLICAE."

THE Mackintoshes of Kyllachy are the oldest cadets of the House of Mackintosh, having branched off in the time of Malcolm, 10th of Mackintosh, who died in 1457. Allan, third son of Malcolm, left posterity, who flourished— though not landholders—until the time of Angus, sometimes called "Angus Williamson," sometimes "Angus of the Brazen Face," a man of great repute in his day, and who, early in the 17th century, acquired the lands of Aldourie and others. Lachlan, eldest son of the above Angus, acquired Kyllachy, Dalmigavie, Farr, and other lands, and of him sprung the subsidiary families of Dalmigavie and Farr. In the beginning of last century, Angus was Laird of Kyllachy, and, though a very old man, took, with his eldest son Lachlan, an active part in the Rising of 1715. Lachlan having died without issue, was succeeded by his brother Alexander, who long carried on business in India, where he died. Alexander married Elizabeth Barbour of Aldourie, and, dying without issue, the succession opened to his nephew, Captain Angus Mackintosh, who died unmarried, and was in time succeeded by his brother, Captain John Mackintosh, father of Sir James Mackintosh. The property had become embarrassed through so many changes, and the widow of Alexander, who lived until about 1790, had a large jointure. By her will Mrs. Mackintosh specially bequeathed a portrait of Angus Williamson to Sir James Mackintosh.

Provost John Mackintosh, afterwards of Aberarder, a cousin of Kyllachy, took charge for many years of the estate, which, during his management, was preserved, but it was a thankless task, as James Mackintosh, from an early age, was extravagant in his expenditure and lived beyond his means. The numerous letters which passed between the Provost and his constituent, some in remonstrance, others in ingenious defence, are painful reading.

Early in 1791 Sir James had written the Provost, saying he had entered into engagements whereby he must, as a man of honour, have a large sum immediately remitted to him to London to meet them, but he did not enter into any particulars, and there was so much concealment and reticence that it was no wonder the Provost sharply replied that he had not the money, and that, as all his remonstrances seemed unavailing, he must ask to be relieved of his charges.

The letter after quoted is the reply. It is interesting in all points, and shows that remarkable power and facility of expression—which would now, however, be considered rather redundant—so characteristic of the writer. Sir James's embarrassments continued, and the Provost having relinquished the administration, which fell under the trusteeship of the Earl of Lauderdale and others—the estate, as is well known, was purchased in the year 1804 by Provost Phineas Mackintosh of Drummond. Other letters written by Sir James Mackintosh may be given hereafter. The following is the letter referred to:—

Little Ealing,
Monday, November 11th, 1791.

My dear Sir,—The length of my late silence to you demands an explanation, which, though it may not be satisfactory, will, I assure you, be sincere. I have really been considerably occupied, and I had real expectations of visiting the Highlands this season, but I will not be so uncandid as not to add that the tone of your last letter was another reason of my long silence. I never, indeed, questioned that right to admonish and to reprove, which, by so long a series of benefits, you had so amply acquired. I felt deference to be due to your experience, respect to your virtues—deference and respect I thought I had paid. That you should have differed in opinion with me on any proposition I made, I should not have wondered, because, from the different points of view at which we stand, objects might have appeared to have a very different degree of relative importance. But I confess my surprise that the proposition should have so suddenly have estranged you. I was placed in a situation, where prudence exacted the preservation of my property and rational ambition enlarged my hopes. I have committed myself and my family in the pursuit of a profession, and I have to conciliate, as well as I am able, that pursuit, with the important object of preserving my property. The proposition which I made appeared to me and others, an excellent mode of conciliating these objects, and whatever general suspicions imprudence may attach to my conduct, the detail of defence and the probability of pursuits could only come under my own observation, and, therefore, only under my own judgment. These reflections, my dear sir, had at least prepared me for a milder denial than I received from you, but their impression has long been effaced by the returning sentiment of that gratitude and respect which I shall never cease to feel for you; and it having been my own good fortune to raise the money I wanted by the unexpected success of my book, I have no further cause to keep alive feelings which never could have been more than temporary. Instead, therefore, of any longer dwelling on emotions which have ceased to prey on my mind, I shall pass to circumstances which will, I am sure, give pleasure to yours. The general popularity and the particular notice of distinguished persons which I have been so lucky to acquire, have so smoothed the way to success at the bar that the least sanguine of my friends are no longer doubtful of me. I may, without vanity, say that the first literary and political characters of the kingdom have courted my commission, and were I disposed to shipwreck my future hopes by the prostitution of my character and pen, the temptation of considerable income is not wanting. But I trust I shall have fortitude enough to fix a steady eye on higher and more honourable objects. I send down by Bain a copy of my third edition, which I beg you will do me the favour to accept as a mark of affection and respect. I shall certainly, early in next summer, visit the Highlands, and make a final arrangement of my little affairs, and you surely will not, after such long experienced goodness, think it presumptuous in me to hope that you will continue your care of them till that time. I am at present induced by various reasons to change my residence to London. In the retirement and cheapness which I expected from this country residence I have been undeceived by experience. Retirement is here less attainable because denial is less easy than in town, where it is so familiarly practised as to escape notice. Cheapness I could only expect originally in the article of house rent, all other expenses being the same. But this difference I have found more than counter-balanced by the expense of those occasional visits to London, which business or connection compelled me to make. The two great objects of keeping alive useful connections and attending the Courts of Law, can here be obtained scarcely at all, and, at best, expensively and imperfectly. Induced by these reasons, I move in two or three weeks to a small house I am about taking in London. After so long a suspension of correspondence, I know not how my affairs stand with you, but if they could bear a remittance of thirty pounds it would be a great accommodation, as expenses crowd on me at a moment of removal. I shall even trespass on your wonted good nature, in so far as to hope that you will remit this amount, though the balance in your hands may not justify the request.

I have nothing for the present to add, but my most earnest wishes for your happiness, and that of your family, and the best wishes of this little fireside to you and yours, and believe me ever, my dear sir, most sincerely yours,

(Signed) JAMES MACKINTOSH.

Readers will be glad to know that the £30 asked for was sent; and the Provost states that he had read the book with interest, and that it created quite a sensation in the North.

No. CLXXVII. ANNO 1792.

COLONEL JOHN BAILLIE OF LEYS.

THE following letter, from Colonel John Baillie of Leys, then an ensign in the East India Company's service, to his uncle, Colonel John Baillie of Dunain, will be read with interest. The writer speaks of it as long and possibly uninteresting. I have, however, seldom fallen upon such an admirable composition, and readers will be glad that it has been preserved. When it is considered that Leys was then only an ensign, little wonder need be felt that a great future was before him, if the chance were given. It was given, and Colonel Baillie came home about 1820 with a brilliant record, familiar to Oriental students, and a handsome fortune. Colonel Baillie rather exaggerated his early misdeeds. These were, that a born soldier, and sent to serve an apprenticeship with a Writer to the Signet against his will and inclinations, the spirit fretted and rebelled. He became dissipated and finally disappeared from Edinburgh. The intervention of a powerful friend in England, whose influence he sought, got him after years of inactivity into the army, when all went well. He behaved most handsomely to his sisters and the other members of the family. A letter from his clever sister, Margaret, who rushed to London to welcome him on his return, says of him that she found him everything the fondest sister could desire. Colonel Baillie, who was born in 1773, in the house bewest the River Ness long known as Ness House, Inverness, was younger son of Dr. George Baillie, who was eldest son of John Baillie, W.S., eldest son of James Baillie, the first possessor of Mid Leys, acquired about the year 1650. Colonel Baillie's mother was Ann, sister of Colonel John Baillie of Dunain. It was he who built Leys Castle—unfinished at his death —and planted with symmetry those fine surrounding woods which so greatly ornament the landscape. Colonel Baillie was able to repay his uncle's kindness in after years. Having been appointed by the Court *curator bonis* to his unfortunate cousin, the last Baillie of Dunain, he accepted the office in a letter full of high feeling, and fulfilled the duties with great prudence, until his sudden and lamented death on the 20th of April, 1833, shortly after his second election for the Inverness District of Burghs.

It may be noted that the gentleman from Dingwall, who is referred to in the letter, was uncle to the late Prime Minister. The attack on Seringapatam occurred in February, 1792, the month after the date of the letter, but the final capture, one of the greatest events in Indian history, did not take place until the 4th of May, 1799.

Follows the letter referred to :—

My dear Uncle,—If to receive intelligence of me or my concerns can afford you any pleasure or satisfaction, or if this will serve to convey to you the smallest idea of those principles of gratitude with which your affectionate attention to me as well as to the general interests of my family can and have never ceased to inspire me, I shall conceive this part of my duty the most fortunate as well as the most pleasant (except that of addressing my immediate parent) in which I have ever been engaged.

On my passage from Madras, I wrote a few lines by the "Queen Indiaman" to Margaret which I suppose you will have seen before this arrives. That, however, was done in great haste, and before I was able to give any just account of the general affairs in this country, or my own prospects as referring to them. I shall therefore not be sorry that that letter should not arrive. I have since, however, and by the same ship as this, wrote a long letter in which I have been as explicit and circumstantial as I could, and am convinced you will see that letter also. Indeed, so little has transpired worth notice since the date of it that I should hardly have troubled you at this time, except as a duty and just tribute to that tender and parental attention which you have always paid with pleasure to the most trifling interests of our family. You will see by that letter, and I am convinced that you will be happy to see that, notwithstanding the many disadvantages which my own imprudence and your just diffidence of my future conduct subjected me to, on my first arrival in this country, I have not been near so unfortunate as might be expected. I have met with several friends and acquaintances, whose kindness has enabled me to live ever since my arrival most agreeably and comfortably, and without a farthing of expense, which you know my purse was very ill calculated to afford. I did not carry with me on shore at Madras £2 of the small sum your bounty allowed in England, and from the want of every kind of necessaries on my arrival I was not able to bring away a single gold mohur of what you kindly authorised your friend, Mr. Tulloch, to allow me. You may easily then conceive how uncomfortable I should have been situated on my arrival here except that my good fortune afforded me an accidental meeting with some old friends. The gentleman I now live with, and most pleasantly I do live, is son of Provost Robertson of Dingwall, and after several misfortunes in India is now settled here for the present pretty comfortably, though I hope his situation will soon be much better and more independent. I have all the time hitherto shared with him all his comforts, both in his own house and with his friends in Calcutta, who are pretty numerous and respectable; and were it in his power, should not want the use of what he knows me very well to be quite destitute of. None of my pay has yet become due, as the army are two months in arrears, and were it even due I should not wish to draw it as I expect very soon, indeed almost every day, to be entitled to draw ensign's allowances, as there are more than vacancies already for all of us, I expect to have some arrears of pay to receive, which will be very acceptable. The allowance of an ensign in garrison, which is only a half batta. station, are 140 rs. per month, and when our promotion appears in general orders, which we expect daily, if I have the luck to be allowed to join a corps in the field, or even up the country, my allowances will be fully double. These you know to be very far superior to those at Madras, and therefore wisely chose this establishment, of which I am now very glad, though the cadets of Madras were certainly sooner promoted. With regard to my brother, who is in camp, I can say no more than what you can see in my former letter. I wrote him twice; my first I suppose from its size is miscarried.

The purport of both my letters was, I think, as nearly as possible the subject of our conversation in London. I explained to him briefly the state of my father's family, and mentioned his extreme anxiety, as well as yours, to hear from him, and pressed him earnestly to write. I concluded with mentioning my own situation, and that, if it was fully in his power, I should wish to be his debtor a short time for the small sum sufficient to furnish the articles immediately requisite for my military appearance, and which my own imprudence at home had prevented my friends from allowing me.

My not hearing from my brother hitherto, and my being joined to an European corps in Fort-William, have forced me, as you will see, to take a step which I much regret.

You will also see the reasons which urged me. I could not appear without the articles which I purchased, and had no credit. I do not even know that my having drawn for the sum will enable me to put off the payment till I receive pay sufficient to discharge it.

This was my sole motive, which you may perhaps condemn, but I am sure my situation justified. Were you to see a list of the articles and the expense attending the purchase, you would, I daresay, think as I do. You will be surprised when I tell you that my only regimental coat, and which I could not appear without, will necessarily cost near 80 rupees, and everything else in proportion. You know very well the expense of Europe articles in India, and need not mention it. They are here even more enormous than at Madras, and you may be sure the sum I have mentioned, and been obliged to draw, would not go far. I will not, however, say that I expect to be accepted, tho' I am sure, if my affairs in Edinr. have not turned out very pressing, you and my father will not wish to return it. I have not a doubt, if I live, of soon being able to pay all that I owe; and I shall be very happy that every farthing I have cost you and my father may be restored in one obligation to my sisters, which, if sent out, I will most gratefully sign, and with my first ability discharge. They are the chief, if not the only, sufferers from my extravagance, and the greatest cause why I now more than ever regret it, tho' I trust it may yet be the means of turning out to their as to my own advantage.

Since my letter to my father, very little new has transpired with regard to the army. Its situation, I believe, I can exactly describe to you from the latest accounts, which are dated the 16th Decr.

Lord Cornwallis, at the head of the greatest army that ever was seen in India, then lay encamped about seven miles from Bangalore. He had lately sent out a large detachment, commanded by Colonel Stewart, to reduce Severndairg, a stong fort, about or near ten miles from the place of his encampment, and he himself with the army remained to cover and protect that detachment in their operations, which have hitherto been successful. Two other smaller detachments upon the same service are encamped at the equal distances of seven miles from the army; the one commanded by Lieut.-Colonel Cockerell, and the other by Captain Walsh. When they succeeded agt. Severndairg, which there seems no doubt of before this time, it was the intention to proceed agt. Seringapatam, the destruction of which it is expected will soon, tho' not till after very hard struggles and severe losses, put a final conclusion to the war. With regard to the motions of the Western Army, under Genl. Abercromby, I am not so well acquainted, and they are not very interesting at present. I shall therefore say nothing of them.

We have of late been a little surprised, tho' not much alarmed, to hear of a smart action off Mangalore, on the coast of Malabar, between a French frigate, with two transports in convoy, and His Majesty's frigate, the "Phœnix," commanded by Sir Richd. Strahan. The transports are supposed to have been loaded with supplys to Tippoo's army, and, upon our Captain's requiring them to bring to, for the purpose of examination, he received a broadside from the French frigate, which did him very little damage, but only called forth his just resentment, which he immediately exercised to the almost final destruction of the Frenchman, whom he instantly boarded and took.

What effect this may have upon the politics of the two nations at home, there is no surmise of. A packet has lately arrived over land to Madras, which bring much interesting news about the French nation in particular, and of the total bankruptcy of the Dutch E. India Coy., as also of the destruction of their dock-yards and store-houses at the instigation of the Empress of Russia, and that a similar attempt had been vainly made in England. But I am only, I suppose, reciting what you are already acquainted with. I do not even know that I have said anything which will afford you amusement, or be considered as news. If it is so, I have at least endeavoured, as I shall always with pleasure do, to inform you of what I think will prove amusing or interesting, and

I have no doubt of your forgiveness if I have failed. I had almost forgot to mention a circumstance which gives me the most sincere regret—the death of Captain Phineas Mackintosh of Holm, in the 71st Regiment, with the grand army. He died in camp some time last month, though I do not know the particular day. His death, I believe, has been much and very justly regretted. I know not if this is the first account of his death that will be received by his friends; if it is, I shall be sorry to be the first relater of such distressing news. The length of this scrawl has, I am afraid, already displeased, if not disgusted, you at me; therefore, conclude it after paying you the compliments of the New Year. You are, I hope, fully persuaded of my most sincere and grateful good wishes (all I can offer) for the health and prosperity of you and your family. May I beg leave to be remembered to Mrs. Baillie and the dear little girl, if she at all remembers her cousin Johnny, whom she used to oblige with the appellation of "Puppy," a term which, though I trust a little reformed, he perhaps has not yet lost all manner of title to. That the Supreme Being may many new years preserve and bless you, my dearest parent and benefactor, and every branch of your family, in which, as a mark of your goodness, I believe many of my own are included, is, believe me, the most ardent and sincere wish of your ever grateful and affectionate nephew.

(Signed)   JOHN BAILLIE.
Calcutta, 30th January, 1792.

I might mention that, as I may not again have an opportunity of this season informing you to what corps I will be posted after promotion—when you are pleased to write me, an address as ensign on this establishment at Fort-William or elsewhere will be sufficient

No. CLXXVIII. ANNO 1793.

LADY MACKENZIE OF GRANDVALE.

THE letter after quoted, regarding the allocation of seats in the Gaelic Church of Inverness, nearly a century ago, is not without interest at present (1886), when many are grumbling at the sums payable for the repair of the Church. An opportunity, which will not soon occur again, to remove the Church altogether from its unsuitable and unhealthy position has unhappily been lost, and where an unsightly fabric remains, an ornamental structure on an appropriate site is a thing of the future. The present Gaelic Church was begun about the year 1790.

The writer of the letter was Dame Elizabeth Reid, otherwise Mackenzie, relict of Sir George Mackenzie of Grandvale and Cromarty, Bart., and in a document of 1791 she is described as daughter of "the deceased Captain John Reid, late of Cromarty."

Mr. Mackenzie, in his *History of the Mackenzies*, states that Sir George's affairs having become embarrassed, he, in the year 1741, sold the estate of Cromarty to Sir William Urquhart of Meldrum; that Sir George died in 1748 and was buried at Dingwall, his lady surviving him fifty-nine years, dying at Inverness in 1807, aged eighty-four. Lady Mackenzie was a very prominent figure in Inverness society for upwards of fifty years. The late Mr. Mackenzie of Woodside, in the year 1826, speaks of his having been acquainted with her from the year 1781, when he first came to Inverness; that her ladyship was highly respected, and he remembered that the Lords of Justiciary at their Circuits used to visit her, as did several respectable families of the name of Mackenzie from the county of Ross. Mr. Mackenzie says he became a favourite with her ladyship, and, being a native of Ross-shire, where the Clan Mackenzie chiefly resided, her ladyship used to tell him the origin and branches of different families of that name, particularly the Earl of Cromarty's family, her own husband—Sir George—being grandson of the first Earl; that she mentioned to him the great trouble she had after her husband's death, relative to his succession, and the exertions she had made as his widow to recover some of his effects; and particularly she mentioned her success in getting a pension from Government out of the residue of the price of the Barony of Royston, which, through the forfeiture of George III., Earl of Cromarty, had fallen to the Crown.

When Captain Kenneth Mackenzie succeeded to the estates of Cromarty, which had been restored to Lord

Macleod, he seems to have behaved very shabbily to Lady Mackenzie, and, in consequence, she had to reduce her establishment. Besides Woodside's testimony as to Lady Mackenzie's position and character, I have several letters regarding her from several of her cotemporaries in the same strain. The baronetcy held by her husband, through his grandfather, Kenneth, with the precedence of that conferred upon Sir John Mackenzie of Tarbat in 1628, was in abeyance for some time, and still exists, an empty title without estate.

Follows the letter referred to, addressed to the Town-Clerk of Inverness :—

Inverness, 21 Jany., 1793.

Lady Mackenzie's compliments to Mr. Mackintosh. She understands that this day at noon there is to be a meeting of the hereditors in the Highland Kirk to have pews. And as you are the factor upon the Dempsters, and by my permission paid five pound sterling for building the Kirk, you will please attend the hour of 12 o'clock at the Kirk, and claim a pew. In the old Kirk there were two pews for the proprietors of the lands upon which you are the factor at present.

No. CLXXIX. Anno 1794.

GLENGARRY, AND THE MEN OF KNOYDART WHO REFUSED TO ENLIST.

PRIOR to 1745, there was little difficulty in getting men in the Highlands to go out to fight, though it was very difficult to keep them long in the field continuously.

The Disarming Acts, prohibitive of the use of the Highland dress, and other severe and repressive measures, cowed to a great extent the martial spirit of the people. Large numbers of those in better circumstances, many of whom had been out in the '45, voluntarily expatriated themselves betwixt 1760 and 1790; and it cannot be alleged that towards the end of last century there was any strong feeling in favour of enlistment. All investigations point in the other direction; but undoubtedly, among the gentry, soldiering as a profession was popular, and the screw of landlordism was unscrupulously used for enlistment. While admiring the bravery and good conduct of the Highland regiments, it is impossible not to protest against the shameful manner in which the people were used—being nearly always sent to unhealthy climates without previous training or gradual assimilation to their altered circumstances and surroundings. It is not pretended that the poor people in the Highlands were excused from paying rent—no—they were called on to pay rent, and blood rent, too, to save themselves and families from eviction which to them was death.

The career of Alexander Macdonell of Glengarry, who died in 1828, is too well known in the Highlands to require lengthened remarks. His father died when he was about fifteen years of age, and he either had, or would suffer, no control from his mother or other guardians. He had hardly reached his majority in 1794 when he was named Colonel, with power to raise a regiment.

How he got on in Knoydart is seen by the letter annexed, addressed to his agent in Inverness; and readers will observe the reference, at the end of the enclosure, to cottars. This unfortunate class, then as now, and now as then, were and are the most hardly dealt with; but it is to be hoped that by-and-bye every honest, hard-working son of the soil will have security and permanence.

Authentic documents, such as that now referred to, are most valuable as illustrating the true history of the Highlands.

Here follow the letter and enclosure referred to:—

Scamadale, 29th Nov., 1794.

Sir,—Enclosed you have a list of small tenants belonging to my Knoydart property—their leases being expired by Whitsunday first—and having refused to serve me, I have fully determined to warn them out, and turn them off my property, without loss of time; and as this is the first order of the kind I have given you since I came of age, I have only to add that your punctuality and expedition

on the present occasion will be marked by me, and I am sir, your humble servant.
(Signed) A. MACDONELL,
Glengarry, Colonel.

A list of the tenants who refused themselves, their sons, or their brothers, to Colonel Macdonell :—

Rithedarroch.—Alex. Mackinnon, Rori Macdonell, Donald Gillies, Catharine Gillies.
Claischoille.—Ranald Macdonell, Donald Macdonell, Dugald Maclachlan.
Iuverimore.—John Macdonell, junior.
Killachoan.—Alex. Macdonell, Ranald Macdonell, Angus Mackinnon, senior.
Skiary.—Jas. Macdougald, Donald Macdougald, John Macdougald, Duncan Macphee, Ewen Cameron.
Lee and Mundle.—Donald Macgregor, Angus Macgregor, Donald Macmillan, Angus Macmillan, Ewen Macmillan.
Samadalan.—Angus Macdougald, Donald Macdonald.
Suthardheas.—Samuel Macdonell.
Salacharry.—John Macdonell, senior.
Kyles.—Rori Macdonell, Lachlan Macdonell.
Grob and Riguol,—Mr. Hugh Gray, Duncan Macdonell.

Their cottars must be particularly specified, as they have a great number of them that refused.

No. CLXXX. ANNO 1795.

JAMES FRASER OF GORTHLICK, C.S., AND LOWLAND SHEEP GRABBERS.

THE letter after given, from Mr. Fraser of Gorthlick to the Procurator-Fiscal of Inverness-shire, is of particular interest at present (1885), when, it is to be hoped, the policy of a century is to be reversed. At the period in question, the invasion of Lowland sheep farmers into the Highlands had become so steady and important, that the enmity of those being dispossessed was aroused, and some strong positions were taken up. Gorthlick was a writer in Edinburgh, much respected, and with a large business from the north, apart from the Lovat affairs. He writes cautiously and diplomatically, but reading between the lines it is easy to see what he meant. The particular lands he was interested in were those of Scotos in Knoydart. Ronald Macdonell of Scotos, a fine old character who had been engaged in the '45 on the Hanovarian side, had disposed of his estate to his eldest son, Eneas, on the marriage of the latter with Ann Fraser of Culbokie. Eneas died suddenly, leaving all his children pupils, and the estate was so embarrassed that it had to be sold to Glenmoriston, and he disposed of it to Glengarry. It is now part of Knoydart estate.

The old gentleman referred to in the letter was Ronald of Scotos above mentioned, who, so far as he had any interest, would not dispossess the old inhabitants. Mr. Stewart was of the family of Ballachulish, and held the office of Barrack-Master of Fort-Augustus. The two adventurers did not get Scothouse, which was afterwards let to a Mr. John Gillespie, but the names of Oliver and Stavert are not unfamiliar in connection with sheep farming in the north.

Follows the letter referred to :—

Edinburgh, 22nd April, 1795.

Dear Sir,—Two gentlemen from the Border have just now left me, who set out to-morrow morning for Ft.-Augustus, to examine the Culachy farm, and from thence they propose to proceed to Scothouse ; but, as they are entire strangers, and, I observe, somewhat alarmed and apprehensive of not being relished by the present possessors or others, I told them that I would write to you, and that you would probably direct them to a proper guide from Ft.-Augustus, which, indeed, would seem to be of no small consequence in order to guard agt. all prejudices or prepossessions from any interested third parties, and I think it somewhat fortunate that I hear the old gentleman is just now on some whimsical excursion to attend the inspection of his Chief's regiment.

As they seem prepared to take the shortest course on foot from Fort-Augustus, and know nothing of the country, they will surely not scruple to pay for a guide, and I should think you will think it advisable to find them a sagacious, intelligent man that will be able to show them the bounds, or bring them to Peter McNab, or others that may be willing as well as able to do so.

Their names are Messrs. Robert Oliver and Thomas Stavert. If your time admits, perhaps you might not be unwilling to meet with them; if not, you may address them at the inn at Fort-Augustus, or to Mr. Stewart's care. They propose being there and in the neighbourhood till Tuesday night, nor do I think they will leave it on Wednesday.—I am, dear sir, your

(Signed)   JAMES FRASER.

No. CLXXXI. ANNO 1796.

MUSIC TEACHING IN INVERNESS. THE KIRK-SESSION AND THE MAGISTRATES.

ALTHOUGH dancing and assemblies were common at Inverness during the last century, there seems to have been a difficulty in having a permanent music-master established in the town. General Wolfe, when stationed at Inverness after 1746, speaks of a ball at Inverness, where one of the beauties was a daughter of Keppoch, who fell at Culloden. Mrs. Duff of Muirtown in 1749, writes a friend that she intended keeping her daughter a few days over the period fixed for the visit, in order that the young lady might attend an assembly. An awkward sailor, writing from Calcutta in 1779, states that he has forwarded by ship to his partner at a ball a piece of Indian chintz, to replace a dress torn at an Inverness assembly. The difficulties with regard to music appears prominently in 1759, when the following advertisement appeared in the *Caledonian Mercury* of the 9th January:—
" A master for the Musick School of Inverness is wanted, qualified to teach vocal and instrumental musick, capable of being a precentor in church, and of a good moral character. Such person may, at Edinburgh, apply to Mr. Wm. Forbes, Writer to the Signet, and at Inverness to the Magistrates." The essential as to character would

denote a shortcoming in that respect in previous masters. In the year 1791 the difficulty again arises. In answer to a notification Mr. John Aitken, dating from Crichton Street, Dundee, applies for the office. From Greenock, Mr. Alexander D'Asti writes, referring to "Sir Wm. Forbes of Pitsligo, who, I hope, will satisfy as to both my character and qualifications. I observe what you are pleased to mention concerning church musick, and have requested Sir Wm. to inform that although I had never precented in church, my knowledge in musick would soon enable me to do it, and that in the meantime I might get a man to officiate for me. If I am so happy as to meet with the approval of the hon. the Magistrates of Inverness, and receive the honour of their commands, I make no doubt but Mrs. D'Asti and her daughter, who are thoroughly qualified to keep a sewing and boarding school, will soon merit the honour of their patronage." It would appear from the above letter as if the Magistrates had at last got the oft'-wished-for settlement; but it was not to be. Five years later the matter again comes up in the letter after given from the Kirk-Session to the Town Clerk. It was not until the time of Mr. Thomson that music-teaching took a permanent hold in Inverness. The town was never better served than during Mr. Thomson's long and honourable career; and precenting in the High Church was at its best in the time of the Hunters, father and son, his contemporaries.

Follows the letter referred to :—

Sir,—As you, no doubt, see the expediency of getting a well-recommended teacher of musick to the town, I am desired to intimate to you that it would be very agreeable to the Session that the person who shall be recommended be likewise qualified to discharge the duties of precentor and Session-Clerk, as it is believed the emoluments arising from teaching music would not, as yet, in Inverness be sufficient encouragement to induce a well-qualifyed man to accept of the office.—I am, sir, respectfully, your very humble servant,

(Signed) ROBERT ROSE, Mod.

Inverness, 19th February, 1796.

No. CLXXXII. ANNO 1797.

LANDING OF THE FRENCH IN WALES, AND THEIR CAPTURE BY LORD CAWDOR.

THE ineffectual expedition of the French to Ireland, in December, 1796, did not put an end to their views of being able to effect a landing in England. The letter, after quoted, from Mr. Macpherson of Ardersier, is interesting in recording the views and testimony of an actor in the curious event which occurred in Wales in the early part of the year 1797. Fourteen hundred men were embarked at Brest, and landed on the coast of Pembroke under great difficulties. The one half were veterans, but the other half are described as galley slaves, or men of that sort, taken out of prison on condition of engaging in the attempt. Their first object in landing was to steal, wherever they could, clothes necessary to cover them. Expecting to be joined by the country people, they found themselves wofully disappointed, being met by upwards of three thousand men, including seven hundred well-trained militia under Lord Cawdor: The French commander proposed terms, which were rejected by his lordship, and the next day the whole force surrendered unconditionally as prisoners of war, with their army, and ammunition in powder and ball sufficient to load seventy carts. The ships which carried the French set sail immediately after debarcation, leaving the French entirely to the chances of fortune. Lord Cawdor deservedly received great credit for the spirited manner in which he had acted.

Follows the letter referred to :—

Ardersier, 22nd March, 1797.

Dear Sir,—On the other side I send you a list of tenants in this parish who are to be removed at the approaching term of Whitsunday (unless they make up their peace by payment of their rents and amendment of their conduct), and to receive warnings accordingly. The officer that you sent last year was a very stupid fellow. I hope this year you will be able to employ a man fitter for the purpose. If not, Lord Cawdor's barony officer will do the business. The process will be raised at the instance of the Right Hon. Lord Cawdor and your humble servant as his factor.

I had a letter from Pembrokeshire two days ago, from an officer in Lord Cawdor's cavalry, which informs me that on the 4th inst. the remainder of the French prisoners taken by his lordship were safely lodged on ship board, and that the day before the papers were got from their officers which contained their directions from the French Government, which were to destroy and lay waste the country wherever they went, and, when joined by the inhabitants, to put them in front of any attack which might be made on them, and, if they did not do their duty, to bayonet them. This invasion was a great surprise to the people of that country, and as there were very few troops that could be collected in a moment, the country was in great danger.—I remain, dear sir, your most humble servant,

(Signed)   JAMES MACPHERSON.

List annexed :—Thomas Turner, at Black Park of Ardersier ; John Mackillican, at Easter Bog of do. ; Alexander Ross, at the Carse of do. ; —— William Sutherland's Widow, do. ; Murdow Mackillican, Taylor, at Campbelltown.

No. CLXXXIII. Anno 1798.

RARE DOINGS IN INVERNESS IN EARLY MAY.

A DUEL and elopement in one day would create a sensation in Inverness even during a Northern Meeting week in these days, when the town is so crowded. A century ago Inverness was very gay, and as early as the month of May the two events alluded to occurred. Subscription balls, now almost unknown, were then common, and the county families mingled freely with those of the principal merchants and officials of the town.

Mrs. Macbean, the writer of the gossiping letter after quoted, was of the former family of Mackintosh of Dalmigavie, and had married Mr. Robert Macbean, a merchant settled in the West Indian island of Tortola, who came home and purchased the estate of Culclachie, on the Nairn, changing its name to Nairnside. It is now part of the property of Raigmore.

In his most interesting memoir of Flora Macdonald, the late lamented Rev. Mr. Macgregor, referring to her descendants, notes Anne, her eldest daughter, as married to Major Macleod, their eldest son (Norman) being killed by Glengarry in a duel arising out of a rencontre at a Northern Meeting ball at Inverness. This Norman Macleod is the person referred to in the letter, but the ball was not a Northern Meeting one. Mrs. Macbean writes of Lieutenant Macleod as being severely, but not mortally, wounded. He unhappily died of his wounds, but in justice to Glengarry, I must own that, from letters and accounts of the matter I have seen, he did all he could to avoid a meeting, offering apologies sufficient to satisfy anyone save a fiery Islander.

The elopement of Provost Chisholm's daughter was spoken of for many years after. Two of her sisters were married respectively to Provost John Mackintosh, afterwards of Aberarder, and Mr. Munro, a wealthy merchant of the Island of Grenada, who bought part of the Fairfield property, and inhabited the "blue house," and are two of those mentioned as going in pursuit.

The references to Mrs. Macbean's household troubles show that the redcoats were popular and sought after in hall and kitchen in Inverness in those stirring and warlike times.

Follows the letter referred to:—

Inverness, May 5th, 1798.

I received your letter, dated the 19th, and I hope this will find you in Edinburgh, and we will soon see you in Inverness. Such wonderful events have happened here within these ten days past; the like have not been heard of in this corner of the world this many a year—an elopement and a duel in one day. I am sure your curiosity is raised, but you must have a little patience until I relate the circumstances as they happened. Well, to begin, there was a grand ball, given by the officers and some of the county gentlemen—among the rest Glengarry. He payed Miss

Forbes, Culloden, a deal of attention. Lieutenant Macleod, of the 42nd, asked her to dance and she did. Glengarry wished her not, and spoke rough to Macleod. After the ball was over they quarrelled. Macleod challenged Macdonald; they fought, and Macleod has got a severe wound, but not mortal; the other has escaped without a scratch; some people would not be sorry if he got a slight wound.

Well, now for the elopement. Can you guess who? But to keep you no longer in suspense, the night after the ball Captain Morrit and Miss Bell Chisholm set off at twelve o'clock at night in a carriage and four, accompanied by another officer. She was not missed until eight o'clock in the morning, and you may be sure her parents were in great distress. Provost John, Mr. Munro, and Mr. Fraser, Kirkhill, set off after them—they went the coast road. It is said the young people asked Mr. Stalker in Fort-George to marry them, but he would not. They were in Elgin that morning at eight o'clock, and would be in Aberdeen that night. Where they intend for I do not know, but the other gentlemen have continued the chase. It was never suspected that she was fond of him, nor was he ever within their house or Mr. Munro's. He did all he could to be introduced, but when any offer Mrs. Chisholm always declined it. Her sister (Emily) knew it; all the officers knew it; perhaps you will meet them. Their intention is to marry her whenever they meet her, and I hope that Captain Morrit never intended anything but what was honourable.

That very day, when I went to my mother's to tea, our servant Nancy went off to marry a soldier. Sally saw her married, and came back, but I paid her wages next morning, and sent her away because she did not let me know that Nancy was to be married. I am not at a loss for servants, for there are three or four in my offer. They say good ones. John is quite well, and so is all our others.

I do not intend to write you again, so make haste home. I am sure you may thank me for writing you all this news. It is so uncommon in this place that it is thought ——. Every person is sorry for Miss Chisholm; for you know what Morrit is.—I remain, your affectionate wife.

(Signed)   MARGARET MACBEAN.

Addressed—" Robert Macbean, Esq., care of Charles Mackintosh, Esq., W.S., Edinburgh."

No. CLXXXIV. Anno 1799.

SHERIFF FRASER OF FARRALINE AND THE STATE OF CRIME IN INVERNESS-SHIRE.

THE circular after given shows the state of the County, in the eyes of the chief legal authority, in a period of transition. No doubt a good deal of theft prevailed, and the horror of laird and farmer at the crime of sheep stealing was overpowering. People protected themselves—first, by paying black mail (not a voluntary tax), then through Captains of the Watch, who undertook districts which voluntarily assessed themselves; then a central authority took the matter in hand, appointing resolute men, like Mackay of Inchnacardoch, who were known in Gaelic as "Caiptin nam mearlach," "Captains, with men under them, to hunt down thieves"—men whose daring and intrepidity, probably from the system not having lasted very long, have not been immortalised like those of their predecessors—Captains of the Watch and the leviers of black mail.

The powers of justices and constables of old were very extensive and largely exercised, but for many years sheriffs and policemen have, in Scotland, almost exclusively taken their place.

Follows the letter referred to :—

Edinburgh, 10th April, 1799.

Sir,—You will probably recollect the state of the county of Inverness at the period I came into office, when a number of armed desperadoes infested some parts of it, and that theftuous practices very much prevailed in the district contiguous to Fort-Augustus. At that time it was judged advisable to have confidential persons stationed at Fort-Augustus, and in the line of communication betwixt it and Fort-William, whereby in a few years the whole culprits were apprehended and punished, or obliged to quit the country; and that district has for several years past been in a state of civilisation equal to any other part of the shire.

It now appears that the only district which is most likely to fall into outbreakings against public police lies to the south and north of Fort-William, where their remote and inaccessible situations have of late induced a few to commit crimes which have hitherto passed with impunity, it not having been in the power of the constables to apprehend them, although repeatedly employed in that service; and if this is permitted to go on, other districts (for there is none that wants some disorderly persons) may probably follow the example.

It occurred to me some years ago that the stations of the public constables ought to have been varied; and I therefore suggested to Mr. John Mackay, to whose vigilance, conduct, and exertions the county is much indebted, to remove to Fort-William, or the neighbourhood thereof; and now that sheep-stealing seems to have come to an alarming height, it has been the unanimous opinion of meetings of several districts of the county that the number of constables should be enlarged, and that their stations should be as follow:—1 at the Bridge-end of Inverness; 1 at the Ferry of Bona; 1 at Fort-Augustus; 1 at Auchteraw, in Abertaff; 1 at Leek, in Abertarff; one at Achadrom, in Glengarry; 1 at Muccomar; 1 at the Ferry of Lochy; 1 at the Ferry of Corran of Ardgour; 1 at Dalwhinnie; 1 at the west end of Loch-Treig, for Leckchirin; 1 at the King's House, at the head of Glencoe; 1 at Lynabirrach upon the water of Tromie; 1 at the Ferry of Invereshie—14 The advantage of such an establishment is abundantly obvious. They could not fail to detect any depredation from the northern counties, which are now sometimes driven southwards without molestation, and, upon the commission of any crime against the government of police of the conntry, a set of confidential men could be had upon short warning, ready to unite in apprehending the guilty or suspicious, in whatever district of the county they might take shelter. I shall only add, what will naturally occur, that such of the present constables as have served the county with vigour and fidelity, shall be preferred to the station most eligible to them, with as large an allowance as our funds can admit of.

As, probably, the foregoing plan may still receive improvement, I write you this circular letter requesting your attendance at Inverness on the first day of May next, in order that the collected wisdom of the county may take this measure under consideration.—I have the honour to be, sir, your most humble servant,

        (Signed)   SIMON FRASER, Sh: D: of Inverness.

No. CLXXXV. ANNO 1800.

THE REV. EDMUND MACQUEEN OF BARRA.

THE holding of large farms was but too common in the Hebrides on the part of clergymen of the Church of Scotland, and this matter, with others, was lately seriously attracting the attention of the leaders of the Supreme Ecclesiastical Court.

In a former letter it was shown that the ministers on the West Coast could not recover their stipends, and by the letter after given it would seem that the Laird of Barra was even claiming glebe lands. About this period all old things, connections, and feelings were subverted. I have just observed a decreet of ejection at the instance of Clanranald and his man Brown against "Lieutenant Angus Macdonald of the 91st Regiment of Foot; Colin Macdonald of Gariwaltus, sons of the deceased Captain Angus Macdonald of Milton ; Margaret Macdonald, Jane Macdonald, Penelope Macdonald, and Isobella Macdonald, daughters of the said deceased Captain Angus Macdonald of Millton, and the tutors and curators of such of them as are under age," from the town lands and grazings of Gariwaltus, Millton, and Kildonan. The Millton family, through its daughters and sons, might and did nobly serve Stuart and Hanoverian, but what of that?—a few pounds more rent quickly turned the balance in favour of strangers.

Mr. Edmund Macqueen was son of the Rev. Donald Macqueen of North Uist, a believer in the second sight. Mr. Macqueen of Barra was admitted in 1774, and died in 1812. Of him it is recorded, by a, perhaps, not very trustworthy traveller, "that he had an easy life, and generally not above half-a-dozen hearers on Sunday." This traveller was, perhaps, not aware of these dangerous proceedings on the part of Macneill and his doers, or he could not say the minister had an easy life.

Follows the letter referred to :—

Barray, February 28th, 1800.

Dear Sir,—I have lately received a summons at the instance of Mr. Macneill of Barray, in order to deprive me of my farms of Green and Luive. I beg you will take this business in hand, and get it put off till I have time to make proper defences. With respect to the farm of Green, Mr. Roderick Macleod, father to Lord Bannatyne Macleod of the Court of Session, at the time agent and sole manager for Mr. Macneill during his absence in America in the last war, and I, exchanged missives for the above farm, which I was to possess during my incumbences. These missives have remained at Edinburgh since that time (being in the year 1778), and will be produced how soon they can be obtained. With respect to Luive, that has been appropriated to the Church for upwards of sixty years back as a glebe, and it must remain with the Presbytery to show their right to it. Therefore, you will by all means prevent any decision in Mr. Macneill's favour until the proper vouchers can be produced, and, if you find it necessary, you will appeal to the Court of Session. That I can show Mr. Macleod's missive, there is no doubt, and the transaction about the glebe will be found (proper time being allowed) in the Tiend Office at Edinburgh.—I am, &c.,

(Signed) EDMUND MACQUEEN.

No. CLXXXVI. ANNO 1801.

MR. JAMES CLARK, OF NAPLES, PAINTER.

A FAMILY named Clark long held a respectable position in Inverness—one of them, Alexander, being Provost for a short period during the first half of last century. His descendant, James Clark, was long settled in Italy as a painter, and he had correspondence and dealings with many of the English nobility and patrons of the Fine Arts. The letter from his brother to the directors of the Inverness Academy is given, whereby the Academy benefitted to the extent of £725. It would seem that the picture which has been long in the Academy is of comparatively little value. As Mr. Clark must have been a thorough judge, it is clear he would not think of bequeathing an inferior painting to be placed in a prominent place in the town of his birth, and the great probability is that those entrusted with the transmission of the picture from Naples substituted the present inferior picture, defeating the wishes of the testator, and doing their best to cast a slur on his knowledge and taste. Such paintings do not entirely disappear, and it would be interesting to know where Mr. Clark's real picture is. Mr. Clark bequeathed valuable articles to his patrons—Lords Cawdor, Berwick, Palmerston, Bolton, Beverly, and others.

Mr. Clark bequeathed to the poor of the town of Inverness a share in his property in England, but not more than two pounds to one person. The share so falling to the poor amounted to £150, and Mr. Alexander Clark, in the distribution, wished that his cousin, Mr. Robert Macbean of Nairnside, and Mr. Wm. Grant, postmaster, be consulted in the choice of proper objects, to whom the charity was to be distributed.

Follows the letter referred to :—

To the Governor and Directors of the new established Academy, Inverness.

Gentlemen,—You will most probably have heard some time since of the death of my much-regretted brother, James Clark, who departed this life at Naples in December, 1799.

He appointed by his will Thomas Coutts, Esq., to be his executor in England, and Charles Lock and R. C. Jones, Esq., then at Naples, executors of the property in Italy.

Mr. Coutts, having declined acting or accepting of the legacy bequeathed him by my brother's will, has recommended my taking upon myself the administration of the effects in this country, I have accordingly administered in due form, and I beg leave to inform you that he has bequeathed to this institution five shares or five-sixtieths parts of his property in England, which consists of money in the Funds, the value of which consists of seven hundred and twenty-five pounds sterling.

The proper receipt from the Stamp Office I shall send with

other papers of a similar nature to my cousin, Mr. Robert Macbean of Nairnside, who will concert with you on the best mode of taking the necessary receipt on payment of the legacy.

My brother has also bequeathed to the said Academy, by the Neapolitan part of his will, a picture of the Holy Family, and for further particulars respecting both these legacys, I beg leave to annex you the words of the will. And I have the honour to be, with great respect, gentlemen, your most obt. servant,

(Signed)   ALEX. CLARK.

No. 10 Haymarket, London, 6 July, 1801.

"From the English will, tenth, I also bequeath five shares towards the support and advancement of the new established Academy in the town of Inverness (the place of my nativity, and which, for many reasons, is particularly dear to my memory), to be placed under the direction of the Governor and the Directors of the said Acadamy for the time being.

From the Neapolitan will, sixth, to the Directors and Governor of the new established Academy in Inverness, a picture of the Holy Family—Jesus Christ, the Virgin Mary, Joseph, and St. John—by Sassoferreatto, to be placed in the hall of the Academy."

No. CLXXXVII. Anno 1802.

SIR GEORGE STUART MACKENZIE OF COUL.

THE papers of this talented though eccentric laird, if preserved, would, if published, be very interesting. In particular his correspondence with many men eminent in literature and science must be valuable.

The annexed letter shows him in a favourable light, standing up for the rights of certain poor intending emigrants to America.

A good deal has been written as to emigration, voluntary and enforced, from the Highlands, but authentic accounts of the hardships and extortions practised on the route are much desiderated. Those which are known make it the more desirable that further information be, if possible, obtained.

Fort-William was, for the concluding twenty-five years

of the last century, and for the first twenty-five of this, the great port of embarkation. I have letters, in different years incidentally referring to the matter, such as, "There are now two vessels here taking in emigrants. Within the next ten days upwards of four hundred will have sailed."

This letter was written to a man of business in Inverness, who had interested himself for certain emigrants who were being swindled by an agent named Clark. The receiver puts on the back the single word "Emigrants."

Follows the letter referred to :—

Coul, 16 August, 1802.

Sir,—In consequence of correspondence with the Lord Advocate of some intending emigrants having been defrauded by Clark, the person who had agreed to take them to America,—I stuck up notices for such to apply to me, or to Mr. Munro at Dingwall, when they would be informed of means to recover their money. Some men were with me this morning, who said they had employed you in their cause, and that each had given you a sum of money for that purpose. Now, as I have got a positive opinion from the Lord Advocate, and have something to say with the Sheriff of Ross, and as the offence was committed in that county, and as I am at hand to see the business carried through; for the sake of expedition in the affair, I beg you will transmit the papers and evidences you have already got, or may get, to me, and that you will tell the people of the way in which the business is to be carried on.

You will also state the expenses which may be already incurred, as I hope either to get them paid by Clark, or have him in prison till we can squeeze it out of him. Your undertaking the cause does you much honour, and I have no doubt of your concurring readily in whatever is proposed to punish a man of so little humanity. If you have got any acknowledgments of Clark's for money received, pray send them, and any documents of a bargain having been made and not fulfilled, and also any information of where Clark is to be found. A list of those (with designations) who could be got to prove the bargain would be needful.—I remain, sir, your most obt. servant,

(Signed) GEORGE S. MACKENZIE.

No. CLXXXVIII. ANNO 1803.

THE HONOURABLE COLONEL ARCHIBALD C. FRASER OF LOVAT.

IN his younger days Archibald Fraser had much to struggle against. Having seen many of his productions, I cannot say that his character has impressed me favourably. He was very loyal to the reigning monarchy, and appears not to have had a spark of Jacobite feeling. He was, however, in his own way, clannish. On this point, writing to one of his tribe, under date, London, 26th March, 1785, he says:—"I never desert persons who show real attachment to my family. I have, last post, received notice that the indulgence I asked for you is to be shown to you, as far as the Lord Advocate's opinion can allow. If that does not reach the wishes of my heart, perhaps I may be some day able to do more myself."

As to his extreme loyalty, he writes to the Laird of Struy, under date, London, 1st July, 1782:—"In such tumults as have lately affected the Empire, every effort is laudable whose motives have a tendency to divert Transatlantick nations, and to make the home subjects conscious that their reasonable prayers will be listened to by a gracious King and Government, and that there are still existing persons who will protect and endeavour to procure every reasonable and expedient means of making them happy at home. And by spreading such sentiments among your people, you will be doing the State and yourself essential good.—Your affectionate Chief and humble servant."

I have given these letters as favourable specimens.

After his brother's death, and nominally succeeding to the estates, he was kept by the operation of General Fraser's trust and other troubles from obtaining the full possession of the estates for about twenty years. So soon as he had a free hand and the Act for relief of entailed proprietors had passed, he set himself busily to improve, according to his lights. Although the annexed curious letter had only of necessity to be sent to three people at the outside, Lovat was so pleased that he had it privately printed.

Follows the letter referred to :—

I, the Honourable Archibald Fraser of Lovat, heir of entail in the lands and estate of Lovat, intimate to you, Alexander Fraser, Esq. of Strichen, the next heir of entail in the said lands, except Simon Fraser, my son, in terms of the Act of Parliament of the tenth, George the Third, chapter fifty-one, entitled an Act for encouraging the improvement of lands in Scotland, held under settlements of strict entail, that I have come to the determination to new roof the family dwelling-house of Beaufort Castle, which has no roof since the estate came to me in 1782 ; that there being but two spare bed-chambers in the whole mansion, I mean to add an attic story at the same time, and also to complete the wings. I further mean to complete the fences of the Mains of Beaufort, and the wall round the garden in a suitable manner, and build a square of offices with accommodation for carriages, horses, implements of husbandry, cattle, and poultry. From time to time, I mean from experience gained by practice, to sub-divide the enclosures into more regular fields, and where needful to fence and bring waste land into tillage or permanent grass.

I propose to repair the family burying-place, now dilapidated. It is also become necessary, for the improvement of the estate, to enclose the two Lovats, Balblair, Donaldstown, Easter and Wester Kirkhills, Wester Dunballochs, the Muir of Easter Dunballoch and Mickle Phones, and throw the same and Cononside into safe enclosures, being fit lands to grow wheat, and shew the example of improvement before the inspection of the farmers of the estate, and thereby complete that face of the country. The Davochs of Ardrenish and Fannellan will be enclosed at the same time, and on the same public principle, for the benefit of posterity, and for the immediate employment of those who propose to emigrate for want of work at home.

I shall also (God willing) build a quay at the Port of Loveth, where, in the mid-channel of the river, under the old castle, there is two fathom and a half depth at low-water neap-tides. And, further, I propose to build a wharff at Beauly, to repair and feu out stances for houses and workshops, and to arrange the circumjacent land into proper lots for gardens, small parks, and the like, for the benefit of the inhabitants, and immediate ameliorating the income of the estate. The farms of Tomich, Barnyard, Beauly, Croyard, and Bridgend, being now liable to every sort of depredation, will also be enclosed and scientifically divided by approved surveyors.

This intimation and states of the expense of these salutary improvements will be made according to Act of Parliament in the Sheriff Court books of Inverness, and from time to time authentic extracts or copies may be had agreeable to law.

(Signed) · A. FRASER OF LOVAT.

Titled on the back—" Letter of intimation by Lovat, 1803."

No. CLXXXIX. ANNO 1804.

THE LORD AND VICE LIEUTENANT OF INVERNESS-SHIRE ON THE THREATENED INVASION.

THE annexed interesting letter and appendices show very clearly how fully alive the authorities were to the necessity of using every precaution to meet with success the threatened French invasion.

The county and burgh authorities were most active, the loyal spirit was very strong, volunteering highly popular, and money freely bestowed.

In the year 1796 nearly £2000 sterling, a great sum in those days, was subscribed in the town and parish of Inverness alone to assist the Government, and when the accounts came to be finally closed, the arrears were under £10, owing in two sums, one of £5 5s. being the amount subscribed by a Writer, who died in poor circumstances.

The present volunteer movement began in 1859, and may now be held to be a permanent and efficient contribution to our national defences.

Follows the letter referred to :—

Castle Grant, 22nd September, 1804.

Sir,—As, from the present intentions of the enemy and the advanced state to which they have brought their preparations for invasion, we have every reason to expect that they will omit no opportunity of making the attempt, it is our duty to neglect no measure of defence ; and, as Lord Moira gives me reason to believe, that the lieutenancy will be applied to immediately by the Generals commanding and the Inspecting Field Officers, to complete the arrangements for carrying the provisions and camp kettles of the Yeomanry and Volunteer corps, and for accelerating the movement of the forces in general, from their respective counties to the points of assembly in North Britain, or to such other quarter as the circumstances of the moment may prescribe ; I trust you have paid attention to the measures recommended by Mr. Yorke in his different letters, which I had the honour of communicating to you in November, January, and February last ; but as some time has elapsed since their dates, I request you will *immediately* take them again under your consideration, and give such directions as will most effectually ensure a ready, prompt, and orderly arrangement of such conveyance and measure for accelerating the movements of the forces in the district under your direction, so as to enable you to answer the call of the General commanding, upon the shortest notice.

You will do me the favour to write me, upon receipt of this (directing your letter to the care of Simon Fraser, Esq. of Farraline, Vice-Lieutenant of the County, at Inverness), stating particularly the measures which have been already, or are forthwith to be adopted in your district, in conjunction with the Commanding Officers of the Volunteer corps, in obedience to the commands of Government ; and, relying on your zealous exertions for promoting the public service, especially at a crisis so momentuous as the present, I subscribe myself, with the utmost regard, sir, your most obedient humble servant,

(Signed) JAMES GRANT,
H. M. Lt. C. Inverness.

(„) SIMON FRASER, V.L.

The Lieutenant of the Division of Inverness-shire.

P.S.—A note of the letters above alluded to is subjoined.

Sir James Grant's letter dated 12th November, 1803, conveyed the directions given in Mr. Yorke's letter of 31st October, 1803, relative to the removal of any boats, barges, waggons, carts, cars or other carriages ; horses, cattle, sheep, hay, straw, corn, meal, flour, or provisions of any kind, or any other things which may be of advantage to an enemy, or useful for the public service, taking the same, if necessary for the public service ; and destroying, or rendering useless such as may be in danger of falling into the hands of the enemy:—And as to the removal of such persons as by reason of infancy, age, or infirmity, are incapable of removing themselves, in case of danger. The same letter recommended the calling of a meeting in each district for fixing upon the appointment of Pioneers, the result of which is still unreported from some of the districts.

Mr. Yorke's circular letter of 16th January, 1804, transmitted by Sir James Grant on the 23rd of that month, referred to the above letter of 31st October; and also directed that one light cart per Company should be alloted, before hand, to each Company of Volunteers within the County of Inverness, and always kept marked and numbered, as the carriage intended for the use of that particular Company for carrying their camp kettles and necessaries on their march. It is proper to remark that, besides the cart per Company here alluded to, one will be requisite for conveying the fourteen days' provisions of such corps as have been directed to purchase these provisions; and, that, for both, a liberal hire will be allowed to the owners, when called for on the public service.

Mr Yorke's letter of 10th February, 1804, communicated by Sir James Grant on the 25th, states that, as the expense of such carriages as may be thought necessary for the use of the Volunteer force, will be defrayed by the public, it is to be presumed that the Lieutenancy will find no difficulty in allocating such as are most fit for the purpose, especially as it is not intended, when the allotment shall have been made, that they should be diverted from their ordinary use, until the exigencies of affairs shall require it.

Besides the directions contained in the above mentioned letters, Sir James Grant wrote, on the 31st of March, 1804, in conveyance of Mr. Yorke's letter of the 23rd, to the Deputy Lieutenants and Volunteer officers in the Islands of Inverness-shire, directing them to lose no time in alloting and marking a sufficient number of boats for the conveyance of the Volunteer force, in case of emergency, which it is hoped has been attended to in all the islands. It is but justice to Captain Campbell of Ensay to mention his spirited offer of furnishing smacks at his own expense, which His Majesty graciously approved and accepted.

No. CXC. Anno 1805.

A DAUGHTER OF THE MANSE ON HER LIVERPOOL EXPERIENCES.

THE annexed amusing letter was written with the greatest freedom, and the writer little thought that eighty years later it would be given to the world, affording, perhaps, fully as much pleasure in its perusal now as it did to the original receiver.

The lady was one of a talented family, with great literary tastes. The best people of their county visited at the Manse on familiar terms. Music, dancing, readings, and literary correspondence relieved the arduous and well-attended duties of parochial clerical life.

On her journey to Liverpool, Miss R—— rode by the old Highland road to Glasgow, and in a letter gives a vivid account of her journey, the first from the paternal roof. The following sentence in reference to the inn at Dalwhinnie is interesting :—" We were not in the room where Burns' inscription is written."

The Hugh so frequently referred to was the lady's brother. The reference to the elder Gladstone and his Ross-shire spouse will be read with interest. Their famous fourth son was not born until some years later. The Mrs. S—— was the writer's sister. Readers will be struck with the gay doings in Liverpool, and how they were kept up day after day, a seven miles drive on Sunday not being unusual or an event to be deprecated.

Follows the letter referred to, addressed to a friend of the family :—

Wednesday, 9th January, 1805.

Dear Sir,—I was interrupted here by a young lady (Miss Rogers), an intimate acquaintance of mine, coming to spend the evening, and on Tuesday I was obliged to go to town to buy commissions, and make indispensible calls, and in the evening went with the rest of this family to Miss Tennant's benefit concert, where we were unusually well entertained. Zancowitz excelled himself, if possible, his fine touches on the violin excelled any other fine sounds that can be produced on earth. Mr. Cizos plays the first violincello at the concerts, and he got Zancowitz, at our request, to introduce "O Nanny wilt thou gang wi' me," a heavenly air, in a fine concerto he played by himself—his style and variations were enchanting, every body listened in such apparent extasy that a breath could not be heard—it was loudly *encored*. I need not add that I was ready to drop down with rapture.

Hugh sat beside me ; he could not express his admiration ! and we looked at each other in a style which served better to give expression for what was inwardly felt than any words could convey.

Hugh went round the room with Mr. Rawlinson to be introduced *by sight!* to the reigning belles and beauties among the ladies! he came back to me and said he had over and *over* lost his heart during this circuit, and he did not wonder tho' they bore the appellation of "Lancashire Witches." (However much I admired them, I had too good a *grip* of my heart to lose it among ladies I knew nothing about. H. R.)

I trusted to Hugh to acquaint you of the birth of a son in this family. I am happy to tell you Mrs. S—— is making as fine a recovery as we can possibly wish. The birth took place on the evening of the 3rd inst. Mr. S—— is very much pleased with having a male *heir!* he says "he is the finest boy in all England." I think it is a happy thing when people are contented and pleased with what Providence grants to their share.

New Year's Day we spent at Mr. Gladstone's, with a party of thirty people, amongst whom were Col. and Mrs. Fraser of Culduthel, with their eldest son, and two daughters, all grown up. We had a dinner with three courses served up in silver plate and crystal, and a fine dessert in rich china, a large lustre over the table, and beautiful figures in bronze round the room supporting lights. Dancing began at 8, and supper announced at 12, which was superb. But I admired the manners of the landlord and his lady more than all the splendour that surrounded them; their's is indeed, "Dignity without pride, and condescension without meanness," which I think, is a happy talent to arrive at. Hugh was delighted with his visit and said, he never had, and never should wish to spend his time more to his mind. It is amusing to observe the effect these interferences have upon a stranger.

Thursday morning—This really is a time of interruptions, and I have my own share of them. I believe fate has decreed against my dispatching this scrawl in the time I had wished. I was called from this yesterday to sit with Miss Calverley, a Cheshire lady, who is on a visit in town, and at whose father's house we received extraordinary civilities the time of Chester races I wrote my mother. We took a trip 7 miles out of town one Sunday, which day we spent at Mr. Calverley's house, "The Old Moss," a most beautiful place. Mr. C., I am sorry to say, died 2 months ago. He was one of the very few men I took a fancy to like. His taste in the liberal arts and sciences was extreme, and universally admitted. He played the violin exquisitely, and painted landscapes and portraits in a very superior style of finishing—all self-taught— and, with all his accomplishments, possessed the greatest politeness, and so unassuming that everyone felt pleased in his company.

He was extremely hospitable and gentlemanly, possessing much of the "milk of human kindness," a tall, dignified figure, long visage and high features. In short, I cannot express how deeply I regretted the death of so estimable a man. There is a very just and pretty account given of him in the *Universal Magazine* for November or December among the deaths. He made a second marriage 7 years ago to a —— of a woman—as different from himself as day to night.

I could easily perceive he felt the contrast extremely, but he carried to her as politely and kindly as tho' she had been an *equal!* If you tire of all this medley, I beg you may burn it. These are kind of subjects I have a fancy for, and the turn of one's mind always shews itself if one does not endeavour to restrain it. With you, my good sir, I take the liberty of dwelling on my favourite subjects, convinced of your *long-suffering* patience on former occasions.

Last night we were out at tea; a ball and supper at Mr. Mullion's, Great George Street. He and his lady are an agreeable hearty pair. He is a lordly spirit! You would like him. He is a *good fellow*. We had a large party, and dispersed about 1 o'clock. To-night, Miss Ferguson and I go to Everton to a ball and supper at Mr. *Backhouse's*. He has four dashing daughters. They are immensely rich people. We are promised grand doings there. Twenty-six couples, Miss B. told me, had been engaged a fortnight ago. To-morrow we go to Mr. Taylor's to tea and cards; on Tuesday to Mr Vanse's to tea and cards; on the 21st to Mr. Sellar's to a famous ball and supper. Mrs. Sellar's sister is married to *Campbell* the *celebrated* poet.

No. CXCI. Anno 1806.

MR. EWEN MACLACHLAN, OF LOCHABER, POET AND SCHOLAR.

I HAVE several letters written by this distinguished scholar and good man. In the early years of this century every family almost of any position in the Highlands sent at least one of their sons to King's College, Aberdeen, and many were boarded with Mr. Maclachlan. He had the art of winning the confidence of his pupils, and interesting them in their studies.

The unpopularity of Glengarry with the county gentlemen and leading townsmen of Inverness greatly contributed to Mr. Maclachlan's losing the appointment to the Inverness Academy, which he ardently desired. Glengarry, who exerted himself in creating votes, was passionately attached to the Gaelic language, and I observe that some of his children were instructed in the language by Mr. Campbell, afterwards minister of Croy.

A native of Lochaber, Maclachlan's countrymen have done themselves honour in raising a monument to the memory of one in all respects a credit to the Highlands.

The letter after given is a fair specimen of Maclachlan's flowery style. The young gentleman he writes about was Simon Macdonald of Morar. The eldest son, Major James, died young abroad, and Simon himself, in his 21st year, lost his life through the accidental discharge of his gun.

The postscript is interesting, inasmuch as it refers to Maclachlan's first published work. It is styled "Attempts in Verse," and was published in 1807. The other works, of which I have copies, by him, besides the foregoing, are, "Elegy on the death of Beattie of Aberdeen, 1810," "Metrical Effusions, second edition, Aberdeen, 1816." Chance has given me the copy of Alexander Macdonald of the celebrated first Gaelic dictionary (published in 1741), which belonged to Mr. Maclachlan, and has many of his notes prepared for revising the dictionary.

Follows the letter referred to, addressed to a friend of the Morar family at Inverness :—

Sir,—With unexpressible pleasure I write you that the conduct of Mr. Simon Macdonald, since the commencement of the session, is such as entitles him to my unqualified approbation. To a most obliging and polite manner, he joins as exemplary an attention to his studies ; in one word he delights in his Greek, and respects Dr. Macpherson almost to adoration. I never saw him but in the genteelest company ; he detests blackguards of every denomination. He very often sits by our fireside, and takes great pleasure in reciting his tasks in my hearing, from which circumstance I know that his diligence is uncommon, and his progress rapid. I never saw a boy who has more attracted my love and esteem. This statement of facts must gratify the feelings of an affectionate mother, and it must please the whole clan of the Macdonalds to observe the vigour with which this elegant young branch is already unfolding its blossoms. I have long made it a business to trace the progressive evolution of the human faculties from the earliest stage of childhood, and from what I have already witnessed in Simon Macdonald, I doubt not but he will give exquisite pleasure to every person within the sphere of his acquaintance. He requested me to intimate that he intends, during the summer, to study arithmetic and mathematics at the Academy, but as he seems to have a strong predilection for the Latin, it would be much in his favour to study it with a private teacher. After so long a letter I conclude by requesting, as a particular favour, that you or his mama will have the goodness to give him some Christmas present, to testify your approbation of his conduct. I feel a lively interest in his welfare, and think no means should be neglected for stimulating his ardour. With respectful compliments to Mrs. Macdonell, Mr. James, and you, I conclude, and am, with unfeigned esteem, sir, your most obedient servant,

(Signed) EWEN MACLACHLAN.

Old Aberdeen, 21st Dec., 1806.

N.B.—I have been compelled by the students to undertake the publication of a few original compositions by subscription. The price of the pamphlet may amount to 1s. 6d. Perhaps some of my Inverness friends might wish for a few copies. The poems have been sent to the printing office, and will be made public in the course of a fortnight.

No. CXCII. Anno 1807.

LACHLAN MACKINTOSH OF RAIGMORE.

THE annexed letter, from the last Raigmore, is a good specimen of clear, but old-fashioned and somewhat rotund style of composition.

Eneas Mackintosh of Raigmore died at Cantraydown about 1788, and his sons had to make their way in the world. Lachlan, the eldest, was for some time a mariner, and afterwards a merchant in Calcutta, in which position he soon earned a large fortune. Before his return he was the means of raising large sums for the Inverness Academy and Northern Infirmary; and his letter shows but little of that contrary spirit which, for the last thirty years of his life, was so strongly displayed in his debates with the authorities of Inverness, and those connected with, or who supported them. In this letter, which, no doubt, at the time truly expressed his views, he speaks of the respect he had for many of the inhabitants. Raigmore received his education at Fortrose, and, in 1817, referring to a visit he had been requested to make, in order to settle some differences betwixt the Directors of the Fortrose Academy and the Magistrates of Fortrose, and which he was successful in accomplishing, he writes to Sir Eneas Mackintosh—"It will, I am sure, give you as much pleasure as it does me, to see the place to which we are both indebted for education, flourish from the almost only source which is capable of giving it prosperity."

Raigmore got a good part of Castlehill, to the north-east of Ault Muirnich, built his house on the terrace, overlooking the Moray Firth, and his successor has been so fortunate as to secure all the Castlehill estate, north and east of the Highland road.

Follows extract from letter by Raigmore, dated Calcutta, 1807 :—

Since my letter to you of the 12th January, it has occurred to me that a possibility may exist of the Castlehill estate remaining still on hand. It is, however, so remote, and so barely a possibility, that it is not with a view to it I at présent trouble you, for, were it really the case, it might, amongst so many Demerara and West India overgrown fortunes, go at a rate which it would be by no means prudent for me to give for it. On account of its situation, however, its contiguity to Inverness, and proximity to the sea, it is a property which would have suited my wishes extremely well, were its price and the manner of paying for it equally unobjectionable. The early age at which I left Scotland, gave me little opportunity of acquiring local knowledge of any part of it, but independent of family connections, the respect in which I hold many of the inhabitants of Inverness and neighbourhood, who are, and some who are not, personally known to me, gives me a strong desire to settle and possess a property amongst them, and as the superintendence of such a property would, perhaps, in a great manner constitute my employment and amusement, I should wish it to be compact, and so situated as to give me an opportunity of a general superintendence, however little I might farm of it myself. Indians, they say, are not fond of living far from towns, and some of my own friends who went home with strong impressions in favour of a country life, after having tried it, now express their disappointment; and, not content even with the neighbourhood of Bath or other equally famous places, are drawing near the Metropolis, as the residence most congenial to their wishes and habits. This would not be my case, yet I should not wish to live any distance from a town, and were I to choose a site for a house, it would, according to my present ideas, be within a mile or less of Inverness, near the sea, and with a good open prospect of the Firth. This, with the Castlehill estate, would, I think, fix me at Inverness. Your observation is strictly just of the satisfaction it must afford every man to have a previous knowledge of landed property before he becomes the proprietor of it. Unfortunately, however, the many thousand miles between us leave to me, in my situation, the option only of becoming proprietor in this way, or not at all. Should we delay until we can personally approve, an opportunity may be lost, and we may be driven to seek that in other countries, which we would prefer in that which gave us birth. In case, therefore, such a thing should offer, I will just sketch my wishes on the subject, and if my mother, uncle, and yourself agree on the subject, be assured that the purchase will be satisfactory to me.

No. CXCIII. Anno 1808.

COLONEL HALKETT AND GLENGARRY AND ROTHIEMURCHUS.

GLENGARRY was engaged in several affairs of honour, but the one referred to in the annexed letter is not well-known, as it was hushed up by the friends of the lady (for there is generally a lady in these cases), as was mentioned to me years ago by a gentleman who was present on the occasion. Glengarry must have led an exciting life, for not long before was pronounced the serious judgment against him for £2000 of damages in

Dr. Macdonald's case, and the recommendation of the Court of Session that he be removed from the Lieutenancy and Magistracy of the County of Inverness.

Follows the letter referred to, addressed to Glengarry, who, according to Mrs. Macdonell, on 11th June wrote in answer in the terms he thought best, so that this matter, she states, "is now amicably settled":—

Inverness, June 10th, 1808.

My dear Sir,—Immediately on receipt of yours of this morning, with its enclosure from Rothiemurchus, I had a conversation with Corrymonie on the subject thereof. This I thought proper to do in the first instance, as he is mentioned by Rothiemurchus in his note to you as his friend.

I afterwards had an interview with Rothiemurchus, at which Colonel Grant of Moy and Corriemony were present. The cause of the altercation and the words which had passed were of course fully canvassed, and from your statement, theirs, and what I myself heard, it was allowed that though there were some warmth shown by both, that still there was no improper language used by either. That this being the case, there could be no necessity for proceeding to extremities, or any call for an apology from either; but that both parties should declare they did not mean to offend. On this Rothiemurchus most readily declared that he had not the most distant idea of any insult to you, and I was statisfied that you had as little intention of that nature towards him, the whole business having grown out of a misunderstanding. I have now to give you my opinion, which is, that as there was no improper expressions on either part, and Rothiemurchus having declared that he had not the most distant idea of insult towards you, that you should declare on your part in a letter to me that you had not the slightest intention of insult to him. This I shall send to Corriemony or Colonel Grant, to be communicated to Rothiemurchus, or I will personally acquaint the latter with the contents of your letter. It appears to me of little consequence which is done; or, if you would prefer it, you might come down here and both parties declare the same sentiments at the same time, but this I do not think at all necessary. I have now given you my opinion on this business and the conduct, were I in your situation, I would pursue. Had any direct insult passed, the case would have been widely different. As it stands, I see no reason why any further proceedings should take place, more than the mutual explanations before mentioned.—I remain, my dear sir, yours very truly,

(Signed)   JOHN C. HALKETT.

I have collected many curious papers concerning Glengarry. One of the most amusing relates to an apartment in the Caledonian Hotel, formerly the Mason Lodge in which Lovat kept a room from year to year, as he was often in Inverness, particularly when on military duty at Fort-George. The particulars will be found in letter CXCV.

No. CXCIV. Anno 1809.
CAPTAIN CHARLES MUNRO, LATE 42ND REGIMENT.

"Young Munro, Charlie agam,
Young Munro, s' tu mo ghaol."

Fifty years ago this song was very popular in the counties of Inverness and Ross, and I have often heard it sung in "ceilidhs," chiefly by girls. The author's name is unknown, but Robert Munro, in his reminiscences, says it was composed by an Inverness lady*; if so, some of the lines are rather free, when literally translated into English, and it must not be forgotten that Captain Munro was a married man, as he himself states. A lady now living (1889) told me she was well acquainted with young Munro.

Some papers relative to an intended duel in the year 1809 having fallen under observation, in which Munro was concerned, I give his declaration.

There can be no doubt he was very popular, and this may have arisen from his fine appearance, skill as a swordsman, and affable manner, all spoken to by Robert Munro, who had his information from people who knew him and the circumstances connected with his unhappy end. A small farmer, named Fergusson, had a grievance of some standing with Munro, and meeting in a smithy in Rossshire, Fergusson was so enraged that he seized a large knife and stabbed Captain Munro, who died within a few hours. Fergusson, whom many commiserated, the affair

* Since this letter first appeared the name has been communicated to me. She died single.—C. F.-M.

not being premediated, was executed at the Longman, Inverness, about 1812.

Militarism was very strong in the Highlands in the beginning of the century, and every man of position was either in the regular army, fencibles, locals, or volunteers. It could not but eventuate at a period when family and neighbour disputes were rife—always breaking out at funerals and gatherings—that the meetings of officers, with hard drinking going on, led to strife and quarrels.

In the month of March, 1808, Hugh Fraser of Eskadale challenged Captain Hugh Chisholm at Midmain, late of the Royals. Both parties had to find caution to keep the peace for twelve months, but immediately, on the expiry of this period, the quarrel was renewed, and a complaint was made to the Sheriff of Inverness-shire on 2nd May, 1809, that Hugh Fraser of Eskadale and Captain Hugh Chisholm, tacksman of Midmain, having had differences, a challenge ensued, wherein Dr. Wm. Kennedy, of Inverness, and Charles Munro, late of the 42nd Regiment, then residing on the Green of Muirtown, were seconds. All parties were brought up, and the principals again ordered to find security. Captain Munro's judicial declaration was as follows, taken at Inverness said 2nd May, 1809. It will be observed that the Captain, finding himself in the hands of justice, minimizes his part:—

> Appeared Captain Charles Munro, late of the Forty-Second, now on half-pay in the Sixty-Second Regiment, married, aged thirty years or thereby, who, being judicially examined and interrogated, declares that yesterday morning a message was sent to the declarant's house, desiring the declarant to come and speak to Captain Hugh Chisholm, tacksman of Midmain, and the declarant not being then in the way, a second message was sent to his house acquainting him that Captain Chisholm and Ensign Kenneth Murchison, of the 78th, had been waiting the declarant at Miss Ettles, and the declarant having gone there, Captain Chisholm asked him if he would be his friend, which the declarant answered that he was well disposed to be so, but wished to know the particular cause now alluded to, upon which Captain Chisholm said that he had some difference with Captain Fraser of Eskadale, and desired the declarant call upon Dr. Kennedy, who would talk to him on the subject. That

the declarant having soon thereafter met Dr. Kennedy, asked him to inform him of the difference subsisting between Eskadale and Captain Chisholm. That Dr. Kennedy declined to give any explanation, but having met him a short time thereafter, said to him that he was determined to have nothing to do with the business formerly alluded to betwixt Eskadale and Captain Chisholm. Declares that the Captain, soon thereafter went home to Midmain, but upon going away told the declarant that he would be glad to see him at the Ferry House upon the north side of Kessock, either that evening or this morning. That in consequence of this, the declarant went to the Ferry House this morning, where he met the said Captain Hugh Chisholm, and communicated to him what passed 'twixt him and Dr. Kennedy. Declares that there was a pair of pistols on the table in the room where Captain Chisholm and the declarant met in the house on the other side of the Ferry. Declares that the declarant told Captain Chisholm that he would have nothing more to do in that business, and mentioned that he had said so to Dr. Kennedy.

(Signed) CHAS. MUNRO.

The object of going to North Kessock, as appears by the procedure, was to get beyond the Sheriff's jurisdiction, it being supposed that the bond was inoperative outside the county of Inverness.

NO. CXCV. ANNO 1810.

THE HONOURABLE ARCHIBALD FRASER OF LOVAT.

THE Northern Meeting has just (1888) been celebrating its centenary in quietness and prosperity.

This seems not an unsuitable opportunity for referring to a singular episode in its early history. Although Lovat was twice Glengarry's age, yet, from his fiery and haughty temperament, it would not have been strange had he, on account of the outrage referred to in the letter after given, sent a challenge which might have been attended with fatal results. Glengarry's behaviour, as detailed in Lovat's letter, was in the highest degree unjustifiable, but, notwithstanding, Lovat delayed, in consequence of Mrs. Macdonell's state, to take any steps for about three months. The circumstances are fully detailed in the letter. The Crown refused to prosecute, but intimated willingness to concur in a criminal process, should Lovat take such a step. This process was raised, and, after certain procedure, was withdrawn, mutual friends having procured a satisfactory adjustment. Lovat was not at all a close church-goer, and his appearance on the Sunday referred to, rather late, and his untimely exit from the Dunain gallery pew, in the High Church, Inverness, attracted much attention. Lovat had on a Fraser tartan doublet and trews, *per se*, and, apart from the individual, rather a startling costume for church. Mr. Gregor Urquhart, afterwards the well-known painter, then juvenile monitor to the late Laird of Inshes, sitting in the Inshes gallery seat in the Church, took a pencil sketch of Lovat, which was afterwards extended in oil. It is a poor work of art, being Urquhart's first attempt in oils. This portrait, after various vicissitudes, came into my hands, and was presented to Sir Willam A. Fraser of Leadclune, great nephew of Lovat's wife, and is now amongst his many and valuable collections connected with the Lovat family.

Follows the letter referred to :—

C. Beaufort, 29th Dec., 1810.

Sir,—Having served the Empire under the best of Sovereigns for upwards of forty years in the Diplomatic and Military departments, my feelings are much impressed and my mind quite made up on the idea that an apartment in any lodging, inn, or hotel, hired by me and of which I keep the key, to preserve my papers, apparel, and effects, is as much my castle as my own house.

On this ground I call on you to establish that proposition legally, in a case relative to myself, and which I do loudly claim the public mind to have full satisfaction, to evince that no person whatever, may be allowed to trespass on sacred right of a free and independent subject, under the protection and enjoying the privilege thereunto annexed ; and this I do most freely now, because I understand from unquestionable authority, that the daughter of my friend Sir William Forbes, married to the person who I have to prosecute, is out of all danger of a miscarriage, which at the time might from a sudden alarm have been apprehended.

The person who, without discretion, broke through all bounds, is no other than Colonel Macdonell of Glengarry, and the facts I now sit down to state.

On Saturday, the last day of the Northern Meeting this last season, in order to amuse the strangers who had come from a distance, a number of young persons wanted the sanction of my name for an additional dance, which, on account of its being the Eve of Sabbath, I at first objected to; but having been offered a condition to have it in my power to end the dance and put out the lights of the ball-room before midnight, the direction fell on myself, and Glengarry was one of the party. The ball finished as I had capitulated for. The ladies supped, and the gentlemen remained in the supper room, or returned after seeing them home, to drink the ladies' health. I thought it my duty to keep up the hilarity, but maintain the decorum of the meeting which the public expected.

By some accident, Glengarry and I exchanged hats. He put up at Ettles, I at Fraser's directly opposite. The moment I came home to Fraser's I sent Glengarry's hat back to the custody of Ettles to be given to Glengarry.

Next day, being Sunday, I went to the High Kirk, when I was summoned in the middle of the sermon, and called out by a message, that Glengarry insisted on seeing me on pressing business. I came out of kirk to the alarm of the whole congregation, who concluded I had got a military express, or was taken ill. Upon going to Fraser's Hotel, not two hundred yards distance [now the Caledonian Hotel—C. F.-M] I found Glengarry gone out of town, after beating open my locked door, in which there was a good deal of money and papers in a law contest I have with him for taking a grant of feu duties due the Crown on my estate of Abertarff but granted to me 15 years ago—my apartment being ransacked, and his hat not found. The door was left open by Glengarry, who in a supercilious, dictatorial tone of voice hallood to the landlord to have the lock mended at his, Glengarry's, expense. The manners of the gentleman I overlook, but as a public man I demand Glengarry and all the world to be made sensible that any man's apartment is his sacred castle, and that it is criminal to break it open under any pretence without legal warrant. I have the honour to be, dear Sir, your faithful humble servant,

     (Signed) AD. FRASER, LOVAT.

Addressed to Simon Fraser, Esq. of Farraline, Sheriff of Inverness-shire.

No. CXCVI. Anno 1811.

AN ALLEGED BREACH OF PROMISE OF MARRIAGE.

I HAVE altered the date and suppressed names in the annexed letter, in case of offence being taken by the representatives of those interested. Of course every one concerned is long dead.

The letter was circulated in print among the writer's friends and the gentlemen of the North. It is singularly well put together, and as the writer by himself could never have concocted it, I have wondered who was the real author. Actions for breach of promise of marriage have become so common as to amount to a scandal, and the ex-Lord Chancellor Herschell introduced a bill many years ago for their abolition. They are nearly always what is called attorney's actions, and as the lady has to put her whole previous life at the mercy of a cross-examination, the ordeal is not submitted to by any one of sensitiveness. Juries of late have also been giving excessive sums, and as a rule never give damages where a man is plaintiff.

In the case referred to in the letter, no proceeding took place, it being understood that the lady was not at all anxious in the matter, but had been egged forward by her father who thought the marriage would be what is termed in common language a "good catch."

Follows the letter referred to :—

However disagreeable it may be intrude upon one's friends, or the public, yet occurrences, or the machinations of enemies, may render such a step not only proper but inevitable. In such a situation I find myself placed, and to be silent, amidst the false representations of a party in confederacy against me, would be to give sanction to deceit. I should naturally feel much greater pain in involving the fair sex in discussion of a public nature than of being myself the subject even of unjust animadversion, but the line of conduct pursued by ——— having showed that he held such motives in contempt it does not belong me to repair what he has thought fit not to prevent. If I can judge by his measures, and report, it would seem that he has given out for a long time that I had given serious promises of connecting myself with his family, and that now I have changed my intentions of this. I was long ignorant of, and both these assertions are untrue. I never inclined, nor did I ever make any promise of the kind, and ——— conduct in my own house, on an occasion but a very short time before he left Inverness, gave me the opportunity of asking him if such was the case before three most respectable gentlemen, who can vouch that he allowed it was not. Had not motives of a nature capable of actuating the breast of a manly honour and feeling been urged to me the next day by ———, I should on this occasion have dropped his acquaintance, but not doing this, during the few days he remained in Inverness, my intentions in continuing in his society did not become less unequivocal. This could easily be proved by the declarations of his own family, and should circumstances put me to the disagreeable necessity I can state facts which though honourable to the ladies, will show that no attention of mine could be construed into a matrimonial view.

Does it result that a young man is to marry every young lady in whose society he sometimes, or often, passes a few hours, or of whom he may entertain a high opinion? or does it result that presenting a few trinkets to a lady, is the certain or even probable pledge of matrimony? If such was the case, I should be under more obligations of this nature than I have yet counted years. I assert that whatever ——— may have thought proper for this year to give out, neither he, nor any part of his family, ever had the smallest ground for believing that my frequent hospitality to him, or my attention to his family, passed the limits of common civility, and good will. In what manner he has returned this line of conduct it is not necessary for me to state. Has ——— conduct been so ungaurded, not to say more, as not to furnish him with the means of showing the contrary of this statement. Was it unfounded? or, had he anything to bring forward, what can prevent him? Can it be believed that he wants the inclination, or that his motives of delicacy influence his conduct.

Nearly nine months had elapsed since ——— and his family left Inverness, when I received a message from him, that it was expected I should fulfil my engagements—that in short——might be still pacified, and I still married. I had no engagement to fulfil, and therefore could only smile at this new sort of manœuvre.

About ten days after this transaction, I happened to be a juryman, when a letter was delivered to me by a servant. The Sheriff of the County, who was then acting as judge, and who, it seems, had heard something of what was going on, urged that the privilege of opening letters given in to jurymen belonged to him, and that if I did not give my word of honour not to open it till Monday (this happened on Saturday), he would keep it. I was forced to comply with this, and on Sunday I gave the letter to a friend, with whom I dined, who informed me that it contained nothing like a challenge. At the very moment this was passing, the Sheriff sent a messenger and some of the volunteers after me, so that the bail bond to which I was subjected, in no way whatever was the result of either my conduct, or that of my friends. Whatever the letter contained, I never read it, though I had every reason to believe it contained no invitation to any meeting, which was the part of his composition I was most anxious to know.

I have ever esteemed an unblemished character of higher consequence in life than every other blessing, since no station or fortune can confer happiness where that is wanting. But a man can have no possibility of keeping free from stain, with the most honourable intentions and conduct, if the voice of a party is to have the effect of tarnishing the character, by the arts of misrepresentation, and the activity of faction.

A. B.

25th October, 1811.

No. CXCVII. Anno 1812.

CAPTAIN ENEAS MACDONELL, 6TH ROYAL VETERANS, FORT-AUGUSTUS.

THE annexed letter from an officer at Fort-Augustus deals with legal fishing questions in a clear and thorough manner. The writer was a member of the Leek Macdonells of Glengarry, and the points at issue, though at the time interesting, have ceased to be so, in consequence of the re-acquisition by the Lovat family of the Fort-Augustus garrison lands.

The salmon fishings of the Ness waters, from the Garry to Inverness, were, prior to the formation of the Caledonian Canal, and after the destruction of cruives, of great value.

Here is an account of the take on the Glengarry portion in the year 1807, not less remarkable for the quantity than for the average weight. Beauly was at the time a great curing centre and place for shipping salmon :—

Fish Caught at Glengarry Fishing in Season 1807.

	Fish.	Weight.
Caught in whole		432
Disposed of as follows :—		
Sent to Beauly	396	3913 lbs.
Sold to Account	28	270
To Glengarry	8	74
	432	4257 lbs.

Above is an exact account of all the fish taken at Glengarry's fishing during last season.

(Signed)   EDWD. NORMAN.

The Canal has been of the greatest service to the Highlands, but, in its construction, sadly destroyed the beauty of the river's course. Starting at Bona narrows, the river flowed in a shallow stream past two pretty islands and the picturesque ruins of Castle Spioradal, whereof two of its towers stood, to the height of three storeys. In Little Loch Ness, now cut up and disfigured by the artificial highway, was a gem of an islet, with some half-dozen old trees. Just opposite Dochgarroch, there were several wooded islands of great beauty covered with timber, the property of which at one time was hotly disputed betwixt Dochgarroch and Borlum, but ultimately adjudged to the former. Near the march between Dochgarroch and Dunain, was the picturesque Mill of Tor; while, on the opposite side, from Bona to Holme, the Borlum Woods sloped thickly to the river's edge, and with the rustic corn and waulk mills of the Dowinsche, added beauty and variety to the landscape. The ugly scars in Torvean Hill did not exist, the river at this place rather trending towards the East, or Holme side.

Now-a-days, from the abstraction of the Canal waters,

improved drainage, etc., the success of the fishings is almost wholly dependent on the season being wet.

Follows the letter referred to :—

Fort-Augustus, Apl. 24th, 1812.

Dear Sir,—Mr. John Mackay served me upon the 23rd, with the warrant accompanying, which I shall comply with by appearing before Mr. Gilzean on Tuesday next. In the meantime, I shall thank you to prepare an answer for me. Having heard the late Governor Brodie often declare an intention of challenging the right of fishing upon the shores of the Government lands exercised by Lovat and his tacksmen, and, after his death, having made inquiries upon the subject, I learned from intelligent persons that Mr. Alexander Trapaud, a former deputy-governor of the Fort, had not only challenged, but actually interrupted Lovat's tacksman, or tacksmen, from fishing for a whole season, and that in like manner Captain Daniel Shaw, of the 35th Foot, had not only interrupted Lovat's fishers, but did also himself, assisted by soldiers of the garrison, fish with a net and caught two salmon. This happened about the year 1788, or 89, as I am informed. You will perceive from the tenor of Lovat's allegiance that he claims the superiority of the Government lands, altho' these lands have been occupied for more than a century for military purposes, and, I am certain, pay no feu either to Lovat or to any other person, nor does the possession in any respect pay any service in the nature of vassalage. Besides, Lovat denies the right of the garrison to cut peats upon his moss (formerly called the Kings moss), by which act, even if he had originally claim to a superiority, he *sua sponte* abdicates all right of superiority, thereby cutting off the servitudes and accommodations belonging to the other parcels of the estate of Abertarff. I stated to Lieut.-General Campbell and to General Ross, Governor and Deputy-Governor, the doubts I had of the sufficiency of Lovat's title to the fishings, and the Lieutenant-General accordingly instructed me to call for Lovat's title, which I did in a very moderate way, having communicated to Mr. Nicol, the tacksman, the instruction I had got, and requesting to be allowed an inspection of Lovat's title, which he promised me should be done. And this not having been done, upon the 8th of April, seeing Nicol's boat upon the Oich, I desired them to desist, which they did, and this is all the interruption I gave them. I should suppose no one existing is more capable than yourself to furnish full information to justify me in the steps I have taken. If analogy could have any weight in such a case as this, you can refer to the practice at Fort-George, where the right of salmon fishing is exclusively exercised by the garrison along the whole extent of the shores of the Government lands. Upon the whole, from everything I can gather upon the

subject, it would seem as if Lovat had no right of fishing either upon Oich or Tarff, the right never having been conveyed to him, consequently not to be seen in his titles. As to any negative argument to be drawn from the abstinence of Governors Trapaud and Brodie, it is to be recollected that they were both of them tenants of Lovat, and so under his influence and fear.—Your very humble servant,
(Signed) ÆNEAS MACDONELL.
Capt. 6 R.V.B.

P.S.—I am told the clause *cum piscationibus* is not in Lovat's conveyance of the lands, consequently, he has no title to the fishings. The day I interrupted the fishers was that upon which Glengarry went last down to Inverness, as I joined him immediately after I did it. Since writing what precedes, I conversed with a man of my company, from whom I learned that he was one of those who assisted Capain Shaw in drawing the net upon the occasion referred to, and that it was understood at the time that Captain Shaw would have followed up the interruption he gave to Lovat's fishers by some other steps, but his regiment changed their quarter immediately after his drawing the net. It is evident the circumstance of Mr. Trapaud being the tenant of Lovat determined him for that reason not to subject himself to the anger of his landlord. It will be evident to you that the point Lovat aims at establishing in this case is his superiority, which established would at once cut off our title, and determine his. But as the Government lands (no matter how the possession was originally acquired) pay no vassalage whatever, they consequently are free.

Æ. M.

No. CXCVIII. Anno 1813.

MR. JOHN MELVILL, ISLAND OF ISAY.

A LETTER from a now uninhabited island, one of the Hebrides, must be deemed a curiosity.

The island of Isay, on the west coast of Skye, has an evil historic episode, too well known to require repetition. This event is fully noticed in Mr. Mackenzie's *History of the Macleods*, recently published.

Isay formed part of the Barony of Waternish, was thickly populated, and contained at least one important residence, that within which the murders were committed. In the latter times it was a considerable fishing station, and I have seen numerous documents connected with large transactions, emanating from it. Towards the end of last century, one Rory Macneill had a general store on the island, dealing with many customers; as also a branch at Lochbay.

From the letter after given it would seem that a Mr. Melvill carried on business in Isay as late as 1813. The letter is well written, evidently that of a man of education who had seen the world. Rory Macneill, above referred to, on 30th September, 1806, draws a bill in favour of Melvill for £29 10s, payable at the Banking Office in Edinburgh of Sir William Forbes & Co., which bill is duly paid.

A wholesale clearance of some twelve crofter families with their dependants, being the entire population of the island, was made about thirty years ago, and it has ever since been practically waste and unproductive. The letter after quoted is in itself not of interest, but it is given for the purpose of illustrating the extent of business formerly carried on in localities where the unhappy process, so often to be met with in the Highlands and Islands, of systematic depopulation with its atendant evils has been effected.

The island of Isay seems to be peculiarly a case for migration, or extension of holdings.

Island Isa, 10th Dec., 1813.

Sir,—I received your favour and observe the contents, and herein enclose two pounds. The article I got from Holmes was Debenture Rum, cleared out at Liverpool for Archangel. This is the fact, and you will please state the matter as you think best. At all events spin out the time as long as possible. I forgot to mention that it is likely Mr Tolmie has not a proper power of Attorney for uplifting Holme's debts should they be legal.—I am, sir, your very obt. servant,

(Signed)   JOHN MELVILL.

P.S.—Examine if Holmes gave me credit on the back of the letter given him for cash, fish, etc., etc., sent him after the letter was granted. I can send a note of them if you require it.

J. M.

No. CXCIX. ANNO 1814.
MR. JOHN LAMONT, PRIEST AT ABERCHALDER.

WE hear a great deal and read so much of the persecutions of the Covenanters, that it would almost seem they were the only ones persecuted in Scotland. The Annals of Episcopacy, after the Revolution, tell a melancholy tale, and nothing more offensive have I ever perused than some of the records of the Presbytery of Chanonry, within whose bounds dwelt so many non-jurants. Men and women of good family, regularly married by their own clergyman, are pursued and persecuted by the Presbytery, and accused of cohabitation, to the scandal of so-called religion. These proceedings occurred in the earlier part of last century, but the proceedings after referred to took place within the memory of people now living. The papers explain themselves, but it may be mentioned that Mr. Lamont, having been tried at the Circuit Court, was acquitted.

Some forty years ago, circumstances made me the guest of the priest at Kinlochunagan. His name was also Lamont, and he was such an enthusiast in regard to Gaelic, that I may say the night I spent at Kinlochunagan had in this respect much influence on my future life.

Follows the proceedings and letter referred to :—

Unto the Honourable the Sheriff-Depute of Inverness-shire, or his Substitute: the petition of Alexander Macdonell, writer in Inverness, Procurator-Fiscal of the Sheriff Court of Inverness, for the public interest :

Humbly sheweth,—That in the course of the months of August and September, 1814, John Macrail, barrack-sergeant in Fort-Augustus, and Isobel Macdonell, was clandestinely married, and about the same time Peter Macdonald, labourer, at the Caledonian Canal, residing at Kytree, and Mary Macdonald his wife; that the celebration of these two marriages was illegal, and, contrary to positive injunction, celebrated by —— Lamont, Roman Catholic priest, residing at Aberchalder; that this being a breach of positive law, and a violation committed upon the Established Church of the country, the petitioner intends to investigate and Crown Counsel to bring to trial the person guilty of the violation; but previous to doing so, it is necessary to take a precognition how the facts stand, and to examine these witnesses who know the facts best, and therefore this application is humbly made to your Lordship.

> May it therefore please your Lordship to consider what is above stated, and in respect thereof to grant warrant to officers of Court for citing witnesses to appear at Inverness upon the eighth day of April next, to be procognosced anent the facts stated in the above petition, according to justice.
> (Signed) ALEX. MACDONELL.

Inverness, 23 March, 1815.

The Sheriff-Substitute, having considered the above petition, grants warrant for citing witnesses to be procognosced at Inverness upon the eighth day of April next, relative to the facts contained in above petition with certification.

(Signed) THO. GILZEAN.

Having examined his witnesses, the Procurator seems to have written to Mr. Lamont to attend at Inverness to be judicially examined, which application evoked the following proper and becoming answer:—

Aberchalder, 27 May, 1815.

Dr. Sir,—Yesterday I received your *welcome* favours. In reply, I have only to say that, please God, I will make my appearance at the Capital of the North on Thursday first at your request. For what I know not, unless we are to be persecuted for religion. If so, I am glad to suffer, hoping to be rewarded.. Meantime, I am, dear sir, your most obt. servant.

(Signed) JOHN LAMONT.

No. CC. Anno 1815.
COLL MACDONELL OF BARISDALE.

IN another place I have given full particulars of this family, extinct, it is understood, in the male line.

Coll, fourth of Barisdale, the writer of the letter after given, was a man of much influence in his day. I find the following note of a conversation I had with the late Sir Alexander Matheson upon 31st January, 1879:—
"Knew the late Coll Macdonell of Barisdale, a very tall man, nearly seven feet high. Saw him in Edinburgh in the year 1822 at George IV. reception, in charge of the Glengarry Highlanders. He lived long at Auchtertyre of Lochalsh, being more convenient and accessible. Went back to Barisdale to live before his death. Archibald, last of Barisdale, was his only surviving son. His father had a commission in the Royal service. Coll of the '45 was one of the keepers of the watch, and regularly levied blackmail. His (Sir Alexander's) grandmother often used to relate that she in her youth had paid blackmail for Fernaig to Coll of the '45, commonly called 'Coll Bàn.'"

The letter after given shows Coll Barisdale in a pleasant light, and is quoted chiefly for the sake of the reference to the marriage of Macdonell of Scammadale. To think that a man who had fought for Prince Charles should be taking a wife seventy years later, and during the period of "the hundred days," seems almost incredible. Yet here it is in black and white. Scammadale had been married in his youth, for I find one of his sons, Archibald, in Sandaig, in the year 1792, referring to his father as then an old man, and he (the son) well on in years. In a letter from Knoydart, dated 23rd August, 1793, Ranald Scammadale is described as granduncle to Simon Macdonald of Morar and to Coll Macdonell of Barisdale.

The following is a specimen of Ranald's letters:—

Dear Sir,—I received payment from Lachlan Macdonald, excepting your expences and charges, for which he gave me his letter that he would pay you at Inverness directly after the first Fort-William market, and get your receipt to me for the said expenses. Lachlan expects that Dugald Macdonell will not charge him 20s for any trouble he was at, as he had other business in the country besides his. I wish you to make it as easy as possible for him. I have given him a sight of your account, and he says that there is part of it that he cannot understand. I wish you would make him sensible of his error, for it defied me to make him understand it. Any money I can put together, I will send it soon after the market by the ground officer, but I am afraid it will not amount to the sum I ought to have paid this day twelvemonth. But you may depend on it I will make it all I can.—I remain, dear sir, your most humble servant,

(Signed) RANALD MACDONELL.
Crowlin, Nov. 7th, 1794.

Follows Barisdale's letter referred to. The William mentioned was his son, who died abroad young :—

Auchtertyre, 6 May, 1815.

My dear Sir,—I received your line of the 28th of last month this day. I shall send an express to John with it on Monday, so that the post of 16th may bring you his answer.

I am already in your debt for him and Col. Macdonald's roup stamps, and till I pay that, I will defer any more engagements for John. Cash is confoundedly scarce here just now, and will be so with us until we sell our wool and sheep. You did not say what John's arrears were. You had better write him by Fort-Augustus, or to my care by Lochalsh.

I was glad to see George pass his trials in London. I have not heard from William since December last. I have forwarded recommendations to Lord Moira on his behalf, and from a friend at the India House who writes me he will be sure of staff promotion when his letters arrive. I hope the female part of the family are well. Christy and my friend Betsy correspond.

Enclosed is a piece of news which I wish you to get inserted in the first *Inverness Journal*, and after you have put it into some better shape. What will my friend, Mrs. Macdonell, say? A foolish man I suppose. For fear of double postage, I will put it on the back. God bless you all. Glengarry will see this piece of news in the *Journal.*—Yours sincerely,

(Signed) COLL MACDONELL.

On the back—"Married at Knoydart, on the 5th of this month, Lieutenant Ranald Macdonell of Sandaig to Miss Catherine Macdonell of Slany. This veteran officer is now in his 95th year, as stout and vigorous as most military men at the age of 60, and thinks it no more than a necessary piece of exercise to ride 30 miles after breakfast. He is one of those gentlemen who, with some of his friends, followed the fortunes of Prince Charles in the year '45, and was not only present but bore a particular share in every engagement which took place on behalf of that Prince, who more than once took notice of him for his activity and courage. He now enjoys half-pay for his services under His present Majesty."

Endorsed—" Barisdale anent Scammadale's marriage."

NOTE.—Since the foregoing letter was first published, I have found a document of 1748, wherein Coll Bàn the 2nd Barisdale, and Ranald Scammadale, are described as Brothers. "Spanish John" of the Scotos family in his memoirs refers to Ranald as "Black Ranald, natural brother of Barisdale, and who had righteously well beaten Allan "Knock" for one of his numerous misdeeds. Ranald's first wife was one of the old family of Glenaladale, and the lady of 1815 above referred to, was a native of Kilchoan.

APPENDIX.

—:o:—

No 1. Anno 1639.

MACDONALD OF SLEAT.

COLONEL BURTON MACKENZIE of Kilcoy has kindly favoured me with the annexed copy of a letter addressed by Lady Macdonald to her uncle, Alexander Mackenzie, first of Kilcoy. The letter is valuable, that of a lady who has all her wits about her, in a period of anxiety, showing herself conciliatory, but also by the postscript, prepared for extremities—possessing all the heroic qualities of her heroic predecessor in Sleat " Mhairie-na-Chaisteall," in short one of the grand sisterhood of Cavalier ladies, such as Lady Airlie and Lady Derby, whose names are held in deserved honour. Whenever harryings and burnings are wanted, "my Lord of Lorne" is always ready for the work which "gangs sae bonnily on" according to the well known clerical zealot. The friend in Ireland referred to was Sir Donald's cousin, the great Earl, afterwards Marquis of Antrim, himself a Macdonald.

I should infer as the letter is dated from "Sleat" and that the writer, who evidently loved the designation "Ladie of Sleat," speaks of "this abode," that it must have been written, not at Duntulm Castle, but in either Dunskaich, or Castle "I' Chamuis," the two ancient habitations of the family, in the parish of Sleat. If so, the letter in itself valuable, is still more so on account of the place in which it was written.

Colonel Burton Mackenzie mentions the very satisfactory fact of their being many old Kilcoy letters still extant, and it is to be hoped they and others belonging to Northern families, may yet see the light by means of a Highland Club.

Here follows the letter :—

Loving Uncle,—My love being remembered to you, I thought meet to write these lines desiring you to send me a part of the surest news that you have for the present, and I hoped for a letter of yours with your best opinions and with news long ago, and since you have forgotten me, yet I cannot forget you nevertheless, and although my friends be offended at my husband for the present, yet I hope in God that is without deserving in him except to go to visit his good friend in Ireland. This is not to dishonour or to displease you his best friend in Scotland, which he will prove and testify to you all at his return by the Grace of God.

It is reported to me for certaintie that my Lord of Lorne is to send men to harry our lands. I desire you therefore earnestly to send me your best advice, with the consent of the rest of the friends thereanent, and to acquaint me what to do if the same come to pass, because my husband is afar off, and if my Lord my brother may get this helped, let him use his best endeavours to hold this abode, as I shall write to my Lord myself, because the best friend that I have under God.

As for that little monies you have of mine, I should fain, if you would spare it, have it, and send me sure word when I should send one to receive it. As for count and reckoning we need not, for we are friends and none of us will distress another. I would fain that you would speir at my Lord what should I do with my own personal goods if sine enemies come on, that his Lordship might send me his best opinion within your own letter. I rest and committing you to God your loving brother's daughter.

      (Signed) DAME JENAT MACKENZIE,
               Ladie of Sleat.

From Sleat, January 23, 1639.

Post Scriptum.—You shall send me some powder and lead to keep me from my enemies, because I cannot get none to buy, or else grant me this favour as to buy it on my behalf, or send me it with this bearer.

Addressed—"To my loving uncle, Mr Alexander Mackenzie of Culcowie."

No. 2. Anno 1739.

DR. COLIN CAMPBELL OF INVERNESS.

UPON a recent occasion, reference was made to the strained relations betwixt the Magistrates of Inverness and the Customs Authorities. The annexed letter clearly indicates the feelings of the worthy Provost Maclean, the chief Magistrate at the time. On the other hand, the powers usurped by the Lord President are not less singular. The powers assumed by the Court of Session may be said to have culminated in the famous Act of Sederunt of 1756, whereby the Lords, in their wisdom, entirely superseded the necessity for an Act of Parliament, and *de facto* made a new Act which, though it does not appear in the Records of Statutes, has been given effect to over and over again in the Court of last resort.

Dr. Campbell was younger son of Sir Archibald Campbell of Clunes, and had an excellent practice, Simon Lord Lovat being one of his patients. He was very particular about his appearance, and I have one of his letters wherein, as he has not a sword sufficiently handsome for his Highland dress he begs a relative to lend him one on the occasion of an approaching festivity.

Being called to attend the Countess of Moray, Dr. Campbell was seized with fever, to which he shortly succumbed. His death occurred at Darnaway Castle, on the 25th October, 1740, and his remains were carried to the family burial place in Bareven on the 31st.

Follows the letter referred to :—

Dear Sir,—All my news is that yesterday morning the President went for Edinr., and Sunday night last the Custom House boat seized a boat of Lodovick Gordon's with brandy and other goods, in which boat was Hugh Campbell; and John Baillie applied the Provost for horses to carry the goods to the Custom House, and for his order to the town's officers to secure all the men as prisoners to the Tolbooth, at which the Provost refused, it being Sunday, upon which the men were set at liberty, and John Baillie went to the Haugh, and got horses from David Baillie, Dunean's brother, to carry the goods, but the Provost, thinking this a breach of the Sabbath, sent David Baillie to prison. Monday John Baillie went to the President to complain of the Provost, and the President, not approving of the Provost's conduct, ordered Mr. Baillie to be liberated ; and yesterday, at a Justice of Peace Court, the boat was condemned to be burnt, but the men have made their escape. This is all that story. I am glad my brother is mending. I have sent by the bearer a pair of shoes for Johnie, and I beg to be acquainted of anything he wants from time to time, and they shall be provided him by, dear sir, your dutiful and affectionate son to serve you,

(Signed) COLIN CAMPBELL.

Inverness, May 26th, 1739.

Addressed to "Sir Archibald Campbell of Clunes, at Budgate."

(This letter appeared under date 1739, as well as letter No. CXXIV.)

No. 3. LETTER No. CXXXI. ANNO 1746.

SINCE this letter was first published considerable light has been thrown on the name of "Kennochan." Accidentally taking up Robert Chambers' History of the '15, I observed that "The Laird of Kynnachin (a small estate in Athole) appeared on the walls to answer the summons (the Duke of Argyle to Borlum to surrender Leith Citadel). As to surrendering, he said they did not understand the word, nor he hoped, ever would. With regard to quarter they were determined in case of being engaged, neither to give nor to take any. Finally, if his Grace was prepared to give an assault they were equally prepared to receive it."

With this clue I applied to Mr. Robertson of Old Blair, who kindly replied in the words after given, under date 10th May, 1889, and his letter is not only valuable as regards Kynachan, but for the other information given connected with an ever-interesting period. "Kynachan, as you surmise, is in the district of Athole, but the estate now belongs to the Marquis of Breadalbane, whose predecessors bought it from the trustees of General Stewart of Garth about 1830. The estate held of the Duke of Athole until about 1814 when John, the fourth Duke, sold the superiority to Robert Stewart of Garth (now Fortingall) who was then proprietor of both Garth and Kynachan. The estate extends (on the right bank of the Tummel) from near the head of Loch Tummel, westward towards Shiechallion, including part of that mountain. The House of Kynachan, now occupied as a farm house, is a plain, high, white harled house, with many narrow windows, situated about two miles below Tummel Bridge.

"I do not know whether the Laird of Kynachan was out in 1715, but David Stewart of Kynachan was a leading Athole man in the '45, and held the rank of Major in the Athole Brigade. He fought at Culloden but never returned, and it is believed that Menzies of Shian and he and about thirty other wounded men were burned to death in a hut fired by the English soldiers the day after the battle. Kynachan House was occupied by one hundred men of the Argyleshire Highlanders (for the King) in March, 1746, when Sir Andrew Agnew held Blair Castle, but a party of the Prince's men, sent by Lord George Murray, who was himself near Blair at the same time, took the garrison by surprise and made them prisoners."

"But I cannot think who the 'Lord H.' can be, unless it is possible that the letter 'H.' may be taken for 'N.' Lord Nairne was of the Prince's party, and connected with this district, and his sister, who was married to Robertson of Drumachaoin (afterwards Robertson of Struan), went to France at that time. I regret that the Duke of Athole is not here at present, otherwise I might get information from him, for his Grace has a minute and accurate knowledge of the history of that time.

"Stewart of Drumacharry and Garth, married the eldest daughter of David Stewart of Kynachan, and these three estates were thereby conjoined, and General David Stewart of Garth was a son of that marriage, and named David after his maternal grandfather. Dr. Irvine, Pitlochry, is son of a sister of General Stewart, who was married to the Rev. Dr. Irvine of Little Dunkeld, and my wife is his niece."

I also observe from "The Book of Garth and Fortingall" an interesting volume compiled in 1888 by Mr. Campbell, of the *Northern Chronicle*, Inverness, by request of the present proprietor of the estates, several references to Kynachan. Amongst others is a Gaelic poem. Allusion is made to Kynachan Woods, that David was among the bravest of the brave, and the most fanatic of Jacobites. That after Culloden Kynachan House was seized and occupied by a small garrison under charge of a serjeant who had a wife and daughter, that the daughter having been accidentally shot, her ghost still haunts the house of Kynachan.

No. 4. LETTER No. CLVI. Anno 1771.

THE second edition of a small volume of Gaelic poems by Margaret Cameron, published by Mr. Young, of Inverness, in 1805, and originally issued in 1785, has lately come into my possession. There are two songs in praise of Tullochcrom. The following, being the larger and more important, has been translated for me by Mr. Whyte, librarian, Inverness, and rendered into metre by Mr. Allan Macdonald. The song is not only generally interesting but is to me particularly so, and seems to have been composed during the time, and refers to those eviction litigations which proved so serious to Tullochcrom in his youth, and resulted in the expatriation of his brother Macdonalds of the house of Achnacoichan.

Follows the translations of the poems :—

A GAELIC SONG TO ALISTER BAN MACDONALD OF TULLOCHROM.

BY MARGARET CAMERON.

Rendered into English metre by Mr. Allan Macdonald, L.L.B., Inverness.

I lately hied me to the Fair,
  My sporran's store being very scant,
But I met kindly clansmen there
  Who helped me in my time of want.

Young Alister from Garvamore
  In Badenoch, with hair so fine,
Gave me an ox of size galore;
  May health and strength be ever thine.

A dark grey ox of size galore,
  So powerful-limbed, so sleek and round;
It's tallow weighed two stones and more,
  It's hide brought me a silver pound.

Alister of the golden hair
  On horseback swifter than the dart,
Well worthy thou of trappings rare,
  Ah! happy she who's won thy heart.

Alister of the beautiful face,
Alister of the golden hair,
  The bloom of the apple is on thy cheek,
  Thy teeth are white as a chalky streak;
Ah! happy she may thy kisses share.

Alister of the locks of gold
  Small wonder thy skill is thy peoples pride;
Thou art head of a family great and old,
  And Macranald's daughter is thy bride.

Small wonder that thou art powerful and strong,
  For strong are thy people in battle array.
When the clansmen of Keppoch arouse them to fight,
With the men of Aberarder to add to their might,
  Foolish those would question their sway!

A handsome youth is he I sing,
  Of stalwart form and well turned leg,
  High-blooded as becomes his Clan,
  Booted and spurred; each inch a man
  In tartan plaid and phillibeg.

Thou never didst the poor distress,
  Their wrongs to right, their rights to gain,
  In Scotland's Courts their cause thou'lt press,
  In England's too, and not in vain.

Alister of the golden hair,
  My pride, my pet, my darling boy,
  On Sassenach soil you meanwhile fare,
  But we long to welcome you back with joy.

A SONG TO ALISTER BAN (FAIR ALEXANDER) MACDONALD OF TULLOCH-CROM.

I made a visit to the market,
And my purse was not as I should have wished,
But there met me most excellent gentlemen,
And they succoured me well in my need.

  E-ho, aoi-ri-ri-u,
  Ho-aoi ri-ri-u
  Hem-u-li-bho-aoi-ri-u.

Young Alister of the beautiful hair,
From Garva more in Badenoch,
Long may health and strength be thine,
Who madest me a gift of the splendid ox.

Thou madest me a gift of the dark-grey ox,
So large, so handsome, and so fine;
There were two stones of tallow or fat in it,
And I got a guinea for its hide.

Alister of the golden ringlets,
Thou rider of the gallant steed,
Well does golden mounting become thy saddle;
Happy the gentle lady who has won thee!

Alister of the golden tresses,
Of countenance most beautiful,
Thy cheeks are like the apple on the tree,
Thy well-set teeth are white as chalk ;
Happy the one to whom thou grantest a kiss !

Alister of the flowing golden locks,
Little wonder that thou art skilful ;
Thou art head of an august family,
And thy lady is the daughter of Macranald.

Little wonder that thou art powerful (commanding),
Thy friends are strong under their banners ;
If once arose the Macranalds of Keppoch,
And the Laird of Aberarder by his side,
I pity the enemy that would rouse them.

I would tell you the aspect of the youth—
A strong-limbed, shapely man,
Of the high-blooded race of Clan Donald ;
Well becomes thee the bonnet, the spur, the boot,
And comely kilt and lovely tartan plaid.

And when thou goest to Edinburgh,
In the Court (*Lit.* " House ") of Law thou wilt be
    listened to ;
Thou never trustedst to injustice,
And thou wilt go to London with it ere thou yield.

My darling, my treasure, and my joy,
Alister of the golden tresses ;
Thou hast gone with thy drove to England,
And hale be thy return home.

No. 5. Anno 1777.

LIEUTENANT THOMAS FRASER OF ERROGIE.

FEW clans sent forth more men or officers to the American wars than that of Fraser. Through the influence of General Fraser, the Chief, scores of young men of respectable family got commissions, and served their country well. The annexed letter from one of the Stratherrick Frasers has been preserved and gives a vivid description of the scenes in America. It would appear that the writer had been a colonist in Virginia, but was obliged to resort to the profession of arms. The uncle referred to was the famous Brigadier-General Simon Fraser, younger son of Alexander Fraser of Balnain, by his second wife, Jean, daughter of Angus Mackintosh of Kyllochy. In the Balnain MS. I find with reference to this distinguished officer the following notes:—"Of this officer it may be said that it falls to the lot of few military men of his rank to obtain so much distinction. The circumstances attending his death, as contained in the narrative of General Burgoyne, cannot fail to leave on the mind an impression highly favourable to his character. He served in the Scots regiment in the Dutch service, and was wounded at Bergen-op-Zoom in 1747, and was afterwards at Minden. He was the officer who answered the hail of the enemies' sentry in French, and made him believe that the troops who surprised the Heights of Abraham were the Regiment-De-La-Reine. Being much noticed by the late Marquis of Townshend, he was appointed his aid-du-campe in Ireland, and subsequently Quartermaster-General to the troops there. This place he quitted to take a command under General Burgoyne, and had the singular good fortune to increase his reputation in that disastrous expedition." John Fraser of Errogie was one of the lieutenants in the Fraser or 78th Highlanders when embodied in 1757. The letter after given has now no address, but is filed by William Fraser, writer in Inverness, thus—" Lieutenant Thomas Fraser, son to Erogie, about sundries, from New York."

Follows the letter referred to :—

Dear Brother,—Mr Thomas Fraser, Farraline, delivered me your letter of the 7th June, and am happy to find by it that you and your family are well. I have not seen Simon for 20 months past, being at that time obliged to leave Virginia for my attachment to Government, and go on board the fleet with Lord Dunmore, where I was so lucky as to get a lieutenancy in a provincial regiment, which he

APPENDIX. 385

embodied of the refugees that were on board with him. He continued in Virginia until August, undergoing every hardship that man could suffer from want of provision and water, till the arrival of General Howe's army at Staten Island, to which place we made the best of our way. It was my lot to go into the New York Volunteers, the first provincial regiment raised on the Continent, and in which I am at present as a Lieutenant and Adjutant. I have not heard from Simon since last June. He was then well, but very much harassed with the rebels. They have obliged him to give security that he will not leave the Colony without their permission, which it will be impossible for him to obtain while the rebellion lasts.

I find by your letter that my father has been carried off suddenly by a fever in May last. I hope your attention to poor Charlie and May will be such as will make the loss they sustained seem light to them. I feel with gratitude the many services you have already rendered us, and only wish that fortune may put it my power to make a suitable return.

It is with sorrow I inform you that in an action that happened the 7th of last month, between General Burgoyne's army and the rebels, my uncle was killed with the greatest part of the troops he commanded. Since that, the northern army have been particularly unfortunate—they advanced so far into the country that they could neither retreat to Ticanderoga or force their way to make a junction with the army under General Clinton. They have been obliged to capitulate. Genl. Burgoyne and the army are to return to England, and not to act during the war.

Upon the 6th of October last the army under General Clinton attacked two forts the rebels had up the Hudson River, where we lost several very brave officers, among which were Lieut.-Col. Campbell, 52 Regiment, and Lieut.-Col. Grant of our regiment. I received a slight wound in the fleshy part of the thigh, but so inconsiderable that I was never confined by it.

Since my being with the army I frequently wrote my uncle begging that he might get my rank exchanged into some of the British regiments. I received a letter dated a few days before his death, in which he promised that as soon as the army joined he would be able to effect it for me. Your acquaintances in the 71st Regt. are all very well. They have been rather inactive this last campaign, and consequently suffered very little. You will be good enough to remember me to all enquiring friends. I am wishing you and my sister many happy days. Direct to Lt. Fraser, New York Volunteers.—Yours affectionately,

(Signed) THOS. FRASER.
Camp, near Powder Hook, 10 Nov., 1777.

No. 6. Anno 1792.

MR. JAMES MACKINTOSH AND GENERAL MACKINTOSH OF SAVANNAH.

IN the latter half of the eighteenth century, an extraordinary movement to foreign parts took place among the enterprising young men of the Highlands. To the East and West Indies, Canada, and the States, there was a constant flow. Many returned with fortunes, but a far larger number succumbed to climatic and other causes. The writer of the annexed letter is described by Provost John Mackintosh of Aberarder as "grandson to his uncle James," and he was evidently in a fair way in 1792, after many ups and downs, of making his fortune—as he says himself, to do or die. Of his future, I am ignorant. James Mackintosh, of New York, returned, and made an attempt to establish a family in Stratherrick, but was unsuccessful.

There was a close connection 'twixt the name of Mackintosh and the early settlement of the great State of Georgia. After the establishment of South Carolina came that of Georgia, and mainly through the great exertions of General and Governor Oglethorpe, a large number sailed from Inverness about 1735 for the new State, and in particular many of those Mackintoshes whose families had never recovered from the effect of the Rising of 1715.

Brigadier Mackintosh, younger of Borlum, had six brothers who came to manhood, his next brother being Lachlan, commonly styled "of Knocknageal." Lachlan did·not go out with his brothers in 1715. His first wife was Mary Lockhart, whose tomb-stone is still extant in the Grey Friars at Inverness; the second being Anne Shaw, of the Tordarroch family. Lachlan's eldest son, John, from his great size, was called "John Mor Mackintosh," and so universally that frequently in his after life in Georgia he is termed "Mor Mackintosh" without the Christian name. John Mor married, about 1727, Miss Fraser of Garthmore, and was, with his family, one of General Oglethorpe's settlers. He was accompanied from Inverness, with others, by Benjamin Mackintosh, a natural son of the Brigadier, who had married Miss Mackintosh, daughter of John Mackintosh of Holme; also by John Mackintosh, third son of Holme. John Mor himself took a considerable part in the earlier wars, but his efforts were as nothing compared to those of his distinguished sons, Colonel William and General Lachlan Mackintosh. These last, at an early period, sided with the Americans, and their achievements are indelibly recorded in American history. This General Lachlan is the person referred to in the letter as being so clannish, and it is satisfactory to find that he had not forgotten the ties of kindred and clanship. A friend some years ago sent me an engraved portrait of the General, which I highly value. There is now, or was lately, living in New Jersey, a descendant of John Mor's, in a high military position, and this gentleman is the male representative of the Borlums, failing any male descendants of Edward Mackintosh, last of Borlum, who disappeared in 1773.

Follows the letter referred to :—

Dear Sir,—Having experienced your friendship and at the same time relying on your good sense to consider my misfortunes, I now make bold to inform you of my good success after suffering very much in a strange country without either money or friends (all the money I had was one sixpence when I landed at Baltimore and no friend). The first person I engaged with got deranged; afterwards was obliged to apply myself to hard labour. I got the length of New York. My cousin, Jas. Mackintosh, behaved like a brother. He sent me to this place, gave me the management of ten thousand pounds sterg. in liquors and grocery, allows me half the profits from the capital for managing the business. As my prospect is so very great, and not doubting if I live but a very short time, I will have in my power to make ample satisfaction to my creditors, and, as I had never reason to doubt but you wished for my prosperity, I think it my duty to inform you first of my success. I left Invss. with the view of either to do or die; if the issue in circumstances would not prove favorable, no man would ever hear from me. I am to request one favor, together with all former favors, that is, if you see it proper to thank Jas. Mackintosh at New York for his friendship to me. I own that I am not deserving just now, but I expect to merit your approbation soon. I got a letter of introduction from my cousin at N. York to General Mackintosh in this place, by whom I was very well received, and as I am a stranger I consult him in every material point of business. He is very friendly, and as clannish as any Mackintosh can be. Mr. James Chapman from Invss. is very attentive to me likewise. I was introduced to Mr. James Macgillivray of Daviot at General Mackintosh's, but no intimacy prevails.

This is the best State of the thirteen for making money, and them that live temperate may enjoy their health here as well as at Invss. I was not an hour sick since I left Scotland. As I do not wish to trouble you with a long letter, I will conclude with my best respects to you and family.—I am, dr. sir, your huble. servt.,

(Signed)   JAS. MACKINTOSH.

Savannah, State of Georgia, 27th Decr., 1792.

(This letter was first published under date 1792, as well letter No. CLXXVII.).

No. 7.   ANNO. 1815.

SHERIFF TYTLER.

IN these days when the conduct of Sheriffs in Scotland, and of Magistrates in Ireland, is so much canvassed, the annexed dignified letter from Mr. Wm. Fraser Tytler, long Sheriff of Inverness-shire, may be perused with advantage. Naithless, the Sheriff was a hasty tempered gentleman, strongly imbued with his own importance, which in some instances led him into undignified apology. Take, in illustrations, his abuse of another dignified personage, Mr. Burnett, Kinchyle, at a roup, and his poaching on Duntelchaig, both occurrences ending to his discredit. In short, he sometimes thought that his official position cloaked private indiscretion. At present county gentlemen are the most inoffensive class in the community. But formerly it was not so. Besides public and private quarrellings, there were breaches of the peace and foolish litigations. In the early part of this century, Glengarry was the chief offender. I do not know what the first part of the Sheriff's letter refers to, but the second related to the well-known "Well of the Heads" connected with a supposed episode in the Keppoch family. This erection, historically incorrect, was a piece of bombast, which gave offence to a section of the great Clan Macdonald, and led to its being damaged. Not being within consecrated ground, or in any sense a public affair, the Procurator-Fiscal of the day declined to prosecute the alleged iconoclasts, it being open to the proprietor to sue for damages. The third matter related to a curious charge, afterwards formulated against the then Sheriff-Clerk of Inverness-shire for exacting fees of Court, exorbitant and unauthorised. Follows the letter referred to, addressed to the Procurator-Fiscal.

Aldourie, 7 June, 1815.

Sir,—I have received a letter from your client, Colonel Macdonell of Glengarry, dated 27 May, 1815, written in a style which certainly entitles it to no answer from me. I permit no individual whatever to animadvert in such a manner on my official conduct; when I err, redress is open to every one in a legal form. On the present occasion I shall take no other notice of this letter than by not replying to it, but if I meet with any repetition of a similar mode of address, I shall consider it my duty to take such steps as shall convince the writer, that such addresses to a judge, on the subject of his official conduct, are liable to a very adequate measure of reprehension and punishment.

With respect to the complaint made to me by Colonel Macdonell, in a former letter and memorial, that in your capacity of Procurator-Fiscal you had refused to prosecute at the public expense the injury done to a monument erected by him, I entirely approve of your having done so; I do not see any ground upon which such an injury can be prosecuted *ad-vindictam publicam*. If your *concurrence* to an action at the instance of the private party is required, that you can give as a matter of course, but I entirely approve of your withholding your insistence in such a case.

With regard to the former memorial, complaining of the conduct of the Sheriff-Clerk, I informed you before what steps I considered it proper you should take. I told you on the first head of the complaint what my own knowledge of the circumstances was and recommended that you should first consult your client, and then prefer a regular complaint. On the 2nd head I desired you to put your charge in a specific form, narrating the actual overcharges complained of, and bring it into Court in a regular manner in form of petition and complaint.

In giving to you these directions on the subject of a memorial sent extrajudicially by your client to me, and which was not in a shape to form a step in any proceedings in Court, I apprehend I did considerably more than I was necessarily called upon to do; and it lies with you and your client to follow out your case. My duty is to judge of it, when it comes before me. The circumstances to which Colonel Macdonell so shortly alludes in a Notabene on his letter, of a house having been set fire to, had been communicated to me in a manner more satisfactory, and more respectful, and you are in possession of your instructions regarding it.—I am, sir, your obedt. humble servant,

(Signed) WM. FRASER TYTLER.

(This letter appeared under date 1815 as well as letter No. CC.)

INDEX OF NAMES.

—:o:—

Agnew, Sir Andrew, 379
Alves, Doctor, of Shipland, 283
Anne, Queen, 122, 158
Argyll, Archibald, Third Duke of, 221
Argyll, The Earl, afterwards Marquis of, 43, 84
Arnell, A., London, 104-5
Arundel and Surrey, Earl of, 17

Baillie, Alexander, of Dunain, 14, 23, 65, 80, 112
Baillie, Alexander, writer in Edinburgh, 193
Baillie, Alexander, of Dochfour, 199, 237, 239
Baillie, Colonel John, of Dunain, 320
Baillie, Colonel John, of Leys, 320
Baillie, Colonel William, of Dunain, 283, 295
Baillie, David, 1st of Dochfour, 79, 80
Baillie, Evan, of Abriachan, 238
Baillie, Hugh, of Dochfour, 253
Baillie, Ian Dubh, London, 238
Baillie, James, son of Dochfour, 253
Baillie, John, of Leys, Clerk to the Signet, 214, 220, 222
Baillie, Rev. Robert, Inverness, 128
Baillie, William, Commissary of Inverness, 112, 214
Barbour, Daniel, of Aldourie, 182
Barbour, Miss Sibilla, of Aldourie, 193
Bayne, Alexander, of Knockbayne, 26, 28
Boswell, James, of Auchinleck, 288
Braco, Lord, 54
Breadalbane, John, 2nd Earl of, 222
Brodie, D., Laird of Lethen, 139, 140

Brodie, James, of Inshoch, 185
Buchan, Alexander, Earl of, 231
Burgoyne, General, 384-5
Burnett, Mr., Kinchyle, 388

Caithness, George Earl of, 5
Cameron, Sir Ewen, of Lochiel, 67, 117, 120
Camerons, The, of Auchindaul, 269
Campbell, Archibald, writer, Edinburgh, 180
Campbell, Colin, of Ardersier, 44
Campbell, Dr., of Inverness, 377
Campbell, John, of Cawdor, afterwards Baron Cawdor, 197, 333
Campbell, Sir Archibald, of Clunes, 164, 171, 175, 180, 182, 186, 198, 337
Campbell, Sir Hugh, of Calder, 143, 163, 187,
Carstairs, Principal William, 143
Charles I., 18, 42, 121
Charles II., 59, 71, 121
Charles Edward, Prince, and his lady supporters at Inverness, 223, 228
Chisholm, Alexander, Sheriff-Depute of Inverness-shire, 105
Chisholm, Captain Hugh, of Midmain, 358
Chisholm, Doctor, Provost of Inverness, 291
Chisholm, The, 124
Clark, Alexander, minister of Inverness, 80, 88-9
Clark, James, of Naples, painter, 340
Clark, Rev. John, of Stornoway, 249
Cromartie, George, 1st Earl of, 149
Cromwell Oliver, 105
Cornwallis, Lord, and Rev. Dr. Alexander Webster, Edinburgh, 299
Cuthbert, David, Town Clerk of Inverness, 25
Cuthbert, James, of Little Drakies, 56
Cuthbert, John, of Castlehill, 66-7, 122, 171
Cuttlebray, the goodman of, 120

Danenberg, Quirinuis, solicitor at the Hague, 229
Douglas, Lord James, Earl of Angus, 120
Duff, Mrs., of Muirtown, 331
Dunbar, James Roy, of Dalcross, 47
Dunbar, John, of Bennetsfield, 27
Dunbar, John, of Burgie, 236

Farquhar, Sir Robert, 77, 79
Ferguson, Captain John, Commander of H.M. ship "Porcupine," 246
Forbes, Arthur, of Culloden, 309
Forbes, Dr., of Elgin, 156

Forbes, Duncan, of Culloden, 36
Forbes, John, 4th of Culloden, 158, 196
Forbes, John, 2nd of Culloden, Provost of Inverness, 55, 77, 99
Forbes, Jonathan, son of Dr. Forbes of Elgin, 162
Forbes, Lord, 271
Forbes, Sir David, of Newhall, Midlothian, Advocate, 109, 110, 111, 135
Fortrose, Kenneth, Lord, 307
Fowler, Bailie, of Inverness, Inshes and Glenmoriston, 83
Fraser, Alexander, of Fairfield, 199
Fraser, Brigadier Simon, 279, 384
Fraser, Captain Simon, of Fanellan, 315
Fraser, Charles, of the Balnain family, 297
Fraser, Colonel James, of Culduthel, 306
Fraser, Duncan, merchant, Inverness, 200
Fraser, General, of Lovat, 258, 277, 294
Fraser, Hector, master of the Grammar School, Inverness, 249
Fraser, Hew, of Balnain, 124
Fraser, James, of Gorthlick, C.S., 329, 331
Fraser, Lieutenant Thomas, of Errogie, 383
Fraser of Phopachie, 8
Fraser, Sheriff, of Farraline, and the year of scarcity, 303, 361
Fraser, The Honourable Colonel Archibald C., of Lovat, 344
Fraser, Thomas, of Gortuleg, 263
Fraser, Thomas, of Struie, 222
Fraser Tytler, Wm., Sheriff of Inverness-shire, 388
Fraser, William, of Balnain, 260
Fraser, William, writer, Inverness, 303
Fraser, Wilson & Co., Inverness, 308

Gascoigne, The Honourable Mrs., 255
Ged, Dougall, of Edinburgh, 230
Godsman, Captain Alexander, of the 89th Highlanders, 177
Gordon, Lord Adam, 277
Gordon, Lord Geoge, 276
Gordon, Sir Alexander, 29
Gordon, Sir Robert, 1st Baronet of Gordonston, 1, 4, 9, 11, 36, 37, 39, 48, 53
Gordon, Sir Robert, 3rd Baronet of Gordonston, 126
Gorme, Sir Donald, 4th Baronet of Sleat, 146
Graham, John, of Claverhouse, Viscount Dundee, 119
Grant, Sir Alexander, of Dalvey, Baronet, 267, 296

Hastings, Warren, 296
Hay, William, last Bishop of Moray, 122
Hill, Colonel, Governor of Fort-William, 126

Holland, Earl of, 42
Hossack, John, Provost of Inverness, 216
Howard, Lady Caroline, 197
Huntly, Alexander, Marquis, afterwards second Duke of Gordon, 156, 170
Huntly, George, 1st Marquis of, 4
Huntly, Anna Campbell, 2nd Marchioness of, 13
Huntly, Marquis of, and the goodwife of Dochgarroch, 102
Hutcheson, Professor, of Edinburgh, 130

Inglis, Bailie, of Kingsmills, 27
Innes, Lieutenant R., 120
Innes, Robert, of Rosskeen, 45
Innes, Sir Harrie, 4th Baronet of Innes, 148
Irvine, Dr., of Little Dunkeld, 380
Irvine, Dr., of Pitlochry, 380

James I., 12, 17
James II., 119

Kay, W., Doer for Lord Reay, 39
Kilcoy, Lady, 259
Kintail, Kenneth, 1st Lord Mackenzie of, 2, 9
Kyde, Captain James, Commander of H.M. sloop "Princess Anne, 246

Lamont, John, priest at Aberchalder, 371
Leslie, A., and the goodwife of Inshes, 60
Leslie, Alexander, writer, Edinburgh 55, 69
Lindsay, Thomas, inmate of Cromarty prison, 91
Linton, Alexander, writer, Edinburgh, 49
Lorn, Lord, and his friends, 71
Lovat, Hugh, Lord, 297
Lovat, Simon, Lord, 23, 48, 128, 200, 203, 217, 220, 221-2, 260, 263, 294

Macandrew, John Beg, Delnahatnich on Dulnan, 126
Macaulay, Mr., of Applecross, 234
Macbean, Bailie William, Inverness, 94
Macbean, Mrs. Margaret, Inverness, 334-6
Macbean, Rev. Angus, Inverness, 117
Macdonald, Alexander, of Tullochcrom, 273
Macdonald, Lady, of Sleat, 375
Macdonald, Lord, 278
Macdonald, Simon, of Morar, 352

INDEX. 395

Macdonald, Sir Donald, 1st Baronet of Sleat, 137
Macdonell, Alexander, of Glengarry, 328
Macdonell and Aros, Lady, 137
Macdonell and Aros, Lord, 137
Macdonell, Captain, 6th Royal Veterans, Fort-Augustus, 364
Macdonell, Captain James, third son of John, the 19th of Glengarry, 311
Macdonell, Coll, of Keppoch, 147
Macdonell, Colonel, of Glengarry, 389
Macdonell, Lord, of Aros, 67
Macdonell, Major Simon, of Morar, 311
Macdonell, Mrs., of Glenmeddle, 311
Macdonell, Ronald, of Scotus, 330
Macgillivray, Alexander, of Dunmaglass, 301
Macgillivray, James of Maviot, 388
Mackay, Angus, cousin to first Lord Reay, 3
Mackay, John, Hereford, 24
Mackenzie, Alexander, 1st of Kilcoy, 375
Mackenzie, Captain Kenneth, of Cromarty, 362
Mackenzie, Colin, of Kincraig, 25, 46
Mackenzie, Colin, of Kintail, 31
Mackenzie, Colin, of Redcastle, 111
Mackenzie, Colonel Burton, of Kilcoy, 375
Mackenzie, Francis Humberston, afterwards Lord Seaforth,
Mackenzie, Hector, minister in Inverness, 124
Mackenzie, John, of Delvin, C.S., 235, 250, 315-6
Mackenzie, Mr., of Woodside, 326
Mackenzie, Kenneth Mor, 1st of Dundonell, 141
Mackenzie, Lady, of Grandville, 325
Mackenzie, Simon, of Allangrange, 142
Mackenzie, Sir George, of Grandville and Cromarty, 326
Mackenzie, Sir George, of Rosehaugh, 97, 150
Mackenzie, Sir George Stuart, of Coul, 342
Mackenzie, Sir John, of Tarbat, 327
Mackenzie, Thomas, of Pluscardine, 120
Mackenzie, William, Udrigill, 231
Mackenzie, William, of Gruinard, 229
Mackintosh, Alexander, of Connage, 68, 98, 106
Mackintosh, Alexander, of Kyllachy, 191
Mackintosh, Angus, of Daviot, 111
Mackintosh, Angus, of Farr, 251
Mackintosh, Angus, of Kyllachy, 125, 384
Mackintosh, Bailie John, of Inverness, 220, 229, 241, 249
Mackintosh, Brigadier William, of Borlum, 152, 205, 211, 241, 386
Mackintosh, Captain Angus, of Kyllachy, 291

Mackintosh, Captain John, of Kyllachy, 305, 306
Mackintosh, Captain John, 73rd Regiment of Foot, Gibralter, 299
Mackintosh, Colonel William, 387
Mackintosh, Duncan, of Castle Leathers, 300-1
Mackintosh, Edward, last of Borlum, 387
Mackintosh, Eneas, of Raigmore. 353
Mackintosh, General Lachlan, 387
Mackintosh, James, of Farr, 251
Mackintosh, James, of Kinrara, 20-1
Mackintosh, James, of New York, 386
Mackintosh, J., from the Castle of Moy, 25
Mackintosh, John, merchant, Inverness, 294
Mackintosh, "John Mor," 386
Mackintosh, John, of the Holme family, 203
Mackintosh, John, Town Treasurer of Inverness, 216
Mackintosh, Lachlan, 5th of Borlum, 205
Mackintosh, Lachlan Mor, 7, 305, 315
Mackintosh, Lachlan, of Balnespick, 117
Mackintosh, Lachlan, of Kinrara, 96
Mackintosh, Lachlan, of Knocknagail, 152-3
Mackintosh, Lachlan, of Kyllachy, 187
Mackintosh, Lachlan, of Raigmore, 353
Mackintosh, Lachlan, of that Ilk, 189
Mackintosh, Lachlan, of Torcastle, 190
Mackintosh, Lady Ann, of Mackintosh, 219
Mackintosh, "Laird Lachlan," 179
Mackintosh, Miss Peggy, milliner, Inverness, 240, 255-7
Mackintosh, Provost John, afterwards of Aberarder, 317, 386
Mackintosh, Shaw, 6th of Borlum, 205
Mackintosh, Sir Eneas, of Mackintosh, 219, 272, 300, 306
Mackintosh, Sir Ewen, of Mackintosh, 291
Mackintosh, Sir James, of Kyllachy, 183, 306, 317
Mackintosh, Sir Lachlan, of Torcastle, 6
Mackintosh, William, an insurgent in 1715, Lieutenant in Borlum's regiment, 165
Mackintosh, William, 1st of Borlum, 128
Mackintosh, William, son of Dalmigavie, 278
Maclachlan, Ewen, of Lochaber, poet and scholar, 351
Maclean, John, of Dochgarroch, 104
Maclean, Provost, of Inverness, 377
Macleod, Lieutenant Norman, of Raasay, 228
Macpherson, Duncan, of Cluny, 107
Macpherson, Ewen, of Cluny, the younger, 211
Macpherson, John, of Ballachroan (The Black Officer), 280
Macpherson, Rev. Robert, Laggan, 272

Macpherson, Mr., of Arderseir, 333
Macpherson, Sir John, Baronet, 313
Macqueen, Rev. Edmund, of Barra, 339
Macra, Anne, the "Wise Woman" of Beauly, 310
Magistrates of Inverness, 114, 177, 245, 247-8
Maitland, William, historian, 215
Mar, The Earl of, 86
Melvill, John, Island of Isay, 367
Moniack, Baron of, 7
Moray, James, 3rd Earl of, 46
Munro, A., writer, Edinburgh, 62
Munro, Captain Charles, late 42nd Regiment, 357
Munro, Mr. and Mrs., of Granada, 291-3
Munro, R., writer, Edinburgh, 57
Munro, Sir Hector, of Novar, 268
Murray, Lord George, 227, 379
Murray, Sir Patrick, of Ochtertyre, 222

Nairn, Lord, 379
Nicoll, John, writer, Edinburgh, 38

Ogilvie, James, 8th Earl of Airlie, 43-4
Old Love Letters, 87

Palmer, Thomas, jr., Boston, 207-9
Pepperill, Sir William, 210
Pitcairn, Dr. Archibald, "The Scot," 153
Polson, David, Sheriff-Depute of Inverness, 199
Polson, John, advocate, late of Kinmylies, 199
Portmore, The Earl of, 138
Preston, Lady, of Valleyfield, 299

Reay, Donald, 1st Lord, 1, 24, 34, 39
Robertson, Eme John, Burgess of Inverness, 17
Robertson, Hew, of the Inshes family, 82
Robertson, H., merchant, Inverness, 76-9
Robertson, H., Nairn, 90
Robertson, John, 1st of Inshes, 22, 39, 51, 56, 64
Robertson, John, of Lude, 134
Robertson, Mrs. Sybilla, Carie, 204
Robertson, William, of Inshes, 116, 121
Robertson, William, of the Inshes family, 32-3, 46, 92, 94, 97
Robertson, William, of the Inshes family, 262
Rose, Alexander, Town Clerk of Inverness, 75
Rose, Forbes, & Paterson, Messrs., Inverness, 63

Ross, Alexander, of Pitcalnie, 236
Ross, Captain, and his thieving recruits, 107-8
Ross, David, of Balnagown, 168, 236
Ross, David, of Holm, 184
Ross, General Charles, 236
Ross, George, of Pitkerrie, 235
Ross, Lord, 236
Ross, Mrs. Naomi, of Pitcalnie, 236

Sage, Rev. Æneas, of Lochcarron, 232
Saltoun, Lady Marjory, 129
Saltoun, Lord, 132-3
Schevis, Robert, of Muirtown, 200
Seaforth, George, Earl of, 30
Seaforth, Kenneth Mor, 3rd Earl of, 101
Seaforth, William, 5th Earl of, 307
Shaw, Governor Alexander, of Tordarroch, 305-6
Shaw Mackenzie, John Andrew, of Newhall, 306
Shaw, Rev. Æneas, of Forres, 266
Shaw, Rev. Lachlan, historian, minister of Kingussie, 166, 175
Sinclair, Henry, writer, Edinburgh, 92
Skoone, The Lord, 6
Stewart, Bailie John, Inverness, of the family of Kincardine, 231-2
Stewart, Doctor, of Elgin, 158
Stewart, General, of Garth, 379
Stewart or Ross, Lady Anna, of Balnagown, 168
Stewart, Robert, of Garth and Kynachan, 379
Stewart, Sir Walter, 1st of Kincardine, 231
Strathnaver, Lord, 88, 89, 90
Sutherland, Countess, afterwards Duchess of, 198
Sutherland, Earl and Countess of, 50
Sutherland, Countess of, 256
Sutherland, James, minister of Inverness, 80
Sutherland, John, 13th Earl of, 48

Thomson, Mr., music teacher, Inverness, 332

Urquhart, Sir Wm., of Meldrum, 326

Vaus, Gilbert, late Burgess of Inverness, 15
Villiers, George, Duke of Buckingham, 18

Wade, General, 94
Washington, George, 291, 292-3
Watson, collector, of Inverness, 61

INDEX OF PLACE NAMES.

—:o:—

Aberarder in Laggan, 269, 272
Aberdeen, City of, 59
Achaydonill (Dundonell), 142
Achindaul, Lower Braes of Lochaber, 269
Airlie, 45
Aldourie, Lands of, 124, 182, 260
Allan, Barony of, 141
Altnaskiach, Castle lands of, 66
Ardersier, 188
Auchinleck, Mains of, 289
Auchtertyre of Lochalsh, 371
Auld Castlehill, Barony of, 174

Ballachcroan, Badenoch, 281
Ballachastell, 81
Balmacaan, 52
Bal-na-cruick, 80
Balnagown, 181, 236
Barra, 340
Bareven, 377
Bochruben, Estate of, 189
Borlum Castle, 128
Boston, U.S.A., 207, 210
Breakachie, 107, 119
Bristol, Church of St. Michael's, 210.
Budzett, 180

Castle Downie, 133
Castlehill, 57

Castle " l' Chamuis," Parish of Sleat, 375
Chanonry, 101, Presbytery of, 369
Clune, Estate of, 190
Coigs, Braes of, Strathdearn, 278
Conachan of Glenmoriston, 224
Corrybrough, (Mackintosh), 290
Corrybrough, (Macqueen), 290
Corryaraick, 207, 260
Cradlehall, 173
Crofterton of Altnaskiach, 282
Cromarty, 246, prison of, 91, estates of, 326
Crubinmore, farm of, 119
Culcabock, 33, Barony of, 52, 61, 66, 83
Culclachie, renamed Nairnside, 98, 335
Culloden, " Dunmaglass Well," 310
Cuttlebray, Banffshire, 128

Dalcross, 187 ; Barony of, 215
Dalmigavie, 317
Darnaway Castle, 377
Delnahatnich on Dulnan, 126
Dochcairn, lands of, 65, 79, 237, 285
Dochfour, 79 (Loch, 79), 237, 283
Dochgarroch, 102, 136, 365
Dochnacraig, or Lochend, 4, 65, 136
Drumchardiny, Barony of, 7, 315, 316
Drumdivan, Barony of Lochardill, 16
Drumochter, Pass of, 107
Dunain and Dochgarroch, Estates of, 60
Dunachton, Barony of, 166
Dunskaich, Parish of Sleat, 375
Duntulm, 146
Durris, Barony of, 128, 148, 183

Edinburgh, Black Friar's Wynd, 49
Eileandonan, Barony of, 31

Farr, 317
Fort-Augustus, 227, 337, 364
Fort-George, 227
Fort-William, 227, 271, 337

Gellovie and Aberarder, Estates of, 189
Glenlui and Loch Arkaig, 85, lands of, 98, 120
Glenmoriston, Estate of, 55

INDEX OF PLACE NAMES. 401

Gordon Castle, " The Bog," 103
Gordonstoun, Barony of, 49, old house of, 54
Grangehall, near Forres, 267

Haugh and Altnaskiach lands, 282
Holme, 184

Inshes, Martin Vaus', 16, Patersons', 16
Inshes, Easter and Wester, 33
Inshock, 183, 186
Inverness, 64, 99, 113, 137, 144, 177, 193, 199, 216, 217, 229, 245, 247, 248, 309, 377.
Inverness, Arms of, 114, 115 ; Castle lands of, 102 ; Citadel, 68, 75; Academy, 313, 314, 340, 341, 354 ; Gaelic Church, 325 ; High Church, 61, 123 ; Queensgate, 256 ; music teaching in, 331 ; rare doings in, 334-5 ; Northern Infirmary, 354 ; Caledonian Hotel, 357, 361 ; Northern Meeting, 359, 361
Inverness-shire, 276 ; state of crime in, 337
Inverquharity, 44
Ireland (Dublin), 298
Isay, Island of, west coast of Skye, 367-8
Islay and Muckairn, Estates of, 197

Kincardine, Barony of, 29, 232
Kingsmills, 64, 66, 99
Kinlochlochy, 297
Kinlochunagan, 369
Kinmylies, Barony of, 199, 235
Kinrara, of the Woods, 96
Knoydart, evictions in, 311-2, 327
Kyllachy, 187, 317
Kynachan, in Athole, 378, 379, 380

Laggan, Davoch of, 117
Leys, Easter, 33 ; Mid, lands of, 214 ; Castle, 215, 321 ; Wester, old house of, 305
Little Loch Ness, 365
Lochaber, Braes of, 86
Lochcarron, 234
Lovat, Lordship of, 215
Lynvuilg, Easter, 126

Mar, Braes of, 5
Millburn, Valley of the, 22
Mill of Tor, 365

Moray and Ross, diocese of, 122

Ness Castle, 129
Newtonmore, 152
North Kessock, 359

Orkney and Zetland, 49

Perth, 178
Pluscardine and Dallas, Baronies of, 54
Presmuckerach, 119
Preston, 165

Raitts, Estate of, 206-7
Raasay, 229
Redcastle, 27
Rosehaugh, 97
Ross, Chanonry of, 45
Ross, Easter, 45
Rosskeen, 45
Ruthven Barracks, 212

Saint Eustatius, 254
Sandside, Caithness, 2
Shipland, mansion house of, 82
South Carolina, 386
Spioradail Castle, 65, 365
State of Georgia, 386
Strathdearn, Braes of, 171, 278
Stratherne, Lordship of, 278

Torbreck, 113
Tordarroch, Castle lands of, 305
Tromie, Glen, 107
Tullochcrom, 276

Urquhart, lands of, 52, 53

Waternish, Barony of, 367
Well of the Heads, 389
Westminster, Steiven's Ally, off King Street, 105

www.ingramcontent.com/pod-product-compliance
Lightning Source LLC
Chambersburg PA
CBHW022109290426
44112CB00008B/613